The Old Testament:

---

with the
Joseph Smith Translation

Includes:

All Textual Changes
made by the
Prophet Joseph Smith

Genesis, Isaiah, & Malachi
in full context
and in Parallel Harmony with
the Books of Moses & Abraham
and Isaiah Texts from the Book of Mormon

Compiled by

**Julie M. Hite, Steven J. Hite
and R. Tom Melville**

Published by

The Veritas Group
Orem, Utah

The Old Testament
with the Joseph Smith Translation
1st edition (2nd printing)

ISBN 0-9642325-2-9

Printed in the U.S.A.

Published by:
The Veritas Group
491 East 450 South
Orem, UT 84097
801-224-2903
hitefam@aol.com

Additional copies may be ordered
from the above address

DEDICATION

To Our Children

Melissa and Craig
Rachel and Albert
David
Shelley
Laurie

INTRODUCTION

In Doctrine and Covenants 45:60-61, 73:3-4, and 76:15, Joseph Smith was commanded by the Lord to "translate" the Bible. While the meaning of "translate" might initially seem obvious, there are actually several interesting and viable possibilities. Dr. Robert L. Millet, Dean of Religious Education at Brigham Young University, has described three perspectives for how one can view Joseph Smith's "translation" (1985, p. 43). He proposes that Joseph's "translation" could be:

1) Inspired prophetic commentary; and/or,

2) Harmonization of the themes, accounts and theologies in the Biblical text with Joseph's progressing understanding of truth, focused by his continuing revelations from the Lord; and/or,

3) Restoration by Joseph of text originally included in the Bible, but lost or changed through centuries of textual transmission and cross-language rendering.

Each of these three possibilities should be especially interesting to Latter-day Saints. Whether a given change represents one or more of these three possibilities, "new" ways of reading the text, and therefrom new insights, are possible.

The Joseph Smith Translation (JST)

After purchasing an 1828 edition of the King James Version (KJV) Bible from E. B. Grandin, the Prophet Joseph Smith spent 16 years, virtually to the time of his martyrdom, following the Lord's commandment to translate. This enormous effort produced changes in over 4,000 verses of the text of the KJV Bible. The marked Bible and accompanying manuscripts produced by Joseph in the translation process were, following his death, left in the private possession of Emma Hale Smith. Later in her life, she donated the manuscript to the Reorganized Church of Jesus Christ of Latter Day Saints (RLDS). The manuscript has remained in their possession to the present time.

For a substantial period of time, access for LDS scholars to the Bible and manuscripts of Joseph's work was very limited. This limited access created some feelings of caution on the part of LDS students of the scriptures concerning the accuracy of the JST texts being published by the RLDS church (such as the *Inspired Bible*). However, since Robert J. Matthews, former Dean of BYU Religious Education, was given full access to the Bible and manuscripts in the 1960's, no serious doubt has survived in the LDS scholarly community that the Joseph Smith Translation, as represented in RLDS publications, is fundamentally reliable and complete when compared to Joseph's original work.

Previous JST Integrations

The numerous past efforts at integrating the JST have produced very different and interesting texts. For example, in 1970 the Herald Press in Independence, Missouri published a comprehensive parallel text of all JST variations against the King James version. The exclusion of non-modified verses, although understandable due to space limitations, makes this text strictly a reference work, rather than a study text. The changes are available in context of the verse, but the verse is not available in the context of the full chapter, or even the surrounding verses. Additionally, the book does not highlight the additions or deletions, leaving the reader to compare verses word by word to determine where the changes have been made.

An interesting problem associated with the Herald Press book was described by Robert Matthews (1971): "Some variant readings that are given are not actually revisions. Differences are due to the use of different editions of the King James Version rather than to deliberate revision by the Prophet Joseph." Matthews points out that the Herald Press did not take into account the fact that KJV Bibles published in England and the United States in the early 1800's sometimes differed in their use of articles, pronouns and the spelling of some words.

The main limitation to *all* of the previous attempts at integrating the JST text is the lack of full context. Perhaps the main barrier to any complete integration is the fact that the actual mechanics (such as which JST words were meant as replacements for which specific KJV words) are nearly impossible to establish[1]. However, it is possible to construct the integration so that the text can be read either as it normally would as KJV text (without the JST changes), or as it would with Joseph's translation, without having to assert the actual mechanical process. This compilation has approached the integration of the JST texts in this fashion.

Integration of the Joseph Smith Translation

The organization of this text was done in such a way as to maximize the ability of the reader to use the current LDS version scriptures, with their extensive footnotes and topical guide references. Specifically, the changes in the numbering of verses made by Joseph Smith in his translation were not represented in this text so that readers could more easily find the passage in the current LDS version scriptures.

In generating the most reasonably reliable text, both in relation to the JST alterations and the paralleling of the text, this project made use of a number of generally available publications[2]. The microfilm copy of the JST manuscripts, in possession of the Harold B. Lee Library at BYU was also consulted when conflicts between sources were encountered. In instances where two sources conflicted, precedence was always given to the most original source (usually the microfilm version). All changes in spelling, words, phrases and verses made by the Prophet Joseph Smith were included in this work (from one letter to multiple verses).

The Old Testament

This volume presents a compilation and integration of the the changes made by the Prophet Joseph Smith to the King James Version of the Old Testament. By far, the most changes were made in the books of Genesis and Isaiah; therefore, these books are presented in their contextual entirety. The JST version of the Book of Genesis has parallels with the Books of Moses and Abraham. In fact, the Book of Moses "is an almost verbatim copy of JST Genesis 1:1-8:18" (Horton, 1985, p. 53). In this volume, the JST Genesis (KJV Genesis 1:1-6:13), Moses and Genesis are presented in harmonized parallel columns with markers embedded within the Book of Moses to indicate when the text of Moses differs from the JST Genesis text (see Description of Text Format).

The integration of JST Isaiah is presented with its parallels in the Book of Mormon Isaiah text. Again, markers are placed in the Book of Mormon Isaiah text to indicate when the text differs from the JST Isaiah. On occasion, other scriptural text is also harmonized when it specifically and directly relates to the Isaiah text.

The Prophet Joseph Smith also made textual changes throughout the remaining books of the Old Testament. The Book of Malachi is presented in its contextual entirety given the high degree of parallel LDS scriptures. However, given that fewer JST changes exist in the remaining books of the Old Testament books, the verses with JST changes are presented in integrated form in the Appendix but not in full context.

The tremendous possibilities that lie in integrating the parallel format with the changes made by the prophet Joseph Smith are clear. With Joseph's textual changes to Genesis, Isaiah and Malachi, in parallel harmony with other LDS scripture, we can broaden our perspective and deepen our scriptural understandings. Our hope is that this text will be useful in the study of the Old Testament.

---

[1] Personal communication received from Dr. Richard P. Howard in 1989, as Church Historian and head of the Archives of the RLDS Church.

[2] See the bibliography at the end of this book.

Description of Text Format

Example:

> **Genesis**
>
> 1:1 . . . ***Yea, i***~~I~~n the beginning ~~God~~ ***I*** created the heaven, and the earth ***upon which thou standest***.

Chapter & Verse Number
~~Strikeout~~ indicates original KJV rendering for the verse
Bold Italics indicates the JST rendering for the verse

Joseph Smith Translation

When reading the text, if the reader were to ignore the words ~~marked by the strikeout line~~, and include the words that are ***bolded and italicized***, the reading of the passage would be that of the complete JST, i.e.:

1:1 . . . Yea, in the beginning I created the heaven, and the earth upon which thou standest.

King James Version

Reversing that process to include the words ~~marked by the strikeout line~~, and ignoring the words that are ***bolded and italicized***, would render the text as the regular KJV This provides a practical way of comparing how the JST might impact the reading of a particular section, i.e.:

1:1 . . . In the beginning God created the heaven, and the earth.

Comparisons with JST Text

The following markers are used to compare parallel LDS scripture from Book of Moses and the Book of Mormon with the JST text:

<u>Underline</u>	indicates words or phrases that are different from, or not found in, the JST rendering.
(-) (- - -)	indicates a word (-) or phrase (- - -) in the JST rendering that is not found in the comparative LDS text.

TABLE OF CONTENTS

Introduction v
Description of Text Format vii

THE BOOK OF GENESIS 1
In Parallel Harmony with the Books of Moses and Abraham

Abraham's Vision 3
Moses' Vision 5
Satan's Rebellion 9

Chapter 1: The Creation: the First Day 11
The Creation: the Second Day 11
The Creation: the Third Day 12
The Creation: the Fourth Day 13
The Creation: the Fifth Day 13
The Creation: the Sixth Day 14

Chapter 2: The Creation: the Seventh Day 15
Generations of Heaven and Earth 15
The Creation of Man 16
The Garden of Eden 16

Chapter 3: The Fall 18
Expulsion from the Garden 20

Chapter 4: Adam Lives in the World 21
Cain and Abel 23
Lamech & Secret Combinations 25
Seth 27

Chapter 5: Adam's Posterity 27
Enoch's Vision 29
Enoch Testifies 31
The Lord Covenants with Enoch 39
Zion Is Fled 42
Methuselah 42

Chapter 6: Prelude to the Flood 43
Noah Builds the Ark 45

For locations of specific verses of Genesis, Isaiah, Malachi, Moses, Abraham, Joseph Smith History, the Book of Mormon and the Doctrine & Covenants that are incorporated into the parallel harmony, please refer to the Verse Index, starting on page 299.

TABLE OF CONTENTS (cont.)

GENESIS (cont.)

Chapter 7: Noah Enters the Ark 46

Chapter 8: The Flood Abates 48
Noah Leaves the Ark and Builds an Altar 49

Chapter 9: God Covenants with Noah 50
Noah's Sons 52

Chapter 10: Nations and Peoples of the Earth 52

Chapter 11: The Tower of Babel 54
The Genealogy of Abram 55
Abram Seeks His Appointment in Ur of the Chaldees 56
Attempt to Offer Abram as Sacrifice 57
Brief History of Egypt 59
Abrah Leaves Ur of the Chaldees 60

Chapter 12: The Lord Appears to Abram 61
Abram Departs and Builds an Altar at Shechem 62
Abram Journeys to Egypt 63
Abram in Egypt 64

Chapter 13: Abram and Lot Separate 64

Chapter 14: The Four Kings 65
Abram Rescues Lot 65
Abram and Melchizedek 66

Chapter 15: Abram's Seed 67

Chapter 16: Hagar & the Birth of Ishmael 68

Chapter 17: Abraham: The Covenant and Circumcision 69

Chapter 18: Abraham and Sarah Visited by Three Holy Men 70
Abraham Intercedes for Sodom 71

Chapter 19: Lot Visited by Three Holy Angels 72
Lot Escapes from Sodom 73
Sodom Destroyed 73

Chapter 20: Abraham, Sarah and Abimelech in Gerar 74

Chapter 21: Birth of Isaac 75
Expulsion of Hagar 75
Abraham and Abimelech at Beersheba 76

TABLE OF CONTENTS (cont.)

GENESIS (cont.)

Chapter 22: The Sacrifice of Isaac 76
Line of Nahor 77

Chapter 23: Death and Burial of Sarah 78

Chapter 24: Isaac and Rebekah 79

Chapter 25: Abraham's Sons by Keturah 81
Death of Abraham 82
The Line of Ishmael 82
Birth of Jacob and Esau 82
Esau Sells His Birthright 83

Chapter 26: Isaac and Abimelech 83
Isaac in Beersheba 84

Chapter 27: Isaac Blesses Jacob 85

Chapter 28: Jacob is Sent to Laban 86
Jacob's Vision at Bethel 87

Chapter 29: Jacob in Haran 87
Jacob Marries Leah and Rachel 88

Chapter 30: Jacob's Children 89
Jacob's Bargain with Laban 90

Chapter 31: Jacob Leaves Laban 91
Laban's Pursuit 92
Contract Between Jacob and Laban 92

Chapter 32: Jacob Prepares to Meet Esau 93
Jacob Wrestles 94

Chapter 33: Jacob Meets Esau 94

Chapter 34: Jacob's Sons Revenge Dinah 95

Chapter 35: Jacob Visits Bethel 96
Death and Burial of Rachel 97
Sons of Jacob 97
Death and Burial of Isaac 98

Chapter 36: Descendants of Esau 98

TABLE OF CONTENTS (cont.)

GENESIS (cont.)

Chapter 37: Joseph's Coat of Many Colors 99
Joseph's Dream 99
Joseph Sold Into Egypt 100

Chapter 38: Judah and Tamar 101
Chapter 39: Joseph and Potiphar's Wife 102
Joseph in Prison 103

Chapter 40: Joseph Interprets Prisoners' Dreams 103

Chapter 41: Joseph Interprets Pharoah's Dream 104
Joseph Second to Pharoah 106
Seven Years of Plenty 106
Birth of Manasseh and Ephriam 106
Seven Years of Famine 106

Chapter 42: First Journey of Jacob's Sons to Egypt 107
Joseph's Brothers Return Home 108

Chapter 43: Second Journey to Egypt 109

Chapter 44: Second Journey to Egypt (cont.) 110

Chapter 45: Joseph Discloses His Identity 111
Joseph's Brothers Return Home 112

Chapter 46: Jacob Goes to Egypt 112
Joseph Meets Jacob 113

Chapter 47: Jacob Meets Pharoah 113
Joseph and the Famine 114
Jacob Lives in Goshen 115

Chapter 48: The Blessing of Ephriam and Manasseh 115

Chapter 49: Jacob's Blessings and Prophecies 116
Death and Burial of Jacob 117

Chapter 50: Joseph Forgives His Brothers 118
Joseph's Prophecy 119
Death of Joseph 120

TABLE OF CONTENTS (cont.)

THE BOOK OF ISAIAH 121
In parallel with the Book of Mormon Isaiah text and other LDS scripture

Isaiah Introduction in the Book of Mormon 123

Chapter 1 124
2 126
3 128
4 130
5 131
6 133
7 134
8 136
9 138
10 140

11 142
12 145
13 145
14 147
15 149
16 150
17 151
18 152
19 153
20 155

21 156
22 157
23 159
24 160
25 162
26 163
27 165
28 166
29 168
30 175

31 176
32 177
33 177
34 178
35 179
36 180
37 181
38 183
39 184
40 184

TABLE OF CONTENTS (cont.)

THE BOOK OF ISAIAH (cont.)

Chapter 41 185
42 187
43 188
44 189
45 190
46 191
47 192
48 193
49 195
50 197

51 299
52 201
53 204
54 205
55 207
56 218
57 209
58 210
59 212
60 214

61 214
62 217
63 218
64 220
65 221
66 223

THE BOOK OF MALACHI

Chapter 1 229
2 230
3 231
4 234

TABLE OF CONTENTS (cont.)

APPENDIX: JST Changes in the Other Books of the Old Testament 237

Genesis (Full Text) 1
Exodus 239
Leviticus 247
Numbers 249
Deuteronomy 250
Joshua 251
Judges 252
Ruth .... (No JST changes)
1st Samuel 253
2nd Samuel 256
1st Kings 258
2nd Kings 262
1st Chronicles 263
2nd Chronicles 266
Ezra .... (No JST changes)
Nehemiah 270
Esther .... (No JST Changes)
Job 271
Psalms 272
Proverbs 283
Ecclesiastes .... (No JST Changes)
Song of Solomon .... (Not included in the JST)
Isaiah (Full Text) 123
Jeremiah 287
Lamentations .... (No JST Changes)
Ezekiel 288
Daniel 290
Hosea 291
Joel 292
Amos 292
Obadiah .... (No JST Changes)
Jonah 293
Micah 294
Nahum 294
Habakkuk 294
Zephaniah 294
Haggai 294
Zechariah 295
Malachi (FULL TEXT) 229

VERSE INDEX 297

REFERENCES 301

THE BOOK OF GENESIS

With
the Joseph Smith Translation

In
in Parallel Harmony with
the Books of Moses and Abraham

ABRAHAM'S VISION

3:1 And I, Abraham, had the Urim
and Thummim, which the Lord my God
had given unto me, in Ur of the
Chaldees;
3:2 And I saw the stars, that they
were very great, and that one of them
was nearest unto the throne of God; and
there were many great ones which were
near unto it;
3:3 And the Lord said unto me:
These are the governing ones; and the
name of the great one is Kolob, because
it is near unto me, for I am the Lord thy
God: I have set this one to govern all
those which belong to the same order as
that upon which thou standest.
3:4 And the Lord said unto me, by
the Urim and Thummim, that Kolob
was after the manner of the Lord,
according to its times and seasons in
the revolutions thereof; that one
revolution was a day unto the Lord,
after his manner of reckoning, it being
one thousand years according to the
time appointed unto that whereon thou
standest. This is the reckoning of the
Lord's time, according to the reckoning
of Kolob.
3:5 And the Lord said unto me: The
planet which is the lesser light, lesser
than that which is to rule the day, even
the night, is above or greater than that
upon which thou standest in point of
reckoning, for it moveth in order more
slow; this is in order because it standeth
above the earth upon which thou
standest, therefore the reckoning of its
time is not so many as to its number of
days, and of months, and of years.
3:6 And the Lord said unto me: Now,
Abraham, these two facts exist, behold
thine eyes see it; it is given unto thee to
know the times of reckoning, and the
set time, yea, the set time of the earth
upon which thou standest, and the set
time of the greater light which is set to
rule the day, and the set time of the
lesser light which is set to rule the
night.
3:7 Now the set time of the lesser
light is a longer time as to its reckoning
than the reckoning of the time of the
earth upon which thou standest.
3:8 And where these two facts exist,
there shall be another fact above them,
that is, there shall be another planet

whose reckoning of time shall be longer still;
3:9 And thus there shall be the reckoning of the time of one planet above another, until thou come nigh unto Kolob, which Kolob is after the reckoning of the Lord's time; which Kolob is set nigh unto the throne of God, to govern all those planets which belong to the same order as that upon which thou standest.
3:10 And it is given unto thee to know the set time of all the stars that are set to give light, until thou come near unto the throne of God.
3:11 Thus I, Abraham, talked with the Lord, face to face, as one man talketh with another; and he told me of the works which his hands had made;
3:12 And he said unto me: My son, my son (and his hand was stretched out), behold I will show you all these. And he put his hand upon mine eyes, and I saw those things which his hands had made, which were many; and they multiplied before mine eyes, and I could not see the end thereof.
3:13 And he said unto me: This is Shinehah, which is the sun. And he said unto me: Kokob, which is star. And he said unto me: Olea, which is the moon. And he said unto me: Kokaubeam, which signifies stars, or all the great lights, which were in the firmament of heaven.
3:14 And it was in the night time when the Lord spake these words unto me: I will multiply thee, and thy seed after thee, like unto these; and if thou canst count the number of sands, so shall be the number of thy seeds.
3:15 And the Lord said unto me: Abraham, I show these things unto thee before ye go into Egypt, that ye may declare all these words.
3:16 If two things exist, and there be one above the other, there shall be greater things above them; therefore Kolob is the greatest of all the Kokaubeam that thou hast seen, because it is nearest unto me.
3:17 Now, if there be two things, one above the other, and the moon be above the earth, then it may be that a planet or a star may exist above it; and there is nothing that the Lord thy God shall take in his heart to do but what he will do it.

3:18 Howbeit that he made the greater
star; as, also, if there be two spirits, and
one shall be more intelligent than the
other, yet these two spirits, notwithstanding one is more intelligent that the
other, have no beginning; they existed
before, they shall have no end, they
shall exist after, for they are gnolaum,
or eternal.
3:19 And the Lord said unto me:
These two facts do exist, that there are
two spirits, one being more intelligent
than the other; there shall be another
more intelligent than they; I am the
Lord thy God, I am more intelligent
than they all.
3:20 The Lord thy God sent his angel
to deliver thee from the hands of the
priest of Elkenah.
3:21 I dwell in the midst of them all; I
now, therefore, have come down unto
thee to declare unto thee the works
which my hands have made, wherein
my wisdom excelleth them all, for I rule
in the heavens above, and in the earth
beneath, in all wisdom and prudence,
over all the intelligences thine eyes
have seen from the beginning; I came
down in the beginning in the midst of
all the intelligences thou hast seen.
3:22 Now the Lord had shown unto
me, Abraham, the intelligences that
were organized before the world was;
and among all these there were many of
the noble and great ones;
3:23 And God saw these souls that
they were good, and he stood in the
midst of them, and he said: These I will
make my rulers; for he stood among
those that were spirits, and he saw that
they were good; and he said unto me:
Abraham, thou art one of them; thou
wast chosen before thou wast born.

MOSES' VISION

1:1 The words of God, which he
spake unto Moses at a time when Moses
was caught up into an exceedingly high
mountain,
1:2 And he saw God face to face, and
he talked with him, and the glory of God
was upon Moses; therefore Moses could
endure his presence.
1:3 And God spake unto Moses,
saying: Behold, I am the Lord God
Almighty, and Endless is my name; for

I am without beginning of days or end
of years; and is not this endless?
1:4 And, behold, thou art my son;
wherefore look, and I will show unto
thee the workmanship of mine hands;
but not all, for my works are without
end, and also my words, for they never
cease.
1:5 Wherefore, no man can behold all
my works, except he behold all my
glory; and no man can behold all my
glory, and afterwards remain in the flesh
on the earth.
1:6 And I have a work for thee,
Moses my son; and thou art in the
similitude of mine Only Begotten; and
mine Only Begotten is and shall be the
Savior, for he is full of grace and truth;
but there is no God beside me, and all
things are present with me, for I know
them all.
1:7 And now, behold, this one thing
I show unto thee, Moses, my son, for
thou art in the world, and now I show it
unto thee.
1:8 And it came to pass that Moses
looked, and beheld the world upon
which he was created; and Moses beheld
the world and all the ends thereof, and
all the children of men which are, and
which were created; of the same he
greatly marveled and wondered.
1:9 And the presence of God
withdrew from Moses, that his glory
was not upon Moses; and Moses was
left unto himself. And as he was left
unto himself, he fell unto the earth.
1:10 And it came to pass that it was for
the space of many hours before Moses
did again receive his natural strength
like unto man; and he said unto himself:
Now, for this cause I know that man is
nothing, which thing I never had
supposed.
1:11 But now mine own eyes have
beheld God; but not my natural, but my
spiritual eyes, for my natural eyes could
not have beheld; for I should have
withered and died in his presence; but
his glory was upon me; and I beheld his
face, for I was transfigured before him.
1:12 And it came to pass that when
Moses had said these words, behold,
Satan came tempting him, saying:
Moses, son of man, worship me.
1:13 And it came to pass that Moses
looked upon Satan and said: Who art

thou? For behold, I am a son of God, in the similitude of his Only Begotten; and where is thy glory, that I should worship thee?
1:14 For behold, I could not look upon God, except his glory should come upon me, and I were transfigured before him. But I can look upon thee in the natural man. Is it not so, surely?
1:15 Blessed be the name of my God, for his Spirit hath not altogether withdrawn from me, or else where is thy glory, for it is darkness unto me? And I can judge between thee and God; for God said unto me: Worship God, for him only shalt thou serve.
1:16 Get thee hence, Satan; deceive me not; for God said unto me: Thou art after the similitude of mine Only Begotten.
1:17 And he also gave me commandments when he called unto me out of the burning bush, saying: Call upon God in the name of mine Only Begotten, and worship me.
1:18 And again Moses said: I will not cease to call upon God, I have other things to inquire of him: for his glory has been upon me, wherefore I can judge between him and thee. Depart hence, Satan.
1:19 And now, when Moses had said these words, Satan cried with a loud voice, and ranted upon the earth, and commanded, saying: I am the Only Begotten, worship me.
1:20 And it came to pass that Moses began to fear exceedingly; and as he began to fear, he saw the bitterness of hell. Nevertheless, calling upon God, he received strength, and he commanded, saying: Depart from me, Satan, for this one God only will I worship, which is the God of glory.
1:21 And now Satan began to tremble, and the earth shook; and Moses received strength, and called upon God, saying: In the name of the Only Begotten, depart hence, Satan.
1:22 And it came to pass that Satan cried with a loud voice, with weeping, and wailing, and gnashing of teeth; and he departed hence, even from the presence of Moses, that he beheld him not.
1:23 And now of this thing Moses bore record; but because of wickedness it is not had among the children of men.

1:24 And it came to pass that when Satan had departed from the presence of Moses, that Moses lifted up his eyes unto heaven, being filled with the Holy Ghost, which beareth record of the Father and the Son;
1:25 And calling upon the name of God, he beheld his glory again, for it was upon him; and he heard a voice, saying: Blessed art thou, Moses, for I, the Almighty, have chosen thee, and thou shalt be made stronger than many waters; for they shall obey thy command as if thou wert God.
1:26 And lo, I am with thee, even unto the end of thy days; for thou shalt deliver my people from bondage, even Israel my chosen.
1:27 And it came to pass, as the voice was still speaking, Moses cast his eyes and beheld the earth, yea, even all of it; and there was not a particle of it which he did not behold, discerning it by the spirit of God.
1:28 And he beheld also the inhabitants thereof, and there was not a soul which he beheld not; and he discerned them by the Spirit of God; and their numbers were great, even numberless as the sand upon the sea shore.
1:29 And he beheld many lands; and each land was called earth, and there were inhabitants on the face thereof.
1:30 And it came to pass that Moses called upon God, saying: Tell me, I pray thee, why these things are so, and by what thou madest them?
1:31 And behold, the glory of the Lord was upon Moses, so that Moses stood in the presence of God, and talked with him face to face. And the Lord God said unto Moses: For mine own purpose have I made these things. Here is wisdom and it remaineth in me.
1:32 And by the word of my power, have I created them, which is mine Only Begotten Son, who is full of grace and truth.
1:33 And worlds without number have I created; and I also created them for mine own purpose; and by the Son I created them, which is mine Only Begotten.
1:34 And the first man of all men have I called Adam, which is many.

1:35 But only an account of this earth, and the inhabitants thereof, give I unto you. For behold, there are many worlds that have passed away by the word of my power. And there are many that now stand, and innumerable are they unto man; but all things are numbered unto me, for they are mine and I know them.
1:36 And it came to pass that Moses spake unto the Lord, saying: Be merciful unto thy servant, O God, and tell me concerning this earth, and the inhabitants thereof, and also the heavens, and then thy servant will be content.
1:37 And the Lord God spake unto Moses, saying: The heavens, they are many, and they cannot be numbered unto man; but they are numbered unto me, for they are mine.
1:38 And as one earth shall pass away, and the heavens thereof even so shall another come; and there is no end to my works, neither to my words.
1:39 For behold, this is my work and my glory to bring to pass the immortality and eternal life of man.
1:40 And now, Moses, my son, I will speak unto thee concerning this earth upon which thou standest; and thou shalt write the things which I shall speak.
1:41 And in a day when the children of men shall esteem my words as naught and take many of them from the book which thou shalt write, behold, I will raise up another like unto thee; and they shall be had again among the children of men among as many as shall believe.
1:42 (These words were spoken unto Moses in the mount, the name of which shall not be known among the children of men. And now they are spoken unto you. Show them not unto any except them that believe. Even so. Amen.)

SATAN'S REBELLION

3:24 And there stood one among them that was like unto God, and he said unto those who were with him: We will go down, for there is space there, and we will take of these materials, and we will make an earth whereon these may dwell;
3:25 And we will prove them herewith, to see if they will do all things whatsoever the Lord their God shall command them;

GENESIS

3:1a ***And I, the Lord God, spake unto Moses, saying,***
That Satan whom thou hast commanded in the name of mine Only Begotten, is the same which was from the beginning;
And he came before me, saying, Behold I, send me, I will be thy Son, and I will redeem all mankind, that one soul shall not be lost, and surely I will do it;
wherefore give me thine honor.
But behold, my beloved Son, which was my beloved and chosen from the beginning, said unto me; Father, thy will be done, and the glory be thine for ever.

Wherefore, because that Satan rebelled against me, and sought to destroy the agency of man, which I, the Lord God, had given him;
and also that I should give unto him mine own power; by the power of mine Only Begotten I caused that he should be cast down;
and he became Satan.
Yea, even the devil, the father of all lies, to deceive, and to blind men, and to lead them captive at his will, even as many as would not hearken unto my voice.

MOSES

4:1 And I, the Lord God, spake unto Moses, saying:
That Satan, whom thou hast commanded in the name of mine Only Begotten, is the same which was from the beginning,

and he came before me, saying--Behold, here am I, send me, I will be thy son, and I will redeem all mankind, that one soul shall not be lost, and surely I will do it;
wherefore give me thine honor.
4:2 But, behold, my Beloved Son, which was my Beloved and Chosen from the beginning, said unto me,
Father, thy will be done, and the glory be thine forever.

4:3 Wherefore, because that Satan rebelled against me, and sought to destroy the agency of man, which I, the Lord God, had given him,
and also, that I should give unto him mine own power; by the power of mine Only Begotten, I caused that he should be cast down;
4:4 And he became Satan,
yea, even the devil, the father of all lies, to deceive and to blind men, and to lead them captive at his will, even as many as would not hearken unto my voice.

ABRAHAM

3:26 And they who keep their first estate shall be added upon; and they who keep not their first estate shall not have glory in the same kingdom with those who keep their first estate; and they who keep their second estate shall have glory added upon their heads for ever and ever.
3:27 And the Lord said: Whom shall I send?
And one answered like unto the Son of Man: Here am I, send me.
And another answered and said: Here am I, send me.

And the Lord said: I will send the first.
3:28 And the second was angry, and kept not his first estate;

and, at that day, many followed after him.

GENESIS King James Version with JST	**MOSES** (With Comparison to JST Genesis)	**ABRAHAM**
THE CREATION: The First Day		
1:1 ***And it came to pass, that the Lord spake unto Moses, saying, Behold, I reveal unto you concerning this heaven and this earth; write the words which I speak.*** ***I am the Beginning and the End; the Almighty God. By mine Only Begotten I created these things.*** ***Yea, i***~~I~~n the beginning ~~God~~ ***I*** created the heaven, and the earth ***upon which thou standest***.	2:1 And it came to pass that the Lord spake unto Moses, saying: Behold, I reveal unto you concerning this heaven, and this earth; write the words which I speak. I am the Beginning and the End, the Almighty God; by mine Only Begotten I created these things; yea, in the beginning I created the heaven, and the earth upon which thou standest.	
		4:1 And then the Lord said: Let us go down. And they went down at the beginning, and they, that is the Gods, organized and formed the heavens and the earth.
1:2 And the earth was without form, and void;	2:2 And the earth was without form, and void;	4:2 And the earth, after it was formed, was empty and desolate, because they had not formed anything but the earth;
and ***I caused*** darkness ~~was~~ ***to come up*** upon the face of the deep. And ~~the~~ ***my*** Spirit ~~of God~~ moved upon the face of the waters***, for I am God***.	and I caused darkness to come up upon the face of the deep; and my Spirit moved upon the face of the water; for I am God.	and darkness reigned upon the face of the deep, and the Spirit of the Gods was brooding upon the face of the waters.
1:3 And ***I,*** God***,*** said, Let there be light**,** ~~:~~ and there was light.	2:3 And I, God, said: Let there be light; and there was light.	4:3 And they (the Gods) said: Let there be light; and there was light.
1:4 And ***I,*** God***,*** saw the light, ***and*** that ~~it~~ ***light*** was good**.** ~~: a~~And ***I,*** God, divided the light from the darkness.	2:4 And I, God, saw the light; and that light was good. And I, God, divided the light from the darkness.	4:4 And they (the Gods) comprehended the light, for it was bright; and they divided the light, or caused it to be divided, from the darkness.
1:5 And ***I,*** God***,*** called the light ~~D~~*d*ay, and the darkness ~~he~~ ***I*** called ~~N~~*n*ight.	2:5 And I, God, called the light Day; and the darkness, I called Night;	4:5 And the Gods called the light Day, and the darkness they called Night. And it came to pass that from the evening until morning they called night;
And this I did by the word of my power; and it was done as I spake. And the evening and the morning were the first day.	and this I did by the word of my power, and it was done as I spake; and the evening and the morning were the first day.	and from the morning until the evening they called day;
THE CREATION: The Second Day		
1:6 And ***again, I,*** God***,*** said, Let there be a firmament in the midst of the waters; and ***it was so, even as I spake. And I said,*** ~~l~~Let it divide the waters from the waters***; and it was done***.	2:6 And again, I, God, said: Let there be a firmament in the midst of the water, and it was so, even as I spake; and I said: Let it divide the waters from the waters; and it was done;	
		and this was the first, or the beginning, of that which they called day and night. 4:6 And the Gods also said: Let there be an expanse in the midst of the waters, and it shall divide the waters from the waters.
1:7 And ***I,*** God***,*** made the firmament, and divided the waters ~~which were~~ ***;***	2:7 And I, God, made the firmament and divided the waters, yea, the great	4:7 And the Gods ordered the expanse, so that it divided the waters

yea, the great waters under the firmament**,** from the waters which were above the firmament**;** ~~:~~	waters under the firmament from the waters which were above the firmament,	which were under the expanse from the waters which were above the expanse;
and it was so ***even as I spake***. 1:8 And ***I,*** God**,** called the firmament ~~H~~***h***eaven.	and it was so even as I spake. 2:8 And I, God, called the firmament Heaven;	and it was so, even as they ordered. 4:8 And the Gods called the expanse, Heaven. And it came to pass that it was from evening until morning that they called night; and it came to pass that it was from morning until evening that
And the evening and the morning were the second day.	and the evening and the morning were the second day.	they called day; and this was the second time that they called night and day.

THE CREATION: The Third Day

1:9 And ***I,*** God**,** said, Let the waters under the heaven be gathered together unto one place***; and it was so.*** ~~a~~***A***nd ***I, God, said,*** ~~l~~***L***et ~~the~~ ***there be*** dry land**;** ~~appear:~~ and it was so. 1:10 And ***I,*** God**,** called the dry land ~~E~~***e***arth; and the gathering together of the waters**,** called ~~he Seas:~~ ***I the sea***.	2:9 And I, God, said: Let the waters under the heaven be gathered together unto one place, and it was so; and I, God, said: Let there be dry land; and it was so. 2:10 And I, God, called the dry land Earth; and the gathering together of the waters, called I the Sea;	4:9 And the Gods ordered, saying: Let the waters under the heaven be gathered together unto one place, and let the earth come up dry; and it was so as they ordered; 4:10 And the Gods pronounced the dry land, Earth; and the gathering together of the waters, pronounced they, Great Waters;
~~a~~***A***nd ***I,*** God**,** saw that ~~it was~~ ***all things which I had made were*** good. 1:11 And **I,** God**,** said, Let the earth bring forth grass**;** ~~,~~ the herb yielding seed**;** ~~, and~~ the fruit tree yielding fruit after his kind~~,~~ **;** ***and the tree yielding fruit,*** whose seed ***should be*** ~~is~~ in itself, upon the earth**;** ~~:~~ and it was so***, even as I spake***.	and I, God, saw that all things which I had made were good. 2:11 And I, God, said: Let the earth bring forth grass, the herb yielding seed, the fruit tree yielding fruit, after his kind, and the tree yielding fruit, whose seed should be in itself upon the earth, and it was so even as I spake.	and the Gods saw that they were obeyed. 4:11 And the Gods said: Let us prepare the earth to bring forth grass; the herb yielding seed; the fruit tree yielding fruit, after his kind, whose seed in itself yieldeth its own likeness upon the earth; and it was so, even as they ordered.
1:12 And the earth brought forth grass**;** ~~, and~~ ***every*** herb yielding seed after his kind**;** ~~,~~	2:12 And the earth brought forth grass, every herb yielding seed after his kind,	4:12 And the Gods organized the earth to bring forth grass from its own seed, and the herb to bring forth herb from its own seed, yielding seed after his kind;
and the tree yielding fruit, whose seed ~~was~~ ***should be*** in itself,	and the tree yielding fruit, whose seed should be in itself,	and the earth to bring forth the tree from its own seed, yielding fruit, whose seed could only bring forth the same in itself,
after his kind**.** ~~:~~	after his kind;	after his kind;
and ***I,*** God**,** saw that ~~it was~~ ***all things which I had made were*** good.	and I, God, saw that all things which I had made were good;	and the Gods saw that they were obeyed.
1:13 And the evening and the morning were the third day.	2:13 And the evening and the morning were the third day.	4:13 And it came to pass that they numbered the days; from the evening until the morning they called night; and it came to pass, from the morning until the evening they called day; and it was the third time.

THE CREATION: The Fourth Day

Genesis

1:14 And **I,** God, said, Let there be lights in the firmament of the heaven, to divide the day from the night;
and let them be for signs, and for seasons, and for days, and ***for*** years:
1:15 And let them be for lights in the firmament of the heaven, to give light upon the earth***;*** ~~:~~ and it was so.
1:16 And **I**, God, made two great lights; the greater light to rule the day, and the lesser light to rule the night~~:~~ ***;***
and the greater light was the sun, and the lesser light was the moon. ~~he made~~

And the stars also ***were made, even according to my word.***
1:17 And ***I,*** God, set them in the firmament of the heaven, to give light upon the earth***;*** ~~,~~
1:18 And ***the sun*** to rule over the day, and ***the moon to rule*** over the night, and to divide the light from the darkness***;*** ~~:~~

and ***I,*** God, saw that ~~it was~~ ***all things which I had made were*** good.

1:19 And the evening and the morning were the fourth day.

Moses

2:14 And I, God, said: Let there be lights in the firmament of the heaven, to divide the day from the night,
and let them be for signs, and for seasons, and for days, and for years;
2:15 And let them be for lights in the firmament of the heaven to give light upon the earth; and it was so.
2:16 And I, God, made two great lights; the greater light to rule the day, and the lesser light to rule the night,
and the greater light was the sun, and the lesser light was the moon;

and the stars also were made even according to my word.
2:17 And I, God, set them in the firmament of the heaven to give light upon the earth.
2:18 And the sun to rule over the day, and the moon to rule over the night, and to divide the light from the darkness;

and I, God, saw that all things which I had made were good;

2:19 And the evening and the morning were the fourth day.

Abraham

4:14 And the Gods organized the lights in the expanse of the heaven, and caused them to divide the day from the night;
and organized them to be for signs and for seasons, and for days and for years;
4:15 And organized them to be for lights in the expanse of the heaven to give light upon the earth; and it was so.
4:16 And the Gods organized the two great lights, the greater light to rule the day, and the lesser light to rule the night;

with the lesser light they set the stars also;
4:17 And the Gods set them in the expanse of the heavens, to give light upon the earth,
and to rule over the day and over the night,
and to cause to divide the light from the darkness.
4:18 And the Gods watched those things which they had ordered until they obeyed.

4:19 And it came to pass that it was from evening until morning that is was night; and it came to pass that it was from morning until evening that it was day; and it was the fourth time.

THE CREATION: The Fifth Day

Genesis

1:20 And ***I,*** God, said, Let the waters bring forth abundantly, the moving creature that hath life, and fowl ~~that~~ ***which*** may fly above the earth, in the open firmament of heaven.
1:21 And ***I,*** God,
created great whales, and every living creature that moveth, which the waters brought forth abundantly, after their kind, and every winged fowl after his kind***;*** ~~:~~
and **I,** God, saw that ~~it was~~ ***all things which I had created were*** good.
1:22 And ***I,*** God, blessed them, saying, Be fruitful, and multiply, and fill the waters in the sea~~s~~,

and let fowl multiply in the earth.

Moses

2:20 And I, God, said: Let the waters bring forth abundantly the moving creature that hath life, and fowl which may fly above the earth in the open firmament of heaven.
2:21 And I, God,
created great whales, and every living creature that moveth, which the waters brought forth abundantly, after their kind, and every winged fowl after his kind;
and I, God, saw that all things which I had created were good.
2:22 And I, God, blessed them, saying: Be fruitful, and multiply, and fill the waters in the sea;

and let fowl multiply in the earth;

Abraham

4:20 And the Gods said: Let us prepare the waters to bring forth abundantly the moving creatures that have life; and the fowl, that they may fly above the earth in the open expanse of heaven.
4:21 And the Gods prepared the waters that they might bring forth great whales, and every living creature that moveth, which the waters were to bring forth abundantly after their kinds; and every winged fowl after their kind.
And the Gods saw that they would be obeyed, and that their plan was good.
4:22 And the Gods said: We will bless them, and cause them to be fruitful and multiply, and fill the waters in the seas or great waters; and cause the fowl to multiply in the earth.

1:23 And the evening and the morning were the fifth day.

2:23 And the evening and the morning were the fifth day.

4:23 And it came to pass that it was from evening until morning that they called night; and it came to pass that it was from morning until evening that they called day; and it was the fifth time.

THE CREATION: The Sixth Day

1:24 And ***I,*** God, said, Let the earth bring forth the living creature, after his kind~~:~~ ***;*** cattle, and creeping thing*s*, and beast*s* of the earth, after ~~his~~ ***their*** kind***;*** ~~:~~ and it was so.
1:25 And ***I,*** God, made the beast*s* of the earth, after ~~his~~ ***their*** kind***;*** ~~,~~ and cattle after their kind***;*** ~~,~~
and ~~every thing that~~ ***everything which*** creepeth upon the earth after his kind:
and ***I,*** God, saw that ~~it was~~ ***all these things were*** good.
1:26 And ***I,*** God, said ***unto mine Only Begotten, which was with me from the beginning***,
Let us make man in our image, after our likeness~~:~~ ***; and it was so.***
And ***I, God, said,*** ~~l~~*L*et them have dominion over the fish*es* of the sea, and over the fowl of the air, and over the cattle, and over all the earth, and over every creeping thing that creepeth upon the earth.
1:27 ~~So~~ ***And I,*** God, created man in ~~his~~ ***mine*** own image, in the image of ~~God~~ ***mine Only Begotten*** created ~~he~~ ***I*** him; male and female created ~~he~~ ***I*** them.
1:28 And ***I,*** God, blessed them, and ~~God~~ said unto them, Be fruitful, and multiply, and replenish the earth, and subdue it***;*** ~~:~~ and have dominion over the fish of the sea, and over the fowl of the air, and over every living thing that moveth upon the earth.

1:29 And ***I,*** God, said ***unto man***, Behold, I have given you every herb, bearing seed, which is upon the face of all the earth***;*** ~~,~~ and every tree~~,~~ in the which ~~is~~ ***shall be*** the fruit of a tree, yielding seed; to you it shall be for meat.
1:30 And to every beast of the earth, and to every fowl of the air, and to ~~every thing~~ ***everything*** that creepeth upon the earth, wherein ~~there is~~ ***I grant*** life,

2:24 And I, God, said: Let the earth bring forth the living creature after his kind, cattle, and creeping things, and beasts of the earth after their kind, and it was so;
2:25 And I, God, made the beasts of the earth after their kind, and cattle after their kind,
and everything which creepeth upon the earth after his kind;
and I, God, saw that all these things were good.
2:26 And I, God, said unto mine Only Begotten, which was with me from the beginning:
Let us make man in our image, after our likeness; and it was so.
And I, God, said: Let them have dominion over the fishes of the sea, and over the fowls of the air, and over the cattle, and over all the earth, and over every creeping thing that creepeth upon the earth.
2:27 And I, God, created man in mine own image, in the image of mine Only Begotten created I him; male and female created I them.
2:28 And I, God, blessed them, and said unto them: Be fruitful, and multiply, and replenish the earth, and subdue it, and have dominion over the fish of the sea, and over the fowl of the air, and over every living thing that moveth upon the earth.

2:29 And I, God, said unto man: Behold, I have given you every herb bearing seed, which is upon the face of all the earth, and every tree in the which shall be the fruit of a tree yielding seed; to you it shall be for meat.

2:30 And to every beast of the earth, and to every fowl of the air, and to everything that creepeth upon the earth, wherein I grant life,

4:24 And the Gods prepared the earth to bring forth the living creature after his kind, cattle and creeping things, and beasts of the earth after their kind; and it was so, as they had said.
4:25 And the Gods organized the earth to bring forth the beasts after their kind, and cattle after their kind,
and every thing that creepeth upon the earth after its kind;
and the Gods saw they would obey.

4:26 And the Gods took counsel among themselves and said:

Let us go down and form man in our image, after our likeness;
and we will give them dominion over the fish of the sea, and over the fowl of the air, and over the cattle, and over all the earth, and over every creeping thing that creepeth upon the earth.

4:27 So the Gods went down to organize man in their own image, in the image of the Gods to form they him, male and female to form they them.
4:28 And the Gods said: We will bless them. And the Gods said: We will cause them to be fruitful and multiply, and replenish the earth, and subdue it, and to have dominion over the fish of the sea, and over the fowl of the air, and over every living thing that moveth upon the earth.
4:29 And the Gods said: Behold, we will give them every herb bearing seed that shall come upon the face of all the earth, and every tree which shall have fruit upon it; yea, the fruit of the tree yielding seed to them we will give it; it shall be for their meat.
4:30 And to every beast of the earth, and to every fowl of the air, and to every thing that creepeth upon the earth, behold, we will give them life,

GENESIS King James Version with JST	MOSES (With Comparison to JST Genesis)	ABRAHAM
~~I have~~ ***there shall be*** given every ~~green~~ ***clean*** herb for meat***;*** ~~:~~	there shall be given every clean herb for meat;	and also we will give to them every green herb for meat, and all these things shall be thus organized. 4:31 And the Gods said: We will do everything that we have said, and organize them; and behold, they shall be very obedient.
and it was so***, even as I spake***. 1:31 And ***I,*** God***,*** saw ~~every thing~~ ***everything*** that ~~he~~ ***I*** had made, and, behold, ~~it was~~ ***all things which I had made were*** very good.	and it was so, even as I spake. 2:31 And I, God, saw everything that I had made, and, behold, all things which I had made were very good;	
And the evening and the morning were the sixth day.	and the evening and the morning were the sixth day.	And it came to pass that it was from evening until morning they called night; and it came to pass that it was from morning until evening that they called day; and they numbered the sixth time.

THE CREATION: The Seventh Day

GENESIS	MOSES	ABRAHAM
2:1 Thus the heaven~~s~~ and the earth were finished, and all the host of them.	3:1 Thus the heaven and the earth were finished, and all the host of them.	5:1 And thus we will finish the heavens and the earth, and all the hosts of them. 5:2 And the Gods said among themselves: On the seventh time we will end our work, which we have counseled; and we will rest on the seventh time from all our work which we have counseled.
2:2 And on the seventh day, ***I,*** God, ended ~~his~~ ***my*** work***, and all things*** which ~~he~~ ***I*** had made; and ~~he~~ ***I*** rested on the seventh day from all ~~his~~ ***my*** work***; and all things*** which ~~he~~ ***I*** had made ***were finished.***	3:2 And on the seventh day I, God, ended my work, and all things which I had made; and I rested on the seventh day from all my work, and all things which I had made were finished,	5:3 And the Gods concluded upon the seventh time, because that on the seventh time they would rest from all their works which they (the Gods) counseled among themselves to form;
And I, God, saw that they were good. 2:3 And ***I,*** God***,*** blessed the seventh day, and sanctified it***;*** ~~:~~ because that in it ~~he~~ ***I*** had rested from all ~~his~~ ***my*** work, which ***I,*** God***, had*** created and made.	and I, God, saw that they were good; 3:3 And I, God, blessed the seventh day, and sanctified it; because that in it I had rested from all my work which I, God, had created and made.	and sanctified it. And thus were their decisions at the time that they counseled among themselves to form the heavens and the earth.

GENERATIONS OF HEAVEN AND EARTH

GENESIS	MOSES	ABRAHAM
2:4 ***And now, behold, I say unto you, that*** ~~T~~*t*hese are the generations of the heaven~~s~~ , and of the earth***,*** when they were created~~;~~ in the day that ***I*** the Lord God made the ***heaven and the*** earth ~~and the heavens~~,	3:4 And now, behold, I say unto you, that these are the generations of the heaven and of the earth, when they were created, in the day that I, the Lord God, made the heaven and the earth,	5:4 And the Gods came down and formed these the generations of the heavens and of the earth, when they were formed in the day that the Gods formed the earth and the heavens,

GENESIS	MOSES	ABRAHAM
2:5 And every plant of the field before it was in the earth, and every herb of the field before it grew***;*** ~~:~~ for ***I,*** the Lord God***, created all things of which I have spoken, spiritually, before they were naturally upon the face of the earth;***	3:5 And every plant of the field before it was in the earth, and every herb of the field before it grew. For I, the Lord God, created all things of which I have spoken, spiritually, before they were naturally upon the face of the earth.	5:5 According to all that which they had said concerning every plant of the field before it was in the earth, and every herb of the field before it grew;
for I, the Lord God had not caused it to rain upon the ***face of the*** earth ~~;~~.	For I, the Lord God, had not caused it to rain upon the face of the earth.	for the Gods had not caused it to rain upon the earth when they counseled to do them,
And I, the Lord God, had created all the children of men, and ~~there was~~ not ***yet*** a man to till the ground, ***for in heaven created I them,*** ***and there was not yet flesh upon the earth, neither in the water, neither in the air;***	And I, the Lord God, had created all the children of men; and not yet a man to till the ground; for in heaven created I them; and there was not yet flesh upon the earth, neither in the water, neither in the air;	and had not formed a man to till the ground.
2:6 But ***I, the Lord God, spake, and*** there went up a mist from the earth, and watered the whole face of the ground.	3:6 But I, the Lord God, spake, and there went up a mist from the earth, and watered the whole face of the ground.	5:6 But there went up a mist from the earth, and watered the whole face of the ground.

THE CREATION OF MAN

GENESIS	MOSES	ABRAHAM
2:7 And ***I,*** the Lord God, formed man ~~of~~ ***from*** the dust of the ground,	3:7 And I, the Lord God, formed man from the dust of the ground,	5:7 And the Gods formed man from the dust of the ground, and took his spirit (that is, the man's spirit), and put it into him;
and breathed into his nostrils the breath of life; and man became a living soul***;*** the first flesh upon the earth, the first man also; Nevertheless, all things were before created, but spiritually were they created and made, according to my word.	and breathed into his nostrils the breath of life; and man became a living soul, the first flesh upon the earth, the first man also; nevertheless, all things were before created; but spiritually were they created and made according to my word.	and breathed into his nostrils the breath of life, and man became a living soul.

THE GARDEN OF EDEN

GENESIS	MOSES	ABRAHAM
2:8 And ***I,*** the Lord God***,*** planted a garden eastward in Eden; and there ~~he~~ ***I*** put the man whom ~~he~~ ***I*** had formed.	3:8 And I, the Lord God, planted a garden eastward in Eden, and there I put the man whom I had formed.	5:8 And the Gods planted a garden, eastward in Eden, and there they put the man, whose spirit they had put into the body which they had formed.
2:9 And out of the ground***,*** made ***I,*** the Lord God***,*** to grow every tree ***naturally,*** that is pleasant to the sight ***of man, and man could behold it, and it became also a living soul; for it was spiritual in the day that I created it; for it remaineth in the sphere in which I, God, created it; yea, even all things which I prepared for the use of man;***	3:9 And out of the ground made I, the Lord God, to grow every tree, naturally, that is pleasant to the sight of man; and man could behold it. And it became also a living soul. For it was spiritual in the day that I created it; for it remaineth in the sphere in which I, God, created it, yea, even all things which I prepared for the use of man;	5:9 And out of the ground made the Gods to grow every tree that is pleasant to the sight
and ***man saw that it was*** good for food~~;~~. ***And I, the Lord God, planted*** the tree of life also, in the midst of the garden***;*** ~~;~~ and ***also*** the tree of knowledge of good and evil.	and man saw that it was good for food. And I, the Lord God, planted the tree of life also in the midst of the garden, and also the tree of knowledge of good and evil.	and good for food; the tree of life, also, in the midst of the garden, and the tree of knowledge of good and evil.

GENESIS King James Version with JST	MOSES (With Comparison to JST Genesis)	ABRAHAM
2:10 And ***I, the Lord God, caused*** a river ~~went~~ ***to go*** out of Eden, to water the garden; and from thence it was parted, and became into four heads.	3:10 And I, the Lord God, caused a river to go out of Eden to water the garden; and from thence it was parted, and became into four heads.	5:10 There was a river running out of Eden, to water the garden, and from thence it was parted and became into four heads.
2:11 ***And I, the Lord God, called*** ~~T~~***t***he name of the first ~~is~~ Pison, ~~: that is it which~~ ***and it*** compasseth the whole land of Havilah, where ~~there is~~ ***I, the Lord, created much*** gold;	3:11 And I, the Lord God, called the name of the first Pison, and it compasseth the whole land of Havilah, where I, the Lord God, created much gold;	
2:12 And the gold of that land ~~is~~ ***was*** good~~:~~ ***, and*** there ~~is~~ ***was*** bdellium and the onyx stone.	3:12 And the gold of that land was good, and there was bdellium and the onyx stone.	
2:13 And the name of the second river ~~is~~ ***was called*** Gihon, ~~:~~ the same ~~is it~~ that compasseth the whole land of Ethiopia.	3:13 And the name of the second river was called Gihon; the same that compasseth the whole land of Ethiopia.	
2:14 And the name of the third river ~~is~~ ***was*** Hiddekel, ~~:~~ that ~~is it~~ which goeth toward the east of Assyria. And the fourth river ~~is~~ ***was*** Euphrates.	3:14 And the name of the third river was Hiddekel; that which goeth toward the east of Assyria. And the fourth river was the Euphrates.	
2:15 And ***I,*** the Lord God, took the man, and put him into the garden of Eden, to dress it, and to keep it.	3:15 And I, the Lord God, took the man, and put him into the Garden of Eden, to dress it, and to keep it.	5:11 And the Gods took the man and put him in the Garden of Eden, to dress it and to keep it.
2:16 And ***I,*** the Lord God, commanded the man, saying, Of every tree of the garden thou mayest freely eat***;*** ~~:~~	3:16 And I, the Lord God, commanded the man, saying: Of every tree of the garden thou mayest freely eat,	5:12 And the Gods commanded the man, saying: Of every tree of the garden thou mayest freely eat,
2:17 But of the tree of the knowledge of good and evil, thou shalt not eat of it: ***Nevertheless, thou mayest choose for thyself, for it is given unto thee; but remember that I forbid it; F***~~f~~or in the day ~~that~~ thou eatest thereof thou shalt surely die.	3:17 But of the tree of the knowledge of good and evil, thou shalt not eat of it, nevertheless, thou mayest choose for thyself, for it is given unto thee; but, remember that I forbid it, for in the day thou eatest thereof thou shalt surely die.	5:13 But of the tree of knowledge of good and evil, thou shalt not eat of it; for in the time that thou eatest thereof, thou shalt surely die. Now I, Abraham, saw that it was after the Lord's time, which was after the time of Kolob; for as yet the Gods had not appointed unto Adam his reckoning.
2:18 And ***I,*** the LORD God, said ***unto mine Only Begotten, that*** it ***was*** ~~is~~ not good that the man should be alone; ***Wherefore,*** I will make ~~him~~ an help meet for him.	3:18 And I, the Lord God, said unto mine Only Begotten, that it was not good that the man should be alone; wherefore, I will make an help meet for him.	
2:19 And out of the ground, ***I,*** the Lord God, formed every beast of the field, and every fowl of the air;	3:19 And out of the ground I, the Lord God, formed every beast of the field, and every fowl of the air;	5:20 And out of the ground the Gods formed every beast of the field, and every fowl of the air,
and ~~brought them~~ ***commanded that they should come*** unto Adam to see what he would call them. ~~:~~	and commanded that they should come unto Adam, to see what he would call them;	and brought them unto Adam to see what he would call them;
		and whatsoever Adam called every living creature, that should be the name thereof.
~~a~~***A***nd ***they were also living souls; for I, God, breathed into them the breath of life, and commanded that*** whatsoever Adam called every living creature, that ~~was~~ ***should be*** the name thereof.	and they were also living souls; for I, God, breathed into them the breath of life, and commanded that whatsoever Adam called every living creature, that should be the name thereof.	
2:20 And Adam gave names to all cattle, and to the fowl of the air, and to every beast of the field;	3:20 And Adam gave names to all cattle, and to the fowl of the air, and to every beast of the field;	5:21a And Adam gave names to all cattle, to the fowl of the air, to every beast of the field;

but ***as*** for Adam there was not found an help meet for him.	but as for Adam, there was not found an help meet for him.	
		5:14 And the Gods said: Let us make an help meet for the man, for it is not good that the man should be alone, therefore we will form an help meet for him.
2:21 And ***I,*** the Lord God***,*** caused a deep sleep to fall upon Adam, and he slept***;*** ~~:~~ and ~~he~~ ***I*** took one of his ribs, and closed up the flesh ~~instead~~ ***in the stead*** thereof;	3:21 And I, the Lord God, caused a deep sleep to fall upon Adam; and he slept, and I took one of his ribs and closed up the flesh in the stead thereof;	5:15 And the Gods caused a deep sleep to fall upon Adam; and he slept, and they took one of his ribs, and closed up the flesh in the stead thereof;
2:22 And the rib, which ***I,*** the Lord God had taken from man, made ~~he~~ ***I*** a woman, and brought her unto the man.	3:22 And the rib which I, the Lord God, had taken from man, made I a woman, and brought her unto the man.	5:16 And of the rib which the Gods had taken from man, formed they a woman, and brought her unto the man.
2:23 And Adam said, This ***I know now*** is ~~now~~ bone of my bones, and flesh of my flesh***.*** ~~: s~~***S***he shall be called ~~W~~***w***oman, because she was taken out of ~~M~~***m***an.	3:23 And Adam said: This I know now is bone of my bones, and flesh of my flesh; she shall be called Woman, because she was taken out of man.	5:17 And Adam said: This was bone of my bones, and flesh of my flesh; now she shall be called Woman, because she was taken out of man;
2:24 Therefore shall a man leave his father and his mother, and shall cleave unto his wife***;*** ~~:~~ and they shall be one flesh.	3:24 Therefore shall a man leave his father and his mother, and shall cleave unto his wife; and they shall be one flesh.	5:18 Therefore shall a man leave his father and his mother, and shall cleave unto his wife, and they shall be one flesh.
2:25 And they were both naked, the man and his wife, and were not ashamed.	3:25 And they were both naked, the man and his wife, and were not ashamed.	5:19 And they were both naked, the man and his wife, and were not ashamed.
		5:21b and for Adam, there was found an help meet for him.

THE FALL

3:1b ***And*** Now the serpent was more subtle than any beast of the field which ***I,*** the LORD God***,*** had made.	4:5 And now the serpent was more subtle than any beast of the field, which I, the Lord God, had made.	
And Satan put it into the heart of the serpent, for he had drawn away many after him; and he sought also to beguile Eve, for he knew not the mind of God; ***wherefore, he sought to destroy the world.***	4:6 And Satan put it into the heart of the serpent, (for he had drawn away many after him,) and he sought also to beguile Eve, for he knew not the mind of God, wherefore he sought to destroy the world.	
And he said unto the woman, Yea, hath God said, Ye shall not eat of every tree of the garden? ***And he spake by the mouth of the serpent.***	4:7 And he said unto the woman: Yea, hath God said ye shall not eat of every tree of the garden? (And he spake by the mouth of the serpent.)	
3:2 And the woman said unto the serpent, We may eat of the fruit of the trees of the garden:	4:8 And the woman said unto the serpent: We may eat of the fruit of the trees of the garden;	
3:3 But of the fruit of the tree which ~~is~~ ***thou beholdest*** in the midst of the garden, God hath said, Ye shall not eat of it, neither shall ye touch it, lest ye die.	4:9 But of the fruit of the tree which thou beholdest in the midst of the garden, God hath said ye shall not eat of it, neither shall ye touch it, lest ye die.	
3:4 And the serpent said unto the woman, Ye shall not surely die:	4:10 And the serpent said unto the woman: Ye shall not surely die;	
3:5 For God doth know that in the day ye eat thereof, then your eyes shall	4:11 For God doth know that in the day ye eat thereof, then your eyes shall	

be opened, and ye shall be as gods, knowing good and evil.

3:6 And when the woman saw that the tree was good for food, and that it was pleasant to the eyes, and a tree to be desired to make ~~one~~ ***her*** wise, she took of the fruit thereof, and did eat, and gave also unto her husband with her; and he did eat.

3:7 And the eyes of them both were opened, and they knew that they ~~were~~ ***had been*** naked; and they sewed fig leaves together, and made themselves aprons.

3:8 And they heard the voice of the LORD God***, as they were*** walking in the garden in the cool of the day. ~~a~~***A***nd Adam and his wife ~~hid~~ ***went to hide*** themselves from the presence of the LORD God amongst the trees of the garden.

3:9 And ***I,*** the LORD God***,*** called unto Adam, and said unto him, Where ~~art~~ ***goest*** thou?

3:10 And he said, I heard thy voice in the garden, and I was afraid, because I ***beheld that I*** was naked; and I hid myself.

3:11 And ~~he~~ ***I, the Lord God,*** said ***unto Adam***, Who told thee that thou wast naked? Hast thou eaten of the tree, whereof I commanded thee that thou shouldst not eat***, if so thou shouldst surely die***?

3:12 And the man said, The woman whom thou gavest ~~to be with~~ me, ***and commanded that she should remain with me,*** she gave me of the ***fruit of*** tree, and I did eat.

3:13 And ***I,*** the LORD God***,*** said unto the woman, What is this ~~that~~ ***thing which*** thou hast done? And the woman said, The serpent beguiled me, and I did eat.

3:14 And ***I,*** the LORD God***,*** said unto the serpent, Because thou hast done this, thou ~~art~~ ***shalt be*** cursed above all cattle, and above every beast of the field; upon thy belly shalt thou go, and dust shalt thou eat all the days of thy life:

3:15 And I will put enmity between thee and the woman, ~~and~~ between thy seed and her seed; ~~it~~ ***and he*** shall bruise thy head, and thou shalt bruise his heel.

3:16 Unto the woman ~~he~~ ***I, the Lord God,*** said, I will greatly multiply thy sorrow and thy conception; in sorrow thou shalt bring forth children; and thy desire

be opened, and ye shall be as gods, knowing good and evil.

4:12 And when the woman saw that the tree was good for food, and that it became pleasant to the eyes, and a tree to be desired to make her wise, she took of the fruit thereof, and did eat, and also gave unto her husband with her, and he did eat.

4:13 And the eyes of them both were opened, and they knew that they had been naked. And they sewed fig-leaves together and made themselves aprons.

4:14 And they heard the voice of the Lord God, as they were walking in the garden, in the cool of the day; and Adam and his wife went to hide themselves from the presence of the Lord God amongst the trees of the garden.

4:15 And I, the Lord God, called unto Adam, and said unto him: Where goest thou?

4:16 And he said: I heard thy voice in the garden, and I was afraid, because I beheld that I was naked, and I hid myself.

4:17 And I, the Lord God, said unto Adam: Who told thee (-) thou wast naked? Hast thou eaten of the tree whereof I commanded thee that thou shouldst not eat, if so thou shouldst surely die?

4:18 And the man said: The woman thou gavest me, and commanded that she should remain with me, she gave me of the fruit of the tree and I did eat.

4:19 And I, the Lord God, said unto the woman: What is this thing which thou hast done? And the woman said: The serpent beguiled me, and I did eat.

4:20 And I, the Lord God, said unto the serpent: Because thou hast done this thou shalt be cursed above all cattle, and above every beast of the field; upon thy belly shalt thou go, and dust shalt thou eat all the days of thy life;

4:21 And I will put enmity between thee and the woman, between thy seed and her seed; and he shall bruise thy head, and thou shalt bruise his heel.

4:22 Unto the woman, I, the Lord God, said: I will greatly multiply thy sorrow and thy conception. In sorrow thou shalt bring forth children, and thy desire shall

shall be to thy husband, and he shall rule over thee.

3:17 And unto Adam ~~he~~ ***I, the Lord God,*** said, Because thou hast hearkened unto the voice of thy wife, and hast eaten of the tree, of which I commanded thee, saying, Thou shalt not eat of it: cursed ~~is~~ ***shall be*** the ground for thy sake; in sorrow shalt thou eat of it all the days of thy life;

3:18 Thorns also and thistles shall it bring forth to thee; and thou shalt eat the herb of the field;

3:19 ~~In~~ ***By*** the sweat of thy face shalt thou eat bread, ~~till~~ ***until*** thou return unto the ground; for ***thou shalt surely die; for*** out of it wast thou taken: for dust thou ~~art~~ ***wast***, and unto dust shalt thou return.

3:20 And Adam called his wife's name Eve; because she was the mother of all living, ***for thus have I, the Lord God, called the first of all women, which are many***.

3:21 Unto Adam, ***and*** also ~~and~~ ***un***to his wife, did ***I***, the LORD God, make coats of skins, and clothed them.

be to thy husband, and he shall rule over thee.

4:23 And unto Adam, I, the Lord God, said: Because thou hast hearkened unto the voice of thy wife, and hast eaten of the fruit of the tree of which I commanded thee, saying --Thou shalt not eat of it, cursed shall be the ground for thy sake; in sorrow shalt thou eat of it all the days of thy life.

4:24 Thorns also, and thistles shall it bring forth to thee, and thou shalt eat the herb of the field.

4:25 By the sweat of thy face shalt thou eat bread, until thou shalt return unto the ground, (- -) for out of it wast thou taken: for dust thou wast, and unto dust shalt thou return.

4:26 And Adam called his wife's name Eve, because she was the mother of all living; for thus have I, the Lord God, called the first of all women, which are many.

4:27 Unto Adam, and also unto his wife, did I, the Lord God, makecoats of skins, and clothed them.

EXPULSION FROM THE GARDEN

3:22 And ***I***, the LORD God said ***unto mine Only Begotten***, Behold, the man is become as one of us, to know good and evil: and now, lest he put forth his hand, and ***par***take also of the tree of life, and eat, and live ~~for ever~~ forever~~:~~ .

3:23 Therefore, ***I***, the LORD God, ~~sent~~ ***will send*** him forth from the garden of Eden, to till the ground from whence he was taken.

For, as I, the Lord God, liveth, even so my words cannot return void, for, as they go forth out of my mouth, they must be fulfilled.

3:24 So ~~he~~ ***I*** drove out the man; and ~~he~~ ***I*** placed at the east of the garden of Eden ~~C~~***c***herubim~~s~~, and a flaming sword, which turned every way, to keep the way of the tree of life.

(And these are the words which I spake unto my servant Moses. And they are true, even as I will.

And I have spoken them unto you. See thou show them unto no man, until I command you, except they that believe.) Amen.

4:28 And I, the Lord God, said unto mine Only Begotten: Behold, the man is become as one of us to know good and evil; and now lest he put forth his hand and partake also of the tree of life, and eat and live forever,

4:29 Therefore I, the Lord God, will send him forth from the Garden of Eden, to till the ground from whence he was taken;

4:30 For as I, the Lord God, liveth, even so my words cannot return void, for as they go forth out of my mouth they must be fulfilled.

4:31 So I drove out the man, and I placed at the east of the Garden of Eden, cherubim and a flaming sword, which turned every way to keep the way of the tree of life.

4:32 (And these are the words which I spake unto my servant Moses, and they are true even as I will;
and I have spoken them unto you. See thou show them unto no man, until I command you, except to them that believe. Amen.)

ADAM LIVES IN THE WORLD

4:1a ***And it came to pass, that after I,***
the Lord God, had driven them out,
that Adam began to till the earth, and
to have dominion over all the beasts of
the field, and to eat his bread by the
sweat of his brow, as I, the Lord had
commanded him, and Eve also, his
wife, did labor with him.
And Adam knew his wife, and
she bare unto him son sand daughters,
and they began to multiply, and to
replenish the earth.
And from that time forth, the
sons and daughters of Adam began to
divide, two and two, in the land, and to
till the land, and to tend flocks; and
they also begat sons and daughters.
And Adam called upon the name
of the Lord, and Eve also, his wife; and
they heard the voice of the Lord, from
the way towards the garden of Eden,
speaking unto them, and they saw him
not; for they were shut out from his
presence.
And he gave unto them
commandments, that they should
worship the Lord their God; and
should offer the firstlings of their
flocks for an offering unto the Lord.
And Adam was obedient unto the
com-mandments of the Lord. And
after many days, an angel of the Lord
appeared unto Adam, saying, Why dost
thou offer sacrifices unto the Lord.
And Adam said unto him, I know not,
save the Lord commanded me.
And then the angel spake,
saying, This thing is a similitude of the
sacrifice of the Only Begotten of the
Father, which is full of grace and
truth;
Wherefore, thou shalt do all that
thou doest, in the name of the Son.
And thou shalt repent, and call upon
God, in the name of the Son for
evermore.
And in that day, the Holy Ghost
fell upon Adam, which beareth record
of the Father and Son, saying, I am the
Only Begotten of the Father from the
beginning, henceforth and for ever;
that, as thou has fallen, thou mayest be

5:1 And it came to pass that after I,
the Lord God, had driven them out, that
Adam began to till the earth, and to
have dominion over all the beasts of the
field, and to eat his bread by the sweat
of his brow, as I the Lord had
commanded him. And Eve, also, his
wife, did labor with him.
5:2 And Adam knew his wife, and
she bare unto him sons and daughters,
and they began to multiply and to
replenish the earth.
5:3 And from that time forth, the sons
and daughters of Adam began to divide
two and two in the land, and to till the
land, and to tend flocks, and they also
begat sons and daughters.
5:4 And Adam <u>and Eve, his wife</u>,
called upon the name of the Lord, (--)
and they heard the voice of the Lord
from the way toward the <u>G</u>arden of
Eden, speaking unto them, and they saw
him not; for they were shut out from his
presence.
5:5 And he gave unto them
commandments, that they should
worship the Lord their God, and should
offer the firstlings of their flocks, for an
offering unto the Lord.
And Adam was obedient unto the
commandments of the Lord.
5:6 And after many days an angel of
the Lord appeared unto Adam, saying:
Why dost thou offer sacrifices unto the
Lord<u>?</u> And Adam said unto him: I know
not, save the Lord commanded me.
5:7 And then the angel spake, saying:
This thing is a similitude of the sacrifice
of the Only Begotten of the Father,
which is full of grace and truth.

5:8 Wherefore, thou shalt do all that
thou doest in the name of the Son,
and thou shalt repent and call upon God
in the name of the Son forevermore.

5:9 And in that day the Holy Ghost
fell upon Adam, which beareth record
of the Father and the Son, saying: I am
the Only Begotten of the Father from
the beginning, henceforth and forever,
that as thou hast fallen thou mayest be

redeemed, and all mankind, even as many as will.

4:1b And in that day Adam blessed God, and was filled, and began to prophesy concerning all the families of the earth; saying, Blessed be the name of God, for because of my transgression my eyes are opened, and in this life I shall have joy, and again, in the flesh I shall see God.

And Eve, his wife, heard all these things and was glad, saying, Were it not for our transgression, we never should have had seed, and never should have known good and evil, and the joy of our redemption, and the eternal life which God giveth unto all the obedient.

And Adam and Eve blessed the name of God; and they made all things known unto their sons and their daughters.

And Satan came among them, saying, I am also a son of God, and he commanded them, saying, Believe it not. And they believed it not; and they loved Satan more than God. And men began from that time forth to be carnal, sensual and devilish.

And the Lord God called upon men, by the Holy Ghost, everywhere, and commanded them that they should repent;

And as many believed in the Son, and repented of their sins, should be saved. And as many as believed not, and repented not, should be damned. And the words went forth out of the mouth of God, in a firm decree, wherefore they must be fulfilled.

And Adam ceased not to call upon God; and Eve also his wife. And Adam knew Eve his wife; and she conceived, and bare Cain, and said, I have gotten a man from the LORD***; wherefore he may not reject his words. But, behold, also Cain hearkened not, saying, Who is the Lord, that I should know him?***

4:2 And she again ***conceived, and*** bare his brother Abel. ***And Abel hearkened unto the voice of the Lord.*** And Abel was a keeper of sheep, but Cain was a tiller of the ground.

redeemed, and all mankind, even as many as will.

5:10 And in that day Adam blessed God and was filled, and began to prophesy concerning all the families of the earth, saying: Blessed be the name of God, for because of my transgression my eyes are opened, and in this life I shall have joy, and again in the flesh I shall see God.

5:11 And Eve, his wife, heard all these things and was glad, saying:
Were it not for our transgression we never should have had seed, and never should have known good and evil, and the joy of our redemption, and the eternal life which God giveth unto all the obedient.

5:12 And Adam and Eve blessed the name of God, and they made all things known unto their sons and their daughters.

5:13 And Satan came among them, saying: I am also a son of God; and he commanded them, saying: Believe it not; and they believed it not; and they loved Satan more than God. And men began from that time forth to be carnal, sensual, and devilish.

5:14 And the Lord God called upon men by the Holy Ghost everywhere and commanded them that they should repent;

5:15 And as many as believed in the Son, and repented of their sins, should be saved; and as many as believed not and repented not, should be damned; and the words went forth out of the mouth of God in a firm decree; wherefore they must be fulfilled.

5:16 And Adam and Eve, his wife, ceased not to call upon God (- -). And Adam knew Eve his wife, and she conceived and bare Cain, and said: I have gotten a man from the Lord; wherefore he may not reject his words. But behold, (-) Cain hearkened not, saying: Who is the Lord that I should know him?

5:17 And she again conceived and bare his brother Abel. And Abel hearkened unto the voice of the Lord. And Abel was a keeper or sheep, but Cain was a tiller of the ground.

CAIN AND ABEL

4:3 ***And Cain loved Satan more than God. And Satan commanded him, saying, Make an offering unto the Lord.***
And in process of time it came to pass, that Cain brought of the fruit of the ground an offering unto the LORD.
4:4 And Abel, he also brought of the firstlings of his flock and of the fat thereof. And the LORD had respect unto Abel, and to his offering:
4:5 But unto Cain, and to his offering, he had not respect. ***Now Satan knew this, and it pleased him.*** And Cain was very wroth, and his countenance fell.
4:6 And the LORD said unto Cain, Why art thou wroth? ~~and~~ why is thy countenance fallen?
4:7 If thou doest well, ***thou*** shalt ~~thou not~~ be accepted ~~?~~, and if thou doest not well, sin lieth at the door~~.~~ ***; and Satan desireth to have thee, and except thou shalt hearken unto my commandments, I will deliver thee up,*** And ***it shall be*** unto thee ~~shall be~~ ***according to*** his desire, and thou shalt rule over him***,***
for from this time forth thou shalt be the father of his lies.
Thou shalt be called Perdition, for thou wast also before the world, and it shall be said in time to come, that these abominations were had from Cain, for he rejected the greater counsel, which was had from God; and this is a cursing which I will put upon thee, except thou repent.
And Cain was wroth, and listened not any more to the voice of the Lord, neither to Abel his brother, who walked in holiness before the Lord.
And Adam also, and his wife, mourned before the Lord, because of Cain and his brethren.
And it came to pass, that Cain took one of his brother's daughters to wife, and they loved Satan more than God.
And Satan said unto Cain, Swear unto me by thy throat, and if thou tell it thou shalt die; and swear thy brethren by their heads,

5:18 And Cain loved Satan more than God. And Satan commanded him, saying: Make an offering unto the Lord.

5:19 And in process of time it came to pass that Cain brought of the fruit of the ground an offering unto the Lord.
5:20 And Abel, he also brought of the firstlings of his flock, and of the fat thereof. And the Lord had respect unto Abel, and to his offering;
5:21 But unto Cain, and to his offering, he had not respect. Now Satan knew this, and it pleased him. And Cain was very wroth, and his countenance fell.
5:22 And the Lord said unto Cain: Why are thou wroth? Why is thy countenance fallen?
5:23 If thou doest well, thou shalt be accepted. And if thou doest not well, sin lieth at the door, and Satan desireth to have thee; and except thou shalt hearken unto my commandments, I will deliver thee up, and it shall be unto thee according to his desire. And thou shalt rule over him;
5:24 For from this time forth thou shalt be the father of his lies;
thou shalt be called Perdition; for thou wast also before the world.
5:25 And it shall be said in time to come that these abominations were had from Cain; for he rejected the greater counsel which was had from God; and this is a cursing which I will put upon thee, except thou repent.
5:26 And Cain was wroth, and listened not any more to the voice of the Lord, neither to Abel, his brother, who walked in holiness before the Lord.
5:27 And Adam and his wife mourned before the Lord, because of Cain and his brethren.
5:28 And it came to pass that Cain took one of his brothers' daughters to wife, and they loved Satan more than God.
5:29 And Satan said unto Cain: Swear unto me by thy throat, and if thou tell it thou shalt die; and swear thy brethren by their heads,

and by the living God, that they tell it not; for if they tell it they shall surely die; and this that thy father may not know it; and this day I will deliver thy brother Abel into thine hands.

And Satan swear unto Cain, that he would do according to his commands. And all these things were done in secret.

And Cain said, Truly I am Mahan, the master of this great secret, that I may murder and get gain. Wherefore Cain was called Master Mahan; and he gloried in his wickedness.

4:8 ***And Cain went into the field,*** And Cain talked with Abel his brother: and it came to pass, ~~when~~ ***that while*** they were in the field, ~~that~~ Cain rose up against Abel his brother, and slew him. ***And Cain gloried in that which he had done, saying, I am free; surely the flocks of my brother falleth into my hands.***

4:9 And the LORD said unto Cain, Where is Abel, thy brother? And he said, I know not: Am I my brother's keeper?

4:10 And ~~he~~ ***the Lord*** said, What hast thou done? the voice of thy brother's blood ~~crieth~~ ***cries*** unto me from the ground.

4:11 And now, ~~art thou~~ ***thou shalt be*** cursed from the earth, which hath opened her mouth to receive thy brother's blood from thy hand;

4:12 When thou tillest the ground, it shall not henceforth yield unto thee her strength; a fugitive and a vagabond shalt thou be in the earth.

4:13 And Cain said unto the LORD, ***Satan tempted me, because of my brother's flock; and I was wroth also, for his offering thou didst accept, and not mine.*** My punishment is greater than I can bear.

4:14 Behold, thou hast driven me out this day from the face of the ~~earth~~; ***Lord,*** and from thy face shall I be hid; and I shall be a fugitive and a vagabond in the earth; and it shall come to pass, that ~~every one~~ ***he*** that findeth me shall slay me***, because of mine iniquities, for these things are not hid from the Lord.***

and by the living God, that they tell it not; for if they tell it, they shall surely die; and this that thy father may not know it; and this day I will deliver thy brother Abel into thine hands.

5:30 And Satan sware unto Cain that he would do according to his commands. And all these things were done in secret.

5:31 And Cain said: Truly I am Mahan, the master of this great secret, that I may murder and get gain. Wherefore Cain was called Master Mahan, and he gloried in his wickedness.

5:32 And Cain went into the field, and Cain talked with Abel, his brother. And it came to pass that while they were in the field, Cain rose up against Abel, his brother, and slew him.

5:33 And Cain gloried in that which he had done, saying: I am free; surely the flocks of my brother falleth into my hands.

5:34 And the Lord said unto Cain: Where is Abel, thy brother? And he said: I know not. Am I my brother's keeper?

5:35 And the Lord said: What hast thou done? The voice of thy brother's blood cries unto me from the ground.

5:36 And now thou shalt be cursed from the earth which hath opened her mouth to receive thy brother's blood from thy hand.

5:37 When thou tillest the ground it shall not henceforth yield unto thee her strength. A fugitive and a vagabond shalt thou be in the earth.

5:38 And Cain said unto the Lord: Satan tempted me because of my brother's flocks. And I was wroth also; for his offering thou didst accept and not mine; my punishment is greater than I can bear.

5:39 Behold thou hast driven me out this day from the face of the Lord, and from thy face shall I be hid; and I shall be a fugitive and a vagabond in the earth; and it shall come to pass, that he that findeth me will slay me, because of mine iniquities, for these things are not hid from the Lord.

Genesis (KJV with JST)	Moses	Abraham
4:15 And*, I,* the LORD*,* said unto him, ~~Therefore~~ whosoever slayeth ~~Cain~~ ***thee***, vengeance shall be taken on him sevenfold. And***, I,*** the LORD***,*** set a mark upon Cain, lest any finding him should kill him.	5:40 And I the Lord said unto him: Whosoever slayeth thee, vengeance shall be taken on him sevenfold. And I the Lord set a mark upon Cain, lest any finding him should kill him.	
4:16 And Cain ~~went~~ ***was shut*** out from the presence of the LORD, and ***with his wife and many of his brethren,*** dwelt in the land of Nod, on the east of Eden.	5:41 And Cain was shut out from the presence of the Lord, and with his wife and many of his brethren dwelt in the land of Nod, on the east of Eden.	

LAMECH & SECRET COMBINATIONS

Genesis (KJV with JST)	Moses	Abraham
4:17 And Cain knew his wife; and she conceived, and bare Enoch~~:~~ , ***and he also began many sons and daughters.*** ~~a~~***A***nd he builded a city, and called the name of the city, after the name of his son, Enoch.	5:42 And Cain knew his wife, and she conceived and bare Enoch, and he also begat many sons and daughters. And he builded a city, and he called the name of the city after the name of his son, Enoch.	
4:18 And unto Enoch was born Irad~~:~~ ***,*** ***and other sons and daughters,*** and Irad begat Mehujael***, and other sons and daughters~~:~~*** . ~~a~~***A***nd Mehujael begat Methusael~~:~~ , ***and other sons and daughters.*** ~~a~~***A***nd Methusael begat Lamech.	5:43 And unto Enoch was born Irad, and other sons and daughters. And Irad begat Mahujael, and other sons and daughters. And Mahujael begat Methusael, and other sons and daughters. And Methusael begat Lamech.	
4:19 And Lamech took unto him***self*** two wives: the name of the one ~~was~~ ***being*** Adah, and the name of the other Zillah.	5:44 And Lamech took unto himself two wives; the name of the one being Adah, and the name of the other, Zillah.	
4:20 And Adah bare Jabal: he was the father of such as dwell in tents, and ~~of such as have~~ ***they were keepers of*** cattle.	5:45 And Adah bare Jabal; he was the father of such as dwell in tents, and they were keepers of cattle;	
4:21 And his brother's name was Jubal***,*** ~~: he~~ ***who*** was the father of all such as handle the harp and organ.	and his brother's name was Jubal, who was the father of all such as handle the harp and organ.	
4:22 And Zillah, she also bare ~~Tubalcain~~ ***Tubal Cain***, an instructor of every artificer in brass and iron: and the sister of ~~Tubalcain~~ ***Tubal Cain*** was Naamah.	5:46 And Zillah, she also bare Tubal Cain, an instructor of every artificer in brass and iron. And the sister of Tubal Cain was called Naamah.	
4:23 And Lamech said unto his wives, Adah and Zillah, Hear my voice; ye wives of Lamech, hearken unto my speech: for I have slain a man to my wounding, and a young man to my hurt.	5:47 And Lamech said unto his wives, Adah and Zillah: Hear my voice, ye wives of Lamech, hearken unto my speech; for I have slain a main to my wounding, and a young man to my hurt.	
4:24a If Cain shall be avenged sevenfold, truly Lamech ***shall be*** seventy and sevenfold.	5:48 If Cain shall be avenged sevenfold, truly Lamech shall be seventy and seven fold;	
For Lamech having entered into a covenant with Satan, after the manner of Cain, wherein he became Master	5:49 For Lamech having entered into a covenant with Satan, after the manner of Cain, wherein he became Master	

Mahan, master of that great secret which was administered unto Cain by Satan;

4:24b And Irad, the son of Enoch, having known their secret, began to reveal it unto the sons of Adam; wherefore, Lamech, being angry, slew him, not like unto Cain his brother Abel for the sake of getting gain; but he slew him for the oath's sake;

For, from the days of Cain, there was a secret combination, and their works were in the dark, and they knew every man his brother.

Wherefore the Lord cursed Lamech and his house, and all they that had covenanted with Satan; for they kept not the commandements of God. And it displeased God, and he ministered not unto them.

And their works were abominations, and began to spread among all the sons of men. And it was among the sons of men.

And among the daughters of men, these things were not spoken; because that Lamech had spoken the secret unto his wives, and they rebelled against him, and declared these things abroad, and had not compassion.

Wherefore Lamech was despised, and cast out, and came not among the sons of men, lest he should die.

And thus the works of darkness began to prevail among all the sons of men.

And God cursed the earth with a sore curse, and was angry with the wicked, with all the sons of men whom he had made,

for they would not hearken unto his voice, nor believe on his Only Begotten Son, even him whom he declared should come in the meridian of time; who was prepared from before the foundation of the world.

And thus the gospel began to be preached from the beginning, being declared by holy angels, sent forth from the presence of God; and by his own voice, and by the gift of the Holy Ghost.

And thus all things were confirmed unto Adam by an holy ordinance; and the gospel preached;

Mahan, master of that great secret which was administered unto Cain by Satan;

and Irad, the son of Enoch, having known their secret, began to reveal it unto the sons of Adam;

5:50 Wherefore Lamech, being angry, slew him, not like unto Cain, his brother Abel, for the sake of getting gain, but he slew him for the oath's sake.

5:51 For, from the days of Cain, there was a secret combination, and their works were in the dark, and they knew every man his brother.

5:52 Wherefore the Lord cursed Lamech, and his house, and all them that had covenanted with Satan; for they kept not the commandments of God, and it displeased God, and he ministered not unto them,

and their works were abominations, and began to spread among all the sons of men. And it was among the sons of men.

5:53 And among the daughters of men these things were not spoken, because that Lamech had spoken the secret unto his wives, and they rebelled against him, and declared these things abroad, and had not compassion;

5:54 Wherefore Lamech was despised, and cast out, and came not among the sons of men, lest he should die.

5:55 And thus the works of darkness began to prevail among all the sons of men.

5:56 And God cursed the earth with a sore curse, and was angry with the wicked, with all the sons of men whom he had made;

5:57 For they would not hearken unto his voice, nor believe on his Only Begotten Son, even him whom he declared should come in the meridian of time, who was prepared from before the foundation of the world.

5:58 And thus the Gospel began to be preached, from the beginning, being declared by holy angels sent forth from the presence of God, and by his own voice, and by the gift of the Holy Ghost.

5:59 And thus all things were confirmed unto Adam, by an holy ordinance, and the Gospel preached, and

and a decree sent forth that it should
be in the world until the end thereof;
and thus it was. Amen.

a decree sent forth, that it should be in
the world, until the end thereof; and
thus it was. Amen.

SETH

And Adam hearkened unto the
voice of God, and called upon his sons
to repent.
4:25 And Adam knew his wife again;
and she bare a son, and called his name
Seth: ~~For God, said she,~~ ***And Adam***
glorified the name of God, for he said,
God hath appointed me another seed
instead of Abel, whom Cain slew.
4:26a And ***God revealed himself un***to
Seth, ***and he rebelled not, but offered***
an acceptable sacrifice like unto his
brother Abel. And to him also ~~there~~
was born a son; and he called his name
Enos:
then began ***these*** men to call upon the
name of the LORD.

6:1 And Adam hearkened unto the
voice of God, and called upon his sons
to repent.
6:2 And Adam knew his wife again,
and she bare a son, and he called his
name Seth. And Adam glorified the
name of God; for he said: God hath
appointed me another seed, instead of
Abel, whom Cain slew.
6:3 And God revealed himself unto
Seth, and he rebelled not, but offered an
acceptable sacrifice, like unto his
brother Abel. And to him also was born
a son, and he called his name Enos.
6:4a And then began these men to call
upon the name of the Lord,

ADAM'S POSTERITY

4:26b ***And the Lord blessed them;***
and a book of remembrance was kept
in the which was recorded in the
language of Adam, for it was given
unto as many as called upon God, to
write by the Spirit of inspiration;
And by them their children were
taught to read and write, having a
language which was pure and
undefiled.
Now this same priesthood which
was in the beginning, shall be in the
end of the world also.
Now this prophecy Adam spake,
as he was moved upon by the Holy
Ghost.
5:1 ***And a genealogy was kept of the***
children of God. And ~~T~~ this ~~is~~ ***was*** the
book of the generations of Adam~~:~~ ,
saying, In the day that God created man,
(in the likeness of God made he him;) ***in***
the image of his own body,
5:2 Male and female created he them;
and blessed them, and called their name
Adam, in the day when they were
created ***and became living souls, in the***
land, upon the footstool of God.

6:4b and the Lord blessed them;
6:5 And a book of remembrance was
kept, in the which was recorded, in the
language of Adam, for it was given unto
as many as called upon God to write by
the spirit of inspiration;
6:6 And by them their children were
taught to read and write, having a
language which was pure and undefiled.

6:7 Now this same Priesthood, which
was in the beginning, shall be in the end
of the world also.
6:8 Now this prophecy Adam spake,
as he was moved upon by the Holy
Ghost,
and a genealogy was kept of the
children of God. And this was the book
of the generations of Adam, saying: In
the day that God created man, (-)in the
likeness of God made he him;(-)
6:9 In the image of his own body,
male and female, created he them, and
blessed them, and called their name
Adam, in the day when they were
created and became living souls in the
land upon the footstool of God.

GENESIS King James Version with JST	MOSES (With Comparison to JST Genesis)	ABRAHAM
5:3 And Adam lived ~~an~~ ***one*** hundred and thirty years, and begat a son in his own likeness, after his ***own*** image; and called his name Seth:	6:10 And Adam lived one hundred and thirty years, and begat a son in his own likeness, after his own image, and called his name Seth.	
5:4 And the days of Adam after he had begotten Seth were eight hundred years: and he begat ***many*** sons and daughters:	6:11 And the days of Adam, after he had begotten Seth, were eight hundred years, and he begat many sons and daughters;	
5:5 And all the days that Adam lived were nine hundred and thirty years: and he died.	6:12 And all the days that Adam lived were nine hundred and thirty years, and he died.	
5:6 And Seth lived an hundred and five years, and begat Enos: ***and prophesied in all his days, and taught his son Enos in the ways of God. Wherefore Enos prophesied also.***	6:13 Seth lived one hundred and five years, and begat Enos, and prophesied in all his days, and taught his son Enos in the ways of God; wherefore Enos prophesied also.	
5:7 And Seth lived after he begat Enos eight hundred and seven years, and begat sons and daughters:	6:14 And Seth lived, after he begat Enos, eight hundred and seven years, and begat many sons and daughters.	
And the children of men were numerous upon all the face of the land. And in those days, Satan had great dominion among men, and raged in their hearts; and from thenceforth came wars and bloodshed.	6:15 And the children of men were numerous upon all the face of the land. And in those days Satan had great dominion among men, and raged in their hearts; and from thenceforth came wars and bloodshed;	
And a man's hand was against his own brother in administering death, because of secret works, seeking for power.	and a man's hand was against his own brother, in administering death, because of secret works, seeking for power.	
5:8 And all the days of Seth were nine hundred and twelve years: and he died.	6:16 All the days of Seth were nine hundred and twelve years, and he died.	
5:9 And Enos lived ninety years, and begat Cainan: ***And Enos, and the residue of the people of God, came out from the land which was called Shulon, and dwelt in a land of promise, which he called after his own son, whom he had named Cainan.***	6:17 And Enos lived ninety years, and begat Cainan. And Enos and the residue of the people of God came out from the land, which was called Shulon, and dwelt in a land of promise, which he called after his own son, whom he had named Cainan.	
5:10 And Enos lived, after he begat Cainan, eight hundred and fifteen years, and begat ***many*** sons and daughters:	6:18 And Enos lived, after he begat Cainan, eight hundred and fifteen years, and begat many sons and daughters.	
5:11 And all the days of Enos were nine hundred and five years: and he died.	And all the days of Enos were nine hundred and five years, and he died.	
5:12 And Cainan lived seventy years, and begat Mahalaleel:	6:19 And Cainan lived seventy years, and begat Mahalaleel;	
5:13 And Cainan lived after he begat Mahalaleel eight hundred and forty years, and begat sons and daughters:	and Cainan lived after he begat Mahalaleel eight hundred and forty years, and begat sons and daughters.	
5:14 And all the days of Cainan were nine hundred and ten years: and he died.	And all the days of Cainan were nine hundred and ten years, and he died.	
5:15 And Mahalaleel lived sixty and five years, and begat Jared:	6:20 And Mahalaleel lived sixty-five years, and begat Jared;	

5:16 And Mahalaleel lived after he begat Jared, eight hundred and thirty years, and begat sons and daughters:

5:17 And all the days of Mahalaleel were eight hundred ~~ninety and five~~ ***and ninety-five*** years: and he died.

5:18 And Jared lived ~~an~~ ***one*** hundred ~~sixty and two~~ ***and sixty-two*** years, and ~~he~~ begat Enoch:

5:19 And Jared lived after he begat Enoch eight hundred years, and begat sons and daughters~~:~~***. And Jared taught Enoch in all the ways of God.***

And this is the genealogy of the sons of Adam, who was the son of God, with whom God himself conversed.

And they were preachers of righteousness, and spake and prophesied, and called upon all men everywhere to repent. And faith was taught unto the children of men.

5:20 And ***it came to pass, that*** all the days of Jared were nine hundred ~~sixty and two~~ ***and sixty-two*** years: and he died.

5:21a And Enoch lived ~~sixty and five~~ ***sixty-five*** years, and begat Methuselah:

and Mahalaleel lived, after he begat Jared, eight hundred and thirty years, and begat sons and daughters.

And all the days of Mahalaleel were eight hundred and ninety-five years, and he died.

6:21 And Jared lived one hundred and sixty-two years, and begat Enoch;

and Jared lived, after he begat Enoch, eight hundred years, and begat sons and daughters. And Jared taught Enoch in all the ways of God.

6:22 And this is the genealogy of the sons of Adam, who was the son of God, with whom God, himself, conversed.

6:23 And they were preachers of righteousness, and spake and prophesied, and called upon all men, everywhere, to repent; and faith was taught unto the children of men.

6:24 And it came to pass that all the days of Jared were nine hundred and sixty-two years, and he died.

6:25 And Enoch lived sixty-five years, and begat Methuselah.

ENOCH'S VISION

5:21b ***And it came to pass that Enoch journeyed in the land, among the people; and as he journeyed the Spirit of God descended out of heaven, and abode upon him.***

And he heard a voice from heaven, saying Enoch, my son, prophesy unto this people, and say unto them, Repent, for thus saith the Lord, I am angry with this people, and my fierce anger is kindled against them; for their hearts have waxed hard, and their ears are dull of hearing, and their eyes cannot see afar off.

And for these many generations, even since the day that I created them, have they gone astray, and have denied me, and have sought their own counsels in the dark; and in their own abominations have they devised murder, and have not kept the commandments which I gave unto their father Adam.

6:26 And it came to pass that Enoch journeyed in the land, among the people; and as he journeyed, the Spirit of God descended out of heaven, and abode upon him.

6:27 And he heard a voice from heaven, saying: Enoch, my son, prophesy unto this people, and say unto them--Repent, for thus saith the Lord: I am angry with this people, and my fierce anger is kindled against them; for their hearts have waxed hard, and their ears are dull of hearing, and their eyes cannot see afar off;

6:28 And for these many generations, ever since the day that I have created them, have they gone astray, and have denied me, and have sought their own counsels in the dark; and in their own abominations have they devised murder, and have not kept the commandments, which I gave unto their father, Adam.

5:21c ***Wherefore, they have forsworn themselves, and by their oaths they have brought upon themselves death.***

And an hell I have prepared for them, if they repent not;

And this is a decree which I have sent forth in the beginning of the world, from mine own mouth, from the foundation thereof; and by the mouths of my servants, thy fathers, have I decreed it; even as it shall be sent forth in the world, unto the end thereof.

And when Enoch had heard these words, he bowed himself to the earth, before the Lord, and spake before the Lord, saying, Why is it that I have found favor in thy sight, and am but a lad, and all the people hate me, for I am slow of speech; wherefore am I thy servant?

And the Lord said unto Enoch, Go forth, and do as I have commanded thee and no man shall pierce thee.

Open thy mouth, and it shall be filled, and I will give thee utterance; for all flesh is in my hands, and I will do as seemeth me good.

Say unto this people, Choose ye this day to serve the Lord God who made you.

Behold, my Spirit is upon you; wherefore all thy words will I justify, and the mountains shall flee before you, and the rivers shall turn from their course; and thou shalt abide in me, and I in you; therefore walk with me.

And the Lord spake unto Enoch, and said unto him, Anoint thine eyes with clay, and wash them, and thou shalt see; and he did so.

And he beheld the spirits that God had created, and he beheld also things which were not visible to the natural eye; and from thenceforth came the saying abroad in the land,
A seer hath the Lord raised up unto his people.

6:29 Wherefore, they have foresworn themselves, and, by their oaths, they have brought upon themselves death; and a hell I have prepared for them, if they repent not;

6:30 And this is a decree, which I have sent forth in the beginning of the world, from my own mouth, from the foundation thereof, and by the mouths of my servants, thy fathers, have I decreed it, even as it shall be sent forth in the world, unto the ends thereof.

6:31 And when Enoch had heard these words, he bowed himself to the earth, before the Lord, and spake before the Lord, saying: Why is it that I have found favor in thy sight, and am but a lad, and all the people hate me; for I am slow of speech; wherefore am I thy servant?

6:32 And the Lord said unto Enoch: Go forth and do as I have commanded thee, and no man shall pierce thee.
Open thy mouth, and it shall be filled, and I will give thee utterance, for all flesh is in my hands, and I will do as seemeth me good.

6:33 Say unto this people: Choose ye this day, to serve the Lord God who made you.

6:34 Behold my Spirit is upon you, wherefore all thy words will I justify; and the mountains shall flee before you, and the rivers shall turn from their course; and thou shalt abide in me, and I in you; therefore walk with me.

6:35 And the Lord spake unto Enoch, and said unto him: Anoint thine eyes with clay, and wash them, and thou shalt see. And he did so.

6:36 And he beheld the spirits that God had created; and he beheld also things which were not visible to the natural eye; and from thenceforth came the saying abroad in the land:
A seer hath the Lord raised up unto his people.

ENOCH TESTIFIES

5:21d And it came to pass, that Enoch went forth in the land, among the people, standing upon the hills, and the high places, and cried with a loud voice, testifying against their works.

And all men were offended because of him;
and they came forth to hear him upon the high places, saying unto the tent-keepers, Tarry ye here and keep the tents, while we go yonder to behold the seer, for he prophesieth; and there is a strange thing in the land, a wild man hath come among us.

And it came to pass when they heard him, no man laid hands on him, for fear came on them all that heard him, for he walked with God.

And there came a man unto him, whose name was Mahijah, and said unto him, Tell us plainly who thou art, and from whence thou comest.

And he said unto them, I came out from the land of Cainan, the land of my fathers, a land of righteousness unto this day; and my father taught me in all the ways of God.

And it came to pass, as I journeyed from the land of Cainan by the sea east, I beheld a vision; and lo, the heavens I saw, and the Lord spake with me, and gave me commandment; wherefore for this cause, to keep the commandment, I speak forth these words.

And Enoch continued his speech, saying, The Lord which spake with me, the same is the God of heaven, and he is my God and your God, and ye are my brethren; and why counsel ye yourselves, and deny the God of heaven?

The heavens he made; the earth is his footstool, and the foundation thereof is his; behold he laid it, and hosts of men hath he brought in upon the face thereof.

And death hath come upon our fathers; nevertheless, we know them, and cannot deny, and even the first of all we know, even Adam;
for a book of remembrance we have written among us, according to the pattern given by the finger of God; and it is given in our own language.

6:37 And it came to pass that Enoch went forth in the land, among the people, standing upon the hills and the high places, and cried with a loud voice, testifying against their works;
and all men were offended because of him.
6:38 And they came forth to hear him, upon the high places, saying unto the tentkeepers: Tarry ye here and keep the tents, while we go yonder to behold the seer, for he prophesieth, and there is a strange thing in the land; a wild man hath come among us.
6:39 And it came to pass when they heard him, no man laid hands on him; for fear came on all them that heard him; for he walked with God.
6:40 And there came a man unto him, whose name was Mahijah, and said unto him: Tell us plainly who thou art, and from whence thou comest?
6:41 And he said unto them: I came out from the land of Cainan, the land of my fathers, a land of righteousness unto this day. And my father taught me in all the ways of God.
6:42 And it came to pass, as I journeyed from the land of Cainan, by the sea east, I beheld a vision; and lo, the heavens I saw, and the Lord spake with me, and gave me commandment; wherefore, for this cause, to keep the commandment, I speak forth these words.
6:43 And Enoch continued his speech, saying: The Lord which spake with me, the same is the God of heaven, and he is my God, and your God, and ye are my brethren, and why counsel ye yourselves, and deny the God of heaven?
6:44 The heavens he made; the earth is his footstool; and the foundation thereof is his. Behold, he laid it, an host of men hath he brought in upon the face thereof.
6:45 And death hath come upon our fathers; nevertheless we know them, and cannot deny, and even the first of all we know, even Adam.
6:46 For a book of remembrance we have written among us, according to the pattern given by the finger of God; and it is given in our language.

5:21e ***And as Enoch spake forth the words of God, the people trembled and could not stand in his presence.***

And he said unto them, Because that Adam fell, we are; and by his fall came death, and we are made partakers of misery and woe.

Behold, Satan hath come among the children of men, and tempteth them to worship him; and men have become carnal, sensual, and devilish, and are shut out from the presence of God.

But God hath made known unto our fathers that all men must repent.

And he called upon our father Adam, by his own voice, saying, I am God; made the world, and men before they were in the flesh.

And he also said unto him, If thou wilt, turn unto me and hearken unto my voice, and believe, and repent of all thy transgressions, and be baptized, even in water, in the name of mine Only Begotten Son, who is full of grace and truth, which is Jesus Christ, the only name which shall be given under heaven, whereby salvation shall come unto the children of men;
and ye shall receive the gift of the Holy Ghost, asking all things in his name, and whatsoever ye shall ask it shall be given you.

And our father Adam spake unto the Lord, and said, Why is it that men must repent, and be baptized in the water?

And the Lord said unto Adam, Behold, I have forgiven thee thy transgression in the garden of Eden.

Hence came the saying abroad among the people, that the Son of God hath atoned for original guilt, wherein the sins of the parents cannot be answered upon the heads of the children, for they are whole from the foundation of the world.

And the Lord spake unto Adam, saying, Inasmuch as thy children are conceived in sin, even so, when they begin to grow up sin conceiveth in their hearts, and they taste the bitter, that they may know to prize the good.

And it is given unto them to know good from evil; wherefore, they are agents until themselves.

6:47 And as Enoch spake forth the words of God, the people trembled, and could not stand in his presence.

6:48 And he said unto them: Because that Adam fell, we are; and by his fall came death; and we are made partakers of misery and woe.

6:49 Behold Satan hath come among the children of men, and tempteth them to worship him; and men have become carnal, sensual, and devilish, and are shut out from the presence of God.

6:50 But God hath made known unto our fathers that all men must repent.

6:51 And he called upon our father Adam by his own voice, saying: I am God; I made the world, and men before they were in the flesh.

6:52 And he also said unto him: If thou <u>wilt turn</u> unto me, and hearken unto my voice, and believe, and repent of all thy transgressions, and be baptized, even in water, in the name of mine Only Begotten Son, who is full of grace and truth, which is Jesus Christ, the only name which shall be given under heaven, whereby salvation shall come unto the children of men,
ye shall receive the gift of the Holy Ghost, asking all things in his name, and whatsoever ye shall ask, it shall be given you.

6:53 And our father Adam spake unto the Lord, and said: Why is it that men must repent and be baptized in (-) water?
And the Lord said unto Adam: Behold I have forgiven thee thy transgression in the Garden of Eden.

6:54 Hence came the saying abroad among the people, that the Son of God hath atoned for original guilt, wherein the sins of the parents cannot be answered upon the heads of the children, for they are whole from the foundation of the world.

6:55 And the Lord spake unto Adam, saying: Inasmuch as thy children are conceived in sin, even so when they begin to grow up, sin conceiveth in their hearts, and they taste the bitter, that they may know to prize the good.

6:56 And it is given unto them to know good and evil; wherefore they are agents unto themselves,

5:21f And I have given unto you another law and commandment; wherefore teach it unto your children, that all men, everywhere, must repent, or they can in no wise inherit the kingdom of God.

For no unclean thing can dwell there, or dwell in his presence; for, in the language of Adam, Man of Holiness is his name; and the name of the Only Begotten is the Son of Man, even Jesus Christ, a righteous judge, who shall come in the meridian of time.

Therefore I give unto you a commandment, to teach these things freely unto your children, saying,
that by reason of transgression cometh the fall, which fall bringeth death; and inasmuch as ye were born into the world by water and blood, and the spirit, which I have made, and so become of dust a living soul;

Even so ye must be born again, into the kingdom of heaven, of water, and of the Spirit, and be cleansed by blood, even the blood of mine Only Begotten; that ye may be sanctified from all sin; and enjoy the words of eternal life in this world, and eternal life in the world to come; even immortal glory.

For, by the water ye keep the commandment; by the Spirit ye are justified; and by the blood ye are sanctified.

Therefore it is given to abide in you, the record of heaven, the Comforter, the peaceable things of immortal glory, the truth of all things, that which quickeneth all things, which maketh alive all things, that which knoweth all things, and hath all power according to wisdom, mercy, truth, justice and judgment.

And now behold, I say unto you, This is the plan of salvation unto all men, through the blood of mine Only Begotten, who shall come in the meridian of time.

And, behold, all things have their likeness; and all things are created and made to bear record of me; both things which are temporal, and things which are spiritual; things which are in the heavens above, and things which are on the earth, and things which are in the earth, and

and I have given unto you another law and commandment.
6:57 Wherefore teach it unto your children, that all men, everywhere, must repent, or they can in nowise inherit the kingdom of God,
for no unclean thing can dwell there, or dwell in his presence; for, in the language of Adam, Man of Holiness is his name, and the name of his Only Begotten is the Son of Man, even Jesus Christ, a righteous Judge, who shall come in the meridian of time.
6:58 Therefore I give unto you a commandment, to teach these things freely unto your children, saying:
6:59 That by reason of transgression cometh the fall, which fall bringeth death, and inasmuch as ye were born into the world by water, and blood, and the spirit, which I have made, and so became of dust a living soul,
even so ye must be born again into the kingdom of heaven, of water, and of the Spirit, and be cleansed by blood, even the blood of mine Only Begotten; that ye might be sanctified from all sin, and enjoy the words of eternal life in this world, and eternal life in the world to come, even immortal glory;

6:60 For by the water ye keep the commandment; by the Spirit ye are justified, and by the blood ye are sanctified;
6:61 Therefore it is given to abide in you; the record of heaven; the Comforter; the peaceable things of immortal glory; the truth of all things; that which quickeneth all things, which maketh alive all things; that which knoweth all things, and hath all power according to wisdom, mercy, truth, justice, and judgment.
6:62 And now, behold, I say unto you: This is the plan of salvation unto all men, through the blood of mine Only Begotten, who shall come in the meridian of time.
6:63 And behold, all things have their likeness, and all things are created and made to bear record of me, both things which are temporal, and things which are spiritual; things which are in the heavens above, and things which are on the earth, and things which are in the earth, and things which are under the

things which are under the earth, both above and beneath, all things bear record of me.

earth, both above and beneath: all things bear record of me.

5:21g And it came to pass, when the Lord had spoken with Adam our father, that Adam cried unto the Lord, and he was caught away by the Spirit of the Lord, and was carried down into the water, and was laid under the water, and was brought forth out of the water; and thus he was baptized.

6:64 And it came to pass, when the Lord had spoken with Adam, our father, that Adam cried unto the Lord, and he was caught away by the Spirit of the Lord, and was carried down into the water, and was laid under the water, and was brought forth out of the water.

6:65 And thus he was baptized,

And the Spirit of God descended upon him, and thus he was born of the Spirit, and became quickened in the inner man.

and the Spirit of God descended upon him, and thus he was born of the Spirit, and became quickened in the inner man.

And he heard a voice out of heaven, saying, Thou art baptized with fire and with the Holy Ghost; this is the record of the Father and the Son, from henceforth and for ever;

6:66 And he heard a voice out of heaven, saying: Thou art baptized with fire, and with the Holy Ghost. This is the record of the Father, and the Son, from henceforth and forever;

And thou art after the order of him who was without beginning of days or end of years, from all eternity to all eternity.

6:67 And thou art after the order of him who was without beginning of days or end of years, from all eternity to all eternity.

Behold, thou are one in me, a son of God; and thus may all become my sons. Amen.

6:68 Behold, thou art one in me, a son of God; and thus may all become my sons. Amen.

And it came to pass, that Enoch continued his speech, saying, Behold, our father Adam taught these things, and many have believed, and become the sons of God; and many have believed not, and have perished in their sins, and are looking forth with fear, in torment, for the fiery indignation of the wrath of God to be poured out upon them.

7:1 And it came to pass that Enoch continued his speech, saying: Behold, our father Adam taught these things, and many have believed and become the sons of God, and many have believed not, and have perished in their sins, and are looking forth with fear, in torment, for the fiery indignation of the wrath of God to be poured out upon them.

And from that time forth, Enoch began to prophesy, saying unto the people, that, as I was journeying, and stood in the place Mahujah, and cried unto the Lord, there came a voice out of heaven, saying, Turn ye and get ye upon the mount Simeon.

7:2 And from that time forth Enoch began to prophesy, saying unto the people, that: As I was journeying, and stood upon the place Mahujah, and cried unto the Lord, there came a voice out of heaven, saying--Turn ye, and get ye upon the mount Simeon.

And it came to pass, that I turned and went up on the mount; and as I stood upon the mount, I beheld the heavens open, and I was clothed upon with glory.

7:3 And it came to pass that I turned and went up on the mount; and as I stood upon the mount, I beheld the heavens open, and I was clothed upon with glory;

And I saw the Lord, and he stood before my face, and he talked with me, even as a man talketh one with another, face to face; and he said unto me, Look, and I will show unto thee the world for the space of many generations.

7:4 And I saw the Lord; and he stood before my face, and he talked with me, even as a man talketh one with another, face to face; and he said unto me: Look, and I will show unto thee the world for the space of many generations.

5:21h And it came to pass, that I beheld in the valley of Shum, and lo! a great people which dwelt in tents, which were the people of Shum.

And again the Lord said unto me, Look, and I looked towards the north, and I beheld the people of Cainan, which dwelt in tents.

And the Lord said unto me, Prophesy; and I prophesied saying, Behold the people of Cainan which are numerous, shall go forth in battle array against the people of Shum, and shall slay them, that they shall be utterly destroyed.

And the people of Cainan shall divide themselves in the land, and the land shall be barren and unfruitful, and none other people shall dwell there, but the people of Cainan;
for, behold, the Lord shall curse the land which much heat, and the barrenness thereof shall go forth for ever.

And there was a blackness came upon all the children of Cainan, that they were despised among all people.

And it came to pass, that the Lord said unto me, Look, and I looked, and I beheld the land of Sharon, and the land of Enoch, and the land of Omner, and the land of Heni, and the land of Shem, and the land of Haner, and the land of Hanannihah, and all the inhabitants thereof.

And the Lord said unto me, Go forth to this people, and say unto them, Repent; lest I come out and smite them with a curse, and they die.

And he gave unto me a commandment, that I should baptize in the name of the Father, and of the Son, who is full of grace and truth, and the Holy Ghost which beareth record of the Father and the Son.

And it came to pass, that Enoch continued to call upon all the people, save it were the people of Cainan, to repent.

And so great was the faith of Enoch, that he led the people of God, and their enemies came to battle against them, and he spake the word of the Lord, and the earth trembled, and the mountains fled, even according to his command.

7:5 And it came to pass that I beheld in the valley of Shum, and lo, a great people which dwelt in tents, which were the people of Shum.

7:6 And again the Lord said unto me: Look; and I looked towards the north, and I beheld the people of Canaan, which dwelt in tents.

7:7 And the Lord said unto me: Prophesy; and I prophesied, saying: Behold the people of Canaan, which are numerous, shall go forth in battle array against the people of Shum, and shall slay them that they shall utterly be destroyed;
and the people of Canaan shall divide themselves in the land, and the land shall be barren and unfruitful, and none other people shall dwell there but the people of Canaan;

7:8 For behold, the Lord shall curse the land with much heat, and the barrenness thereof shall go forth forever;
and there was a blackness came upon all the children of Canaan, that they were despised among all people.

7:9 And it came to pass that the Lord said unto me: Look; and I looked, and I beheld the land of Sharon, and the land of Enoch, and the land of Omner, and the land of Heni, and the land of Shem, and the land of Haner, and the land of Hanannihah, and all the inhabitants thereof;

7:10 And the Lord said unto me: Go to this people, and say unto them--Repent, lest I come out and smite them with a curse, and they die.

7:11 And he gave unto me a commandment that I should baptize in the name of the Father, and of the Son, which is full of grace and truth, and of the Holy Ghost, which beareth record of the Father and the Son.

7:12 And it came to pass that Enoch continued to call upon all the people, save it were the people of Canaan, to repent;

7:13 And so great was the faith of Enoch that he led the people of God, and their enemies came to battle against them; and he spake the word of the Lord, and the earth trembled, and the mountains fled, even according to his command;

5:21i And the rivers of water were turned out of their course, and the roar of the lions was heard out of the wilderness.

And all nations feared greatly, so powerful was the word of Enoch, and so great was the power of the language which God had given him.

There also came up a land out of the depths of the sea; and so great was the fear of the enemies of the people of God, that they fled and stood afar off, and went upon the land which came up out of the depths of the sea.

And the giants of the land also stood afar off; and there went forth a curse upon all the people which fought against God.

And from that time forth, there were wars, and bloodshed among them; but the Lord came and dwelt with his people, and they dwelt in righteousness.

And the fear of the Lord was upon all nations, so great was the glory of the Lord which was upon his people.

And the Lord blessed the land, and they were blessed upon the mountains, and upon the high places, and did flourish.

And the Lord called his people, Zion, because they were of one heart and of one mind, and dwelt in righteousness; and there were no poor among them.

And Enoch continued his preaching in righteousness unto the people of God. And it came to pass in his days, that he built a city that was called the city of Holiness, even Zion.

And it came to pass that Enoch talked with the Lord; and he said unto the Lord: Surely, Zion shall dwell in safety for ever. But the Lord said unto Enoch: Zion have I blessed, but the residue of the people have I cursed.

And it came to pass that the Lord showed unto Enoch all the inhabitants of the earth, and he beheld, and lo! Zion in process of time was taken up into heaven.

And the Lord said unto Enoch, Behold mine abode for ever.

And Enoch also beheld the residue of the people which were the sons of Adam, and they were a mixture

and the rivers of water were turned out of their course; and the roar of the lions was heard out of the wilderness;

and all nations feared greatly, so powerful was the word of Enoch, and so great was the power of the language which God had given him.

7:14 There also came up a land out of the depth of the sea, and so great was the fear of the enemies of the people of God, that they fled and stood afar off and went upon the land which came up out of the depth of the sea.

7:15 And the giants of the land, also, stood afar off; and there went forth a curse upon all people that fought against God;

7:16 And from that time forth there were wars and bloodshed among them; but the Lord came and dwelt with his people, and they dwelt in righteousness.

7:17 The fear of the Lord was upon all nations, so great was the glory of the Lord, which was upon his people.
And the Lord blessed the land, and they were blessed upon the mountains, and upon the high places, and did flourish.

7:18 And the Lord called his people ZION, because they were of one heart and one mind, and dwelt in righteousness; and there were no poor among them.

7:19 And Enoch continued his preaching in righteousness unto the people of God. And it came to pass in his days, that he built a city that was called the City of Holiness, even ZION.

7:20 And it came to pass that Enoch talked with the Lord; and he said unto the Lord: Surely Zion shall dwell in safety forever. But the Lord said unto Enoch: Zion have I blessed, but the residue of the people have I cursed.

7:21 And it came to pass that the Lord showed unto Enoch all the inhabitants of the earth; and he beheld, and lo, Zion, in process of time, was taken up into heaven.
And the Lord said unto Enoch: Behold mine abode forever.

7:22 And Enoch also beheld the residue of the people which were the sons of Adam; and they were a mixture

of all the seed of Adam, save it were the seed of Cain; for the seed of Cain were black, and had not place among them.

5:21j And after that Zion was taken up into heaven, Enoch beheld, and lo, all the nations of the earth were before him; and there came generation upon generation.

And Enoch was high and lifted up, even in the bosom of the Father and the Son of Man; and behold, the powers of Satan were upon all the face of the earth;

and he saw angels descending out of heaven, and he heard a loud voice, saying, Woe! woe! be unto the inhabitants of the earth!

And he beheld Satan, and he had a great chain in his hand, and it veiled the whole face of the earth with darkness; and he looked up and laughed, and his angels rejoiced.

And Enoch beheld angels descending out of heaven, bearing testimony of the Father and of the Son.

And the Holy Ghost fell on many, and they were caught up by the powers of heaven into Zion.

And it came to pass, that the God of heaven looked upon the residue of the people, and wept; and Enoch bore record of it, saying, How is it that the heavens weep, and shed forth their tears as the rain upon the mountains?

And Enoch said unto the Lord, How is it that thou canst weep, seeing thou art holy, and from all eternity to all eternity?

And were it possible that man could number the particles of the earth, yea, millions of earths like this, it would not be a beginning to the number of thy creations;

And thy curtains are stretched out still, and thou art there, and thy bosom is there; and also, thou art just, thou art merciful and kind forever;

Thou hast taken Zion to thine own bosom, from all thy creations, from all eternity to all eternity; and naught but peace, justice, and truth is the habitation of thy throne; and mercy shall go before thy face and have no end. How is it that thou canst weep?

The Lord said unto Enoch, Behold, these thy brethren, they are the workmanship of mine own hands, and

of all the seed of Adam save it was the seed of Cain, for the seed of Cain were black, and had not place among them.

7:23 And after that Zion was taken up into heaven, Enoch beheld, and lo, all the nations of the earth were before him;

7:24 And there came generation upon generation;

and Enoch was high and lifted up, even in the bosom of the Father, and of the Son of Man; and behold, the power of Satan was upon all the face of the earth.

7:25 And he saw angels descending out of heaven; and he heard a loud voice saying: Wo, wo be unto the inhabitants of the earth.

7:26 And he beheld Satan; and he had a great chain in his hand, and it veiled the whole face of the earth with darkness; and he looked up and laughed, and his angels rejoiced.

7:27 And Enoch beheld angels descending out of heaven, bearing testimony of the Father and Son;

and the Holy Ghost fell on many, and they were caught up by the powers of heaven into Zion.

7:28 And it came to pass that the God of heaven looked upon the residue of the people, and he wept; and Enoch bore record of it, saying: How is it that the heavens weep, and shed forth their tears as the rain upon the mountains?

7:29 And Enoch said unto the Lord: How is it that thou canst weep, seeing thou art holy, and from all eternity to all eternity?

7:30 And were it possible that man could number the particles of the earth, yea, millions of earths like this, it would not be a beginning to the number of thy creations;

and thy curtains are stretched out still; and yet thou art there, and thy bosom is there; and also thou art just; thou art merciful and kind forever;

7:31 And thou hast taken Zion to thine own bosom, from all thy creations, from all eternity to all eternity; and naught but peace, justice, and truth is the habitation of thy throne; and mercy shall go before thy face and have no end; how is it thou canst weep?

7:32 The Lord said unto Enoch: Behold these thy brethren; they are the workmanship of mine own hands, and I

I gave unto them their knowledge in the day that I created them.
5:21k And in the garden of Eden, gave I unto man his agency;
and unto thy brethren have I said, and also gave commandment, that they should love one another; and that they should choose me their Father.

But, behold, they are without affection, and they hate their own blood; and the fire of mine indignation is kindled against them; and in my hot displeasure will I send in the floods upon them; for my fierce anger is kindled against them.

Behold, I am God; Man of Holiness is my name; Man of Counsel is my name; and Endless and Eternal is my name also.
Wherefore I can stretch forth mine hands and hold all the creations which I have made, and mine eye can pierce them also.

And among all the workmanship of my hands there has not been so great wickedness as among thy brethren;
but, behold, their sins shall be upon the heads of their fathers; Satan shall be their father, and misery shall be their doom; and the whole heavens shall weep over them, even all the workmanship of mine hands.

Wherefore should not the heavens weep, seeing these shall suffer?
But, behold, these which thine eyes are upon shall perish in the floods; and, behold, I will shut them up; a prison have I prepared for them,
and he whom I have chosen has plead before my face;

Wherefore he suffereth for their sins, inasmuch as they will repent, in the day that my chosen shall return unto me; and until that day they shall be in torment.

Wherefore for this shall the heavens weep, yea, and all the workmanship of my hands.

gave unto them their knowledge, in the day I created them;
and in the Garden of Eden, gave I unto man his agency;
7:33 And unto thy brethren have I said, and also given commandment, that they should love one another, and that they should choose me, their Father;
but behold, they are without affection, and they hate their own blood;
7:34 And the fire of mine indignation is kindled against them; and in my hot displeasure will I send in the floods upon them, for my fierce anger is kindled against them.
7:35 Behold, I am God; Man of Holiness is my name; Man of Counsel is my name; and Endless and Eternal is my name, also.
7:36 Wherefore, I can stretch forth mine hands and hold all the creations which I have made; and mine eye can pierce them also,
and among all the workmanship of mine hands there has not been so great wickedness as among thy brethren.

7:37 But behold, their sins shall be upon the heads of their fathers; Satan shall be their father, and misery shall be their doom; and the whole heavens shall weep over them, even all the workmanship of mine hands;
wherefore should not the heavens weep, seeing these shall suffer?

7:38 But behold, these which thine eyes are upon shall perish in the floods; and behold, I will shut them up; a prison have I prepared for them.
7:39 And That which I have chosen hath pled before my face.
Wherefore, he suffereth for their sins; inasmuch as they will repent in the day that my Chosen shall return unto me,
and until that day they shall be in torment;
7:40 Wherefore, for this shall the heavens weep, yea, and all the workmanship of mine hands.

THE LORD COVENANTS WITH ENOCH

GENESIS King James Version with JST	MOSES (With Comparison to JST Genesis)	ABRAHAM
5:211 ***And it came to pass, that the Lord spake unto Enoch, and told Enoch all the doings of the children of men.***	7:41 And it came to pass that the Lord spake unto Enoch, and told Enoch all the doings of the children of men;	
Wherefore Enoch knew and looked upon their wickedness, and their misery; and wept, and stretched forth his arms, and his heart swelled wide as eternity, and his bowels yearned, and all eternity shook.	wherefore Enoch knew, and looked upon their wickedness, and their misery, and wept and stretched forth his arms, and his heart swelled wide as eternity; and his bowels yearned; and all eternity shook.	
And Enoch saw Noah also, and his family, that the posterity of all the sons of Noah should be saved with a temporal salvation.	7:42 And Enoch also saw Noah, and his family; that the posterity of all the sons of Noah should be saved with a temporal salvation;	
Wherefore Enoch saw that Noah built an ark, and that the Lord smiled upon it, and held it in his own hand; but upon the residue of the wicked came the floods and swallowed them up.	7:43 Wherefore Enoch saw that Noah built an ark; and that the Lord smiled upon it, and held it in his own hand; but upon the residue of the wicked the floods came and swallowed them up.	
And as Enoch saw thus, he had bitterness of soul, and wept over his brethren, and said unto the heavens, I will refuse to be comforted.	7:44 And as Enoch saw this, he had bitterness of soul, and wept over his brethren, and said unto the heavens: I will refuse to be comforted;	
But the Lord said unto Enoch, Lift up your heart and be glad, and look.	but the Lord said unto Enoch: Lift up your heart, and be glad; and look.	
And it came to pass, that Enoch looked, and from Noah, he beheld all the families of the earth, and he cried unto the Lord, saying: When shall the day of the Lord come? When shall the blood of the righteous be shed, that all they that mourn may be sanctified, and have eternal life?	7:45 And it came to pass that Enoch looked; and from Noah, he beheld all the families of the earth; and he cried unto the Lord, saying: When shall the day of the Lord come? When shall the blood of the Righteous be shed, that all they that mourn may be sanctified and have eternal life?	
And the Lord said: It shall be in the meridian of time; in the days of wickedness and vengeance.	7:46 And the Lord said: It shall be in the meridian of time, in the days of wickedness and vengeance.	
And, behold, Enoch saw the day of the coming of the Son of Man, even in the flesh; and his soul rejoiced, saying, The righteous is lifted up; and the Lamb is slain from the foundation of the world; and through faith I am in the bosom of the Father; and behold, Zion is with me!	7:47 And behold, Enoch saw the day of the coming of the Son of Man, even in the flesh; and his soul rejoiced, saying: The Righteous is lifted up, and the Lamb is slain from the foundation of the world; and through faith I am in the bosom of the Father, and behold, Zion is with me.	
And it came to pass, that Enoch looked upon the earth, and he heard a voice from the bowels thereof, saying, Woe! woe! is me, the mother of men! I am pained, I am weary, because of the wickedness of my children! When shall I rest, and be cleansed from the filthiness which has gone forth out of me?	7:48 And it came to pass that Enoch looked upon the earth; and he heard a voice from the bowels thereof, saying: Wo, wo is me, the mother of men; I am pained, I am weary, because of the wickedness of my children. When shall I rest, and be cleansed from the filthiness which is gone forth out of me?	

When will my Creator sanctify me, that I may rest, and righteousness for a season abide upon my face?
5:21m And when Enoch heard the earth mourn, he wept, and cried unto the Lord, saying, O Lord, wilt thou not have compassion upon the earth? wilt thou not bless the children of Noah?

And it came to pass, that Enoch continued his cry unto the Lord, saying, I ask thee, O Lord, in the name of thine Only Begotten, even Jesus Christ, that thou wilt have mercy upon Noah, and his seed, that the earth might never more be covered by the floods.

And the Lord could not withhold; and he covenanted with Enoch, and sware unto him with an oath, that he would stay the floods; that he would call upon the children of Noah;
and he sent forth an unalterable decree, that a remnant of his seed should always be found among all nations, while the earth should stand.

And the Lord said, Blessed is he through whose seed Messiah shall come; for he saith, I am Messiah, the King of Zion, the Rock of heaven, which is broad as eternity; whoso cometh in at the gate and climbeth up by me shall never fall.

Wherefore, blessed are they of whom I have spoken, for they shall come forth with songs of everlasting joy.

And it came to pass, that Enoch cried unto the Lord, saying, When the Son of Man cometh in the flesh shall the earth rest? I pray thee, show me these things.

And the Lord said unto Enoch, Look; and he looked, and beheld the Son of Man lifted up on the cross, after the manner of men.

And he heard a loud voice, and the heavens were veiled; and all the creations of God mourned, and the earth groaned; and the rocks were rent; and the saints arose, and were crowned at the right hand of the Son of Man, with crowns of glory.

And as many of the spirits as were in prison came forth, and stood on the right hand of God. And the remainder were reserved in chains of darkness until the judgment of the great day.

When will my Creator sanctify me, that I may rest, and righteousness for a season abide upon my face?
7:49 And when Enoch heard the earth mourn, he wept, and cried unto the Lord, saying: O Lord, wilt thou not have compassion upon the earth? Wilt thou not bless the children of Noah?
7:50 And it came to pass that Enoch continued his cry unto the Lord, saying: I ask thee, O Lord, in the name of thine Only Begotten, even Jesus Christ, that thou wilt have mercy upon Noah and his seed, that the earth might never more be covered by the floods.

7:51 And the Lord could not withhold; and he covenanted with Enoch, and sware unto him with an oath, that he would stay the floods; that he would call upon the children of Noah;
7:52 And he sent forth an unalterable decree, that a remnant of his seed should always be found among all nations, while the earth should stand;
7:53 And the Lord said: Blessed is he through whose seed Messiah shall come; for he saith I am Messiah, the King of Zion, the Rock of Heaven, which is broad as eternity; whoso cometh in at the gate and climbeth up by me shall never fall;
wherefore, blessed are they of whom I have spoken, for they shall come forth with songs of everlasting joy.
7:54 And it came to pass that Enoch cried unto the Lord, saying: When the Son of Man cometh in the flesh, shall the earth rest? I pray thee, show me these things.
7:55 And the Lord said unto Enoch: Look, and he looked and beheld the Son of Man lifted up on the cross, after the manner of men;
7:56 And he heard a loud voice; and the heavens were veiled; and all the creations of God mourned; and the earth groaned; and the rocks were rent; and the saints arose, and were crowned at the right hand of the Son of Man, with crowns of glory;
7:57 And as many of the spirits as were in prison came forth, and stood on the right hand of God; and the remainder were reserved in chains of darkness until the judgment of the great day.

5:21n And again Enoch wept, and cried unto the Lord, saying, When shall the earth rest?

And Enoch beheld the Son of Man ascend up unto the Father; and he called unto the Lord, saying, Wilt thou not come again upon the earth? for inasmuch as thou art God, and I know thee, and thou hast sworn unto me, and commanded me that I should ask in the name of thine Only Begotten; thou hast made me, and given unto me a right to thy throne, and not of myself, but through thine own grace; wherefore I ask thee if thou wilt not come again on the earth?

And the Lord said unto Enoch, As I live, even so will I come in the last days, in the days of wickedness and vengeance, to fulfil the oath which I made unto you concerning the children of Noah.

And the day shall come that the earth shall rest. But before that day the heavens shall be darkened,
and a veil of darkness shall cover the earth; and the heavens shall shake, and also the earth.

And great tribulations shall be among the children of men, but my people will I preserve;
and righteousness will I send down out of heaven, and truth will I send forth out of the earth, to bear testimony of mine Only Begotten; his resurrection from the dead; yea, and also the resurrection of all men.

And righteousness and truth will I cause to sweep the earth as with a flood, to gather out mine elect from the four quarters of the earth, unto a place which I shall prepare; an holy city, that my people may gird up their loins, and be looking forth for the time of my coming; for there shall be my tabernacle, and it shall be called Zion; a New Jerusalem.

And the Lord said unto Enoch, Then shalt thou and all thy city meet them there; and we will receive them into our bosom; and they shall see us, and we will fall upon their necks, and they shall fall upon our necks, and we will kiss each other;

And there shall be mine abode, and it shall be Zion, which shall come forth out of all the creations which I

7:58 And again Enoch wept _ and cried unto the Lord, saying: When shall the earth rest?

7:59 And Enoch beheld the Son of Man ascend up unto the Father; and he called unto the Lord, saying: Wilt thou not come again upon the earth? Forasmuch as thou art God, and I know thee, and thou hast sworn unto me, and commanded me that I should ask in the name of thine Only Begotten; thou hast made me, and given unto me a right to thy throne, and not of myself, but through thine own grace; wherefore, I ask thee if thou wilt not come again on the earth.

7:60 And the Lord said unto Enoch: As I live, even so will I come in the last days, in the days of wickedness and vengeance, to fulfil the oath which I have made unto you concerning the children of Noah;

7:61 And the day shall come that the earth shall rest, but before that day the heavens shall be darkened,
and a veil of darkness shall cover the earth; and the heavens shall shake, and also the earth;
and great tribulations shall be among the children of men, but my people will I preserve;

7:62 And righteousness will I send down out of heaven; and truth will I send forth out of the earth, to bear testimony of mine Only Begotten; his resurrection from the dead; yea, and also the resurrection of all men;
and righteousness and truth will I cause to sweep the earth as with a flood,
to gather out mine elect from the four quarters of the earth, unto a place which I shall prepare, an Holy City, that my people may gird up their loins, and be looking forth for the time of my coming; for there shall be my tabernacle, and it shall be called Zion, a New Jerusalem.

7:63 And the Lord said unto Enoch: Then shalt thou and all thy city meet them there, and we will receive them into our bosom, and they shall see us; and we will fall upon their necks, and they shall fall upon our necks, and we will kiss each other;

7:64 And there shall be mine abode, and it shall be Zion, which shall come forth out of all the creations which I

have made; and for the space of a thousand years the earth shall rest.
5:21o And it came to pass that Enoch saw the day of the coming of the Son of Man, in the last days, to dwell on the earth in righteousness for the space of a thousand years.

But before that day, he saw great tribulation among the wicked; and he also saw the sea, that it was troubled, and men's hearts failing them, looking forth with fear for the judgment of the Almighty God, which should come upon the wicked.

And the Lord showed Enoch all things, even unto the end of the world. And he saw the day of the righteous, the hour of their redemption, and received a fulness of joy.

have made; and for the space of a thousand years the earth shall rest.
7:65 And it came to pass that Enoch saw the day of the coming of the Son of Man, in the last days, to dwell on the earth in righteousness for the space of a thousand years;
7:66 But before that day he saw great tribulations among the wicked; and he also saw the sea, that it was troubled, and men's hearts failing them, looking forth with fear for the judgments of the Almighty God, which should come upon the wicked.
7:67 And the Lord showed Enoch all things, even unto the end of the world; and he saw the day of the righteous, the hour of their redemption, and received a fulness of joy;

ZION IS FLED

5:21p ***And all the days of Zion, in the days of Enoch, were three hundred and sixty-five years.***
5:22 And Enoch ***and all his people*** walked with God, ~~after he began Methuselah three hundred years, and he began sons and daughters:~~
and he dwelt in the midst of Zion.
5:24a ***And it came to pass, that Zion was not, for God received it up into his own bosom; and from thence went forth the saying, Zion is fled.*** ~~And Enoch walked with God: and he was not; for God took him.~~
5:23 And all the days of Enoch were ~~three hundred sixty and five~~ ***four hundred and thirty*** years.
[verse order changed by JST]

7:68 And all the days of Zion, in the days of Enoch, were three hundred and sixty-five years.
7:69 And Enoch and all his people walked with God,

and he dwelt in the midst of Zion;
and it came to pass that Zion was not, for God received it up into his own bosom; and from thence went forth the saying, ZION IS FLED.

8:1 And all the days of Enoch were four hundred and thirty years.

METHUSELAH

5:24b ***And it came to pass, that Methuselah the son of Enoch, was not taken, that the covenants of the Lord might be fulfilled, which he made to Enoch; for he truly covenanted with Enoch, that Noah should be of the fruit of his loins.***

And it came to pass, that Methuselah prophesied that from his loins should spring all the kingdoms of the earth; (through Noah,) and he took glory unto himself.

8:2 And it came to pass that Methuselah, the son of Enoch, was not taken, that the covenants of the Lord might be fulfilled, which he made to Enoch; for he truly covenanted with Enoch that Noah should be of the fruit of his loins.
8:3 And it came to pass that Methuselah prophesied that from his loins should spring all the kingdoms of the earth (through Noah), and he took glory unto himself.

Genesis	Moses
And there came forth a great famine into the land, and the Lord cursed the earth with a sore curse, and many of the inhabitants thereof died.	8:4 And there came forth a great famine into the land, and the Lord cursed the earth with a sore curse, and many of the inhabitants thereof died.
5:25 And ***it came to pass that*** Methuselah lived ~~an~~ ***one*** hundred ***and*** eighty ~~and~~ seven years, and begat Lamech;	8:5 And it came to pass that Methuselah lived one hundred and eighty-seven years, and begat Lamech;
5:26 And Methuselah lived, after he begat Lamech, seven hundred ***and*** eighty ~~and~~ two years, and begat sons and daughters;	8:6 And Methuselah lived, after he begat Lamech, seven hundred and eighty-two years, and begat sons and daughters;
5:27 And all the days of Methuselah were nine hundred ***and*** sixty ~~and~~ nine years, and he died.	8:7 And all the days of Methuselah were nine hundred and sixty-nine years, and he died.

PRELUDE TO THE FLOOD

Genesis	Moses
5:28 And Lamech lived ~~an~~ ***one*** hundred ***and*** eighty ~~and~~ two years, and begat a son,	8:8 And Lamech lived one hundred and eighty-two years, and begat a son,
5:29 And he called his name Noah, saying: This ~~same~~ ***son*** shall comfort us concerning our work, and toil of our hands, because of the ground which the LORD hath cursed.	8:9 And he called his name Noah, saying: This son shall comfort us concerning our work and toil of our hands, because of the ground which the Lord hath cursed.
5:30 And Lamech lived after he begat Noah five hundred ***and*** ninety ~~and~~ five years, and begat sons and daughters~~;~~ **.**	8:10 And Lamech lived, after he begat Noah, five hundred and ninety-five years, and begat sons and daughters;
5:31 And all the days of Lamech were seven hundred ***and*** seventy ~~and~~ seven years; and he died.	8:11 And all the days of Lamech were seven hundred and seventy-seven years, and he died.
5:32 And Noah was ***four hundred and fifty years old, and begat Japheth, and forty-two years afterward he begat Shem of her who was the mother of Japheth, and when he was*** five hundred years old ~~: and Noah~~ ***, he*** begat ***Ham*** ~~Shem, Ham, and Japeth~~ .	8:12 And Noah was four hundred and fifty years old, and begat Japheth; and forty-two years afterward he begat Shem of her who was the mother of Japheth, and when he was five hundred years old he begat Ham.
6:1 ***And Noah and his sons hearkened unto the Lord, and gave heed; and they were called the sons of God.***	8:13 And Noah and his sons hearkened unto the Lord, and gave heed, and they were called the sons of God.
And ~~it came to pass,~~ when ***these*** men began to multiply on the face of the earth, and daughters were born unto them,	8:14 And when these men began to multiply on the face of the earth, and daughters were born unto them,
6:2 ~~That~~ the sons of ~~God~~ ***men*** saw ~~the daughters of men that they~~ ***that their daughters*** were fair, and they took them wives ***even as*** ~~, all of which~~ they chose.	the sons of men saw that <u>those</u> daughters were fair, and they took them wives, even as they chose.
And the Lord said unto Noah, The daughters of thy sons have sold themselves, for behold, mine anger is kindled against the sons of men, for they will not hearken to my voice.	8:15 And the Lord said unto Noah: The daughters of thy sons have sold themselves; for behold mine anger is kindled against the sons of men, for they will not hearken to my voice.

And it came to pass that Noah prophesied, and taught the things of God, even as it was in the beginning.
6:3 And the LORD said ***unto Noah***: My ~~s~~*S*pirit shall not always strive with man, for ~~that he is also flesh:~~ ***he shall know that all flesh shall die***, yet his days shall be an hundred and twenty years; ***and if men do not repent, I will send in the floods upon them.***
6:4 ***And in those days*** there were giants ~~in~~ ***on*** the earth ~~in those days;~~ ***, and they sought Noah to take away his life;***

But the Lord was with Noah, and the power of the Lord was upon him;
and the Lord ordained Noah after his own order, and commanded him that he should go forth and declare his gospel unto the children of men, even as it was given unto Enoch.

And it came to pass that Noah called upon the children of men, that they should repent, but they hearkened not unto his words.

~~And also after that, when the sons of God came in unto the daughters of men, and they bare children to them,~~
And also, after that they had heard him, they came up before him, saying: Behold, we are the sons of God, have we not taken unto ourselves the daughters of men?
And are we not eating and drinking, and marrying and giving in marriage?
And our wives bear unto us children, and the same ~~became~~ are mighty men, which are ~~like unto men~~ ***like them*** of old, men of ***great*** renown. ***And they hearkened not unto the words of Noah.***
6:5 And God saw that the wickedness of man ~~was~~ ***had become*** great in the earth; and every ***man was lifted up in the*** imagination of the thoughts of his heart***;*** ~~was~~ ***being*** only evil continually.

And it came to pass that Noah continued his preaching unto the people, saying, Hearken, and give heed unto my words,
believe and repent of your sins and be baptized in the name of Jesus Christ, the Son of God, even as our fathers did, and ye shall receive the Holy Ghost, that ye may have all things made manifest;

8:16 And it came to pass that Noah prophesied, and taught the things of God, even as it was in the beginning.
8:17 And the Lord said unto Noah: My Spirit shall not always strive with man, for he shall know that all flesh shall die; yet his days shall be an hundred and twenty years;
and if men do not repent, I will send in the floods upon them.
8:18 And in those days there were giants on the earth, and they sought Noah to take away his life;

but the Lord was with Noah, and the power of the Lord was upon him.

8:19 And the Lord ordained Noah after his own order, and commanded him that he should go forth and declare his <u>G</u>ospel unto the children of men, even as it was given unto Enoch.
8:20 And it came to pass that Noah called upon the children of men that they should repent; but they hearkened not unto his words;

8:21 And also, after that they had heard him, they came up before him, saying: Behold, we are the sons of God; have we not taken unto ourselves the daughters of men?
And are we not eating and drinking, and marrying and giving in marriage?
And our wives bear unto us children, and the same are mighty men, which are like unto men of old, men of great renown. And they hearkened not unto the words of Noah.
8:22 And God saw that the wickedness of men had become great in the earth; and every man was lifted up in the imagination of the thoughts of his heart, being only evil continually.
8:23 And it came to pass that Noah continued his preaching unto the people, saying: Hearken, and give heed unto my words;
8:24 Believe and repent of your sins and be baptized in the name of Jesus Christ, the Son of God, even as our fathers, and ye shall receive the Holy Ghost, that ye may have all things made manifest;

And if you do not this, the floods will come in upon you; nevertheless, they hearkened not.
6:6 And it repented ~~the Lord~~ ***Noah, and his heart was pained,*** that ~~he~~ ***the Lord*** had made man on the earth, and it grieved him at his heart.
6:7 And the LORD said, I will destroy man whom I have created***,*** from the face of the earth~~;~~ ***,*** both man, and beast, and the creeping thing***s***, and the fowls of the air***.*** ~~;~~
~~f~~***F***or it repenteth ~~me~~ ***Noah that I have created them, and*** that I have made them***; and he hath called upon me, for they have sought his life***.
6:8 ~~But~~ ***And thus*** Noah found grace in the eyes of the LORD~~.~~ ***;***
6:9 ~~These are the generations of Noah:~~ ***for*** Noah was a just man, and perfect in his generation~~s;~~ ***;*** and ~~Noah~~ ***he*** walked with God ***,***
6:10 ~~A~~***a***nd ~~Noah begat~~ ***also his*** three sons, Shem, Ham, and Japheth.
6:11 The earth ~~also~~ was corrupt before God, and ~~the earth~~ ***it*** was filled with violence.
6:12 And God looked upon the earth, and, behold, it was corrupt~~;~~ ***,*** for all flesh had corrupted ~~his~~ ***its*** way upon the earth.

and if ye do not this, the floods will come in upon you; nevertheless they hearkened not.
8:25 And it repented Noah, and his heart was pained that the Lord had made man on the earth, and it grieved him at <u>the</u> heart.
8:26 And the Lord said: I will destroy man whom I have created, from the face of the earth, both man and beast, and the creeping things, and the fowls of the air;
for it repenteth Noah that I have created them, and that I have made them; and he hath called upon me; for they have sought his life.
8:27 And thus Noah found grace in the eyes of the Lord;
for Noah was a just man, and perfect in his generation; and he walked with God,
<u>as did</u> also his three sons, Shem, Ham, and Japheth.
8:28 The earth was corrupt before God, and it was filled with violence.
8:29 And God looked upon the earth, and behold, it was corrupt, for all flesh had corrupted its way upon the earth.

NOAH BUILDS THE ARK

6:13 And God said unto Noah, The end of all flesh is come before me; for the earth is filled with violence ~~through them;~~ ***,*** and, behold, I will destroy ~~them with~~ ***all flesh from off*** the earth.
6:14 Make thee ***therefore,*** an ark of gopher wood; rooms shalt thou make in the ark, and ***thou*** shalt pitch it within and without with pitch.
6:15 And ~~this is the fashion which thou shalt make it of:~~ The length of the ark ~~shall be~~ ***thou shalt make*** three hundred cubits, the breadth of it fifty cubits, and the height of it thirty cubits.
6:16 ~~A window~~ ***And windows*** shalt thou make to the ark, and in a cubit shalt thou finish it above; and the door of the ark shalt thou set in the side thereof; ~~with~~ lower, second, and third ~~stories~~ ***chambers*** shalt thou make ***in*** it.
6:17 And, behold, I, even I, ~~do~~ ***will*** bring ***in*** a flood of water~~s~~ upon the earth, to destroy all flesh, wherein is the

8:30 And God said unto Noah: The end of all flesh is come before me, for all the earth is filled with violence, and behold I will destroy all flesh from off the earth.

breath of life, from under heaven; and every thing that ~~is in~~ ***liveth on*** the earth shall die.
6:18 But with thee will I establish my covenant~~;~~***, even as I have sworn unto thy father, Enoch, that of thy posterity shall come all nations.*** ~~a~~***A***nd thou shalt come into the ark, ***and*** thou~~,~~ and thy sons, and thy wife, and thy sons' wives with ~~thee~~ ***them***.
6:19 And of every living thing of all flesh, two of every ~~sort~~ ***kind*** shalt thou bring into the ark, to keep ~~them~~ alive with thee; they shall be male and female.
6:20 Of fowls after their kind, and of cattle after their kind, of every creeping thing of the earth after his kind, two of every ~~sort shall come unto thee~~ ***kind shalt thou take into the ark***, to keep ~~them~~ alive.
6:21 And take thou unto thee of all food that is eaten, and thou shalt gather ~~it~~ ***fruit of every kind un***to thee ***in the ark***; and it shall be for food for thee, and for them.
6:22 Thus did Noah~~;~~***,*** according to all that God commanded him~~, so did he~~ .

NOAH ENTERS THE ARK

7:1 And the LORD said unto Noah, Come thou and all thy house, into the ark; for thee ***only*** have I seen righteous before me, in this generation.
7:2 Of every clean beast thou shalt take to thee by sevens, the male and his female: and of beasts that are not clean by two, the male and his female.
7:3 Of fowls also of the air by sevens, the male and ~~the~~ ***his*** female; to keep seed alive upon the face of all the earth.
7:4 For yet seven days, and I will cause it to rain upon the earth forty days, and forty nights; and every living substance that I have made will I destroy from off the face of the earth.
7:5 And Noah did according ~~un~~to all that the LORD commanded him.
7:6 And Noah was six hundred years old when the flood of waters was upon the earth.
7:7 And Noah went in, and his sons, and his wife, and his sons' wives with him, into the ark, because of the waters of the flood.

7:8 Of clean beasts, and of beasts that ~~are~~ ***were*** not clean, and of fowls, and of every thing that creepeth upon the earth,

7:9 ~~T~~*t*here went in two and two unto Noah into the ark, the male and the female, as God had commanded Noah.

7:10 And it came to pass**,** after seven days, that the waters of the flood were upon the earth.

7:11 In the six hundredth year of Noah's life, in the second month, ***and*** the seventeenth day of the month, the same day were all the fountains of the great deep broken up, and the windows of heaven were opened.

7:12 And the rain was upon the earth forty days and forty nights.

7:13 In the selfsame day entered Noah, and Shem, and Ham, and Japheth, the sons of Noah, and Noah's wife, and the three wives of his sons with them~~,~~ into the ark;

7:14 They, and every beast after his kind, and all the cattle after their kind, and every creeping thing that creepeth upon the earth after his kind, and every fowl after his kind, every bird of every sort.

7:15 And they went ~~in~~ unto Noah into the ark, two and two of all flesh, wherein is the breath of life.

7:16 And they that went in, went in male and female of all flesh, as God had commanded him~~:~~***,*** and the LORD shut him in.

7:17 And the flood was forty days upon the earth; and the waters increased, and bare up the ark, and it was lift***ed*** up above the earth.

7:18 And the waters prevailed, and ~~were~~ increased greatly upon the earth; and the ark went upon the face of the waters.

7:19 And the waters prevailed exceedingly upon the ***face of the*** earth; and all the high hills, ~~that were~~ under the whole heavens~~,~~ were covered.

7:20 Fifteen cubits ***and*** upward did the waters prevail; and the mountains were covered.

7:21 And all flesh died that moved upon the ***face of the*** earth, both of fowl, and of cattle, and of beast***s***, and of every creeping thing that creepeth upon the earth, and every man~~:~~***.***

7:22 All in whose nostrils ~~was~~ ***the Lord had breathed*** the breath of life, of all that ~~was in~~ ***were on*** the dry land, died.

7:23 And every living substance was destroyed which was upon the face of the ground, both man, and cattle, and the creeping things, and the fowl***s*** of the ~~heaven~~***air***; and they were destroyed from the earth: and Noah only remained ~~alive~~, and they that were with him in the ark.

7:24 And the waters prevailed ~~up~~on the earth ~~an~~ ***one*** hundred and fifty days.

THE FLOOD ABATES

8:1 And God remembered Noah, and ~~every living thing, and all the cattle that was~~ ***all that were*** with him in the ark ~~,~~**.** ~~a~~***A***nd God made a wind to pass over the earth, and the waters assuaged;

8:2 The fountains also of the deep and the windows of heaven were stopped, and the rain from heaven was restrained;

8:3 And the waters returned from off the earth ~~continually:~~ **.** ~~a~~***A***nd after the end of the hundred and fifty days**,** the waters were abated.

8:4 And the ark rested in the seventh month, on the seventeenth day of the month, upon the mountain~~s~~ of Ararat.

8:5 And the waters decreased continually until the tenth month; in the tenth month, on the first day of the month, were the tops of the mountains seen.

8:6 And it came to pass, at the end of forty days, that Noah opened the window of the ark which he had made:

8:7 And he sent forth a raven, which went forth to and fro, until the waters were dried up from off the earth.

8:8 ~~Also~~ he ***also*** sent forth a dove from him, to see if the waters were abated from off the face of the ground;

8:9 But the dove found no rest for the sole of her foot, and she returned unto him into the ark, for the waters ~~were on~~ ***had not receded from off*** the face of the whole earth: then he put forth his hand, and took her, and pulled her in unto him into the ark.

8:10 And he stayed yet other seven days; and again he sent forth the dove out of the ark;

8:11 And the dove came in to him in the evening; and, lo, in her mouth ~~was~~ an olive leaf plucked off: so Noah knew that the waters were abated from off the earth.

8:12 And he stayed yet other seven days; and sent forth ~~the~~ ***a*** dove; which returned not again unto him any more.

8:13 And it came to pass in the six hundred~~th~~ and first year, in the first month, the first day of the month, the waters were dried up from off the earth: and Noah removed the covering of the ark, and looked, and, behold, the face of the ground was dry.

8:14 And in the second month, on the seven and twentieth day of the month, was the earth dried.

NOAH LEAVES THE ARK AND BUILDS AN ALTAR

8:15 And God spake unto Noah, saying,

8:16 Go forth of the ark, thou, and thy wife, and thy sons, and thy sons' wives with thee.

8:17 Bring forth with thee every living thing that is with thee, of all flesh, both of fowl, and of cattle, and of every creeping thing that creepeth upon the earth; that they may breed abundantly in the earth, and be fruitful, and multiply upon the earth.

8:18 And Noah went forth, and his sons, and his wife, and his sons' wives with him:

8:19 ***And*** Every beast, every creeping thing, and every fowl~~, and whatsoever creepeth~~ upon the earth, after their kinds, went forth out of the ark.

8:20 And Noah builded an altar unto the LORD; and took of every clean beast, and of every clean fowl, and offered burnt offerings on the altar***; and gave thanks unto the Lord, and rejoiced in his heart***.

8:21 And the LORD ***spake unto Noah, and he blessed him. And Noah*** smelled a sweet ~~savour~~ ***savor***; and ~~the LORD~~ ***he*** said in his heart, I will ***call on the name of the Lord, that he will*** not again curse the ground any more for man's sake; for the imagination of man's heart is evil from his youth; ~~neither will I~~ ***and that he will not*** again smite any more every thing living, as ~~I have~~ ***he hath*** done**,**

8:22 ~~W~~***w***hile the earth remaineth~~,~~ ***;***
And, that seed-time and harvest, and
cold and heat, and summer and winter,
and day and night ~~shall~~ ***may*** not cease
with man.

GOD COVENANTS WITH NOAH

9:1 And God blessed Noah and his
sons, and said unto them, Be fruitful,
and multiply, and replenish the earth.
9:2 And the fear of you and the dread
of you shall be upon every beast of the
earth, and upon every fowl of the air,
upon all that moveth upon the earth, and
upon all the fishes of the sea; into your
hand are they delivered.
9:3 Every moving thing that liveth
shall be meat for you; even as the green
herb have I given you all things.
9:4 But ***, the blood of all the*** flesh
~~with the~~ ***which I have given you for***
meat, shall be shed upon the ground,
which taketh life thereof, ~~which is~~ ***and***
the blood ~~thereof, shall~~ ye ***shall*** not eat.
9:5 And surely ~~your~~ blood ~~of your~~
~~lives will I require; at the hand~~ ***shall not***
be shed, only for meat, to save your
lives; and the blood of every beast will
I require ~~it, and at the hand of man; at~~
~~the hand of every man's brother will I~~
~~require the life of man~~ ***at your hands.***
9:6 ***And*** Whoso sheddeth man's
blood, by man shall his blood be shed:
for man shall not shed the blood of
man. For a commandment I give, that
every man's brother shall preserve the
life of man, for in ~~the~~ ***mine own*** image
~~of God~~ ***have I*** made ~~he~~ man.
9:7 And ***a commandment I give unto***
you, be ye fruitful, and multiply; bring
forth abundantly ~~in~~ ***on*** the earth, and
multiply therein.
9:8 And God spake unto Noah, and to
his sons with him, saying,
9:9 And I, behold, I ***will*** establish my
covenant with you, ~~and with~~ ***which I***
made unto your father Enoch,
concerning your seed after you;
9:10 And ~~with~~ ***it shall come to pass,***
that every living creature that is with
you, of the fowl, ***and*** of the cattle, and
of ~~every~~ ***the*** beast of the earth ***that is***
with you; ~~from all that~~ ***which shall*** go
out of the ark, ~~to every beast of the earth~~
shall not altogether perish.

9:11 ~~And I will establish my covenant with you;~~ neither shall all flesh be cut off any more by the waters of a flood; neither shall there any more be a flood to destroy the earth. ***And I will establish my covenant with you, which I made unto Enoch, concerning the remnants of your posterity.***

9:12 And God ***made a covenant with Noah, and*** said, This ~~is~~ ***shall be*** the token of the covenant ~~which~~ I make between me and you~~,~~ and ***for*** every living creature ~~that is~~ with you, for perpetual generations:

9:13 I ~~do~~ ***will*** set my bow in the cloud, and it shall be for a token of a covenant between me and the earth.

9:14 And it shall come to pass, when I bring a cloud over the earth, that the bow shall be seen in the cloud:

9:15 And I will remember my covenant, which ~~is~~ ***I have made*** between me and you, ~~and~~ ***for*** every living creature of all flesh; and the waters shall no more become a flood to destroy all flesh.

9:16 And the bow shall be in the cloud; and I will look upon it, that I may remember the everlasting covenant ***which I made unto thy father Enoch; that, when men should keep all my commandments, Zion should again come on the earth, the city of Enoch which I have caught up unto myself.***

And this is mine everlasting covenant, that when thy posterity shall embrace the truth, and look upward, then shall Zion look downward, and all the heavens shall shake with gladness, and the earth shall tremble with joy.

And the general assembly of the church of the first-born shall come down out of heaven, and possess the earth, and shall have place until the end come. And this is mine everlasting covenant, which I made with thy father Enoch.

And the bow shall be in the cloud, and I will establish my covenant unto thee, which I have made between ~~God and~~ ***me and thee, for*** every living creature of all flesh that ~~is~~ ***shall be*** upon the earth.

9:17 And God said unto Noah, This is the token of the covenant, which I have established between me and ***thee;*** ~~all~~ ***for*** flesh that ~~is~~ ***shall be*** upon the earth.

NOAH'S SONS

9:18 And the sons of Noah, that went forth of the ark, were Shem, and Ham, and Japheth: and Ham ~~is~~ ***was*** the father of Canaan.
9:19 These ~~are~~ ***were*** the three sons of Noah: and of them was the whole earth overspread.
9:20 And Noah began to ~~be~~ ***till the earth, and he was*** an husbandman, and he planted a vineyard:
9:21 And he drank of the wine, and was drunken; and he was uncovered within his tent.
9:22 And Ham, the father of Canaan, saw the nakedness of his father, and told his ~~two~~ brethren without.
9:23 And Shem and Japheth took a garment, and laid ~~it~~ upon both their shoulders, and went backward, and covered the nakedness of their father; ~~and their faces were backward,~~ and they saw not their father's nakedness.
9:24 And Noah awoke from his wine, and knew what his ~~younger~~ ***youngest*** son had done unto him.
9:25 And he said, Cursed be Canaan; a servant of servants shall he be unto his brethren.
9:26 And he said, Blessed be the LORD God of Shem; and Canaan shall be his servant***, and a veil of darkness shall cover him, that he shall be known among all men***.
9:27 God shall enlarge Japheth, and he shall dwell in the tents of Shem; and Canaan shall be his servant.
9:28 And Noah lived after the flood, three hundred and fifty years.
9:29 And all the days of Noah were nine hundred and fifty years: and he died.

NATIONS AND PEOPLES OF THE EARTH

10:1 Now these ~~are~~ ***were*** the generations of the sons of Noah, Shem, Ham, and Japheth: and unto them were sons born after the flood.
10:2 The sons of Japheth; Gomer, and Magog, ~~and~~ Madai, and Javan, and Tubal, and Mes*c*hech, and Tiras.
10:3 And ***these are the*** the sons of Gomer; Ashkenaz, and Riphath, and Togarmah.

10:4 And the sons of Javan; Elishah, and Tarshish, Kittim, and Dodanim.
10:5 By these were the isles of the Gentiles divided in their lands; every one after ~~his~~ ***the same*** tongue, after their families, in their nations.
10:6 And the sons of Ham; Cush, and Mizraim, and Phut, and Canaan.
10:7 And the sons of Cush; Seba, and Havilah, and Sabtah, and Raamah, and Sabtecha~~h~~: and the sons of Raamah; Sheba, and Dedan.
10:8 And Cush begat Nimrod: he began to be a mighty one in the earth.
10:9 He was a mighty hunter ~~before the LORD:~~ ***in the land.*** ~~w~~***W***herefore it is said, Even as Nimrod, the mighty hunter ~~before the LORD~~ ***in the land***.
10:10 And ***he began a kingdom, and*** the beginning of his kingdom was Babel, and Erech, and Accad, and Calneh, in the land of Shinar.
10:11 Out of that land went forth Asshur, and builded Nineveh, and the city Rehoboth, and Calah,
10:12 And Resen between Nineveh and Calah: the same ~~is~~ ***was*** a great city.
10:13 And Mizraim begat Ludim, and Anamim, and Lehabim, and Naphtuhim,
10:14 And Pathrusim, and Casluhim, (out of whom came Philistim,) and Caphtorim.
10:15 And Canaan begat Sidon his firstborn, and Heth,
10:16 And the Jebusite, and the Amorite, and the Girgas***h***ite,
10:17 And the Hivite, and the Arkite, and the Sinite,
10:18 And the Arvadite, and the Zemarite, and the Hamathite: and afterward were the families of the Canaanites spread abroad.
10:19 And the border of the Canaanites ~~was~~ ***were*** from Sidon, as thou comest to Gerar, unto Gaza; as thou goest, unto Sodom, and Gomorrah, and Admah, and Zeboi***i***m, even unto Lasha.
10:20 These ~~are~~ ***were*** the sons of Ham, after their families, after ~~their tongues~~ ***the same tongue***, in their countries, and in their nations.
10:21 Unto Shem also, ***which was the elder, children were born; and he was*** the father of ~~all the children of~~ Eber, ~~the brother of Japheth the elder,~~ even to him were children born.

10:22 ***And these are*** the children of Shem; ***Eber, and*** Elam, and Asshur, and Arphaxad, and Lud, and Aram.
10:23 And ***these were the*** the children of Aram; ~~Uz~~, ***Us,*** and Hul, and Gether, and Mash.
10:24 And Arphaxad begat Salah; and Salah begat Eber.
10:25 And unto Eber were born two sons: the name of one, ~~was~~ Peleg; ***the other Joktan. And Peleg was a mighty man,*** for in his days was the earth divided; ~~and his brother's name was Joktan.~~
10:26 And Joktan begat Almodad, and Sheleph, and Hazarmaveth, and Jerah,
10:27 And Hadoram, and Uzal, and Diklah,
10:28 And Obal, and Abimael, and Sheba,
10:29 And ~~Ophir~~ ***Ophar***, and Havilah, and Jobab: ~~all~~ ***and*** these were the sons of Joktan.
10:30 And their dwelling was from Mesha, as thou goest unto Sephar, a mount of the east.
10:31 These ~~are~~ ***were*** the sons of Shem, after their families, after their tongues, in their lands, after their nations.
10:32 These ~~are~~ ***were*** the families of the sons of Noah, after their generations, in their nations: and by these were the nations divided ~~in~~ ***on*** the earth after the flood.

THE TOWER OF BABEL

11:1 And the whole earth was of ~~one~~ ***the same*** language, and of ~~one~~ ***the same*** speech.
11:2 And it came to pass, ~~as they~~ ***that many*** journeyed from the east, ***and as they journeyed from the east,*** ~~that~~ they found a plain in the land of Shinar; and they dwelt there ***in the plain of Shinar***.
11:3 And they said one to another, ***Come,*** Go to, let us make brick, and burn them thoroughly. And they had brick for stone, and ***they had*** slime ~~had they~~ for mortar.
11:4 And they said, ***Come,*** Go to, let us build us a city and a tower, whose top ~~may reach~~ ***will be high, nigh*** unto heaven; and let us make us a name, lest we be scattered abroad upon the face of the whole earth.

11:5 And the Lord came down***,*** ~~to see~~ ***beholding*** the city and the tower, which the children of men ~~builded~~ ***were building***.

11:6 And the Lord said, Behold, the people ~~is one~~ ***are the same***, and they ***all*** have ~~all one~~ ***the same*** language; and this ***tower*** they begin to ~~do:~~ ***build,*** and now, nothing will be restrained from them, which they have imagined ~~to do~~ ,

11:7 ***except I, the Lord,*** ~~Go to, let us go down, and there~~ confound their language, that they may not understand one another's speech.

11:8 So***, I,*** the Lord ***will*** scatter~~ed~~ them abroad from thence upon ***all*** the face of all the ~~earth:~~ ***land, and unto every quarter of the earth. And they were confounded,*** and they left off to build the city, ***and they hearkened not unto the Lord,***

11:9 Therefore***,*** is the name of it called Babel; because the Lord ***was displeased with their works, and*** did there confound the language of all the earth: and from thence did the Lord scatter them abroad upon the face ~~of all the earth~~ ***thereof***.

THE GENEALOGY OF ABRAM

11:10 ***And*** ~~T~~***these*** ~~are~~ ***were*** the generations of Shem~~:~~ ***. And*** Shem ~~was~~ ***being*** an hundred years old, and begat Arphaxad two years after the flood:

11:11 And Shem lived after he begat Arphaxad five hundred years, and begat sons and daughters.

11:12 And Arphaxad lived five and thirty years, and begat Salah:

11:13 And Arphaxad lived after he begat Salah four hundred and three years, and begat sons and daughters.

11:14 And Salah lived thirty years, and begat Eber:

11:15 And Salah lived after he begat Eber four hundred and three years, and begat sons and daughters.

11:16 And Eber lived four and thirty years, and begat Peleg:

11:17 And Eber lived after he begat Peleg four hundred and thirty years, and begat sons and daughters.

11:18 And Peleg lived thirty years, and begat Reu:

11:19 And Peleg lived after he begat Reu two hundred and nine years, and begat sons and daughters.
11:20 And Reu lived two and thirty years, and begat Serug:
11:21 And Reu lived after he begat Serug two hundred and seven years, and begat sons and daughters.
11:22 And Serug lived thirty years, and begat Nahor:
11:23 And Serug lived after he begat Nahor two hundred years, and begat sons and daughters.
11:24 And Nahor lived nine and twenty years, and begat Terah:
11:25 And Nahor lived after he begat Terah an hundred and nineteen years, and begat sons and daughters.
11:26 And Terah lived seventy years, and begat Abram, Nahor, and Haran.
11:27 Now these ~~are~~ ***were*** the generations of Terah: Terah begat Abram, Nahor, and Haran; and Haran begat Lot.

ABRAM SEEKS HIS APPOINTMENT IN UR OF THE CHALDEES

1:1 In the land of the Chaldeans, at the residence of my fathers, I, Abraham, saw that it was needful for me to obtain another place of residence;
1:2 And finding there was greater happiness and peace and rest for me, I sought for the blessings of the fathers, and the right whereunto I should be ordained to administer the same; having been myself a follower of righteousness, desiring also to be one who possessed great knowledge, and to be a greater follower of righteousness, and to possess a greater knowledge, and to be a father of many nations, a prince of peace, and desiring to receive instructions, and to keep the commandments of God, I became a rightful heir, a High Priest, holding the right belonging to the fathers.
1:3 It was conferred upon me from the fathers; it came down from the fathers, from the beginning of time, yea, even from the beginning, or before the foundation of the earth, down to the present time, even the right of the firstborn, or the first man, who is Adam, or first father, through the fathers unto me.

1:4 I sought for mine appointment unto the Priesthood according to the appointment of God unto the fathers concerning the seed.
1:5 My fathers, having turned from their righteousness, and from the holy commandments which the Lord their God had given unto them, unto the worshiping of the gods of the heathen, utterly refused to hearken to my voice;
1:6 For their hearts were set to do evil, and were wholly turned to the god of Elkenah, and the god of Libnah, and the god of Mahmackrah, and the god of Korash, and the god of Pharoah, king of Egypt;

ATTEMPT TO OFFER ABRAM AS SACRIFICE

1:7 Therefore they turned their hearts of the sacrifice of the heathen in offering up their children unto these dumb idols, and hearkened not unto my voice, but endeavored to take away my life by the hand of the priest of Elkenah was also the priest of Pharoah.
1:8 Now, at this time it was the custom of the priest of Pharoah, the king of Egypt, to offer up upon the altar which was built in the land of Chaldea, for the offering unto these strange gods, men, women, and children.
1:9 And it came to pass that the priest made an offering unto the god of Pharoah, and also unto the god of Shagreel, even after the manner of the Egyptians. Now the god of Shagreel was the sun.
1:10 Even the thank-offering of a child did the priest of Pharaoh offer upon the altar which stood by the hill called Potiphar's Hill, at the head of the plain of Olishem.
1:11 Now, this priest had offered upon this altar three virgins at one time, who were the daughters of Onitah, one of the royal descent directly from the loins of Ham. These virgins were offered up because of their virtue; they would not bow down to worship gods of wood or of stone, therefore they were killed upon this altar, and it was done after the manner of the Egyptians.
1:12 And it came to pass that the priests laid violence upon me, that they might slay me also, as they did those virgins upon this altar; and that you may

have a knowledge of this altar, I will refer you to the representation at the commencement of this record.
1:13 It was made after the form of a bedstead, such as was had among the Chaldeans, and it stood before the gods of Elkenah, Libnah, Mahmackrah, Korash, and also a god like unto that of Pharoah, king of Egypt.
1:14 That you may have an understanding of these gods, I have given you the fashion of them in the figures at the beginning, which manner of figures is called by the Chaldeans Rahleenos, which signifies hieroglyphics.
1:15 And as they lifted up their hands upon me, that they might offer me up and take away my life, behold, I lifted up my voice unto the Lord my God, and the Lord hearkened and heard, and he filled me with the vision of the Almighty, and the angel of his presence stood by me, and immediately unloosed my bands;
1:16 And his voice was unto me: Abraham, Abraham, behold, my name is Jehovah, and I have heard thee, and have come down to deliver thee, and to take thee away from thy father's house, and from all thy kinsfolk, into a strange land which thou knowest not of;
1:17 And this because they have turned their hearts away from me, to worship the god of Elkenah, and the god of Libnah, and the god of Mahmackrah, and the god of Korash, and the god of Pharoah, king of Egypt; therefore I have come down to visit them, and to destroy him who hath lifted up against thee, Abraham, my son, to take away thy life.
1:18 Behold, I will lead thee by my hand, and I will take thee, to put upon thee my name, even the Priesthood of thy father, and my power shall be over thee.
1:19 As it was with Noah so shall it be with thee; but through thy ministry my name shall be known in the earth forever, for I am thy God.
1:20 Behold, Potiphar's Hill was in the land of Ur, of Chaldea. And the Lord broke down the altar of Elkenah, and of the gods of the land, and utterly destroyed them, and smote the priest that he died; and there was great mourning in Chaldea, and also in the

court of Pharoah; which Pharoah signifies king by royal blood.

BRIEF HISTORY OF EGYPT

1:21 Now this king of Egypt was a descendant from the loins of Ham, and was a partaker of the blood of the Canaanites by birth.
1:22 From this descent sprang all the Egyptians, and thus the blood of the Canaanites was preserved in the land.
1:23 The land of Egypt being first discovered by a woman, who was the daughter of Ham, and the daughter of Egyptus, which in the Chaldean signifies Egypt, which signifies that which is forbidden;
1:24 When this woman discovered the land it was under water, who afterward settled her sons in it; and thus, from Ham, sprang that race which preserved the curse in the land.
1:25 Now the first government of Egypt was established by Pharoah, the eldest son of Egyptus, the daughter of Ham, and it was after the manner of the government of Ham, which was patriarchal.
1:26 Pharoah, being a righteous man, established his kingdom and judged his people wisely and justly all his days, seeking earnestly to imitate that order established by the fathers in the first generations, in the days of the first patriarchal reign, even in the reign of Adam, and also of Noah, his father, who blessed him with the blessings of the earth, and with the blessings of wisdom, but cursed him as pertaining to the Priesthood.
1:27 Now, Pharoah being of that lineage by which he could not have the right of Priesthood, notwithstanding the Pharoahs would fain claim it from Noah, through Ham, therefore my father was led away by their idolatry;
1:28 But I shall endeavor, hereafter, to delineate the chronology running back from myself to the beginning of the creation, for the records have come into my hands, which I hold unto this present time.
1:29 Now, after the priest of Elkenah was smited that he died, there came a fulfilment of those things which were said unto me concerning the land of

Chaldea, that there should be a famine in the land.

1:30 Accordingly a famine prevailed throughout all the land of Chaldea, and my father was sorely tormented because of the famine, and he repented of the evil which he had determined against me, to take away my life.

1:31 But the records of the fathers, even the patriarchs, concerning the right of Priesthood, the Lord my God preserved in mine own hands; therefore a knowledge of the beginning of the creation, and also of the planets, and of the stars, as they were made known unto the fathers, have I kept even unto this day, and I shall endeavor to write some of these things upon this record, for the benefit of my posterity that shall come after me.

ABRAM LEAVES UR OF THE CHALDEES

11:28 And Haran died before his father Terah, in the land of his nativity, in Ur of the Chaldees.

11:29 And Abram and Nahor took them wives: the name of Abram's wife was Sarai; and the name of Nahor's wife, Milcah, the daughter of Haran, the father of Milcah, and the father of Iscah.

11:30 But Sarai was barren; she ~~had~~ ***bear*** no child.

11:31 And Terah took Abram his son, and Lot the son of Haran, his son's son, and Sarai his daughter-in-law, his son Abram's wife; and they went forth with them from Ur of the Chaldees, to go into the land of Canaan; and they came unto Haran,

and dwelt there.

11:32 And the days of Terah were two hundred and five years: and Terah died in Haran.

2:1 Now the Lord God caused the famine to wax sore in the land of Ur, insomuch that Haran, my brother, died; but Terah, my father, yet lived in the land of Ur, of the Chaldees.

2:2 And it came to pass that I, Abraham, took Sarai to wife, and Nehor, my brother, took Milcah to wife, who was the daughter of Haran.

2:3 Now the Lord had said unto me: Abraham, get thee out of thy country, and from thy kindred, and from thy father's house, unto a land that I will show thee.

2:4 Therefore I left the land of Ur, of the Chaldees, to go into the land of Canaan; and I took Lot, my brother's son, and his wife, and Sarai my wife; and also my father followed after me, unto the land which we denominated Haran.

2:5 And the famine abated; and my father tarried in Haran and dwelt there, as there were many flocks in Haran; and my father turned again unto his idolatry, therefore he continued in Haran.

LORD APPEARS TO ABRAM

Genesis	Moses	Abraham
12:1 Now the LORD had said unto Abram,		2:6 But I, Abraham, and Lot, my brother's son, prayed unto the Lord, and the Lord appeared unto me, and said unto me: Arise, and take Lot with thee; for I have purposed to take thee away out of Haran,
Get thee out of thy country, and from thy kindred, and from thy father's house, unto a land that I will show thee:		and to make of thee a minister to bear record of my name in a strange land which I will give unto thy seed after thee for an everlasting possession, when they hearken to my voice.
		2:7 For I am the Lord thy God; I dwell in heaven; the earth is my footstool; I stretch my hand over the sea, and it obeys my voice; I cause the wind and the fire to be my chariot; I say to the mountains depart hence, and behold, they are taken away by a whirlwind, in an instant, suddenly.
		2:8 My name is Jehovah, and I know the end from the beginning; therefore my hand shall be over thee.
12:2 And I will make of thee a great nation, and I will bless thee, and make thy name great;		2:9 And I will make of thee a great nation, and I will bless thee above measure, and make thy name great among all nations,
and thou shalt be a blessing:		and thou shalt be a blessing unto thy seed after thee, that in their hands they shall bear this ministry and Priesthood unto all nations;
		2:10 And I will bless them through thy name; for as many as receive this Gospel shall be called after thy name, and shall be accounted thy seed, and shall rise up and bless thee, as their father;
12:3 And I will bless them that bless thee, and curse ~~him~~ ***them*** that curse~~th~~ thee: and in thee		2:11 And I will bless them that bless thee, and curse them that curse thee; and in thee (that is, in thy Priesthood) and in thy seed (that is, thy Priesthood), for I give unto thee a promise that this right shall continue in thee, and in thy seed after thee (that is to say, the literal seed, or the seed of the body)
shall ~~all~~ ***the*** families of the earth be blessed.		shall all the families of the earth be blessed, even with the blessings of the Gospel, which are the blessings of salvation, even of life eternal.
		2:12 Now, after the Lord had withdrawn from speaking to me, and withdrawn his face from me, I said in

my heart: Thy servant has sought thee earnestly; now I have found thee;
2:13 Thou didst send thine angel to deliver me from the gods of Elkenah, and I will do well to hearken unto thy voice, therefore let thy servant rise up and depart in peace.

ABRAM DEPARTS AND BUILDS AN ALTAR AT SHECHEM

12:4 So Abram departed, as the Lord had spoken unto him; and Lot went with him: and Abram was seventy and five years old when he departed out of Haran.
12:5 And Abram took Sarai, his wife,

and Lot his brother's son, and all their substance that they had gathered, and the souls that they had gotten in Haran; and they went forth to go into the land of Canaan; and into the land of Canaan they came.

12:6 And Abram passed through the land unto the place of Sichem, ~~unto~~ ***and*** the plain of Moreh.

And the Canaanite*s* ~~was~~ ***were*** then in the land.

12:7 And the Lord appeared unto Abram, and said,
Unto thy seed will I give this land:
and there builded he an altar unto the Lord, who appeared unto him.

12:8 And he removed from thence unto a mountain on the east of Bethel, and pitched his tent, ~~having~~ ***leaving*** Bethel on the west, and Hai on the east: and there he builded an altar unto the Lord, and called upon the name of the Lord.

2:14 So I, Abraham, departed as the Lord had said unto me, and Lot with me; and I, Abraham, was sixty and two years old when I departed out of Haran.

2:15 And I took Sarai, whom I took to wife when I was in Ur, in Chaldea,
and Lot, my brother's son, and all our substance that we had gathered, and the souls that we had won in Haran, and came forth in the way to the land of Canaan, and dwelt in tents as we came on our way;
2:16 Therefore, eternity was our covering, and our rock and our salvation, as we journeyed from Haran by the way of Jershon, to come to the land of Canaan.
2:17 Now I, Abraham, built an altar in the land of Jershon, and made an offering unto the Lord, and prayed that the famine might be turned away from my father's house, that they might not perish.
2:18 And then we passed from Jershon through the land unto the place of Sechem; it was situated in the plains of Moreh, and we had already come into the borders of the land of the Canaanites,
and I offered sacrifice there in the plains of Moreh, and called on the Lord devoutly, because we had already come into the land of this idolatrous nation.
2:19 And the Lord appeared unto me in answer to my prayers, and said unto me: Unto thy seed will I give this land.
2:20 And I, Abraham, arose from the place of the altar which I had built unto the Lord,
and removed from thence unto a mountain on the east of Bethel, and pitched my tent there, Bethel on the west, and Hai on the east; and there I built another altar unto the Lord, and called again upon the name of the Lord.

ABRAM JOURNEYS TO EGYPT

GENESIS	MOSES	ABRAHAM
12:9 And Abram journeyed, going on still toward the south. 12:10 And there was a famine in the land: and Abram went down into Egypt to sojourn there; for the famine ~~was~~ ***became*** grievous in the land. 12:11 And it came to pass, when he was come near to enter into Egypt,		2:21 And I, Abraham, journeyed, going on still towards the south; and there was a continuation of a famine in the land; and I, Abraham, concluded to go down into Egypt, to sojourn there, for the famine became very grievous. 2:22 And it came to pass when I was come near to enter into Egypt, the Lord said unto me: Behold, Sarai, thy wife, is a very fair woman to look upon; 2:23 Therefore it shall come to pass, when the Egyptians shall see her, they will say--She is his wife; and they will kill you, but they will save her alive; therefore see that ye do on this wise: 2:24 Let her say unto the Egyptians, she is thy sister, and thy soul shall live.
that he said unto Sarai his wife,		2:25 And it came to pass that I, Abraham, told Sarai, my wife, all that the Lord had said unto me--
Behold now, I know ~~that thou art~~ ***thee to be*** a fair woman to look upon: 12:12 Therefore it shall come to pass, when the Egyptians shall see thee, that they shall say, This is his wife: and they will kill me, but they will save thee alive.		
12:13 Say, I pray thee ***unto them***, ~~thou art my sister:~~ ***I am his sister;*** that it may be well with me for thy sake; and my soul shall live because of thee.		Therefore say unto them, I pray thee, thou art my sister, that it may be well with me for thy sake, and my soul shall live because of thee.

ABRAM IN EGYPT

12:14 And it came to pass, that, when Abram was come into Egypt, the Egyptians beheld the woman that she was very fair.
12:15 The princes also of Pharaoh saw her, and ~~commended~~ ***commanded*** her ***to be brought*** before Pharaoh: and the woman was taken into Pharaoh's house.
12:16 And he entreated Abram well for her sake: and he had sheep, and oxen, and he asses, and menservants, and maidservants, and she asses, and camels.
12:17 And the Lord plagued Pharaoh and his house with great plagues, because of Sarai, Abram's wife.
12:18 And Pharaoh called Abram, and said, What ~~is this that thou~~ hast ***thou*** done unto me ***in this thing***? why didst thou not tell me that she was thy wife?
12:19 Why saidst thou, She is my sister? so I might have taken her to me to wife: now therefore, behold ***I say unto thee, Take*** thy wife, ~~take her,~~ and go thy way.
12:20 And Pharaoh commanded ~~his~~ men concerning him: and they sent him away, and his wife, and all that he had.

ABRAM AND LOT SEPARATE

13:1 And Abram went up out of Egypt, he, and his wife, and all that he had, and Lot with him, ~~into~~ ***unto*** the south.
13:2 And Abram was very rich in cattle, in silver, and in gold.
13:3 And he went on his journey~~s~~ from the south, even to Bethel, unto the place where his tent had been at the beginning, between Bethel and Hai;
13:4 Unto the place of the altar, which he had made there at the first: and there Abram called on the name of the Lord.
13:5 And Lot also, which went with Abram, had flocks, and herds, and tents.
13:6 And the land was not able to bear them, that they might dwell together; for their substance was great, so that they could not dwell together.
13:7 And there was a strife between the herdmen of Abram's cattle and the herdmen of Lot's cattle: ***that they could not dwell together.*** ~~a~~***A***nd the Canaanite and the Perizzite dwelled then in the land.
13:8 And Abram said unto Lot, Let there be no strife, I pray thee, between me and thee, and between my herdmen and thy herdmen; for we ~~be~~ ***are*** brethren.
13:9 Is not the whole land before thee? ~~s~~***S***eparate thyself, I pray thee, from me: if thou ~~wilt take~~ ***go to*** the left hand, then I will go to the right; or if thou ~~depart~~ ***go*** to the right hand, then I will go to the left.
13:10 And Lot lifted up his eyes, and beheld all the plain of Jordan, that it was well watered every where, before the Lord destroyed Sodom and Gomorrah, ~~even~~ ***like*** as the garden of the Lord, like the land of Egypt~~, as thou comest unto Zoar~~ .
13:11 Then Lot chose him all the plain of Jordan; and Lot journeyed east: and they separated themselves the one from the other.
13:12 Abram dwelled in the land of Canaan, and Lot dwelled in the cities of the plain, and pitched his tent toward Sodom.
13:13 But the men of Sodom ~~were~~ ***becoming sinners, and exceedingly*** wicked ~~and sinners~~ before the Lord ~~exceedingly~~ , ***the Lord was angry with them***.
13:14 And the Lord said unto Abram, after that Lot was separated from him, Lift up now thine eyes, and look from the place where thou art, northward, and southward, and eastward, and westward: ***And remember the covenant which I make with thee; for it shall be an everlasting covenant; and thou shalt remember the days of Enoch thy father;***
13:15 For all the land which thou seest, ~~to thee~~ will I give ~~it~~ ***thee***, and to thy seed for ever.
13:16 And I will make thy seed as the dust of the earth: so that if a man can number the dust of the earth, ~~then shall~~ thy seed also be numbered.

13:17 Arise, walk through the land in the length of it and in the breadth of it; for I will give it unto thee.
13:18 Then Abram removed his tent, and came and dwelt in the plain of Mamre, which ~~is~~ ***was*** in Hebron, and built there an altar unto the LORD.

THE FOUR KINGS

14:1 And it came to pass, in the days of Amraphel, king of Shinar, ***and*** Arioch king of Ellasar, ***and*** Chedorlaomer king of Elam, and Tidal king of nations;
14:2 That these ***kings*** made war with Bera king of Sodom, and with Birsha king of Gomorrah, Shinab king of Admah, and Shemeber king of Zeboiim, and the king of Bela, which is Zoar.
14:3 All these were joined together in the vale of Siddim, which is the salt sea.
14:4 Twelve years they served Chedorlaomer, and in the thirteenth year they rebelled.
14:5 And in the fourteenth year came Chedorlaomer, and the kings that were with him, and smote the Rephaims in Ashteroth Karnaim, and the Zuzims in Ham, and the Emims in Shaveh Kiriathaim,
14:6 And the Horites in their mount Seir, unto Elparan, which ~~is~~ ***was*** by the wilderness.
14:7 And they returned, and came to Enmishpat, which is Kadesh, and smote all the country of the Amalekites, and also the Amorites, ~~that dwelt~~ in Hazezontamar.
14:8 And there went out the king of Sodom, and the king of Gomorrah, and the king of Admah, and the king of Zeboiim, and the king of Bela, ~~(the same~~ ***which*** is Zoar;~~)~~ and they joined battle with them in the vale of Siddim;
14:9 With Chedorlaomer ~~the~~ king of Elam, and with Tidal king of nations, and Amraphel king of Shinar, and Arioch king of Ellasar; four kings with five.
14:10 And the vale of Siddim was ~~full of~~ ***filled with*** slimepits; and the kings of Sodom and Gomorrah fled, and fell there; and they that remained fled to the mountain ***which was called Hanabal***.
14:11 And they took all the goods of Sodom and Gomorrah, and all their victuals, and went their way.
14:12 And they took Lot, Abram's brother's son, who dwelt in Sodom, and his goods, and departed.

ABRAM RESCUES LOT

14:13 And there came one that had escaped, and told Abram the Hebrew; ***the man of God,*** for he dwelt in the plain of Mamre the Amorite, brother of Eshcol, and brother of Aner: and these were confederate with Abram.
14:14 And when Abram heard that ***Lot,*** his brother***'s son,*** was taken captive, he armed his trained ~~servants~~ ***men, and they which were*** born in his own house, three hundred and eighteen, and pursued ~~them~~ unto Dan.
14:15 And he divided himself against them, he and his ~~servants~~ ***men***, by night, and smote them, and pursued them unto Hobah, which ~~is~~ ***was*** on the left hand of Damascus.
14:16 And he brought back ~~all the goods, and also brought again his brother~~ Lot, ***his brother's son,*** and ***all*** his goods, and the women also, and the people.
14:17 And the king of Sodom ***also*** went out to meet him after his return from the slaughter of Chedorlaomer, and of the kings that were with him, at the valley of Shaveh, which ~~is~~ ***was*** the king's dale.

ABRAM AND MELCHIZEDEK

14:18 And Melchizedek, king of Salem, brought forth bread and wine: and he ***break bread and blest it; and he blest the wine, he being*** ~~was~~ the priest of the most high God.

14:19 ***And he gave to Abram,*** And he blessed him, and said, Blessed ~~be~~ Abram, ***thou are a man*** of the most high God, possessor of heaven and earth:

14:20 And blessed ~~be~~ ***is*** the ***name of the*** most high God, which hath delivered thine enemies into ~~thy~~ ***thine*** hand. And ~~he~~ ***Abram*** gave him tithes of all ***he had taken***.

14:21 And the king of Sodom said ~~un~~to Abram, Give me the persons, and take the goods to thyself.

14:22 And Abram said to the king of Sodom, I have lift***ed*** up mine hand unto the Lord, the most high God, the possessor of heaven and earth,

14:23 ***And have sworn*** That I will not take ***of thee*** from a thread even to a shoelatchet, and that I will not take any thing that is thine, *(*lest thou shouldest say, I have made Abram rich:*)*

14:24 Save only that which the young men have eaten, and the portion of the men which went with me, ~~Aner~~ ***Ener***, Eshcol, and Mamre; let them take their portion.

And Melchizedek lifted up his voice and blessed Abram.

Now Melchizedek was a man of faith, who wrought righteousness; and when a child he feared God, and stopped the mouths of lions, and quenched the violence of fire.

And thus, having been approved of God, he was ordained an high priest after the order of the covenant which God made with Enoch,

It being after the order of the Son of God; which order came, not by man, nor the will of man; neither by father nor mother; neither by beginning of days nor end of years; but of God;

And it was delivered unto men by the calling of his own voice, according to his own will, unto as many as believed on his name.

For God having sworn unto Enoch and unto his seed with an oath by himself; that every one being ordained after this order and calling should have power, by faith, to break mountains, to divide the seas, to dry up waters, to turn them out of their course;

To put at defiance the armies of nations, to divide the earth, to break every band, to stand in the presence of God; to do all things according to his will, according to his command, subdue principalities and powers; and this by the will of the Son of God which was from before the foundation of the world.

And men having this faith, coming up unto this order of God, were translated and taken up into heaven.

And now, Melchizedek was a priest of this order; therefore he obtained peace in Salem, and was called the Prince of peace.

And his people wrought righteousness, and obtained heaven, which sought for the city of Enoch which God had before taken, separating it from the earth, having reserved it unto the latter days, or the end of the world;

And hath said, and sworn with an oath, that the heavens and the earth should come together; and the sons of God should be tried so as by fire.

And this Melchizedek, having thus established righteousness, was called the king of heaven by his people, or, in other words, the King of peace.

And he lifted up his voice, and he blessed Abram, being the high priest, and the keeper of the storehouse of God;

Him whom God had appointed to receive tithes for the poor.

Wherefore, Abram paid unto him tithes of all that he had, of all the riches which he possessed, which God had given him more than that which he had need.

And it came to pass, that God blessed Abram, and gave unto him riches, and honor, and lands for an everlasting possession; according to the covenant which he had made, and according to the blessing wherewith Melchizedek had blessed him.

ABRAM'S SEED

15:1 ***And it came to pass, that*** After these things*,* the word of the Lord came
unto Abram in a vision, saying, Fear not, Abram: I ~~am~~ ***will be*** thy shield, ~~and~~ ***I***
will be thy exceeding great reward. ***And according to the blessings of my***
servant, I will give unto thee.
15:2 And Abram said, Lord God, what wilt thou give me, seeing I go childless,
and ~~the steward of my house is this~~ Eliezer of Damascus ***was made the steward***
of my house?
15:3 And Abram said, Behold, to me thou hast given no seed: and, lo, one born
in my house is mine heir.
15:4 And, behold, the word of the Lord came unto him~~,~~ ***again,*** saying, This ~~shall~~
shalt not be thine heir; but he that shall come forth out of thine own bowels shall
be thine heir.
15:5 And he brought him forth abroad, and ***he*** said, Look now toward heaven,
and tell the stars, if thou be able to number them~~:~~***.*** ~~a~~***A***nd he said unto him, So
shall thy seed be.

And Abram said, Lord God, how wilt thou give me this land for an everlasting inheritance?

And the Lord said, Though thou wast dead, yet am I not abel to give it thee?

And if thou shalt die, yet thou shalt possess it, for the day cometh, that the Son of Man shall live; but how can he live if he be not dead? he must first be quickened.

15:6 ***And it came to pass, that Abram looked forth and saw the days of the Son***
of Man, and was glad, and his soul found rest, And he believed in the Lord; and
~~he~~ ***the Lord*** counted it ***un***to him for righteousness.
15:7 And ~~he~~ ***the Lord*** said unto him, I*,* ~~am~~ the LORD*,* ~~that~~ brought thee out of
Ur*,* of the Chaldees, to give thee this land to inherit it.
15:8 And ~~he~~ ***Abram*** said, Lord ~~God~~, whereby shall I know that I shall inherit it?
yet he believed God.
15:9 And ~~he~~ ***the Lord*** said unto him, Take me a~~n~~ heifer of three years old, and
a she goat of three years old, and a ram of three years old, and a turtledove, and
a young pigeon.
15:10 And he took unto him all these, and ***he*** divided them in the midst, and laid
each piece one against another: but the birds divided he not.
15:11 And when the fowls came down upon the carcas*s*es, Abram drove them
away.
15:12 And when the sun was going down, a deep sleep fell upon Abram; and, lo,
~~an horror of~~ ***a*** great ***horror of*** darkness fell upon him.
15:13 ***And the Lord spake,*** And he said unto Abram, Know of a surety that thy
seed shall be a stranger in a land ~~that is not~~ ***which shall not be*** theirs, and shall
serve ~~them~~ ***strangers***; and they shall ***be*** afflict***ed; and serve*** them four hundred
years;
15:14 And also that nation, whom they shall serve~~,~~ will I judge: and afterward*s*
shall they come out with great substance.
15:15 And thou shalt ***die, and*** go to thy fathers in peace; thou shalt be buried in
a good old age.
15:16 But in the fourth generation they shall come hither again: for the iniquity
of the Amorites is not yet full.

15:17 And it came to pass, that~~;~~ when the sun went down, and it was dark, behold a smoking furnace, and a burning lamp ~~that~~ ***which*** passed between those pieces ***which Abram had divided***.
15:18 ***And*** In ~~the~~ ***that*** same day the Lord made a covenant with Abram, saying, Unto thy seed have I given this land, from the river of Egypt unto the great river ~~, the river~~ Euphrates:
15:19 The Kenites, and the ~~Kenizzites~~ ***Kenazites***, and the Kadmonites,
15:20 And the Hittites, and the Perizzites, and the Rephaims,
15:21 And the Amorites, and the Canaanites, and the Girgashites, and the Jebusites.

HAGAR AND THE BIRTH OF ISHMAEL

16:1 Now Sarai Abram's wife bare him no children: and she had an handmaid, an Egyptian, whose name was Hagar.
16:2 And Sarai said unto Abram, Behold now, the Lord hath restrained me from bearing: I pray thee, go in unto my maid; it may be that I may obtain children by her. And Abram hearkened ***un***to the voice of Sarai.
16:3 And Sarai Abram's wife took Hagar her maid the Egyptian, after Abram had dwelt ten years in the land of Canaan, and gave her to her husband Abram to be his wife.
16:4 And he went in unto Hagar, and she conceived: and when she saw that she had conceived, her mistress was despised in her eyes.
16:5 And Sarai said unto Abram, My wrong ~~be~~ ***is*** upon thee: I have given my maid into thy bosom; and when she saw that she had conceived, I was despised in her eyes: the Lord judge between me and thee.
16:6 But Abram said unto Sarai, Behold, thy maid is in thy hand***s***; do to her as it pleaseth thee. And when Sarai dealt hardly with her, she fled from her face.
16:7 And ~~the~~ ***an*** angel of the Lord found her by a fountain of water in the wilderness, by the fountain in the way to Shur.
16:8 And he said, Hagar, Sarai's maid, whence camest thou,~~?~~ and whither wilt thou go? And she said, I flee from the face of my mistress Sarai.
16:9 And the angel of the Lord said unto her, Return to thy mistress, and submit thyself ~~under~~ ***unto*** her hands.
16:10 And the angel of the Lord said unto her, ~~I~~ ***The Lord*** will multiply thy seed exceedingly, ***so*** that it shall not be numbered for multitude.
16:11 And the angel of the Lord said unto her, Behold, thou art with child, and shalt bear a son, and shalt call his name Ishmael; because the Lord hath heard thy affliction***s***.
16:12 And he will be a wild man; ***and*** his hand will be against every man, and every man's hand against him; and he shall dwell in the presence of all his brethren.
16:13 And she called the name of the ***angel of the*** Lord ~~that~~***.*** ***And he*** spake unto her ***saying***, ***Knowest*** Thou ***that*** God seest ~~me: for~~ ***thee?*** ***And*** she said, ***I know that God seest me, for I*** Have ~~I~~ also here looked after him ~~that seeth me?~~***.***
16:14 ***And there was a well between Kadesh and Bered, near where Hagar saw the angel. And the name of the angel was Beer-la-hai-roi;*** Wherefore the well was called Beer-la-hai-roi~~; behold, it is between Kadesh and Bered~~ ***for a memorial***.
16:15 And Hagar bare Abram a son: and Abram called his son's name, which Hagar bare, Ishmael.
16:16 And Abram was fourscore and six years old, when Hagar bare Ishmael to Abram.

ABRAM: THE COVENANT AND CIRCUMCISION

17:1 And when Abram was ninety ***and nine*** years old ~~and nine~~, the Lord appeared to Abram, and said unto him, I***,*** ~~am~~ the Almighty God***, give unto thee a commandment***; ***that thou shalt*** walk ***uprightly*** before me, and be ~~thou~~ perfect.

17:2 And I will make my covenant between me and thee, and ***I*** will multiply thee exceedingly.

17:3 And ***it came to pass, that*** Abram fell on his face: ***and called upon the name of the Lord.*** ~~a~~***A***nd God talked with him, saying, ***My people have gone astray from my precepts, and have not kept mine ordinances, which I gave unto their fathers;***

And they have not observed mine anointing, and the burial, or baptism wherewith I commanded them;

But have turned from the commandment, and taken unto themselves the washing of children, and the blood of sprinkling;

And have said that the blood of the righteous Abel was shed for sins; and have not known wherein they are accountable before me.

17:4 ***But*** As for ~~me~~ ***thee***, behold, ***I will make*** my covenant ~~is~~ with thee, and thou shalt be a father of many nations.

17:5 ***And this covenant I make, that thy children may be known among all nations.*** Neither shall thy name any more be called Abram, but thy name shall be Abraham; for***,*** a father of many nations have I made thee.

17:6 And I will make thee exceeding fruitful, and I will make nations of thee, and kings shall come ~~out~~ of thee***, and of thy seed***.

17:7 And I will establish ***a covenant of circumcision with thee, and it shall be*** my covenant between me and thee***,*** and thy seed after thee***,*** in their generations***;*** ~~for an everlasting covenant, to~~ ***that thou mayest know for ever that children are not accountable before me until they are eight years old.***

And thou shalt observe to keep all my covenants wherein I covenanted with thy fathers; and thou shalt keep the commandments which I have given thee with mine own mouth, and I will be a God unto thee, and ~~to~~ thy seed after thee.

17:8 And I will give unto thee, and ~~to~~ thy seed after thee, ~~the~~ ***a*** land wherein thou art a stranger, all the land of Canaan, for an everlasting possession; and I will be their God.

17:9 And God said unto Abraham, ***Therefore*** Thou shalt keep my covenant ~~therefore~~, thou, and thy seed after thee***,*** in their generations.

17:10 ***And*** This ~~is~~ ***shall be*** my covenant, which ye shall keep, between me and ~~you~~ ***thee*** and thy seed after thee; Every man child among you shall be circumcised.

17:11 And ye shall circumcise the flesh of your foreskin; and it shall be a token of the covenant betwixt me and you.

17:12 And he that is eight days old shall be circumcised among you, every man child in your generations, he that is born in the house, or bought with money of any stranger, which is not of thy seed.

17:13 He that is born in thy house, and he that is bought with thy money, must needs be circumcised: and my covenant shall be in your flesh for an everlasting covenant.

17:14 And the uncircumcised man child whose flesh of his foreskin is not circumcised, that soul shall be cut off from his people; he hath broken my covenant.

17:15 And God said unto Abraham, As for Sarai thy wife, thou shalt not call her name Sarai, but Sarah ~~shall~~ ***thou shalt*** her name ~~be~~.

17:16 And I will bless her, and ***I will*** give thee a son ~~also~~ of her: yea, I will bless her, and she shall be ***blessed, The*** ~~a~~ mother of nations; kings ~~of~~ ***and*** people shall be of her.

17:17 Then Abraham fell ~~up~~on his face, and ~~laughed~~ ***rejoiced***, and said in his heart, ***There*** Shall ***be*** a child ~~be~~ born unto him that is an hundred years old~~?~~***,*** and ~~shall~~ Sarah ~~,~~ that is ninety years old ~~,~~ ***shall*** bear~~?~~***.***

17:18 And Abraham said unto God, O that Ishmael might live ***uprightly*** before thee!
17:19 And God said, Sarah thy wife shall bear thee a son ~~indeed~~; and thou shalt call his name Isaac: and I will establish my covenant with him ***also,*** for an everlasting covenant ~~, and~~ with his seed after him.
17:20 And as for Ishmael, I have heard thee: Behold, I have blessed him, and will make him fruitful, and will multiply him exceedingly; twelve princes shall he beget, and I will make him a great nation.
17:21 But my covenant will I establish with Isaac, which Sarah shall bear unto thee at this set time in the next year.
17:22 And he left off talking with him, and God went up from Abraham.
17:23 And Abraham took Ishmael his son, and all that were born in his house, and all that were bought with his money, every male among the men of Abraham's house; and circumcised the flesh of their foreskin in the selfsame day, as God had said unto him.
17:24 And Abraham was ninety ***and nine*** years old ~~and nine~~, when he was circumcised in the flesh of his foreskin.
17:25 And Ishmael his son was thirteen years old, when he was circumcised in the flesh of his foreskin.
17:26 In the selfsame day was Abraham circumcised, and Ishmael his son.
17:27 And all the men of his house, ***which were*** born in the house, and bought with money of ~~the~~ stranger***s***, were ***also*** circumcised with him.

ABRAHAM AND SARAH VISITED BY THREE HOLY MEN

18:1 And the Lord appeared unto ~~him~~ ***Abraham*** in the plains of Mamre: and he sat in the tent door in the heat of the day;
18:2 And he lift***ed*** up his eyes and looked, and, lo, three men stood by him: and when he saw ~~them~~, he ran to meet them from ~~the~~ ***his*** tent door, and bowed himself toward the ground,
18:3 And said, My ~~Lord~~ ***brethren***, if now I have found ~~favour~~ ***favor*** in ~~thy~~ your sight, pass not away, I pray ~~thee,~~ ***you*** from thy servant:
18:4 Let a little water, I pray you, be fetched, and wash your feet, and rest yourselves under the tree:
18:5 And I will fetch a morsel of bread, and comfort ye your hearts; after that ~~ye~~ ***you*** shall pass on: for therefore are ye come to your servant. And they said, So do, as thou hast said.
18:6 And Abraham hastened into the tent unto Sarah, and said, Make ready quickly three measures of fine meal, knead ~~it~~, and make cakes upon the hearth.
18:7 And Abraham ran unto the herd, and fetched a calf***,*** tender and good, and gave it unto a young man; and he hasted to dress it.
18:8 And he took butter, and milk, and the calf which he had dressed, and set ~~it~~ ***them*** before them; and he stood by them under the tree, and they did eat.
18:9 And they said unto him, Where is Sarah thy wife? And he said, Behold, in the tent.
18:10 ***And one of them blessed Abraham,*** And he said, I will certainly return unto thee ***from my journey, and lo,*** according to the time of life~~; and, lo~~ , Sarah thy wife shall have a son. And Sarah heard ~~it~~ ***him*** in the tent door~~, which was behind him~~ .
18:11 ***And*** Now Abraham and Sarah ~~were~~ ***being*** old***,*** and ~~well~~ stricken in age; ~~and~~ ***therefore*** it ***had*** ceased to be with Sarah after the manner of women.
18:12 Therefore Sarah laughed within herself, saying, After I ~~am~~ ***have*** waxed old shall I have pleasure, my lord being old also?
18:13 And the ***angel of the*** Lord said unto Abraham, Wherefore did Sarah laugh, saying, Shall I of a surety bear a child, which am old?

18:14 Is any thing too hard for the Lord? At the time appointed, ***behold,*** I will return unto thee ***from my journey, which the Lord hath sent me; and*** according to the time of life~~, and~~ ***thou mayest know that*** Sarah shall have a son.

18:15 Then Sarah denied, saying, I laughed not; for she was afraid. And he said, Nay; but thou didst laugh.

ABRAHAM INTERCEDES FOR SODOM

18:16 And the ~~men~~ ***angels*** rose up from thence, and looked toward Sodom: and Abraham went with them to bring them on the way.

18:17 And the ***angel of the*** Lord said, Shall I hide from Abraham that thing which ~~I~~ ***the Lord will*** do ***for him***;

18:18 Seeing that Abraham shall surely become a great and mighty nation, and all the nations of the earth shall be blessed in him?

18:19 For I know him, that he will command his children, and his household after him, and they shall keep the way of the Lord, to do justice and judgment; that the Lord may bring upon Abraham that which he ~~hath~~ ***has*** spoken of him.

18:20 And the ***angel of the*** Lord said ***unto Abraham, The Lord said unto us***, Because the cry of Sodom and Gomorrah is great, and because their sin is very grievous, ***I will destroy them***;

18:21 I will ***will send you, and ye shall*** go down now, and see ***that their iniquities are rewarded unto them. And ye shall have all things done*** ~~whether they have done~~ altogether according to the cry of it, which is come unto me; and if ***ye do it*** not, ~~I will know~~ ***it shall be upon your heads; for I will destroy them, and you shall know that I will do it, for it shall be before your eyes***.

18:22 And the ***angels which were holy*** men, ***and were sent forth after the order of God,*** turned their faces from thence, and went toward Sodom: but Abraham stood yet before the Lord, ***remembering the things which had been told him***.

18:23 And Abraham drew near ***to Sodom***, and said ***unto the Lord, calling upon his name, saying***, Wilt thou also destroy the righteous with the wicked? ***Wilt thou not spare them?***

18:24 Peradventure there be fifty righteous within the city: wilt thou also destroy and not spare the place for the fifty righteous that ~~are~~ ***may be*** therein?

18:25 ***O may*** That be far from thee to do after this manner, to slay the righteous with the wicked: and that the righteous should be as the wicked. ***O God, may*** that be far from thee: ***for*** Shall not the Judge of all the earth do right?

18:26 And the Lord said ***unto Abraham***, If ~~I~~ ***thou*** find***est*** in Sodom fifty righteous within the city, then I will spare all the place for their sakes.

18:27 And Abraham answered and said, Behold now, I have taken upon me to speak unto the Lord, which ***is able to destroy the city, and lay all the people in*** ~~am but~~ dust and ashes:

18:28 ***Will the Lord spare them*** Peradventure there shall lack five of the fifty righteous: wilt thou destroy all the city for ~~lack of five? And he said,~~ ***their wickedness,*** If I find there forty and five ***righteous? And he said***, I will not destroy ~~it~~ ***but spare them***.

18:29 And he spake unto him ~~yet~~ again, and said, Peradventure there shall be forty found there~~.~~ ***?*** And he said, I will not ~~do~~ ***destroy*** it for forty's sake.

18:30 And he said ***again*** unto ~~him~~ ***the Lord***, O~~h~~, let not the Lord be angry, and I will speak: Peradventure there shall thirty be found there~~.~~ ***?*** And he said, I will not ~~do it,~~ ***destroy them*** if ~~I~~ ***thou shalt*** find thirty there.

18:31 And he said, Behold now, I have taken upon me to speak unto the Lord: ***wilt thou destroy them if*** Peradventure there shall ~~be~~ twenty ***be*** found there~~.~~ ***?*** And he said, I will not destroy ~~it~~ ***them*** for twenty's sake.

18:32 And ~~he~~ ***Abraham*** said ***unto the Lord***, O~~h~~ ***,*** let not the Lord be angry, and I will speak yet but this once: Peradventure ten shall be found there~~.~~ ***?*** And ~~he~~ ***the Lord*** said, I will not destroy ~~it~~ ***them*** for ten's sake. ***And the Lord ceased speaking with Abraham.***

18:33 And ~~the LORD went his way,~~ as soon as he had left communing with ***the Lord,*** Abraham ***went his way. And it came to pass that*** ~~and~~ Abraham returned unto his ~~place~~ ***tent***.

LOT VISITED BY THREE HOLY ANGELS

19:1 And ***it came to pass, that*** there came ~~two~~ ***three*** angels to Sodom ~~at even~~ ***in the evening***; and Lot sat in the ~~gate~~ ***door of his house, in the city*** of Sodom~~:~~ **.** ~~a~~***A***nd Lot, seeing ~~them~~ ***the angels,*** rose up to meet them; and he bowed himself with his face toward the ground;

19:2 And he said, Behold now, my lords, turn in, I pray you, into your servant's house, and tarry all night, and wash your feet, and ye shall rise up early, and go on your ways. And they said, Nay; but we will abide in the street all night.

19:3 And he pressed upon them greatly; and they turned in unto him, and entered into his house; and he made them a feast, and did bake unleavened bread, and they did eat.

19:4 But before they lay down ***to rest***, the men of the city ~~, even the men~~ of Sodom, compassed the house round, ***even men which were*** both old and young, ~~all~~ ***even*** the people from every quarter:

19:5 And they called unto Lot, and said unto him, Where are the men which came in ***un***to thee this night? bring them out unto us, that we may know them.

19:6 And Lot went out ~~at~~ ***of*** the door, unto them, and shut the door after him,

19:7 And said, I pray you, brethren, do not so wickedly.

19:9a And they said ***unto him***, Stand back. ***And they were angry with him.*** And they said ~~again~~ ***among themselves***, This one ~~fellow~~ ***man*** came in to sojourn ***among us***, and he will needs ~~be~~ ***now make himself to be*** a judge: now will we deal worse with ~~thee,~~ ***him*** than with them.

Wherefore they said unto the man, We will have the men, and thy daughters also; and we will do with them as seemeth us good.

Now this was after the wickedness of Sodom.

19:8 ***And Lot said,*** Behold now, I have two daughters which have not known man; let me, I pray you, ***plead with my brethren that I may not*** bring them out unto you, and ***ye shall not*** do ~~ye to~~ ***unto*** them as ~~is~~ ***seemeth*** good in your eyes~~:~~ **.**

For God will not justify his servant in this thing; wherefore, let me plead with my brethren, this once only, ***that*** unto these men ***ye*** do nothing, ***that they may have peace in my house***; for therefore came they under the shadow of my roof. (*verse order changed by JST*)

19:9b And they ~~pressed sore upon the man, even~~ ***were angry with Lot*** and came near to break the door.

19:10 But the ***angels of God, which were holy*** men, put forth their hand, and pulled Lot into the house ***un***to them, and shut ~~to~~ the door.

19:11 And they smote the men ~~that were at the door of the house~~ with blindness, both small and grea~~t:~~ ***, that they could not come at the door. And they were angry,*** so that they wearied themselves to find the door, ***and could not find it***.

19:12 And ~~the~~ ***these holy*** men said unto Lot, Hast thou ~~here~~ any ***here*** besides~~?~~ ***thy*** son***s***-in- law, and thy ***son's*** sons, and thy daughters~~,~~ ***? And they commanded Lot, saying,*** ~~w~~***W***hatsoever thou hast in the city, ***thou shalt*** bring ~~them~~ out of this place~~:~~ **,**

19:13 ~~F~~***f***or we will destroy this place, because the cry of them is waxen great, ***and their abominations have come up*** before the face of the Lord; and the Lord hath sent us to destroy it.

19:14 And Lot went out, and spake unto his sons-in-law, which married his daughters, and said, Up, get you out of this place; for the Lord will destroy this city. But he seemed as one that mocked, unto his sons in law.

LOT ESCAPES FROM SODOM

19:15 And when the morning ~~arose~~ ***came***, ~~then~~ the angels hastened Lot, saying, Arise, take thy wife, and thy two daughters, which are here; lest thou be consumed in the iniquity of the city.
19:16 And while he lingered, the ~~men~~ ***angels*** laid hold upon his hand, and upon the hand of his wife, and upon the hand of his two daughters; the Lord being merciful unto ~~him~~ ***them***: and they brought ~~him~~ ***them*** forth, and set ~~him~~ ***them down*** without the city.
19:17 And it came to pass, when they had brought them forth abroad, that ~~he~~ ***they*** said ***unto them***, Escape for ~~thy life~~ ***your lives***; look not behind ~~thee~~ ***you***, neither stay ~~thou~~ ***you*** in all the plain; escape to the mountain, lest ~~thou~~ ***you*** be consumed.
19:18 And Lot said unto ***one*** them, Oh, not so, my Lord~~:~~ ***!***
19:19 Behold now, thy servant ~~hath~~ ***has*** found grace in thy sight, and thou hast magnified thy mercy, which thou hast showed unto me in saving my life; and I cannot escape to the mountain, lest some evil ***over***take me, and I die:
19:20 Behold now, ~~this~~ ***here is another*** city***, and this*** is near to flee unto, and it is a little one: Oh, let me escape thither, ~~(is it not a little one?)~~ ***and may theLord not destroy it,*** and my soul shall live.
19:21 And ~~he~~ ***the angel*** said unto him, See, I have accepted thee concerning this thing also, that I will not overthrow this city, for the which thou hast spoken.
19:22 Haste thee, escape thither; for I cannot do any thing ~~till~~ ***until*** thou be come thither. ~~Therefore~~ ***And*** the name of the city was called Zoar.
19:23 ***Therefore*** The sun was risen upon the earth when Lot entered into Zoar. ***And the Lord did not destroy Sodom until Lot had entered into Zoar.***

SODOM DESTROYED

19:24 ***And*** Then***, when Lot had entered into Zoar,*** the Lord rained upon Sodom and upon Gomorrah***; for the angels called upon the name of the Lord for*** brimstone and fire from the Lord out of heaven;
19:25 And ~~he~~ ***thus they*** overthrew those cities, and all the plain, and all the inhabitants of the cities, and that which grew upon the ground.
19:26 But ***it came to pass, when Lot fled,*** his wife looked back from behind him, and ~~she~~ became a pillar of salt.
19:27 And Abraham ~~gat~~ ***got*** up early in the morning to the place where he stood before the Lord:
19:28 And he looked toward Sodom and Gomorrah, and toward all the land of the plain, and ~~beheld, and~~ ***behold***, lo, the smoke of the country went up as the smoke of a furnace.
19:29 And it came to pass, when God destroyed the cities of the plain, that God ~~remembered~~ ***spake unto*** Abraham ***saying, I have remembered Lot***, and sent ~~Lot~~ ***him*** out of the midst of the overthrow, ***that thy brother might not be destroyed,*** when ~~he~~ ***I*** overthrew the ~~cities~~ ***city*** in the which ***thy brother*** Lot dwelt.
19:30 *And Abraham was comforted.* And Lot went up out of Zoar, and dwelt in the mountain, and his two daughters with him; for he feared to dwell in Zoar: and he dwelt in a cave, he and his two daughters.
19:31 And the firstborn ***dealt wickedly, and*** said unto the younger, Our father ~~is~~ ***has become*** old, and ~~there is~~ ***we have*** not a man ~~in~~ ***on*** the earth to come in unto us***, to live with us*** after the manner of all ***that live on*** the earth:
19:32 ***Therefore,*** Come, let us make our father drink wine, and we will lie with him, that we may preserve seed of our father.
19:33 And they ***did wickedly, and*** made their father drink wine that night: and the firstborn went in, and lay with her father; and he perceived not when she lay down, nor when she arose.

19:34 And it came to pass on the morrow, that the firstborn said unto the younger, Behold, I lay yesternight with my father: let us make him drink wine this night also; and go thou in, and lie with him, that we may preserve seed of our father.
19:35 And they made their father drink wine that night also: and the younger arose, and lay with him; and he perceived not when she lay down, nor when she arose.
19:36 Thus were both the daughters of Lot with child by their father.
19:37 And the firstborn bare a son, and called his name Moab: ~~the same is~~ the father of the Moabites***, the same which are*** unto this day.
19:38 And the younger, she also bare a son, and called his name Ben-ammi: ~~the same is~~ the father of the children ~~of Ammon~~ ***which are Ammonites; the same which are*** unto this day.

ABRAHAM, SARAH AND ABIMELECH IN GERAR

20:1 And Abraham journeyed from thence toward the south country, and dwelled between Kadesh and Shur, and sojourned in Gerar.
20:2 And Abraham said ***again*** of Sarah his wife, She is my sister~~:~~ ***.*** ~~a~~***A***nd Abimelech king of Gerar sent, and took Sarah.
20:3 But God came to Abimelech in a dream by night, and said ***un***to him, Behold, thou ~~art but a dead man, for the woman which thou~~ hast taken ***a woman which is not thine own***; for she is ~~a man's~~ ***Abraham's*** wife. ***And the Lord said unto him, Thou shalt return her unto Abraham, for if thou do it not thou shalt die.***
20:4 ~~But~~ ***And*** Abimelech had not come near her: ***for the Lord had not suffered him.*** ~~a~~***A***nd he said, Lord, wilt thou slay ***me, and*** also a righteous nation?
20:5 ***Behold,*** Said he not unto me, She is my sister? ~~a~~***A***nd she, even she herself said, He is my brother; in the integrity of my heart and innocency of my hands have I done this.
20:6 And God said unto him in a dream, Yea, I know that thou didst ***do*** this in the integrity of thy heart; for I also withheld thee from sinning against me: therefore suffered I ***not*** thee ~~not~~ to touch her.
20:7 Now***,*** therefore***,*** restore the man***'s*** ~~his~~ wife ***to him***; for he is a prophet, and he shall pray for thee, and thou shalt live: and if thou restore her not ***to him***, know thou that thou shalt surely die, thou, and all that are thine.
20:8 Therefore Abimelech rose early in the morning, and called all his servants, and told all these things in their ears: and the men were sore afraid.
20:9 Then Abimelech called Abraham, and said unto him, What hast thou done unto us? and ***in*** what have I offended thee, that thou hast brought on me and on my kingdom a great sin? ~~t~~***T***hou hast done deeds unto me that ought not to be done.
20:10 And Abimelech said unto Abraham, What sawest thou, that thou hast done this thing?
20:11 And Abraham said, Because I thought, ~~Surely~~ ***assuredly*** the fear of God ~~is~~ ***was*** not in this place; and they ~~will~~ ***would*** slay me for my wife's sake.
20:12 And yet indeed she ~~is~~ ***was*** my sister; she ~~is~~ ***was*** the daughter of my father, but not the daughter of my mother; and she became my wife.
20:13 And it came to pass, when God caused me to wander from my father's house, that I said unto her, This ~~is~~ ***shall be*** thy kindness which thou shalt show unto me; at every place whither we shall come, say of me, He is my brother.
20:14 And Abimelech took sheep, and oxen, and ~~menservants~~ ***men servants***, and ~~womenservants~~ ***women servants***, and gave ~~them~~ unto Abraham, and restored ***unto*** him Sarah his wife.
20:15 And Abimelech said, Behold, my land ~~is~~ ***lieth*** before thee: dwell where it pleaseth thee.

20:16 And unto Sarah he said, Behold, I have given thy brother a thousand pieces of silver: behold, he ~~is to~~ ***shall give unto*** thee a covering of the eyes, ~~unto all that are with thee, and with all other:~~ ***and it shall be a token unto all that thou mayest not be taken again from Abraham thy husband. And*** thus she was reproved.
20:17 So Abraham prayed unto God: and God healed Abimelech, and his wife, and his ~~maidservants~~; ***maid servants*** and they bare ***unto him*** children.
20:18 For ***because of Sarah, Abraham's wife,*** the Lord had fast closed up all the wombs of the house of Abimelech~~, because of Sarah Abraham's wife~~ .

BIRTH OF ISAAC

21:1 And the Lord visited Sarah as he had said, and the Lord did unto Sarah as he had spoken ***by the mouth of his angels***.
21:2 For Sarah conceived, and ~~bare~~ ***bear*** Abraham a son in his old age, at the set time of which ***the angels of*** God had spoken to him.
21:3 And Abraham called the name of his son that was born unto him, whom Sarah ~~bare~~ ***bear un***to him, Isaac.
21:4 And Abraham circumcised his son Isaac***, he*** being eight days old, as God had commanded him.
21:5 And Abraham was an hundred years old, when his son Isaac was born unto him.
21:6 And Sarah said, God ~~hath~~ ***has*** made me to ~~laugh, so that all that hear will laugh~~ ***rejoice; and also all that know me will rejoice*** with me.
21:7 And she said ***unto Abraham***, Who would have said ~~unto Abraham,~~ that Sarah should have given children suck? ~~f~~***F***or I ***was barren, but the Lord promised, and I*** have born***e*** ~~him~~ ***unto Abraham*** a son in his old age.
21:8 And the child grew, and was weaned~~:~~ ***.*** ~~a~~***A***nd ~~Abraham made a great feast the same~~ ***the*** day that Isaac was weaned***, Abraham made a great feast,***

EXPULSION OF HAGAR

21:9 And Sarah saw the son of Hagar the Egyptian, which ~~she~~ ***Hagar*** had born***e*** unto Abraham, mocking***; and she was troubled***.
21:10 Wherefore she said unto Abraham, Cast out this bond-woman and her son: for the son of this bond-woman shall not be heir with my son, ~~even with~~ Isaac.
21:11 And the thing was very grievous ~~in Abraham's sight~~ ***unto Abraham*** because of his son.
21:12 And God said unto Abraham, Let it not be grievous in thy sight because of the lad, and because of thy bond-woman; in all that Sarah ~~hath~~ ***has*** said unto thee, hearken unto her voice; for in Isaac shall thy seed be called.
21:13 And also of the son of the bondwoman will I make a nation, because he is thy seed.
21:14 And Abraham rose up early in the morning, and took bread, and a bottle of water, and gave ~~it~~ unto Hagar, ~~putting it on her shoulder,~~ and ***she took*** the child, and ***he*** sent her away: and she departed, and wandered in the wilderness of Beersheba.
21:15 And ***it came to pass that*** the water was spent in the bottle, and she cast the child under one of the shrubs.
21:16 And she went, and sat her down over against ~~him~~ ***the child,*** a good way off, as it were a bowshot: for she said, Let me not see the death of the child. And she sat over against ~~him~~ ***the child***, and lift***ed*** up her voice, and wept.
21:17 And God heard the voice of the lad; and the angel of ~~God~~ ***the Lord*** called to Hagar out of heaven, and said unto her, What aileth thee, Hagar? fear not; for God hath heard the voice of the lad where he ~~is~~ ***lieth***.

21:18 Arise, lift up the lad, and hold him in thine hand; for I will make ***of*** him a great nation.
21:19 And God opened her eyes, and she saw a well of water; and she went, and filled the bottle with water, and gave the lad drink.
21:20 And God was with the lad; and he grew, and dwelt in the wilderness, and became an archer.
21:21 And he dwelt in the wilderness of Paran: ***he and*** and his mother***. And he*** took him a wife out of the land of Egypt.

ABRAHAM AND ABIMELECH AT BEERSHEBA

21:22 And it came to pass at that time, that Abimelech and ~~Phichol~~ ***Phicol*** the chief captain of his host spake unto Abraham, saying, God is with thee in all that thou doest~~:~~***.***
21:23 Now therefore ~~swear~~***, swear*** unto me here***, that,*** by ***the help of*** God***,*** ~~that~~ thou wilt not deal falsely with me, nor with my son, nor with my son's son: but ***that*** according to the kindness that I have ~~done~~ ***shown*** unto thee, thou shalt do unto me, and to the land wherein thou hast sojourned.
21:24 And Abraham said, I will swear.
21:25 And Abraham reproved Abimelech***,*** because of a well of water, which Abimelech's servants had violently taken away.
21:26 And Abimelech said, ***Thou didst not tell me; and*** I ~~wot~~ ***know*** not who hath done this thing: ~~neither didst thou tell me;~~ neither yet ***have I*** heard ~~I of it, but to~~ ***that it was done until this*** day.
21:27 And Abraham took sheep and oxen, and gave them unto Abimelech; and both of them made a covenant.
21:28 And Abraham set seven ewe lambs of the flock by themselves.
21:29 And Abimelech said unto Abraham, What ~~mean~~ ***wilt thou do with*** these seven ewe lambs which thou hast set by themselves?
21:30 And he said, ~~For these~~ ~~s~~***S***even ewe lambs shalt thou take of my hand, that they may be a witness unto me, that I have digged this well.
21:31 ***And because they sware, both of them,*** Wherefore he called that place Beersheba ~~because there they sware both of them~~ .
21:32 Thus they made a covenant at Beersheba~~:~~***.*** ~~t~~***T***hen Abimelech ~~rose up~~ , and ~~Phichol~~ ***Phicol,*** the chief captain of his host***s***, ***rose up, and they planted a grove in Beer-sheba, and called there on the name of the Lord;*** and they returned into the land of the Philistines.
21:33 And Abraham ~~planted a grove in Beersheba, and called there on the name of the Lord,~~ ***worshipped*** the everlasting God***,***
21:34 And ~~Abraham~~ sojourned in the ***land of the*** Philistines~~'~~ ~~land~~ many days.

THE SACRIFICE OF ISAAC

22:1 And it came to pass after these things, that God did ~~tempt~~ ***try*** Abraham, and said unto him, Abraham: and ~~he~~ ***Abraham*** said, Behold, here I am.
22:2 And ~~he~~ ***the Lord*** said, Take now thy son, thine only ~~son~~ Isaac, whom thou lovest, and get thee into the land of Moriah; and offer him there for a burnt offering upon one of the mountains ***of*** which I will tell thee ~~of~~.
22:3 And Abraham rose up early in the morning, and saddled his ass, and took two of his young men with him, and Isaac his son, and clave the wood for the burnt offering, and rose up, and went unto the place of which God had told him.
22:4 Then on the third day***,*** Abraham lifted up his eyes, and saw the place afar off.

22:5 And Abraham said unto his young men, Abide ~~ye~~ ***you*** here with the ass; and I and the lad will go yonder and worship, and come ~~again~~ to you ***again***.

22:6 And Abraham took the wood of the burnt offering, and laid it upon ~~Isaac his son~~ ***his back***; and he took the fire in his hand, and a knife***, and Isaac his son***; and they went both of them together.

22:7 And Isaac spake unto Abraham his father, and said, My father~~:~~ ***!*** ~~a~~***A***nd he said, Here am I, my son. And he said, Behold the fire and the wood: but where is the lamb for a burnt offering?

22:8 And Abraham said, My son, God will provide himself a lamb for a burnt offering: so they went both of them together.

22:9 And they came to the place ***of*** which God had told him ~~of;~~***.*** ~~a~~***A***nd Abraham built an altar there, and laid the wood in order, and bound Isaac his son, and laid him on the altar upon the wood.

22:10 And Abraham stretched forth his hand, and took the knife to slay his son.

22:11 And the angel of the Lord called unto him out of heaven, and said, Abraham~~;~~ ***!*** Abraham~~:~~ ***!*** ~~and he~~ ***And Abraham*** said, Here am I.

22:12 And ~~he~~ ***the angel*** said, Lay not thine hand upon the lad, neither do thou ~~any thing~~ ***anything*** unto him: for now I know that thou fearest God, seeing thou hast not withheld thy son, thine only ~~son~~ ***Isaac*** from me.

22:13 And Abraham lifted up his eyes, and looked, and behold***,*** behind ~~him~~ ***a thicket, there was*** a ram caught in ~~a thicket~~ ***it*** by his horns~~:~~***.*** ~~a~~***A***nd Abraham went and took the ram, and offered him up for a burnt offering***,*** in the stead of his son.

22:14 And Abraham called the name of that place Jehovahjireh: as it is said ***un***to this day, In the mount of the Lord it shall be seen.

22:15 And the angel of the Lord called unto Abraham out of heaven the second time,

22:16 ~~A~~***a***nd said, ***Thus saith the Lord, I have sworn*** By myself ~~have I sworn, saith the LORD, for~~ ***that*** because thou hast done this thing, and hast not withheld thy son, thine only ~~son:~~ ***Isaac from me;***

22:17 That in blessing I will bless thee, and in multiplying I will multiply thy seed as the stars of ~~the~~ heaven, and as the sand which is upon the sea-shore; and thy seed shall possess the gate of his enemies;

22:18 And in thy seed shall all the nations of the earth be blessed; because thou hast obeyed my voice.

22:19 So Abraham returned unto his young men, and they rose up and went ~~together~~ to Beersheba; and Abraham dwelt at Beersheba.

LINE OF NAHOR

22:20 And it came to pass after these things, that it was told Abraham, saying, Behold, Milcah, she hath also born***e*** children unto thy brother Nahor;

22:21 Huz ***is his*** his firstborn, and Buz ***is*** his brother, and Kemuel ***is*** the father of Aram,

22:22 And Chesed, and ~~Hazo~~ ***Haza***, and ~~Pildash~~ ***Bildash***, and Jidlaph, and Bethuel.

22:23 And Bethuel begat Rebekah~~:~~***.*** ~~t~~***T***hese eight Milcah did bear to Nahor, Abraham's brother.

22:24 And his concubine, whose name was Reumah, she bare also Tebah, and Gaham, and Thahash, and Maachah.

DEATH AND BURIAL OF SARAH

23:1 And Sarah was an hundred and ~~seven and~~ twenty-***seven*** years old, ~~these were~~ ***and she died***: ***and thus ended*** the years of the life of Sarah.
23:2 And Sarah died in Kirjatharba; the same is ***now called*** Hebron, in the land of Canaan: and Abraham came to mourn for Sarah, and to weep for her, ***his wife which was dead***.
23:3 And Abraham stood up from before his dead, and spake unto the sons of Heth, saying,
23:4 I am a stranger and a sojourner with you: give me a possession of a burying-place with you, that I may bury my dead out of my sight.
23:5 And the children of Heth answered Abraham, saying unto him,
23:6 Hear us, my lord: thou art a mighty prince among us: in the choice***st*** of our sepulchres bury ***thou*** thy dead; none of us shall withhold from thee his sepulchre, but that thou mayest bury thy dead.
23:7 And Abraham stood up, and bowed himself to the people of the land, even to the children of Heth.
23:8 And he communed with them, saying, If it be your mind that I should bury my dead out of my sight; hear me, and entreat ~~for me to~~ Ephron the son of Zohar ***for me***,
23:9 That he may give me the cave of Machpelah, which he hath~~, which is~~ in the end of his field; for as much money as it is worth he shall ***have, if he will*** give it me for a possession of a burying-place among~~st~~ you.
23:10 And Ephron dwelt among the children of Heth~~:~~***.*** ~~a~~***A***nd Ephron, the Hittite, answered Abraham in the audience of the children of Heth, ~~even of~~ ***among*** all ***of them*** that went in at the gate***s*** of ~~his~~ ***the*** city, saying,
23:11 ~~Nay,~~ ***Hearken,*** my lord, ***and*** hear me: the field ~~give~~ I ***give*** thee, and the cave that is therein; I give it thee, in the presence of the sons of my people***; and*** ~~give~~ I ***give*** it thee: ***therefore,*** bury thy dead.
23:12 And Abraham bowed down himself before the people of the land.
23:13 And he spake unto Ephron in the audience of the people of the land, saying, ~~But if thou wilt give it,~~ I pray thee, hear me~~:~~***; If thou wilt take it of me,*** I will give thee money for the field; ~~take it of me;~~ and I will bury my dead there***, but I will give thee money for it***.
23:14 And Ephron answered Abraham, saying unto him,
23:15 My lord, hearken unto me: the land ~~is worth~~ ***thou shalt have for*** four hundred shekels of silver; what ~~is~~ ***shall*** that ***be*** betwixt me and thee? ~~b~~***B***ury therefore thy dead.
23:16 And Abraham hearkened unto Ephron; and Abraham weighed ***un***to Ephron the silver, which he had named in the audience of the sons of Heth, four hundred shekels of silver, ***which was the*** current ~~money~~ with the merchant.
23:17 And the field of Ephron, which was in Machpelah, which was before Mamre, the field, and the cave which was therein, and all the trees that were in the field, ***and*** that were in all the borders round about, were made sure
23:18 ~~U~~***u***nto Abraham for a possession, in the presence of the children of Heth, before all that went in at the gate of ~~his~~ ***the*** city.
23:19 And after this, Abraham buried Sarah his wife in the cave of the field of Machpelah, ***which is*** before Mamre: the same is ***called*** Hebron, in the land of Canaan.
23:20 And the field, and the cave that ~~is~~ ***was*** therein, were made sure unto Abraham for a possession of a burying-place by the sons of Heth.

ISAAC AND REBEKAH

24:1 And Abraham was old, ~~and~~ ***being*** well stricken in age: and the Lord had blessed Abraham in all things.
24:2 And Abraham said unto his eldest servant of his house, that ruled over all that he had, Put ***forth***, I pray thee, thy hand under my ~~thigh:~~ ***hand,***
24:3 And I will make thee swear by the Lord, the God of heaven, and the God of the earth, that thou shalt not take a wife unto my son**,** of the daughters of the Canaanites, among whom I dwell:
24:4 But thou shalt go unto my country, and to my kindred, and take a wife unto my son Isaac.
24:5 And the servant said unto him, ~~Peradventure~~ ***Perhaps*** the woman will not be willing to follow me unto this land: ***then I*** must ~~I~~ needs bring thy son again unto the land from whence thou camest~~?~~**.**
24:6 And Abraham said unto him, Beware thou that thou bring not my son thither again.
24:7 The Lord God of heaven, which took me from my father's house, and from the land of my kindred, and which spake unto me, and that ~~sware~~ ***swear*** unto me, saying, Unto ~~thy seed~~ ***thee*** will I give this land; he shall send his angel before thee, and thou shalt take a wife unto my son from thence.
24:8 And if the woman will not be willing to follow thee, then thou shalt be clear from this ~~my~~ ***thine*** oath: only bring not my son thither again.
24:9 And the servant put his hand under the ~~thigh~~ ***hand*** of Abraham his master, and sware to him concerning that matter.
24:10 And the servant took ten camels of the camels of his master, and departed; for all the goods of his master were in his hand: and he arose, and went to Mesopotamia, unto the city of Nahor.
24:11 And he made his camels to kneel down without the city**,** by a well of water**,** at ~~the time of the~~ evening, ~~even~~ the time that women go out to draw water.
24:12 And he said, O Lord God of my master Abraham, I pray thee ***this day,*** ~~send me good speed this day, and~~ ***that thou wouldst*** show kindness unto my master Abraham**,** ***and send me good speed.***.
24:13 Behold, I stand here by the well of water; and the daughters of the men of the city come out to draw water:
24:14 And let it come to pass, that the damsel to whom I shall say, Let down thy pitcher, I pray thee, that I may drink; and she shall say, Drink, and I will give thy camels drink also: let ~~the same~~ ***her*** be ~~she that~~ ***the one whom*** thou hast appointed for thy servant Isaac; and thereby shall I know that thou hast showed kindness unto my master.
24:15 And it came to pass, before he had done speaking, that, behold, Rebekah came out, who was born to Bethuel, son of Milcah, the wife of Nahor, Abraham's brother, with her pitcher upon her shoulder.
24:16 And the damsel ***being a virgin,*** ~~was~~ very fair to look upon, ~~a virgin~~, ***such as the servant of Abraham had not seen,*** neither had any man known ***the like unto*** her: and she went down to the well, and filled her pitcher, and came up.
24:17 And the servant ran to meet her, and said, Let me, I pray thee, drink a little water of thy pitcher.
24:18 And she said, Drink, my lord: and she hasted, and let down her pitcher upon her hand, and gave him drink.
24:19 And when she had done giving him drink, she said, I will draw ~~water~~ for thy camels also, until they have done drinking.
24:20 And she hasted, and emptied her pitcher into the trough, and ran again unto the well to draw ~~water~~, and drew for all his camels.
24:21 And the man**,** wondering at her**,** held his peace, ~~to wit~~ ***pondering in his heart*** whether the Lord had made his journey prosperous or not.
24:22 And it came to pass, as the camels had done drinking, that the man took a gold~~en~~ ear-ring of half a shekel weight, and two bracelets for her hands of ten shekels weight of gold;

24:23 And said, Whose daughter art thou? tell me, I pray thee: ***and*** is there room in thy father's house for us to lodge in?

24:24 And she said unto him, I am the daughter of Bethuel**,** the son of Milcah, which she bare unto Nahor.

24:25 She said moreover**,** unto him, We have both straw and provender enough, and room to lodge in.

24:26 And the man bowed down his head, and worshipped the Lord.

24:27 And he said, Blessed ~~be~~ ***is*** the Lord God of my master Abraham, who hath not left ~~destitute~~ my master ***destitute*** of his mercy and his truth: ~~being~~ ***and when*** I ***was*** in the way, the Lord led me to the house of my master's brethren.

24:28 And the damsel ran ***to the house***, and told ~~them of~~ her mother~~'s house~~ these things.

24:29 And Rebekah had a brother, ~~and his~~ ***whose*** name was Laban: and Laban ran out ~~un~~to the man, unto the well.

24:30 And it came to pass, when he saw the ear-ring***s*****,** and bracelets upon his sister's hands, and when he heard the word~~s~~ of Rebekah his sister, saying, Thus spake the man unto me; ~~that he~~ ***and I*** came unto the man; and, behold, he stood by the camels at the well.

24:31 And he said, Come in, thou blessed of the Lord; wherefore standest thou without? for I have prepared the house, and room for the camels.

24:32 And the man came into the house: and he ~~ungirded~~ ***unburdened*** his camels, and gave straw and provender for the camels, and water to wash his feet, and the men's feet that ~~were~~ ***came*** with him.

24:33 And there was set ~~meat~~ before him ***food*** to eat: but he said, I will not eat, until I have told mine errand. And ~~he~~ ***Laban*** said, Speak on.

24:34 And he said, I am Abraham's servant.

24:35 And the Lord hath blessed my master greatly; and he is become great: and he hath given him flocks, and herds, and silver, and gold, and menservants, and maidservants, and camels, and asses.

24:36 And Sarah my master's wife bare a son to my master when she was old: and unto him hath he given all that he hath.

24:37 And my master made me swear, saying, Thou shalt not take a wife to my son of the daughters of the Canaanites, in whose land I dwell:

24:38 But thou shalt go unto my father's house, and to my kindred, and take a wife unto my son.

24:39 And I said unto my master, ~~Peradventure~~ ***Perhaps*** the woman will not follow me.

24:40 And he said unto me, The Lord, before whom I walk, will send his angel with thee, and ***he will*** prosper thy way; and thou shalt take a wife for my son of my kindred, and of my father's house:

24:41 Then shalt thou be clear ~~from this~~ ***of*** my oath~~;~~**.** ~~w~~***W***hen thou comest to my kindred~~;~~ **,** and if they give ***thee*** not ~~one~~ ***a wife*** for my son, thou shalt be clear from my oath.

24:42 And I came this day unto the well, and said, O Lord God of my master Abraham, if now thou ~~do~~ ***wilt*** prosper my way which I go:

24:43 Behold, I stand by the well of water; and it shall come to pass, that when the virgin cometh forth to draw water, and I say to her, Give me, I pray thee, a little water of thy pitcher to drink;

24:44 And ***if*** she say to me, Both drink thou, and I will also draw for thy camels***;*** ~~let~~ the same ~~be~~ ***is*** the woman whom the Lord hath appointed out for my master's son.

24:45 And before I had done speaking in ~~mine~~ ***my*** heart, behold, Rebekah came forth with her pitcher on her shoulder; and she went down unto the well, and drew water: and I said unto her, Let me drink, I pray thee.

24:46 And she made haste, and let down her pitcher from her shoulder, and said, Drink, and I will give thy camels drink also: so I drank, and she made the camels drink also.

24:47 And I asked her, and said, Whose daughter art thou? And she said, The daughter of Bethuel, Nahor's son, whom Milcah bare unto him: and I ~~put~~ ***gave*** the ear-ring*s* ~~upon~~ ***unto*** her ~~face~~, ***to put into her ears,*** and the bracelets upon her hands.
24:48 And I bowed down my head, and worshipped the Lord, and blessed the Lord God of my master Abraham, ~~which~~ ***who*** had led me in the right way to take my master's brother's daughter unto his son.
24:49 And now**,** if ~~ye will~~ ***thou wilt*** deal kindly and truly with my master, tell me: and if not, tell me; that I may turn to the right hand, or to the left.
24:50 Then Laban and Bethuel answered and said, The thing proceedeth from the Lord: we cannot speak unto thee bad or good.
24:51 Behold, Rebekah is before thee, take her, and go, and let her be thy master's son's wife, as the Lord hath spoken.
24:52 And it came to pass, that, when Abraham's servant heard ~~their~~ ***these*** words, he worshipped the Lord, bowing himself to the earth.
24:53 And the servant brought forth jewels of silver, and jewels of gold, and raiment, and gave them to Rebekah~~:~~**.** ~~h~~***H***e gave also to her brother**,** and to her mother**,** precious things.
24:54 And they did eat and drink, he and the men that were with him, and tarried all night; and they rose up in the morning, and he said, Send me away unto my master.
24:55 And her brother and her mother said, Let the damsel abide with us ~~a few~~ ***at the least ten*** days ~~, at the least ten~~; after that she shall go.
24:56 And he said unto them, Hinder me not, seeing the Lord hath prospered my way; send me away**,** that I may go ***un***to my master.
24:57 And they said, We will call the damsel, and ~~inquire~~ ***enquire*** at her mouth.
24:58 And they called Rebekah, and said unto her, Wilt thou go with this man? And she said, I will go.
24:59 And they sent away Rebekah their sister, and her nurse, and Abraham's servant, and his men.
24:60 And they blessed Rebekah, and said unto her, ***O*** Thou**,** ~~art~~ our sister, be thou ~~the mother~~ ***blessed*** of thousands **--** of millions, and let thy seed possess the gate of those ~~which~~ ***who*** hate them.
24:61 And Rebekah arose, and her damsels, and they rode upon the camels, and followed the man: and the servant took Rebekah, and went his way.
24:62 And Isaac came from the way of the well La-hai-roi; for he dwelt in the south country.
24:63 And Isaac went out to meditate in the field at the eventide: and he lifted up his eyes, and saw, and, behold, the camels ~~were~~ coming.
24:64 And Rebekah lifted up her eyes, and when she saw Isaac, she lighted off the camel.
24:65 For she ~~had~~ said unto the servant, What man is this that walketh in the field to meet us? And the servant had said, It is my master: therefore she took a veil, and covered herself.
24:66 And the servant told Isaac all things that he had done.
24:67 And Isaac brought her into his mother Sarah's tent, and took Rebekah, and she became his wife; and he loved her: and Isaac was comforted after his mother's death.

ABRAHAM'S SONS BY KETURAH

25:1 Then again Abraham took a wife, and her name was Keturah.
25:2 And she bare him Zimran, and Jokshan, and Medan, and Midian, and Ishbak, and Shuah.
25:3 And Jokshan begat Sheba, and Dedan. And the sons of Dedan were Asshurim, and Letushim, and Leummim.

25:4 And the sons of Midian; Ephah, and Epher, and Hanoch, and Abidah, and Eldaah. All these were the children of Keturah.
25:5 And Abraham gave all that he had unto Isaac.
25:6 But unto the sons of the concubines, which Abraham had, Abraham gave gifts, and sent them away from Isaac his son, while he yet lived, eastward, unto the east country.
25:7 And these are the ~~days~~ ***number*** of the years of Abraham's life, which he lived, ~~an~~ ***a*** hundred threescore and fifteen years.

DEATH OF ABRAHAM

25:8 Then Abraham gave up the ghost, and died in a good old age, an old man, and full of years; and was gathered to his people.
25:9 And his sons Isaac and Ishmael buried him in the cave of Machpelah, in the field of Ephron the son of Zohar the Hittite, which is before Mamre;
25:10 The field which Abraham purchased of the sons of Heth: there was Abraham buried, and Sarah his wife.
25:11 And it came to pass after the death of Abraham, that God blessed his son Isaac; and Isaac dwelt by the well Lahairoi.

THE LINE OF ISHMAEL

25:12 Now these are the generations of Ishmael, Abraham's son, whom Hagar the Egyptian, Sarah's handmaid, bare unto Abraham:
25:13 And these are the names of the sons of Ishmael, by their names, according to their generations: the firstborn of Ishmael, Nebajoth; and Kedar, and Adbeel, and Mibsam,
25:14 And Mishma, and Dumah, and Massa,
25:15 Hadar, and Tema, Jetur, Naphish, and Kedemah:
25:16 These are the sons of Ishmael, and these are their names, by their towns, and by their castles; twelve princes according to their nations.
25:17 And these are the ***number of the*** years of the life of Ishmael, ~~an~~ ***a*** hundred and thirty and seven years: and he gave up the ghost and died; and was gathered unto his people.
25:18 And they dwelt from Havilah unto Shur, that is before Egypt, as thou goest toward Assyria: and he died in the presence of all his brethren.

BIRTH OF JACOB AND ESAU

25:19 And these are the generations of Isaac, Abraham's son: Abraham begat Isaac:
25:20 And Isaac was forty years old when he took Rebekah to wife, the daughter of Bethuel the Syrian of Padanaram, the sister to Laban the Syrian.
25:21 And Isaac entreated the Lord for his wife, ***that she might bare children,*** because she was barren: and the Lord was entreated of him, and Rebekah his wife conceived.
25:22 And the children struggled together within her ***womb***; and she said, If ~~it be so~~ ***I am with child***, why ~~am I~~ ***is it*** thus ***with me***? And she went to ~~inquire~~ ***enquire*** of the Lord.
25:23 And the Lord said unto her, Two nations are in thy womb, and two manner of people shall be separated from thy bowels; and the one people shall be stronger than the other people; and the elder shall serve the younger.
25:24 And when her days to be delivered were fulfilled, behold, there were twins in her womb.

25:25 And the first came out red, all over like ~~an~~ ***a*** hairy garment; and they called
his name Esau.
25:26 And after that came his brother out, and his hand took hold on Esau's heel;
and his name was called Jacob: and Isaac was threescore years old when she bare
them.
25:27 And the boys grew: and Esau was a cunning hunter, a man of the field; and
Jacob was a plain man, dwelling in tents.
25:28 And Isaac loved Esau, because he did eat of his venison: but Rebekah loved
Jacob.

ESAU SELLS HIS BIRTHRIGHT

25:29 And Jacob sod pottage: and Esau came from the field, and he was faint:
25:30 And Esau said to Jacob, Feed me, I pray thee, with that same red pottage;
for I am faint: therefore was his name called Edom.
25:31 And Jacob said, Sell me this day thy birthright.
25:32 And Esau said, Behold, I am at the point ~~to die:~~ ***of dying;*** and what ~~profit~~
shall this birthright ~~do to~~ ***profit*** me?
25:33 And Jacob said, Swear to me this day; and he sware unto him: and he sold
his birthright unto Jacob.
25:34 Then Jacob gave Esau bread and pottage of lentiles; and he did eat and
drink, and rose up, and went his way: thus Esau despised his birthright.

ISAAC AND ABIMELECH

26:1 And there was a famine in the land, beside the first famine that was in the
days of Abraham. And Isaac went unto Abimelech king of the Philistines unto
Gerar.
26:2 And the Lord appeared unto him, and said, Go not down into Egypt; dwell
in the land which I shall tell thee of:
26:3 Sojourn in this land, and I will be with thee, and will bless thee; for unto
thee, and unto thy seed, I will give all these countries, and I will perform the oath
which I sware unto Abraham thy father;
26:4 And I will make thy seed to multiply as the stars of heaven, and will give
unto thy seed all these countries; and in thy seed shall all the nations of the earth
be blessed;
26:5 Because that Abraham obeyed my voice, and kept my charge, my
commandments, my statutes, and my laws.
26:6 And Isaac dwelt in Gerar:
26:7 And the men of the place asked him ~~of~~ ***concerning*** his wife; and he said,
She is my sister: for he feared to say, She is my wife; lest, ~~said he,~~ the men of the
place should kill me for ***to get*** Rebekah; because she was fair to look upon.
26:8 And it came to pass, when he had been there a long time, that Abimelech
king of the Philistines looked out at a window, and saw, and, behold, Isaac was
sporting with Rebekah his wife.
26:9 And Abimelech called Isaac, and said, Behold, of a surety she is thy wife:
and how saidst thou, She is my sister? And Isaac said unto him, ***I said it*** Because
I ~~said,~~ ***feared*** Lest I die for her.
26:10 And Abimelech said, What is this thou hast done unto us? one of the people
might lightly have lien with thy wife, and thou shouldest have brought guiltiness
upon us.
26:11 And Abimelech charged all his people, saying, He that toucheth this man
or his wife shall surely be put to death.
26:12 Then Isaac sowed in that land, and received in the same year ~~an~~ ***a***
hundredfold: and the Lord blessed him.

26:13 And the man waxed great, and went forward, and grew until he became very great:
26:14 For he had possession of flocks, and possession of herds, and great store of servants: and the Philistines envied him.
26:15 For all the wells which his father's servants had digged in the days of Abraham his father, the Philistines had stopped them, and filled them with earth.
26:16 And Abimelech said unto Isaac, Go from us; for thou art much mightier than we.
26:17 And Isaac departed thence, and pitched his tent in the valley of Gerar, and dwelt there.
26:18 And Isaac digged again the wells of water, which they had digged in the days of Abraham his father; for the Philistines had stopped them after the death of Abraham: and he called their names after the names by which his father had called them.
26:19 And Isaac's servants digged in the valley, and found there a well of springing water.
26:20 And the herdmen of Gerar did strive with Isaac's herdmen, saying, The water is ours: and he called the name of the well Esek; because they strove with him.
26:21 And they digged another well, and strove for that also: and he called the name of it Sitnah.
26:22 And he removed from thence, and digged another well; and for that they strove not: and he called the name of it Rehoboth; and he said, For now the Lord hath made room for us, and we shall be fruitful in the land.

ISAAC IN BEERSHEBA

26:23 And he went up from thence to Beersheba.
26:24 And the Lord appeared unto him the same night, and said, I am the God of Abraham thy father: fear not, for I am with thee, and will bless thee, and multiply thy seed for my servant Abraham's sake.
26:25 And he builded an altar there, and called upon the name of the Lord, and pitched his tent there: and there Isaac's servants digged a well.
26:26 Then Abimelech went to him from Gerar, and Ahuzzath one of his friends, and Phichol the chief captain of his army.
26:27 And Isaac said unto them, Wherefore come ye to me, seeing ye hate me, and have sent me away from you?
26:28 And they said, We saw certainly that the Lord was with thee: and we said, Let there be now an oath betwixt us, even betwixt us and thee, and let us make a covenant with thee;
26:29 That thou wilt do us no hurt, as we have not touched thee, and as we have done unto thee nothing but good, and have sent thee away in peace: thou art now the blessed of the Lord.
26:30 And he made them a feast, and they did eat and drink.
26:31 And they rose up betimes in the morning, and sware one to another: and Isaac sent them away, and they departed from him in peace.
26:32 And it came to pass the same day, that Isaac's servants came, and told him concerning the well which they had digged, and said unto him, We have found water.
26:33 And he called it Shebah: therefore the name of the city is Beersheba unto this day.
26:34 And Esau was forty years old when he took to wife Judith the daughter of Beeri the Hittite, and Bashemath the daughter of Elon the Hittite:
26:35 Which were a grief of mind unto Isaac and to Rebekah.

ISAAC BLESSES JACOB

27:1 And it came to pass, that when Isaac was old, and his eyes were dim, so that
he could not see, he called Esau his eldest son, and said unto him, My son: and he
said unto him, Behold, here am I.
27:2 And he said, Behold now, I am old, I know not the day of my death:
27:3 Now therefore take, I pray thee, thy weapons, thy quiver and thy bow, and
go out to the field, and take me some venison;
27:4 And make me savoury meat, such as I love, and bring it to me, that I may
eat; that my soul may bless thee before I die.
27:5 And Rebekah heard when Isaac spake to Esau his son. And Esau went to the
field to hunt for venison, and to bring it.
27:6 And Rebekah spake unto Jacob her son, saying, Behold, I heard thy father
speak unto Esau thy brother, saying,
27:7 Bring me venison, and make me savoury meat, that I may eat, and bless thee
before the LORD before my death.
27:8 Now therefore, my son, obey my voice according to that which I command
thee.
27:9 Go now to the flock, and fetch me from thence two good kids of the goats;
and I will make them savoury meat for thy father, such as he loveth:
27:10 And thou shalt bring it to thy father, that he may eat, and that he may bless
thee before his death.
27:11 And Jacob said to Rebekah his mother, Behold, Esau my brother is a hairy
man, and I am a smooth man:
27:12 My father peradventure will feel me, and I shall seem to him as a deceiver;
and I shall bring a curse upon me, and not a blessing.
27:13 And his mother said unto him, Upon me be thy curse, my son: only obey my
voice, and go fetch me them.
27:14 And he went, and fetched, and brought them to his mother: and his mother
made savoury meat, such as his father loved.
27:15 And Rebekah took goodly raiment of her eldest son Esau, which were with
her in the house, and put them upon Jacob her younger son:
27:16 And she put the skins of the kids of the goats upon his hands, and upon the
smooth of his neck:
27:17 And she gave the savoury meat and the bread, which she had prepared, into
the hand of her son Jacob.
27:18 And he came unto his father, and said, My father: and he said, Here am I;
who art thou, my son?
27:19 And Jacob said unto his father, I am Esau thy firstborn; I have done
according as thou badest me: arise, I pray thee, sit and eat of my venison, that thy
soul may bless me.
27:20 And Isaac said unto his son, How is it that thou hast found it so quickly, my
son? And he said, Because the LORD thy God brought it to me.
27:21 And Isaac said unto Jacob, Come near, I pray thee, that I may feel thee, my
son, whether thou be my very son Esau or not.
27:22 And Jacob went near unto Isaac his father; and he felt him, and said, The
voice is Jacob's voice, but the hands are the hands of Esau.
27:23 And he discerned him not, because his hands were hairy, as his brother
Esau's hands: so he blessed him.
27:24 And he said, Art thou my very son Esau? And he said, I am.
27:25 And he said, Bring it near to me, and I will eat of my son's venison, that my
soul may bless thee. And he brought it near to him, and he did eat: and he brought
him wine, and he drank.
27:26 And his father Isaac said unto him, Come near now, and kiss me, my son.
27:27 And he came near, and kissed him: and he smelled the smell of his raiment,
and blessed him, and said, See, the smell of my son is as the smell of a field which
the LORD hath blessed:

27:28 Therefore God give thee of the dew of heaven, and the fatness of the earth,
and plenty of corn and wine:
27:29 Let people serve thee, and nations bow down to thee: be lord over thy
brethren, and let thy mother's sons bow down to thee: cursed be every one that
curseth thee, and blessed be he that blesseth thee.
27:30 And it came to pass, as soon as Isaac had made an end of blessing Jacob, and
Jacob was yet scarce gone out from the presence of Isaac his father, that Esau his
brother came in from his hunting.
27:31 And he also had made savoury meat, and brought it unto his father, and said
unto his father, Let my father arise, and eat of his son's venison, that thy soul may
bless me.
27:32 And Isaac his father said unto him, Who art thou? And he said, I am thy son,
thy firstborn Esau.
27:33 And Isaac trembled very exceedingly, and said, Who? where is he that hath
taken venison, and brought it me, and I have eaten of all before thou camest, and
have blessed him? yea, and he shall be blessed.
27:34 And when Esau heard the words of his father, he cried with a great and
exceeding bitter cry, and said unto his father, Bless me, even me also, O my father.
27:35 And he said, Thy brother came with subtlety, and hath taken away thy
blessing.
27:36 And he said, Is not he rightly named Jacob? for he hath supplanted me these
two times: he took away my birthright; and, behold, now he hath taken away my
blessing. And he said, Hast thou not reserved a blessing for me?
27:37 And Isaac answered and said unto Esau, Behold, I have made him thy lord,
and all his brethren have I given to him for servants; and with corn and wine have
I sustained him: and what shall I do now unto thee, my son?
27:38 And Esau said unto his father, Hast thou but one blessing, my father? bless
me, even me also, O my father. And Esau lifted up his voice, and wept.
27:39 And Isaac his father answered and said unto him, Behold, thy dwelling shall
be the fatness of the earth, and of the dew of heaven from above;
27:40 And by thy sword shalt thou live, and shalt serve thy brother; and it shall
come to pass when thou shalt have the dominion, that thou shalt break his yoke
from off thy neck.
27:41 And Esau hated Jacob because of the blessing wherewith his father blessed
him: and Esau said in his heart, The days of mourning for my father are at hand;
then will I slay my brother Jacob.

JACOB IS SENT TO LABAN

27:42 And these words of Esau her elder son were told to Rebekah: and she sent
and called Jacob her younger son, and said unto him, Behold, thy brother Esau,
as touching thee, doth comfort himself, purposing to kill thee.
27:43 Now therefore, my son, obey my voice; and arise, flee thou to Laban my
brother to Haran;
27:44 And tarry with him a few days, until thy brother's fury turn away;
27:45 Until thy brother's anger turn away from thee, and he forget that which thou
hast done to him: then I will send, and fetch thee from thence: why should I be
deprived also of you both in one day?
27:46 And Rebekah said to Isaac, I am weary of my life because of the daughters
of Heth: if Jacob take a wife of the daughters of Heth, such as these which are of
the daughters of the land, what good shall my life do me?
28:1 And Isaac called Jacob, and blessed him, and charged him, and said unto
him, Thou shalt not take a wife of the daughters of Canaan.
28:2 Arise, go to Padanaram, to the house of Bethuel thy mother's father; and
take thee a wife from thence of the daughters of Laban thy mother's brother.

28:3 And God Almighty bless thee, and make thee fruitful, and multiply thee, that thou mayest be a multitude of people;
28:4 And give thee the blessing of Abraham, to thee, and to thy seed with thee; that thou mayest inherit the land wherein thou art a stranger, which God gave unto Abraham.
28:5 And Isaac sent away Jacob: and he went to Padanaram unto Laban, son of Bethuel the Syrian, the brother of Rebekah, Jacob's and Esau's mother.
28:6 When Esau saw that Isaac had blessed Jacob, and sent him away to Padanaram, to take him a wife from thence; and that as he blessed him he gave him a charge, saying, Thou shalt not take a wife of the daughters of Canaan;
28:7 And that Jacob obeyed his father and his mother, and was gone to Padanaram;
28:8 And Esau seeing that the daughters of Canaan pleased not Isaac his father;
28:9 Then went Esau unto Ishmael, and took unto the wives which he had Mahalath the daughter of Ishmael Abraham's son, the sister of Nebajoth, to be his wife.

JACOB'S VISION AT BETHEL

28:10 And Jacob went out from Beersheba, and went toward Haran.
28:11 And he lighted upon a certain place, and tarried there all night, because the sun was set; and he took of the stones of that place, and put them for his pillows, and lay down in that place to sleep.
28:12 And he dreamed, and behold a ladder set up on the earth, and the top of it reached to heaven: and behold the angels of God ascending and descending ***up***on it.
28:13 And, behold, the LORD stood above it, and said, I am the LORD God of Abraham thy father, and the God of Isaac: the land whereon thou liest, to thee will I give it, and to thy seed;
28:14 And thy seed shall be as the dust of the earth, and thou shalt spread abroad to the west, and to the east, and to the north, and to the south: and in thee and in thy seed shall all the families of the earth be blessed.
28:15 And, behold, I am with thee, and will keep thee in all places whither thou goest, and will bring thee again into this land; for I will not leave thee, until I have done that which I have spoken to thee of.
28:16 And Jacob awaked out of his sleep, and he said, Surely the LORD is in this place; and I knew it not.
28:17 And he was afraid, and said, How dreadful is this place! this is none other but the house of God, and this is the gate of heaven.
28:18 And Jacob rose up early in the morning, and took the stone that he had put for his pillows, and set it up for a pillar, and poured oil upon the top of it.
28:19 And he called the name of that place Bethel: but the name of that city was called Luz at the first.
28:20 And Jacob vowed a vow, saying, If God will be with me, and will keep me in this way that I go, and will give me bread to eat, and raiment to put on,
28:21 So that I come again to my father's house in peace; then shall the LORD be my God:
28:22 And ***the place of*** this stone, which I have set for a pillar, shall be ***the place of*** God's house: and of all that thou shalt give me I will surely give the tenth unto thee.

JACOB IN HARAN

29:1 Then Jacob went on his journey, and came into the land of the people of the east.
29:2 And he looked, and behold a well in the field, and, lo, there were three flocks of sheep lying by it; for out of that well they watered the flocks: and a great stone was upon the well's mouth.

29:3 And thither were all the flocks gathered: and they rolled the stone from the well's mouth, and watered the sheep, and put the stone again upon the well's mouth in his place.
29:4 And Jacob said unto them, My brethren, ***from*** whence ~~be~~ ***are*** ye? And they said, ~~Of~~ ***From*** Haran ~~are we~~.
29:5 And he said unto them, Know ye Laban the son of Nahor? And they said, We know him.
29:6 And he said unto them, Is he well? And they said, He is well: and, behold, Rachel his daughter cometh with the sheep.
29:7 And he said, Lo, it is yet high day, neither is it time that the cattle should be gathered together: water ye the sheep, and go and feed them.
29:8 And they said, We cannot, until all the flocks be gathered together, and till they roll the stone from the well's mouth; then we water the sheep.
29:9 And while he yet spake with them, Rachel came with her father's sheep: for she kept them.
29:10 And it came to pass, when Jacob saw Rachel the daughter of Laban his mother's brother, and the sheep of Laban his mother's brother, that Jacob went near, and rolled the stone from the well's mouth, and watered the flock of Laban his mother's brother.
29:11 And Jacob kissed Rachel, and lifted up his voice, and wept.
29:12 And Jacob told Rachel that he was her father's brother, and that he was Rebekah's son: and she ran and told her father.
29:13 And it came to pass, when Laban heard the tidings of Jacob his sister's son, that he ran to meet him, and embraced him, and kissed him, and brought him to his house. And he told Laban all these things.
29:14 And Laban said to him, Surely thou art my bone and my flesh. And he abode with him the space of a month.
29:15 And Laban said unto Jacob, Because thou art my brother, shouldest thou therefore serve me for nought? tell me, what shall thy wages be?
29:16 And Laban had two daughters: the name of the elder was Leah, and the name of the younger was Rachel.
29:17 Leah was tender eyed; but Rachel was beautiful and well favoured.
29:18 And Jacob loved Rachel; and said, I will serve thee seven years for Rachel thy younger daughter.
29:19 And Laban said, It is better that I give her to thee, than that I should give her to another man: abide with me.
29:20 And Jacob served seven years for Rachel; and they seemed unto him but a few days, for the love he had to her.

JACOB MARRIES LEAH AND RACHEL

29:21 And Jacob said unto Laban, Give ***unto*** me my wife, ***that I may go and take her,*** for my days ***of serving thee*** are fulfilled~~, that I may go in unto her~~ .
29:22 And Laban ***gave her to Jacob, and*** gathered together all the men of the place, and made a feast.
29:23 And it came to pass in the evening, that he took Leah his daughter, and brought her to ~~him~~ ***Jacob***; and ***s***he went in ~~unto her~~ ***and slept with him***.
29:24 And Laban gave unto his daughter Leah, Zilpah, his ***hand***maid ~~for an~~ ***, to be a*** handmaid ***for her***.
29:25 And it came to pass, that in the morning, behold, it was Leah: and he said to Laban, What is this thou hast done unto me? did not I serve with thee for Rachel? wherefore then hast thou beguiled me?
29:26 And Laban said, It must not be so done in our country, to give the younger before the firstborn.
29:27 Fulfil her week, and we will give thee this also for the service which thou shalt serve with me yet seven other years.

29:28 And Jacob did so, and fulfilled her week: and he gave him Rachel his daughter to wife also.
29:29 And Laban gave to Rachel his daughter Bilhah his handmaid to be her maid.
29:30 And he went in also ~~unto~~ ***and slept with*** Rachel, and he loved ~~also~~ Rachel ***also,*** more than Leah, and served with ~~him~~ ***Laban*** yet seven other years.

JACOB'S CHILDREN

29:31 And when the Lord saw that Leah was hated, he opened her womb: but Rachel was barren.
29:32 And Leah conceived, and bare a son, and she called his name Reuben: for she said, Surely the Lord hath looked upon my affliction; now therefore my husband will love me.
29:33 And she conceived again, and bare a son; and said, Because the Lord hath heard that I was hated, he hath therefore given me this son also: and she called his name Simeon.
29:34 And she conceived again, and bare a son; and said, Now this time will my husband be joined unto me, because I have born him three sons: therefore was his name called Levi.
29:35 And she conceived again, and bare a son: and she said, Now will I praise the Lord: therefore she called his name Judah; and left bearing.
30:1 And when Rachel saw that she bare Jacob no children, Rachel envied her sister; and said unto Jacob, Give me children, or else I die.
30:2 And Jacob's anger was kindled against Rachel: and he said, Am I in God's stead, who hath withheld from thee the fruit of the womb?
30:3 And she said, Behold my maid Bilhah, go in ~~unto~~ ***and lie with*** her; and she shall bear upon my knees, that I may also have children by her.
30:4 And she gave him Bilhah her handmaid to wife: and Jacob went ~~in unto~~ ***and lay with*** her.
30:5 And Bilhah conceived, and bare Jacob a son.
30:6 And Rachel said, God hath judged me, and hath also heard my voice, and hath given me a son: therefore called she his name Dan.
30:7 And Bilhah Rachel's maid conceived again, and bare Jacob a second son.
30:8 And Rachel said, With great wrestlings have I wrestled with my sister, and I have prevailed: and she called his name Naphtali.
30:9 When Leah saw that she had left bearing, she took Zilpah her maid, and gave her ***unto*** Jacob to wife.
30:10 And Zilpah Leah's maid bare Jacob a son.
30:11 And Leah said, A troop cometh: and she called his name Gad.
30:12 And Zilpah Leah's maid bare Jacob a second son.
30:13 And Leah said, Happy am I, for the daughters will call me blessed: and she called his name Asher.
30:14 And Reuben went in the days of wheat harvest, and found mandrakes in the field, and brought them unto his mother Leah. Then Rachel said to Leah, Give me, I pray thee, of thy son's mandrakes.
30:15 And she said unto her, Is it a small matter that thou hast taken my husband? and wouldest thou take away my son's mandrakes also? And Rachel said, Therefore he shall lie with thee to night for thy son's mandrakes.
30:16 And Jacob came out of the field in the evening, and Leah went out to meet him, and said, Thou must come in ~~unto~~ ***and lie with*** me; for surely I have hired thee with my son's mandrakes. And he lay with her that night.
30:17 And God hearkened unto Leah, and she conceived, and bare Jacob the fifth son.
30:18 And Leah said, God hath given me my hire, because I have given my maiden to my husband: and she called his name Issachar.
30:19 And Leah conceived again, and bare Jacob the sixth son.

30:20 And Leah said, God hath endued me with a good dowry; now will my husband dwell with me, because I have born him six sons: and she called his name Zebulun.
30:21 And afterwards she bare a daughter, and called her name Dinah.
30:22 And God remembered Rachel, and God hearkened to her, and opened her womb.
30:23 And she conceived, and bare a son; and said, God hath taken away my reproach:
30:24 And she called his name Joseph; and said, The Lord shall add to me another son.

JACOB'S BARGAIN WITH LABAN

30:25 And it came to pass, when Rachel had born Joseph, that Jacob said unto Laban, Send me away, that I may go unto mine own place, and to my country.
30:26 Give me my wives and my children, for whom I have served thee, and let me go: for thou knowest my service which I have done thee.
30:27 And Laban said unto him, I pray thee, if I have found favour in thine eyes, tarry: for I have learned by experience that the Lord hath blessed me for thy sake.
30:28 And he said, Appoint me thy wages, and I will give it.
30:29 And he said unto him, Thou knowest how I have served thee, and how thy cattle was with me.
30:30 For it was little which thou hadst before I came, and it is now increased unto a multitude; and the Lord hath blessed thee since my coming: and now when shall I provide for mine own house also?
30:31 And he said, What shall I give thee? And Jacob said, Thou shalt not give me any thing: if thou wilt do this thing for me, I will again feed and keep thy flock.
30:32 I will pass through all thy flock to day, removing from thence all the speckled and spotted cattle, and all the brown cattle among the sheep, and the spotted and speckled among the goats: and of such shall be my hire.
30:33 So shall my righteousness answer for me in time to come, when it shall come for my hire before thy face: every one that is not speckled and spotted among the goats, and brown among the sheep, that shall be counted stolen with me.
30:34 And Laban said, Behold, I would it might be according to thy word.
30:35 And he removed that day the he goats that were ringstreaked and spotted, and all the she goats that were speckled and spotted, and every one that had some white in it, and all the brown among the sheep, and gave them into the hand of his sons.
30:36 And he set three days' journey betwixt himself and Jacob: and Jacob fed the rest of Laban's flocks.
30:37 And Jacob took him rods of green poplar, and of the hazel and chestnut tree; and pilled white streaks in them, and made the white appear which was in the rods.
30:38 And he set the rods which he had pilled before the flocks in the gutters in the watering troughs when the flocks came to drink, that they should conceive when they came to drink.
30:39 And the flocks conceived before the rods, and brought forth cattle ringstreaked, speckled, and spotted.
30:40 And Jacob did separate the lambs, and set the faces of the flocks toward the ringstreaked, and all the brown in the flock of Laban; and he put his own flocks by themselves, and put them not unto Laban's cattle.
30:41 And it came to pass, whensoever the stronger cattle did conceive, that Jacob laid the rods before the eyes of the cattle in the gutters, that they might conceive among the rods.

30:42 But when the cattle were feeble, he put them not in: so the feebler were Laban's, and the stronger Jacob's.
30:43 And the man increased exceedingly, and had much cattle, and maidservants, and menservants, and camels, and asses.
31:1 And he heard the words of Laban's sons, saying, Jacob hath taken away all that was our father's; and of that which was our father's hath he gotten all this glory.
31:2 And Jacob beheld the countenance of Laban, and, behold, it was not toward him as before.
31:3 And the LORD said unto Jacob, Return unto the land of thy fathers, and to thy kindred; and I will be with thee.
31:4 And Jacob sent and called Rachel and Leah to the field unto his flock,
31:5 And said unto them, I see your father's countenance, that it is not toward me as before; but the God of my father hath been with me.
31:6 And ye know that with all my power I have served your father.
31:7 And your father hath deceived me, and changed my wages ten times; but God suffered him not to hurt me.
31:8 If he said thus, The speckled shall be thy wages; then all the cattle bare speckled: and if he said thus, The ringstreaked shall be thy hire; then bare all the cattle ringstreaked.
31:9 Thus God hath taken away the cattle of your father, and given them to me.
31:10 And it came to pass at the time that the cattle conceived, that I lifted up mine eyes, and saw in a dream, and, behold, the rams which leaped upon the cattle were ringstreaked, speckled, and grisled.
31:11 And the angel of God spake unto me in a dream, saying, Jacob: And I said, Here am I.
31:12 And he said, Lift up now thine eyes, and see, all the rams which leap upon the cattle are ringstreaked, speckled, and grisled: for I have seen all that Laban doeth unto thee.
31:13 I am the God of Bethel, where thou anointedst the pillar, and where thou vowedst a vow unto me: now arise, get thee out from this land, and return unto the land of thy kindred.
31:14 And Rachel and Leah answered and said unto him, Is there yet any portion or inheritance for us in our father's house?
31:15 Are we not counted of him strangers? for he hath sold us, and hath quite devoured also our money.
31:16 For all the riches which God hath taken from our father, that is ours, and our children's: now then, whatsoever God hath said unto thee, do.

JACOB LEAVES LABAN

31:17 Then Jacob rose up, and set his sons and his wives upon camels;
31:18 And he carried away all his cattle, and all his goods which he had gotten, the cattle of his getting, which he had gotten in Padanaram, for to go to Isaac his father in the land of Canaan.
31:19 And Laban went to shear his sheep: and Rachel had stolen the images that were her father's.
31:20 And Jacob stole away unawares to Laban the Syrian, in that he told him not that he fled.
31:21 So he fled with all that he had; and he rose up, and passed over the river, and set his face toward the mount Gilead.
31:22 And it was told Laban on the third day, that Jacob ~~was~~ ***had*** fled.
31:23 And he took his brethren with him, and pursued after him seven days' journey; and they overtook him in the mount Gilead.
31:24 And God came to Laban the Syrian in a dream by night, and said unto him, Take heed that thou speak not to Jacob either good or bad.

LABAN'S PURSUIT

31:25 Then Laban overtook Jacob. Now Jacob had pitched his tent in the mount: and Laban with his brethren pitched in the mount of Gilead.
31:26 And Laban said to Jacob, What hast thou done, that thou hast stolen away unawares to me, and carried away my daughters, as captives taken with the sword?
31:27 Wherefore didst thou flee away secretly, and steal away from me; and didst not tell me, that I might have sent thee away with mirth, and with songs, with tabret, and with harp?
31:28 And hast not suffered me to kiss my sons and my daughters? thou hast now done foolishly in so doing.
31:29 It is in the power of my hand to do you hurt: but the God of your father spake unto me yesternight, saying, Take thou heed that thou speak not to Jacob either good or bad.
31:30 And now, though thou wouldest needs be gone, because thou sore longedst after thy father's house, yet wherefore hast thou stolen my gods?
31:31 And Jacob answered and said to Laban, Because I was afraid: for I said, Peradventure thou wouldest take by force thy daughters from me.
31:32 With whomsoever thou findest thy gods, let him not live: before our brethren discern thou what is thine with me, and take it to thee. For Jacob knew not that Rachel had stolen them.
31:33 And Laban went into Jacob's tent, and into Leah's tent, and into the two maidservants' tents; but he found them not. Then went he out of Leah's tent, and entered into Rachel's tent.
31:34 Now Rachel had taken the images, and put them in the camel's furniture, and sat upon them. And Laban searched all the tent, but found them not.
31:35 And she said to her father, Let it not displease my lord that I cannot rise up before thee; for the custom of women is upon me. And he searched, but found not the images.
31:36 And Jacob was wroth, and chided with Laban: and Jacob answered and said to Laban, What is my trespass? what is my sin, that thou hast so hotly pursued after me?
31:37 Whereas thou hast searched all my stuff, what hast thou found of all thy household stuff? set it here before my brethren and thy brethren, that they may judge betwixt us both.
31:38 This twenty years have I been with thee; thy ewes and thy she goats have not cast their young, and the rams of thy flock have I not eaten.
31:39 That which was torn of beasts I brought not unto thee; I bare the loss of it; of my hand didst thou require it, whether stolen by day, or stolen by night.
31:40 Thus I was; in the day the drought consumed me, and the frost by night; and my sleep departed from mine eyes.
31:41 Thus have I been twenty years in thy house; I served thee fourteen years for thy two daughters, and six years for thy cattle: and thou hast changed my wages ten times.
31:42 Except the God of my father, the God of Abraham, and the fear of Isaac, had been with me, surely thou hadst sent me away now empty. God hath seen mine affliction and the labour of my hands, and rebuked thee yesternight.

CONTRACT BETWEEN JACOB AND LABAN

31:43 And Laban answered and said unto Jacob, These daughters are my daughters, and these children are my children, and these cattle are my cattle, and all that thou seest is mine: and what can I do this day unto these my daughters, or unto their children which they have born?
31:44 Now therefore come thou, let us make a covenant, I and thou; and let it be for a witness between me and thee.

31:45 And Jacob took a stone, and set it up for a pillar.
31:46 And Jacob said unto his brethren, Gather stones; and they took stones, and made an heap: and they did eat there upon the heap.
31:47 And Laban called it Jegarsahadutha: but Jacob called it Galeed.
31:48 And Laban said, This heap is a witness between me and thee this day. Therefore was the name of it called Galeed;
31:49 And Mizpah; for he said, The Lord watch between me and thee, when we are absent one from another.
31:50 If thou shalt afflict my daughters, or if thou shalt take other wives beside my daughters, no man is with us; see, God is witness betwixt me and thee.
31:51 And Laban said to Jacob, Behold this heap, and behold this pillar, which I have cast betwixt me and thee;
31:52 This heap be witness, and this pillar be witness, that I will not pass over this heap to thee, and that thou shalt not pass over this heap and this pillar unto me, for harm.
31:53 The God of Abraham, and the God of Nahor, the God of their father, judge betwixt us. And Jacob sware by the fear of his father Isaac.
31:54 Then Jacob offered sacrifice upon the mount, and called his brethren to eat bread: and they did eat bread, and tarried all night in the mount.
31:55 And early in the morning Laban rose up, and kissed his sons and his daughters, and blessed them: and Laban departed, and returned unto his place.

JACOB PREPARES TO MEET ESAU

32:1 And Jacob went on his way, and the angels of God met him.
32:2 And when Jacob saw them, he said, This is God's host: and he called the name of that place Mahanaim.
32:3 And Jacob sent messengers before him to Esau his brother unto the land of Seir, the country of Edom.
32:4 And he commanded them, saying, Thus shall ye speak unto my lord Esau; Thy servant Jacob saith thus, I have sojourned with Laban, and stayed there until now:
32:5 And I have oxen, and asses, flocks, and menservants, and womenservants: and I have sent to tell my lord, that I may find grace in thy sight.
32:6 And the messengers returned to Jacob, saying, We came to thy brother Esau, and also he cometh to meet thee, and four hundred men with him.
32:7 Then Jacob was greatly afraid and distressed: and he divided the people that was with him, and the flocks, and herds, and the camels, into two bands;
32:8 And said, If Esau come to the one company, and smite it, then the other company which is left shall escape.
32:9 And Jacob said, O God of my father Abraham, and God of my father Isaac, the Lord which saidst unto me, Return unto thy country, and to thy kindred, and I will deal well with thee:
32:10 I am not worthy of the least of all the mercies, and of all the truth, which thou hast ~~shewed~~ ***showed*** unto thy servant; for with my staff I passed over this Jordan; and now I am become two bands.
32:11 Deliver me, I pray thee, from the hand of my brother, from the hand of Esau: for I fear him, lest he will come and smite me, and the mother*s* with the children.
32:12 And thou saidst, I will surely do thee good, and make thy seed as the sand of the sea, which cannot be numbered for multitude.
32:13 And he lodged there that same night; and took of that which came to his hand a present for Esau his brother;
32:14 Two hundred she goats, and twenty he goats, two hundred ewes, and twenty rams,
32:15 Thirty milch camels with their colts, forty kine, and ten bulls, twenty she asses, and ten foals.

32:16 And he delivered them into the hand of his servants, every drove by themselves; and said unto his servants, Pass over before me, and put a space betwixt drove and drove.
32:17 And he commanded the foremost, saying, When Esau my brother meeteth thee, and asketh thee, saying, Whose art thou? and whither goest thou? and whose are these before thee?
32:18 Then thou shalt say, They be thy servant Jacob's; it is a present sent unto my lord Esau: and, behold, also he is behind us.
32:19 And so commanded he the second, and the third, and all that followed the droves, saying, On this manner shall ye speak unto Esau, when ye find him.
32:20 And say ye moreover, Behold, thy servant Jacob is behind us. For he said, I will appease him with the present that goeth before me, and afterward I will see his face; peradventure he will accept of me.
32:21 So went the present over before him: and himself lodged that night in the company.
32:22 And he rose up that night, and took his two wives, and his two womenservants, and his eleven sons, and passed over the ford Jabbok.
32:23 And he took them, and sent them over the brook, and sent over that he had.

JACOB WRESTLES

32:24 And Jacob was left alone; and there wrestled a man with him until the breaking of the day.
32:25 And when he saw that he prevailed not against him, he touched the hollow of his thigh; and the hollow of Jacob's thigh was out of joint, as he wrestled with him.
32:26 And he said, Let me go, for the day breaketh. And he said, I will not let thee go, except thou bless me.
32:27 And he said unto him, What is thy name? And he said, Jacob.
32:28 And he said, Thy name shall be called no more Jacob, but Israel: for as a prince hast thou power with God and with men, and hast prevailed.
32:29 And Jacob asked him, and said, Tell me, I pray thee, thy name. And he said, Wherefore is it that thou dost ask after my name? And he blessed him there.
32:30 And Jacob called the name of the place Peniel: for I have seen God face to face, and my life is preserved.
32:31 And as he passed over Penuel the sun rose upon him, and he halted upon his thigh.
32:32 Therefore the children of Israel eat not of the sinew which shrank, which is upon the hollow of the thigh, unto this day: because he touched the hollow of Jacob's thigh in the sinew that shrank.

JACOB MEETS ESAU

33:1 And Jacob lifted up his eyes, and looked, and, behold, Esau came, and with him four hundred men. And he divided the children unto Leah, and unto Rachel, and unto the two handmaids.
33:2 And he put the handmaids and their children foremost, and Leah and her children after, and Rachel and Joseph hindermost.
33:3 And he passed over before them, and bowed himself to the ground seven times, until he came near to his brother.
33:4 And Esau ran to meet him, and embraced him, and fell on his neck, and kissed him: and they wept.
33:5 And he lifted up his eyes, and saw the women and the children; and said, Who are those with thee? And he said, The children which God hath graciously given thy servant.

33:6 Then the handmaidens came near, they and their children, and they bowed themselves.
33:7 And Leah also with her children came near, and bowed themselves: and after came Joseph near and Rachel, and they bowed themselves.
33:8 And he said, What meanest thou by all this drove which I met? And he said, These are to find grace in the sight of my lord.
33:9 And Esau said, I have enough, my brother; keep that thou hast unto thyself.
33:10 And Jacob said, Nay, I pray thee, if now I have found grace in thy sight, then receive my present at my hand: for therefore I have seen thy face, as though I had seen the face of God, and thou wast pleased with me.
33:11 Take, I pray thee, my blessing that is brought to thee; because God hath dealt graciously with me, and because I have enough. And he urged him, and he took it.
33:12 And he said, Let us take our journey, and let us go, and I will go before thee.
33:13 And he said unto him, My lord knoweth that the children are tender, and the flocks and herds with young are with me: and if men should overdrive them one day, all the flock will die.
33:14 Let my lord, I pray thee, pass over before his servant: and I will lead on softly, according as the cattle that goeth before me and the children be able to endure, until I come unto my lord unto Seir.
33:15 And Esau said, Let me now leave with thee some of the folk that are with me. And he said, What needeth it? let me find grace in the sight of my lord.
33:16 So Esau returned that day on his way unto Seir.
33:17 And Jacob journeyed to Succoth, and built him ~~an~~ ***a*** house, and made booths for his cattle: therefore the name of the place is called Succoth.
33:18 And Jacob came to Shalem, a city of Shechem, which is in the land of Canaan, when he came from Padanaram; and pitched his tent before the city.
33:19 And he bought a parcel of a field, where he had spread his tent, at the hand of the children of Hamor, Shechem's father, for an hundred pieces of money.
33:20 And he erected there an altar, and called it Elelohe-Israel.

JACOB'S SONS REVENGE DINAH

34:1 And Dinah the daughter of Leah, which she bare unto Jacob, went out to see the daughters of the land.
34:2 And when Shechem the son of Hamor the Hivite, prince of the country, saw her, he took her, and lay with her, and defiled her.
34:3 And his soul clave unto Dinah the daughter of Jacob, and he loved the damsel, and spake kindly unto the damsel.
34:4 And Shechem spake unto his father Hamor, saying, Get me this damsel to wife.
34:5 And Jacob heard that he had defiled Dinah his daughter: now his sons were with his cattle in the field: and Jacob held his peace until they were come.
34:6 And Hamor the father of Shechem went out unto Jacob to commune with him.
34:7 And the sons of Jacob came out of the field when they heard it: and the men were grieved, and they were very wroth, because he had wrought folly in Israel in lying with Jacob's daughter; which thing ought not to be done.
34:8 And Hamor communed with them, saying, The soul of my son Shechem longeth for your daughter: I pray you give her him to wife.
34:9 And make ye marriages with us, and give your daughters unto us, and take our daughters unto you.
34:10 And ye shall dwell with us: and the land shall be before you; dwell and trade ye therein, and get you possessions therein.
34:11 And Shechem said unto her father and unto her brethren, Let me find grace in your eyes, and what ye shall say unto me I will give.

34:12 Ask me never so much dowry and gift, and I will give according as ye shall say unto me: but give me the damsel to wife.
34:13 And the sons of Jacob answered Shechem and Hamor his father deceitfully, and said, because he had defiled Dinah their sister:
34:14 And they said unto them, We cannot do this thing, to give our sister to one that is uncircumcised; for that were a reproach unto us:
34:15 But in this will we consent unto you: If ye will be as we be, that every male of you be circumcised;
34:16 Then will we give our daughters unto you, and we will take your daughters to us, and we will dwell with you, and we will become one people.
34:17 But if ye will not hearken unto us, to be circumcised; then will we take our daughter, and we will be gone.
34:18 And their words pleased Hamor, and Shechem Hamor's son.
34:19 And the young man deferred not to do the thing, because he had delight in Jacob's daughter: and he was more honourable than all the house of his father.
34:20 And Hamor and Shechem his son came unto the gate of their city, and communed with the men of their city, saying,
34:21 These men are peaceable with us; therefore let them dwell in the land, and trade therein; for the land, behold, it is large enough for them; let us take their daughters to us for wives, and let us give them our daughters.
34:22 Only herein will the men consent unto us for to dwell with us, to be one people, if every male among us be circumcised, as they are circumcised.
34:23 Shall not their cattle and their substance and every beast of theirs be ours? only let us consent unto them, and they will dwell with us.
34:24 And unto Hamor and unto Shechem his son hearkened all that went out of the gate of his city; and every male was circumcised, all that went out of the gate of his city.
34:25 And it came to pass on the third day, when they were sore, that two of the sons of Jacob, Simeon and Levi, Dinah's brethren, took each man his sword, and came upon the city boldly, and slew all the males.
34:26 And they slew Hamor and Shechem his son with the edge of the sword, and took Dinah out of Shechem's house, and went out.
34:27 The sons of Jacob came upon the slain, and spoiled the city, because they had defiled their sister.
34:28 They took their sheep, and their oxen, and their asses, and that which was in the city, and that which was in the field,
34:29 And all their wealth, and all their little ones, and their wives took they captive, and spoiled even all that was in the house.
34:30 And Jacob said to Simeon and Levi, Ye have troubled me to make me to stink among the inhabitants of the land, among the Canaanites and the Perizzites: and I being few in number, they shall gather themselves together against me, and slay me; and I shall be destroyed, I and my house.
34:31 And they said, Should he deal with our sister as with ~~an~~ ***a*** harlot?

JACOB VISITS BETHEL

35:1 And God said unto Jacob, Arise, go up to Bethel, and dwell there: and make there an altar unto God, that appeared unto thee when thou fleddest from the face of Esau thy brother.
35:2 Then Jacob said unto his household, and to all that were with him, Put away the strange gods that are among you, and be clean, and change your garments:
35:3 And let us arise, and go up to Bethel; and I will make there an altar unto God, who answered me in the day of my distress, and was with me in the way which I went.

35:4 And they gave unto Jacob all the strange gods which were in their hand, and all their earrings which were in their ears; and Jacob hid them under the oak which was by Shechem.
35:5 And they journeyed: and the terror of God was upon the cities that were round about them, and they did not pursue after the sons of Jacob.
35:6 So Jacob came to Luz, which is in the land of Canaan, that is, Bethel, he and all the people that were with him.
35:7 And he built there an altar, and called the place Elbethel: because there God appeared unto him, when he fled from the face of his brother.
35:8 But Deborah Rebekah's nurse died, and she was buried beneath Bethel under an oak: and the name of it was called Allonbachuth.
35:9 And God appeared unto Jacob again, when he came out of Padanaram, and blessed him.
35:10 And God said unto him, Thy name is Jacob: thy name shall not be called any more Jacob, but Israel shall be thy name: and he called his name Israel.
35:11 And God said unto him, I am God Almighty: be fruitful and multiply; a nation and a company of nations shall be of thee, and kings shall come out of thy loins;
35:12 And the land which I gave Abraham and Isaac, to thee I will give it, and to thy seed after thee will I give the land.
35:13 And God went up from him in the place where he talked with him.
35:14 And Jacob set up a pillar in the place where he talked with him, even a pillar of stone: and he poured a drink offering thereon, and he poured oil thereon.
35:15 And Jacob called the name of the place where God spake with him, Bethel.

DEATH AND BURIAL OF RACHEL

35:16 And they journeyed from Bethel; and there was but a little way to come to Ephrath: and Rachel travailed, and she had hard labour.
35:17 And it came to pass, when she was in hard labour, that the midwife said unto her, Fear not; thou shalt have this son also.
35:18 And it came to pass, as her soul was in departing, (for she died) that she called his name Benoni: but his father called him Benjamin.
35:19 And Rachel died, and was buried in the way to Ephrath, which is Bethlehem.
35:20 And Jacob set a pillar upon her grave: that is the pillar of Rachel's grave unto this day.
35:21 And Israel journeyed, and spread his tent beyond the tower of Edar.
35:22a And it came to pass, when Israel dwelt in that land, that Reuben went and lay with Bilhah his father's concubine: and Israel heard it.

SONS OF JACOB

35:22b Now the sons of Jacob were twelve:
35:23 The sons of Leah; Reuben, Jacob's firstborn, and Simeon, and Levi, and Judah, and Issachar, and Zebulun:
35:24 The sons of Rachel; Joseph, and Benjamin:
35:25 And the sons of Bilhah, Rachel's handmaid; Dan, and Naphtali:
35:26 And the sons of Zilpah, Leah's handmaid; Gad, and Asher: these are the sons of Jacob, which were born to him in Padanaram.

DEATH AND BURIAL OF ISAAC

35:27 And Jacob came unto Isaac his father unto Mamre, unto the city of Arbah, which is Hebron, where Abraham and Isaac sojourned.
35:28 And the days of Isaac were an hundred and fourscore years.
35:29 And Isaac gave up the ghost, and died, and was gathered unto his people, being old and full of days: and his sons Esau and Jacob buried him.

DESCENDANTS OF ESAU

36:1 Now these are the generations of Esau, who is Edom.
36:2 Esau took his wives of the daughters of Canaan; Adah the daughter of Elon the Hittite, and Aholibamah the daughter of Anah the daughter of Zibeon the Hivite;
36:3 And Bashemath Ishmael's daughter, sister of Nebajoth.
36:4 And Adah bare to Esau Eliphaz; and Bashemath bare Reuel;
36:5 And Aholibamah bare Jeush, and Jaalam, and Korah: these are the sons of Esau, which were born unto him in the land of Canaan.
36:6 And Esau took his wives, and his sons, and his daughters, and all the persons of his house, and his cattle, and all his beasts, and all his substance, which he had got in the land of Canaan; and went into the country from the face of his brother Jacob.
36:7 For their riches were more than that they might dwell together; and the land wherein they were strangers could not bear them because of their cattle.
36:8 Thus dwelt Esau in mount Seir: Esau is Edom.
36:9 And these are the generations of Esau the father of the Edomites in mount Seir:
36:10 These are the names of Esau's sons; Eliphaz the son of Adah the wife of Esau, Reuel the son of Bashemath the wife of Esau.
36:11 And the sons of Eliphaz were Teman, Omar, Zepho, and Gatam, and Kenaz.
36:12 And Timna was concubine to Eliphaz Esau's son; and she bare to Eliphaz Amalek: these were the sons of Adah Esau's wife.
36:13 And these are the sons of Reuel; Nahath, and Zerah, Shammah, and Mizzah: these were the sons of Bashemath Esau's wife.
36:14 And these were the sons of Aholibamah, the daughter of Anah the daughter of Zibeon, Esau's wife: and she bare to Esau Jeush, and Jaalam, and Korah.
36:15 These were dukes of the sons of Esau: the sons of Eliphaz the firstborn son of Esau; duke Teman, duke Omar, duke Zepho, duke Kenaz,
36:16 Duke Korah, duke Gatam, and duke Amalek: these are the dukes that came of Eliphaz in the land of Edom; these were the sons of Adah.
36:17 And these are the sons of Reuel Esau's son; duke Nahath, duke Zerah, duke Shammah, duke Mizzah: these are the dukes that came of Reuel in the land of Edom; these are the sons of Bashemath Esau's wife.
36:18 And these are the sons of Aholibamah Esau's wife; duke Jeush, duke Jaalam, duke Korah: these were the dukes that came of Aholibamah the daughter of Anah, Esau's wife.
36:19 These are the sons of Esau, who is Edom, and these are their dukes.
36:20 These are the sons of Seir the Horite, who inhabited the land; Lotan, and Shobal, and Zibeon, and Anah,
36:21 And Dishon, and Ezer, and Dishan: these are the dukes of the Horites, the children of Seir in the land of Edom.
36:22 And the children of Lotan were Hori and Hemam; and Lotan's sister was Timna.
36:23 And the children of Shobal were these; Alvan, and Manahath, and Ebal, Shepho, and Onam.

36:24 And these are the children of Zibeon; both Ajah, and Anah: this was that Anah that found the mules in the wilderness, as he fed the asses of Zibeon his father.
36:25 And the children of Anah were these; Dishon, and Aholibamah the daughter of Anah.
36:26 And these are the children of Dishon; Hemdan, and Eshban, and Ithran, and Cheran.
36:27 The children of Ezer are these; Bilhan, and Zaavan, and Akan.
36:28 The children of Dishan are these; Uz, and Aran.
36:29 These are the dukes that came of the Horites; duke Lotan, duke Shobal, duke Zibeon, duke Anah,
36:30 Duke Dishon, duke Ezer, duke Dishan: these are the dukes that came of Hori, among their dukes in the land of Seir.
36:31 And these are the kings that reigned in the land of Edom, before there reigned any king over the children of Israel.
36:32 And Bela the son of Beor reigned in Edom: and the name of his city was Dinhabah.
36:33 And Bela died, and Jobab the son of Zerah of Bozrah reigned in his stead.
36:34 And Jobab died, and Husham of the land of Temani reigned in his stead.
36:35 And Husham died, and Hadad the son of Bedad, who smote Midian in the field of Moab, reigned in his stead: and the name of his city was Avith.
36:36 And Hadad died, and Samlah of Masrekah reigned in his stead.
36:37 And Samlah died, and Saul of Rehoboth by the river reigned in his stead.
36:38 And Saul died, and Baalhanan the son of Achbor reigned in his stead.
36:39 And Baalhanan the son of Achbor died, and Hadar reigned in his stead: and the name of his city was Pau; and his wife's name was Mehetabel, the daughter of Matred, the daughter of Mezahab.
36:40 And these are the names of the dukes that came of Esau, according to their families, after their places, by their names; duke Timnah, duke Alvah, duke Jetheth,
36:41 Duke Aholibamah, duke Elah, duke Pinon,
36:42 Duke Kenaz, duke Teman, duke Mibzar,
36:43 Duke Magdiel, duke Iram: these be the dukes of Edom, according to their habitations in the land of their possession: he is Esau the father of the Edomites.
37:1 And Jacob dwelt in the land wherein his father was a stranger, in the land of Canaan.
37:2a ~~These are~~ ***And this is the history of*** the generations of Jacob.

JOSEPH'S COAT OF MANY COLORS

37:2b Joseph, being seventeen years old, was feeding the flock with his brethren; and the lad was with the sons of Bilhah, and with the sons of Zilpah, his father's wives: and Joseph brought unto his father their evil report.
37:3 Now Israel loved Joseph more than all his children, because he was the son of his old age: and he made him a coat of many colours.
37:4 And when his brethren saw that their father loved him more than all his brethren, they hated him, and could not speak peaceably unto him.

JOSEPH'S DREAM

37:5 And Joseph dreamed a dream, and he told it his brethren: and they hated him yet the more.
37:6 And he said unto them, Hear, I pray you, this dream which I have dreamed:
37:7 For, behold, we were binding sheaves in the field, and, lo, my sheaf arose, and also stood upright; and, behold, your sheaves stood round about, and made obeisance to my sheaf.

37:8 And his brethren said to him, Shalt thou indeed reign over us? or shalt thou indeed have dominion over us? And they hated him yet the more for his dreams, and for his words.
37:9 And he dreamed yet another dream, and told it his brethren, and said, Behold, I have dreamed a dream more; and, behold, the sun and the moon and the eleven stars made obeisance to me.
37:10 And he told it to his father, and to his brethren: and his father rebuked him, and said unto him, What is this dream that thou hast dreamed? Shall I and thy mother and thy brethren indeed come to bow down ourselves to thee to the earth?
37:11 And his brethren envied him; but his father observed the saying.

JOSEPH SOLD INTO EGYPT

37:12 And his brethren went to feed their father's flock in Shechem.
37:13 And Israel said unto Joseph, Do not thy brethren feed the flock in Shechem? come, and I will send thee unto them. And he said to him, Here am I.
37:14 And he said to him, Go, I pray thee, see whether it be well with thy brethren, and well with the flocks; and bring me word again. So he sent him out of the vale of Hebron, and he came to Shechem.
37:15 And a certain man found him, and, behold, he was wandering in the field: and the man asked him, saying, What seekest thou?
37:16 And he said, I seek my brethren: tell me, I pray thee, where they feed their flocks.
37:17 And the man said, They are departed hence; for I heard them say, Let us go to Dothan. And Joseph went after his brethren, and found them in Dothan.
37:18 And when they saw him afar off, even before he came near unto them, they conspired against him to slay him.
37:19 And they said one to another, Behold, this dreamer cometh.
37:20 Come now therefore, and let us slay him, and cast him into some pit, and we will say, Some evil beast hath devoured him: and we shall see what will become of his dreams.
37:21 And Reuben heard it, and he delivered him out of their hands; and said, Let us not kill him.
37:22 And Reuben said unto them, Shed no blood, but cast him into this pit that is in the wilderness, and lay no hand upon him; that he might rid him out of their hands, to deliver him to his father again.
37:23 And it came to pass, when Joseph was come unto his brethren, that they stripped Joseph out of his coat, his coat of many colours that was on him;
37:24 And they took him, and cast him into a pit: and the pit was empty, there was no water in it.
37:25 And they sat down to eat bread: and they lifted up their eyes and looked, and, behold, a company of Ishmeelites came from Gilead with their camels bearing spicery and balm and myrrh, going to carry it down to Egypt.
37:26 And Judah said unto his brethren, What profit is it if we slay our brother, and conceal his blood?
37:27 Come, and let us sell him to the Ishmeelites, and let not our hand be upon him; for he is our brother and our flesh. And his brethren were content.
37:28 Then there passed by Midianites merchantmen; and they drew and lifted up Joseph out of the pit, and sold Joseph to the Ishmeelites for twenty pieces of silver: and they brought Joseph into Egypt.
37:29 And Reuben returned unto the pit; and, behold, Joseph was not in the pit; and he rent his clothes.
37:30 And he returned unto his brethren, and said, The child is not; and I, whither shall I go?
37:31 And they took Joseph's coat, and killed a kid of the goats, and dipped the coat in the blood;

37:32 And they sent the coat of many colours, and they brought it to their father; and said, This have we found: know now whether it be thy son's coat or no.
37:33 And he knew it, and said, It is my son's coat; an evil beast hath devoured him; Joseph is without doubt rent in pieces.
37:34 And Jacob rent his clothes, and put sackcloth upon his loins, and mourned for his son many days.
37:35 And all his sons and all his daughters rose up to comfort him; but he refused to be comforted; and he said, For I will go down into the grave unto my son mourning. Thus his father wept for him.
37:36 And the Midianites sold him into Egypt unto Potiphar, an officer of Pharaoh's, and captain of the guard.

JUDAH AND TAMAR

38:1 And it came to pass at that time, that Judah went down from his brethren, and turned in to a certain Adullamite, whose name was Hirah.
38:2 And Judah saw there a daughter of a certain Canaanite, whose name was Shuah; and he took her, and went in ~~unto~~ ***and lay with*** her.
38:3 And she conceived, and bare a son; and he called his name Er.
38:4 And she conceived again, and bare a son; and she called his name Onan.
38:5 And she yet again conceived, and bare a son; and called his name Shelah: and he was at Chezib, when she bare him.
38:6 And Judah took a wife for Er his firstborn, whose name was Tamar.
38:7 And Er, Judah's firstborn, was wicked in the sight of the Lord; and the Lord slew him.
38:8 And Judah said unto Onan, Go ~~in unto~~ ***and marry*** thy brother's wife, ~~and marry her,~~ and raise up seed ***un***to thy brother.
38:9 And Onan knew that the seed should not be his; and it came to pass, when he ~~went in unto~~ ***married*** his brother's wife, that he ~~spilled it on the ground~~ ***would not lie with her***, lest ~~that~~ he should ~~give~~ ***raise up*** seed ***un***to his brother.
38:10 And the thing which he did displeased the Lord: wherefore he slew him also.
38:11 Then said Judah to Tamar his daughter in law, Remain a widow at thy father's house, till Shelah my son be grown: for he said, Lest peradventure he die also, as his brethren did. And Tamar went and dwelt in her father's house.
38:12 And in process of time the daughter of Shuah Judah's wife died; and Judah was comforted, and went up unto his sheepshearers to Timnath, he and his friend Hirah the Adullamite.
38:13 And it was told Tamar, saying, Behold thy father in law goeth up to Timnath to shear his sheep.
38:14 And she put her widow's garments off from her, and covered her with a veil, and wrapped herself, and sat in an open place, which is by the way to Timnath; for she saw that Shelah was grown, and she was not given unto him to wife.
38:15 When Judah saw her, he thought her to be ~~an~~ ***a*** harlot; because she had covered her face.
38:16 And he turned unto her by the way, and said, Go to, I pray thee, let me come in ~~untoa~~ ***and lie with*** thee; (for he knew not that she was his daughter-in-law.) And she said, What wilt thou give me, that thou mayest come in ~~unto~~ ***and lie with*** me?
38:17 And he said, I will send thee a kid from the flock. And she said, Wilt thou give me a pledge, till thou send it?
38:18 And he said, What pledge shall I give thee? And she said, Thy signet, and thy bracelets, and thy staff that is in thine hand. And he gave it her, and came in ~~unto~~ ***and slept with*** her, and she conceived by him.
38:19 And she arose, and went away, and laid by her veil from her, and put on the garments of her widowhood.

38:20 And Judah sent the kid by the hand of his friend the Adullamite, to receive his pledge from the woman's hand: but he found her not.

38:21 Then he asked the men of that place, saying, Where is the harlot, that was openly by the way side? And they said, There was no harlot in this place.

38:22 And he returned to Judah, and said, I cannot find her; and also the men of the place said, that there was no harlot in this place.

38:23 And Judah said, Let her take it to her, lest we be shamed: behold, I sent this kid, and thou hast not found her.

38:24 And it came to pass about three months after, that it was told Judah, saying, Tamar thy daughter in law hath played the harlot; and also, behold, she is with child by whoredom. And Judah said, Bring her forth, and let her be burnt.

38:25 When she was brought forth, she sent to her father in law, saying, By the man, whose these are, am I with child: and she said, Discern, I pray thee, whose are these, the signet, and bracelets, and staff.

38:26 And Judah acknowledged them, and said, She hath been more righteous than I; because that I gave her not to Shelah my son. And he knew her again no more.

38:27 And it came to pass in the time of her travail, that, behold, twins were in her womb.

38:28 And it came to pass, when she travailed, that the one put out his hand: and the midwife took and bound upon his hand a scarlet thread, saying, This came out first.

38:29 And it came to pass, as he drew back his hand, that, behold, his brother came out: and she said, How hast thou broken forth? this breach be upon thee: therefore his name was called Pharez.

38:30 And afterward came out his brother, that had the scarlet thread upon his hand: and his name was called Zarah.

JOSEPH AND POTIPHAR'S WIFE

39:1 And Joseph was brought down to Egypt; and Potiphar, an officer of Pharaoh, captain of the guard, an Egyptian, bought him of the hands of the Ishmeelites, which had brought him down thither.

39:2 And the Lord was with Joseph, and he was a prosperous man; and he was in the house of his master the Egyptian.

39:3 And his master saw that the Lord was with him, and that the Lord made all that he did to prosper in his hand.

39:4 And Joseph found grace in his sight, and he served him: and he made him overseer over his house, and all that he had he put into his hand.

39:5 And it came to pass from the time that he had made him overseer in his house, and over all that he had, that the Lord blessed the Egyptian's house for Joseph's sake; and the blessing of the Lord was upon all that he had in the house, and in the field.

39:6 And he left all that he had in Joseph's hand; and he knew not ought he had, save the bread which he did eat. And Joseph was a goodly person, and well favoured.

39:7 And it came to pass after these things, that his master's wife cast her eyes upon Joseph; and she said, Lie with me.

39:8 But he refused, and said unto his master's wife, Behold, my master ~~wotteth~~ ***knoweth*** not what is with me in the house, and he hath committed all that he hath to my hand;

39:9 There is none greater in this house than I; neither hath he kept back any thing from me but thee, because thou art his wife: how then can I do this great wickedness, and sin against God?

39:10 And it came to pass, as she spake to Joseph day by day, that he hearkened not unto her, to lie by her, or to be with her.

39:11 And it came to pass about this time, that Joseph went into the house to do his business; and there was none of the men of the house there within.
39:12 And she caught him by his garment, saying, Lie with me: and he left his garment in her hand, and fled, and got him out.
39:13 And it came to pass, when she saw that he had left his garment in her hand, and was fled forth,
39:14 That she called unto the men of her house, and spake unto them, saying, See, he hath brought in an Hebrew unto us to mock us; he came in unto me to lie with me, and I cried with a loud voice:
39:15 And it came to pass, when he heard that I lifted up my voice and cried, that he left his garment with me, and fled, and got him out.
39:16 And she laid up his garment by her, until his lord came home.
39:17 And she spake unto him according to these words, saying, The Hebrew servant, which thou hast brought unto us, came in unto me to mock me:
39:18 And it came to pass, as I lifted up my voice and cried, that he left his garment with me, and fled out.
39:19 And it came to pass, when his master heard the words of his wife, which she spake unto him, saying, After this manner did thy servant to me; that his wrath was kindled.

JOSEPH IN PRISON

39:20 And Joseph's master took him, and put him into the prison, a place where the king's prisoners were bound: and he was there in the prison.
39:21 But the Lord was with Joseph, and showed him mercy, and gave him favour in the sight of the keeper of the prison.
39:22 And the keeper of the prison committed to Joseph's hand all the prisoners that were in the prison; and whatsoever they did there, he was the ~~doer~~ ***overseer*** of it.
39:23 The keeper of the prison looked not to any thing that was under his hand; because the Lord was with him, and that which he did, the Lord made it to prosper.

JOSEPH INTERPRETS PRISONERS' DREAMS

40:1 And it came to pass after these things, that the butler of the king of Egypt and his baker had offended their lord the king of Egypt.
40:2 And Pharaoh was wroth against two of his officers, against the chief of the butlers, and against the chief of the bakers.
40:3 And he put them in ward in the house of the captain of the guard, into the prison, the place where Joseph was bound.
40:4 And the captain of the guard charged Joseph with them, and he served them: and they continued a season in ward.
40:5 And they dreamed a dream both of them, each man his dream in one night, each man according to the interpretation of his dream, the butler and the baker of the king of Egypt, which were bound in the prison.
40:6 And Joseph came in unto them in the morning, and looked upon them, and, behold, they were sad.
40:7 And he asked Pharaoh's officers that were with him in the ward of his lord's house, saying, Wherefore look ye so sadly to day?
40:8 And they said unto him, We have dreamed a dream, and there is no interpreter of it. And Joseph said unto them, Do not interpretations belong to God? tell me them, I pray you.
40:9 And the chief butler told his dream to Joseph, and said to him, In my dream, behold, a vine was before me;

40:10 And in the vine were three branches: and it was as though it budded, and
her blossoms shot forth; and the clusters thereof brought forth ripe grapes:
40:11 And Pharaoh's cup was in my hand: and I took the grapes, and pressed them
into Pharaoh's cup, and I gave the cup into Pharaoh's hand.
40:12 And Joseph said unto him, This is the interpretation of it: The three
branches are three days:
40:13 Yet within three days shall Pharaoh lift up thine head, and restore thee unto
thy place: and thou shalt deliver Pharaoh's cup into his hand, after the former
manner when thou wast his butler.
40:14 But think on me when it shall be well with thee, and show kindness, I pray
thee, unto me, and make mention of me unto Pharaoh, and bring me out of this
house:
40:15 For indeed I was stolen away out of the land of the Hebrews: and here also
have I done nothing that they should put me into the dungeon.
40:16 When the chief baker saw that the interpretation was good, he said unto
Joseph, I also was in my dream, and, behold, I had three white baskets on my
head:
40:17 And in the uppermost basket there was of all manner of bakemeats for
Pharaoh; and the birds did eat them out of the basket upon my head.
40:18 And Joseph answered and said, This is the interpretation thereof: The three
baskets are three days:
40:19 Yet within three days shall Pharaoh lift up thy head from off thee, and shall
hang thee on a tree; and the birds shall eat thy flesh from off thee.
40:20 And it came to pass the third day, which was Pharaoh's birthday, that he
made a feast unto all his servants: and he lifted up the head of the chief butler and
of the chief baker among his servants.
40:21 And he restored the chief butler unto his butlership again; and he gave the
cup into Pharaoh's hand:
40:22 But he hanged the chief baker: as Joseph had interpreted to them.
40:23 Yet did not the chief butler remember Joseph, but forgat him..

JOSEPH INTERPRETS PHAROAH'S DREAM

41:1 And it came to pass at the end of two full years, that Pharaoh dreamed: and,
behold, he stood by the river.
41:2 And, behold, there came up out of the river seven well favoured kine and
fatfleshed; and they fed in a meadow.
41:3 And, behold, seven other kine came up after them out of the river, ill
favoured and leanfleshed; and stood by the other kine upon the brink of the river.
41:4 And the ill favoured and leanfleshed kine did eat up the seven well favoured
and fat kine. So Pharaoh awoke.
41:5 And he slept and dreamed the second time: and, behold, seven ears of corn
came up upon one stalk, rank and good.
41:6 And, behold, seven thin ears and blasted with the east wind sprung up after
them.
41:7 And the seven thin ears devoured the seven rank and full ears. And Pharaoh
awoke, and, behold, it was a dream.
41:8 And it came to pass in the morning that his spirit was troubled; and he sent
and called for all the magicians of Egypt, and all the wise men thereof: and
Pharaoh told them his dream; but there was none that could interpret them unto
Pharaoh.
41:9 Then spake the chief butler unto Pharaoh, saying, I do remember my faults
this day:
41:10 Pharaoh was wroth with his servants, and put me in ward in the captain of
the guard's house, both me and the chief baker:

41:11 And we dreamed a dream in one night, I and he; we dreamed each man according to the interpretation of his dream.
41:12 And there was there with us a young man, an Hebrew, servant to the captain of the guard; and we told him, and he interpreted to us our dreams; to each man according to his dream he did interpret.
41:13 And it came to pass, as he interpreted to us, so it was; me he restored unto mine office, and him he hanged.
41:14 Then Pharaoh sent and called Joseph, and they brought him hastily out of the dungeon: and he shaved himself, and changed his raiment, and came in unto Pharaoh.
41:15 And Pharaoh said unto Joseph, I have dreamed a dream, and there is none that can interpret it: and I have heard say of thee, that thou canst understand a dream to interpret it.
41:16 And Joseph answered Pharaoh, saying, It is not in me: God shall give Pharaoh an answer of peace.
41:17 And Pharaoh said unto Joseph, In my dream, behold, I stood upon the bank of the river:
41:18 And, behold, there came up out of the river seven kine, fatfleshed and well favoured; and they fed in a meadow:
41:19 And, behold, seven other kine came up after them, poor and very ill favoured and leanfleshed, such as I never saw in all the land of Egypt for badness:
41:20 And the lean and the ill favoured kine did eat up the first seven fat kine:
41:21 And when they had eaten them up, it could not be known that they had eaten them; but they were still ill favoured, as at the beginning. So I awoke.
41:22 And I saw in my dream, and, behold, seven ears came up in one stalk, full and good:
41:23 And, behold, seven ears, withered, thin, and blasted with the east wind, sprung up after them:
41:24 And the thin ears devoured the seven good ears: and I told this unto the magicians; but there was none that could declare it to me.
41:25 And Joseph said unto Pharaoh, The dream of Pharaoh is one: God hath showed Pharaoh what he is about to do.
41:26 The seven good kine are seven years; and the seven good ears are seven years: the dream is one.
41:27 And the seven thin and ill favoured kine that came up after them are seven years; and the seven empty ears blasted with the east wind shall be seven years of famine.
41:28 This is the thing which I have spoken unto Pharaoh: What God is about to do he showeth unto Pharaoh.
41:29 Behold, there come seven years of great plenty throughout all the land of Egypt:
41:30 And there shall arise after them seven years of famine; and all the plenty shall be forgotten in the land of Egypt; and the famine shall consume the land;
41:31 And the plenty shall not be known in the land by reason of that famine following; for it shall be very grievous.
41:32 And for that the dream was doubled unto Pharaoh twice; it is because the thing is established by God, and God will shortly bring it to pass.
41:33 Now therefore let Pharaoh look out a man discreet and wise, and set him over the land of Egypt.
41:34 Let Pharaoh do this, and let him appoint officers over the land, and take up the fifth part of the land of Egypt in the seven plenteous years.
41:35 And let them gather all the food of those good years that come, and lay up corn under the hand of Pharaoh, and let them keep food in the cities.
41:36 And that food shall be for store to the land against the seven years of famine, which shall be in the land of Egypt; that the land perish not through the famine.
41:37 And the thing was good in the eyes of Pharaoh, and in the eyes of all his servants.

JOSEPH SECOND TO PHAROAH

41:38 And Pharaoh said unto his servants, Can we find such a one as this is, a man in whom the Spirit of God is?
41:39 And Pharaoh said unto Joseph, Forasmuch as God hath showed thee all this, there is none so discreet and wise as thou art:
41:40 Thou shalt be over my house, and according unto thy word shall all my people be ruled: only in the throne will I be greater than thou.
41:41 And Pharaoh said unto Joseph, See, I have set thee over all the land of Egypt.
41:42 And Pharaoh took off his ring from his hand, and put it upon Joseph's hand, and arrayed him in vestures of fine linen, and put a gold chain about his neck;
41:43 And he made him to ride in the second chariot which he had; and they cried before him, Bow the knee: and he made him ruler over all the land of Egypt.
41:44 And Pharaoh said unto Joseph, I am Pharaoh, and without thee shall no man lift up his hand or foot in all the land of Egypt.
41:45 And Pharaoh called Joseph's name Zaphnathpaaneah; and he gave him to wife Asenath the daughter of Potipherah priest of On. And Joseph went out over all the land of Egypt.
41:46 And Joseph was thirty years old when he stood before Pharaoh king of Egypt. And Joseph went out from the presence of Pharaoh, and went throughout all the land of Egypt.

SEVEN YEARS OF PLENTY

41:47 And in the seven plenteous years the earth brought forth by handfuls.
41:48 And he gathered up all the food of the seven years, which were in the land of Egypt, and laid up the food in the cities: the food of the field, which was round about every city, laid he up in the same.
41:49 And Joseph gathered corn as the sand of the sea, very much, until he left numbering; for it was without number.

BIRTH OF MANASSEH AND EPHRAIM

41:50 And unto Joseph were born two sons before the years of famine came, which Asenath the daughter of Potipherah priest of On bare unto him.
41:51 And Joseph called the name of the firstborn Manasseh: For God, said he, hath made me forget all my toil, and all my father's house.
41:52 And the name of the second called he Ephraim: For God hath caused me to be fruitful in the land of my affliction.

SEVEN YEARS OF FAMINE

41:53 And the seven years of plenteousness, that was in the land of Egypt, were ended.
41:54 And the seven years of dearth began to come, according as Joseph had said: and the dearth was in all lands; but in all the land of Egypt there was bread.
41:55 And when all the land of Egypt was famished, the people cried to Pharaoh for bread: and Pharaoh said unto all the Egyptians, Go unto Joseph; what he saith to you, do.
41:56 And the famine was over all the face of the earth: And Joseph opened all the storehouses, and sold unto the Egyptians; and the famine waxed sore in the land of Egypt.

41:57 And all countries came into Egypt to Joseph for to buy corn; because that the famine was so sore in all lands.

FIRST JOURNEY OF JACOB'S SONS TO EGYPT

42:1 Now when Jacob saw that there was corn in Egypt, Jacob said unto his sons, Why do ye look one upon another?
42:2 And he said, Behold, I have heard that there is corn in Egypt: get you down thither, and buy for us from thence; that we may live, and not die.
42:3 And Joseph's ten brethren went down to buy corn in Egypt.
42:4 But Benjamin, Joseph's brother, Jacob sent not with his brethren; for he said, Lest peradventure mischief befall him.
42:5 And the sons of Israel came to buy corn among those that came: for the famine was in the land of Canaan.
42:6 And Joseph was the governor over the land, and he it was that sold to all the people of the land: and Joseph's brethren came, and bowed down themselves before him with their faces to the earth.
42:7 And Joseph saw his brethren, and he knew them, but made himself strange unto them, and spake roughly unto them; and he said unto them, Whence come ye? And they said, From the land of Canaan to buy food.
42:8 And Joseph knew his brethren, but they knew not him.
42:9 And Joseph remembered the dreams which he dreamed of them, and said unto them, Ye are spies; to see the nakedness of the land ye are come.
42:10 And they said unto him, Nay, my lord, but to buy food are thy servants come.
42:11 We are all one man's sons; we are true men, thy servants are no spies.
42:12 And he said unto them, Nay, but to see the nakedness of the land ye are come.
42:13 And they said, Thy servants are twelve brethren, the sons of one man in the land of Canaan; and, behold, the youngest is this day with our father, and one is not.
42:14 And Joseph said unto them, That is it that I spake unto you, saying, Ye are spies:
42:15 Hereby ye shall be proved: By the life of Pharaoh ye shall not go forth hence, except your youngest brother come hither.
42:16 Send one of you, and let him fetch your brother, and ye shall be kept in prison, that your words may be proved, whether there be any truth in you: or else by the life of Pharaoh surely ye are spies.
42:17 And he put them all together into ward three days.
42:18 And Joseph said unto them the third day, This do, and live; for I fear God:
42:19 If ye be true men, let one of your brethren be bound in the house of your prison: go ye, carry corn for the famine of your houses:
42:20 But bring your youngest brother unto me; so shall your words be verified, and ye shall not die. And they did so.
42:21 And they said one to another, We are verily guilty concerning our brother, in that we saw the anguish of his soul, when he besought us, and we would not hear; therefore is this distress come upon us.
42:22 And Reuben answered them, saying, Spake I not unto you, saying, Do not sin against the child; and ye would not hear? therefore, behold, also his blood is required.
42:23 And they knew not that Joseph understood them; for he spake unto them by an interpreter.
42:24 And he turned himself about from them, and wept; and returned to them again, and communed with them, and took from them Simeon, and bound him before their eyes.

42:25 Then Joseph commanded to fill their sacks with corn, and to restore every man's money into his sack, and to give them provision for the way: and thus did he unto them.
42:26 And they laded their asses with the corn, and departed thence.
42:27 And as one of them opened his sack to give his ass provender in the inn, he espied his money; for, behold, it was in his sack's mouth.
42:28 And he said unto his brethren, My money is restored; and, lo, it is even in my sack: and their heart failed them, and they were afraid, saying one to another, What is this that God hath done unto us?

JOSEPH'S BROTHERS RETURN HOME

42:29 And they came unto Jacob their father unto the land of Canaan, and told him all that befell unto them; saying,
42:30 The man, who is the lord of the land, spake roughly to us, and took us for spies of the country.
42:31 And we said unto him, We are true men; we are no spies:
42:32 We be twelve brethren, sons of our father; one is not, and the youngest is this day with our father in the land of Canaan.
42:33 And the man, the lord of the country, said unto us, Hereby shall I know that ye are true men; leave one of your brethren here with me, and take food for the famine of your households, and be gone:
42:34 And bring your youngest brother unto me: then shall I know that ye are no spies, but that ye are true men: so will I deliver you your brother, and ye shall traffic in the land.
42:35 And it came to pass as they emptied their sacks, that, behold, every man's bundle of money was in his sack: and when both they and their father saw the bundles of money, they were afraid.
42:36 And Jacob their father said unto them, Me have ye bereaved of my children: Joseph is not, and Simeon is not, and ye will take Benjamin away: all these things are against me.
42:37 And Reuben spake unto his father, saying, Slay my two sons, if I bring him not to thee: deliver him into my hand, and I will bring him to thee again.
42:38 And he said, My son shall not go down with you; for his brother is dead, and he is left alone: if mischief befall him by the way in the which ye go, then shall ye bring down my gray hairs with sorrow to the grave.
43:1 And the famine was sore in the land.
43:2 And it came to pass, when they had eaten up the corn which they had brought out of Egypt, their father said unto them, Go again, buy us a little food.
43:3 And Judah spake unto him, saying, The man did solemnly protest unto us, saying, Ye shall not see my face, except your brother be with you.
43:4 If thou wilt send our brother with us, we will go down and buy thee food:
43:5 But if thou wilt not send him, we will not go down: for the man said unto us, Ye shall not see my face, except your brother be with you.
43:6 And Israel said, Wherefore dealt ye so ill with me, as to tell the man whether ye had yet a brother?
43:7 And they said, The man asked us straitly of our state, and of our kindred, saying, Is your father yet alive? have ye another brother? and we told him according to the tenor of these words: could we certainly know that he would say, Bring your brother down?
43:8 And Judah said unto Israel his father, Send the lad with me, and we will arise and go; that we may live, and not die, both we, and thou, and also our little ones.
43:9 I will be surety for him; of my hand shalt thou require him: if I bring him not unto thee, and set him before thee, then let me bear the blame for ever:
43:10 For except we had lingered, surely now we had returned this second time.

43:11 And their father Israel said unto them, If it must be so now, do this; take of the best fruits in the land in your vessels, and carry down the man a present, a little balm, and a little honey, spices, and myrrh, nuts, and almonds:
43:12 And take double money in your hand; and the money that was brought again in the mouth of your sacks, carry it again in your hand; peradventure it was an oversight:
43:13 Take also your brother, and arise, go again unto the man:
43:14 And God Almighty give you mercy before the man, that he may send away your other brother, and Benjamin. If I be bereaved of my children, I am bereaved.

SECOND JOURNEY TO EGYPT

43:15 And the men took that present, and they took double money in their hand, and Benjamin; and rose up, and went down to Egypt, and stood before Joseph.
43:16 And when Joseph saw Benjamin with them, he said to the ruler of his house, Bring these men home, and slay, and make ready; for these men shall dine with me at noon.
43:17 And the man did as Joseph bade; and the man brought the men into Joseph's house.
43:18 And the men were afraid, because they were brought into Joseph's house; and they said, Because of the money that was returned in our sacks at the first time are we brought in; that he may seek occasion against us, and fall upon us, and take us for bondmen, and our asses.
43:19 And they came near to the steward of Joseph's house, and they communed with him at the door of the house,
43:20 And said, O sir, we came indeed down at the first time to buy food:
43:21 And it came to pass, when we came to the inn, that we opened our sacks, and, behold, every man's money was in the mouth of his sack, our money in full weight: and we have brought it again in our hand.
43:22 And other money have we brought down in our hands to buy food: we cannot tell who put our money in our sacks.
43:23 And he said, Peace be to you, fear not: your God, and the God of your father, hath given you treasure in your sacks: I had your money. And he brought Simeon out unto them.
43:24 And the man brought the men into Joseph's house, and gave them water, and they washed their feet; and he gave their asses provender.
43:25 And they made ready the present against Joseph came at noon: for they heard that they should eat bread there.
43:26 And when Joseph came home, they brought him the present which was in their hand into the house, and bowed themselves to him to the earth.
43:27 And he asked them of their welfare, and said, Is your father well, the old man of whom ye spake? Is he yet alive?
43:28 And they answered, Thy servant our father is in good health, he is yet alive. And they bowed down their heads, and made obeisance.
43:29 And he lifted up his eyes, and saw his brother Benjamin, his mother's son, and said, Is this your younger brother, of whom ye spake unto me? And he said, God be gracious unto thee, my son.
43:30 And Joseph made haste; for his bowels did yearn upon his brother: and he sought where to weep; and he entered into his chamber, and wept there.
43:31 And he washed his face, and went out, and refrained himself, and said, Set on bread.
43:32 And they set on for him by himself, and for them by themselves, and for the Egyptians, which did eat with him, by themselves: because the Egyptians might not eat bread with the Hebrews; for that is an abomination unto the Egyptians.
43:33 And they sat before him, the firstborn according to his birthright, and the youngest according to his youth: and the men marvelled one at another.

43:34 And he took and sent messes unto them from before him: but Benjamin's mess was five times so much as any of theirs. And they drank, and were merry with him.

44:1 And he commanded the steward of his house, saying, Fill the men's sacks with food, as much as they can carry, and put every man's money in his sack's mouth.

44:2 And put my cup, the silver cup, in the sack's mouth of the youngest, and his corn money. And he did according to the word that Joseph had spoken.

44:3 As soon as the morning was light, the men were sent away, they and their asses.

44:4 And when they were gone out of the city, and not yet far off, Joseph said unto his steward, Up, follow after the men; and when thou dost overtake them, say unto them, Wherefore have ye rewarded evil for good?

44:5 Is not this it in which my lord drinketh, and whereby indeed he divineth? ye have done evil in so doing.

44:6 And he overtook them, and he spake unto them these same words.

44:7 And they said unto him, Wherefore saith my lord these words? God forbid that thy servants should do according to this thing:

44:8 Behold, the money, which we found in our sacks' mouths, we brought again unto thee out of the land of Canaan: how then should we steal out of thy lord's house silver or gold?

44:9 With whomsoever of thy servants it be found, both let him die, and we also will be my lord's bondmen.

44:10 And he said, Now also let it be according unto your words: he with whom it is found shall be my servant; and ye shall be blameless.

44:11 Then they speedily took down every man his sack to the ground, and opened every man his sack.

44:12 And he searched, and began at the eldest, and left at the youngest: and the cup was found in Benjamin's sack.

44:13 Then they rent their clothes, and laded every man his ass, and returned to the city.

44:14 And Judah and his brethren came to Joseph's house; for he was yet there: and they fell before him on the ground.

44:15 And Joseph said unto them, What deed is this that ye have done? ~~wot~~ ***knew*** ye not that such a man as I can certainly divine?

44:16 And Judah said, What shall we say unto my lord? what shall we speak? or how shall we clear ourselves? God hath found out the iniquity of thy servants: behold, we are my lord's servants, both we, and he also with whom the cup is found.

44:17 And he said, God forbid that I should do so: but the man in whose hand the cup is found, he shall be my servant; and as for you, get you up in peace unto your father.

44:18 Then Judah came near unto him, and said, Oh my lord, let thy servant, I pray thee, speak a word in my lord's ears, and let not thine anger burn against thy servant: for thou art even as Pharaoh.

44:19 My lord asked his servants, saying, Have ye a father, or a brother?

44:20 And we said unto my lord, We have a father, an old man, and a child of his old age, a little one; and his brother is dead, and he alone is left of his mother, and his father loveth him.

44:21 And thou saidst unto thy servants, Bring him down unto me, that I may set mine eyes upon him.

44:22 And we said unto my lord, The lad cannot leave his father: for if he should leave his father, his father would die.

44:23 And thou saidst unto thy servants, Except your youngest brother come down with you, ye shall see my face no more.

44:24 And it came to pass when we came up unto thy servant my father, we told him the words of my lord.

44:25 And our father said, Go again, and buy us a little food.
44:26 And we said, We cannot go down: if our youngest brother be with us, then
will we go down: for we may not see the man's face, except our youngest brother
be with us.
44:27 And thy servant my father said unto us, Ye know that my wife bare me two
sons:
44:28 And the one went out from me, and I said, Surely he is torn in pieces; and
I saw him not since:
44:29 And if ye take this also from me, and mischief befall him, ye shall bring
down my gray hairs with sorrow to the grave.
44:30 Now therefore when I come to thy servant my father, and the lad be not with
us; seeing that his life is bound up in the lad's life;
44:31 It shall come to pass, when he seeth that the lad is not with us, that he will
die: and thy servants shall bring down the gray hairs of thy servant our father with
sorrow to the grave.
44:32 For thy servant became surety for the lad unto my father, saying, If I bring
him not unto thee, then I shall bear the blame to my father for ever.
44:33 Now therefore, I pray thee, let thy servant abide instead of the lad a
bondman to my lord; and let the lad go up with his brethren.
44:34 For how shall I go up to my father, and the lad be not with me? lest
peradventure I see the evil that shall come on my father.

JOSEPH DISCLOSES IDENTITY

45:1 Then Joseph could not refrain himself before ~~all~~ them ***all*** that stood by him;
and he cried, Cause every man to go out from me. And there stood no man with
him, while Joseph made himself known unto his brethren.
45:2 And he wept aloud: and the Egyptians and the house of Pharaoh heard.
45:3 And Joseph said unto his brethren, I am Joseph; doth my father yet live?
And his brethren could not answer him; for they were troubled at his presence.
45:4 And Joseph said unto his brethren, Come near to me, I pray you. And they
came near. And he said, I am Joseph your brother, whom ye sold into Egypt.
45:5 Now therefore be not grieved, nor angry with yourselves, that ye sold me
hither: for God did send me before you to preserve life.
45:6 For these two years hath the famine been in the land: and yet there are five
years, in the which there shall neither be earing nor harvest.
45:7 And God sent me before you to preserve you a posterity in the earth, and to
save your lives by a great deliverance.
45:8 So now it was not you that sent me hither, but God: and he hath made me
a father to Pharaoh, and lord of all his house, and a ruler throughout all the land
of Egypt.
45:9 Haste ye, and go up to my father, and say unto him, Thus saith thy son
Joseph, God hath made me lord of all Egypt: come down unto me, tarry not:
45:10 And thou shalt dwell in the land of Goshen, and thou shalt be near unto me,
thou, and thy children, and thy children's children, and thy flocks, and thy herds,
and all that thou hast:
45:11 And there will I nourish thee; for yet there are five years of famine; lest
thou, and thy household, and all that thou hast, come to poverty.
45:12 And, behold, your eyes see, and the eyes of my brother Benjamin, that it is
my mouth that speaketh unto you.
45:13 And ye shall tell my father of all my glory in Egypt, and of all that ye have
seen; and ye shall haste and bring down my father hither.
45:14 And he fell upon his brother Benjamin's neck, and wept; and Benjamin wept
upon his neck.
45:15 Moreover he kissed all his brethren, and wept upon them: and after that his
brethren talked with him.

45:16 And the fame thereof was heard in Pharaoh's house, saying, Joseph's brethren are come: and it pleased Pharaoh well, and his servants.
45:17 And Pharaoh said unto Joseph, Say unto thy brethren, This do ye; lade your beasts, and go, get you unto the land of Canaan;
45:18 And take your father and your households, and come unto me: and I will give you the good of the land of Egypt, and ye shall eat the fat of the land.
45:19 Now thou art commanded, this do ye; take you wagons out of the land of Egypt for your little ones, and for your wives, and bring your father, and come.
45:20 Also regard not your stuff; for the good of all the land of Egypt is yours.
45:21 And the children of Israel did so: and Joseph gave them wagons, according to the commandment of Pharaoh, and gave them provision for the way.
45:22 To all of them he gave each man changes of raiment; but to Benjamin he gave three hundred pieces of silver, and five changes of raiment.
45:23 And to his father he sent after this manner; ten asses laden with the good things of Egypt, and ten she asses laden with corn and bread and meat for his father by the way.
45:24 So he sent his brethren away, and they departed: and he said unto them, See that ye fall not out by the way.

JOSEPH'S BROTHERS RETURN HOME

45:25 And they went up out of Egypt, and came into the land of Canaan unto Jacob their father,
45:26 And told him, saying, Joseph is yet alive, and he is governor over all the land of Egypt. And Jacob's heart fainted, for he believed them not.
45:27 And they told him all the words of Joseph, which he had said unto them: and when he saw the wagons which Joseph had sent to carry him, the spirit of Jacob their father revived:
45:28 And Israel said, It is enough; Joseph my son is yet alive: I will go and see him before I die.

JACOB GOES TO EGYPT

46:1 And Israel took his journey with all that he had, and came to Beersheba, and offered sacrifices unto the God of his father Isaac.
46:2 And God spake unto Israel in the visions of the night, and said, Jacob, Jacob. And he said, Here am I.
46:3 And he said, I am God, the God of thy father: fear not to go down into Egypt; for I will there make of thee a great nation:
46:4 I will go down with thee into Egypt; and I will also surely bring thee up again: and Joseph shall put his hand upon thine eyes.
46:5 And Jacob rose up from Beersheba: and the sons of Israel carried Jacob their father, and their little ones, and their wives, in the wagons which Pharaoh had sent to carry him.
46:6 And they took their cattle, and their goods, which they had gotten in the land of Canaan, and came into Egypt, Jacob, and all his seed with him:
46:7 His sons, and his sons' sons with him, his daughters, and his sons' daughters, and all his seed brought he with him into Egypt.
46:8 And these are the names of the children of Israel, which came into Egypt, Jacob and his sons: Reuben, Jacob's firstborn.
46:9 And the sons of Reuben; Hanoch, and Phallu, and Hezron, and Carmi.
46:10 And the sons of Simeon; Jemuel, and Jamin, and Ohad, and Jachin, and Zohar, and Shaul the son of a Canaanitish woman.
46:11 And the sons of Levi; Gershon, Kohath, and Merari.

46:12 And the sons of Judah; Er, and Onan, and Shelah, and Pharez, and Zarah: but Er and Onan died in the land of Canaan. And the sons of Pharez were Hezron and Hamul.
46:13 And the sons of Issachar; Tola, and Phuvah, and Job, and Shimron.
46:14 And the sons of Zebulun; Sered, and Elon, and Jahleel.
46:15 These be the sons of Leah, which she bare unto Jacob in Padanaram, with his daughter Dinah: all the souls of his sons and his daughters were thirty and three.
46:16 And the sons of Gad; Ziphion, and Haggi, Shuni, and Ezbon, Eri, and Arodi, and Areli.
46:17 And the sons of Asher; Jimnah, and Ishuah, and Isui, and Beriah, and Serah their sister: and the sons of Beriah; Heber, and Malchiel.
46:18 These are the sons of Zilpah, whom Laban gave to Leah his daughter, and these she bare unto Jacob, even sixteen souls.
46:19 The sons of Rachel Jacob's wife; Joseph, and Benjamin.
46:20 And unto Joseph in the land of Egypt were born Manasseh and Ephraim, which Asenath the daughter of Potipherah priest of On bare unto him.
46:21 And the sons of Benjamin were Belah, and Becher, and Ashbel, Gera, and Naaman, Ehi, and Rosh, Muppim, and Huppim, and Ard.
46:22 These are the sons of Rachel, which were born to Jacob: all the souls were fourteen.
46:23 And the sons of Dan; Hushim.
46:24 And the sons of Naphtali; Jahzeel, and Guni, and Jezer, and Shillem.
46:25 These are the sons of Bilhah, which Laban gave unto Rachel his daughter, and she bare these unto Jacob: all the souls were seven.
46:26 All the souls that came with Jacob into Egypt, which came out of his loins, besides Jacob's sons' wives, all the souls were threescore and six;
46:27 And the sons of Joseph, which were born him in Egypt, were two souls: all the souls of the house of Jacob, which came into Egypt, were threescore and ten.
46:28 And he sent Judah before him unto Joseph, to direct his face unto Goshen; and they came into the land of Goshen.

JOSEPH MEETS JACOB

46:29 And Joseph made ready his chariot, and went up to meet Israel his father, to Goshen, and presented himself unto him; and he fell on his neck, and wept on his neck a good while.
46:30 And Israel said unto Joseph, Now let me die, since I have seen thy face, because thou art yet alive.
46:31 And Joseph said unto his brethren, and unto his father's house, I will go up, and show Pharaoh, and say unto him, My brethren, and my father's house, which were in the land of Canaan, are come unto me;
46:32 And the men are shepherds, for their trade hath been to feed cattle; and they have brought their flocks, and their herds, and all that they have.
46:33 And it shall come to pass, when Pharaoh shall call you, and shall say, What is your occupation?
46:34 That ye shall say, Thy servants' trade hath been about cattle from our youth even until now, both we, and also our fathers: that ye may dwell in the land of Goshen; for every shepherd is an abomination unto the Egyptians.

JACOB MEETS PHAROAH

47:1 Then Joseph came and told Pharaoh, and said, My father and my brethren, and their flocks, and their herds, and all that they have, are come out of the land of Canaan; and, behold, they are in the land of Goshen.

47:2 And he took some of his brethren, even five men, and presented them unto
Pharaoh.
47:3 And Pharaoh said unto his brethren, What is your occupation? And they
said unto Pharaoh, Thy servants are shepherds, both we, and also our fathers.
47:4 They said moreover unto Pharaoh, For to sojourn in the land are we come;
for thy servants have no pasture for their flocks; for the famine is sore in the land
of Canaan: now therefore, we pray thee, let thy servants dwell in the land of
Goshen.
47:5 And Pharaoh spake unto Joseph, saying, Thy father and thy brethren are
come unto thee:
47:6 The land of Egypt is before thee; in the best of the land make thy father and
brethren to dwell; in the land of Goshen let them dwell: and if thou knowest any
men of activity among them, then make them rulers over my cattle.
47:7 And Joseph brought in Jacob his father, and set him before Pharaoh: and
Jacob blessed Pharaoh.
47:8 And Pharaoh said unto Jacob, How old art thou?
47:9 And Jacob said unto Pharaoh, The days of the years of my pilgrimage are
~~an~~ ***a*** hundred and thirty years: few and evil have the days of the years of my life
been, and have not attained unto the days of the years of the life of my fathers in
the days of their pilgrimage.
47:10 And Jacob blessed Pharaoh, and went out from before Pharaoh.
47:11 And Joseph placed his father and his brethren, and gave them a possession
in the land of Egypt, in the best of the land, in the land of Rameses, as Pharaoh
had commanded.
47:12 And Joseph nourished his father, and his brethren, and all his father's
household, with bread, according to their families.

JOSEPH AND THE FAMINE

47:13 And there was no bread in all the land; for the famine was very sore, so that
the land of Egypt and all the land of Canaan fainted by reason of the famine.
47:14 And Joseph gathered up all the money that was found in the land of Egypt,
and in the land of Canaan, for the corn which they bought: and Joseph brought the
money into Pharaoh's house.
47:15 And when money failed in the land of Egypt, and in the land of Canaan, all
the Egyptians came unto Joseph, and said, Give us bread: for why should we die
in thy presence? for the money faileth.
47:16 And Joseph said, Give your cattle; and I will give you for your cattle, if
money fail.
47:17 And they brought their cattle unto Joseph: and Joseph gave them bread in
exchange for horses, and for the flocks, and for the cattle of the herds, and for the
asses: and he fed them with bread for all their cattle for that year.
47:18 When that year was ended, they came unto him the second year, and said
unto him, We will not hide it from my lord, how that our money is spent; my lord
also hath our herds of cattle; there is not ought left in the sight of my lord, but our
bodies, and our lands:
47:19 Wherefore shall we die before thine eyes, both we and our land? buy us and
our land for bread, and we and our land will be servants unto Pharaoh: and give
us seed, that we may live, and not die, that the land be not desolate.
47:20 And Joseph bought all the land of Egypt for Pharaoh; for the Egyptians sold
every man his field, because the famine prevailed over them: so the land became
Pharaoh's.
47:21 And as for the people, he removed them to cities from one end of the
borders of Egypt even to the other end thereof.

47:22 Only the land of the priests bought he not; for the priests had a portion assigned them of Pharaoh, and did eat their portion which Pharaoh gave them: wherefore they sold not their lands.
47:23 Then Joseph said unto the people, Behold, I have bought you this day and your land for Pharaoh: lo, here is seed for you, and ye shall sow the land.
47:24 And it shall come to pass in the increase, that ye shall give the fifth part unto Pharaoh, and four parts shall be your own, for seed of the field, and for your food, and for them of your households, and for food for your little ones.
47:25 And they said, Thou hast saved our lives: let us find grace in the sight of my lord, and we will be Pharaoh's servants.
47:26 And Joseph made it a law over the land of Egypt unto this day, that Pharaoh should have the fifth part; except the land of the priests only, which became not Pharaoh's.

JACOB LIVES IN GOSHEN

47:27 And Israel dwelt in the land of Egypt, in the country of Goshen; and they had possessions therein, and grew, and multiplied exceedingly.
47:28 And Jacob lived in the land of Egypt seventeen years: so the whole age of Jacob was ~~an~~ ***a*** hundred forty and seven years.
47:29 And the time drew nigh that Israel must die: and he called his son Joseph, and said unto him, If now I have found grace in thy sight, put, I pray thee, thy hand under my thigh, and deal kindly and truly with me; bury me not, I pray thee, in Egypt:
47:30 But I will lie with my fathers, and thou shalt carry me out of Egypt, and bury me in their buryingplace. And he said, I will do as thou hast said.
47:31 And he said, Swear unto me. And he sware unto him. And Israel bowed himself upon the bed's head.

THE BLESSING OF EPHRAIM AND MANASSEH

48:1 And it came to pass after these things, that ~~one~~ ***it was*** told Joseph, ***saying,*** Behold, thy father is sick: and he took with him his two sons, Manasseh and Ephraim.
48:2 And ~~one~~ ***it was*** told Jacob, ~~and said,~~ ***saying, Look, and*** Behold, thy son Joseph cometh unto thee: and Israel strengthened himself, and sat upon the bed.
47:3 And Jacob said unto Joseph, God Almighty appeared unto me at Luz in the land of Canaan, and blessed me,
48:4 And said unto me, Behold, I will make thee fruitful, and multiply thee, ***saith the Lord,*** and I will make of thee a multitude of people; and will give this land to thy seed after thee, for an everlasting possession.
48:5 And now, ***of*** thy two sons, Ephraim and Manasseh, which were born unto thee in the land of Egypt, before I came unto thee into Egypt***; behold, they*** are mine; ***and the God of my fathers shall bless them, even*** as Reuben and Simeon, they shall be ***blessed, for they are*** mine; ***wherefore they shall be called after my name. (Therefore they were called Israel.)***
48:6a And thy issue, which thou begettest after them, shall be thine, and shall be called after the name of their brethren in their inheritance, ***in the tribes; therefore they were called the tribes of Manasseh and of Ephraim***.

And Jacob said unto Joseph when the God of my fathers appeared unto me in Luz, in the land of Canaan; he sware unto me, that he would give unto me, and unto my seed, the land for an everlasting possession.

Therefore, O my son, he hath blessed me in raising thee up to be a servant unto me, in saving my house from death;

48:6b In delivering my people, thy brethren, from famine which was sore in the land; wherefore the God of thy fathers shall bless thee, and the fruit of thy loins, that they shall be blessed above thy brethren, and above thy father's house.

For thou has prevailed, and thy father's house hast bowed down unto thee, even as it was shown unto thee, before thou wast sold into Egypt by the hands of thy brethren; wherefore thy brethren shall bow down unto thee, from generation to generation, unto the fruit of thy loins for ever;

For thou shalt be a light unto my people, to deliver them in the days of their captivity, from bondage; and to bring salvation unto them, when they are altogether bowed down under sin.

48:7 And ***therefore,*** as for me, when I came from Padan, Rachel died by me in the land of Canaan, in the way, when ***we were*** yet ~~there was~~ but a little way to come unto Ephrath: and I buried her there in the way of Ephrath; the same is ***called*** Bethlehem.

48:8 And Israel beheld Joseph's sons, and said, Who are these?

48:9 And Joseph said unto his father, They are my sons, whom God hath given me in this place. And he said, Bring them, I pray thee, unto me, and I will bless them.

48:10 Now the eyes of Israel were dim for age, so that he could not see ***well***. And he brought them near unto him; and he kissed them, and embraced them.

48:11 And Israel said unto Joseph, I had not thought to see thy face: and, lo, God hath showed me also thy seed.

48:12 And Joseph brought them out from between his knees, and he bowed himself with his face to the earth.

48:13 And Joseph took them both, Ephraim in his right hand toward Israel's left hand, and Manasseh in his left hand, toward Israel's right hand, and brought them near unto him.

48:14 And Israel stretched out his right hand, and laid it upon Ephraim's head, who was the younger, and his left hand upon Manasseh's head, guiding his hands wittingly; for Manasseh was the firstborn.

48:15 And he blessed Joseph, and said, God, before whom my fathers Abraham and Isaac did walk, the God which fed me all my life long unto this day,

48:16 The Angel which redeemed me from all evil, bless the lads; and let my name be named on them, and the name of my fathers Abraham and Isaac; and let them grow into a multitude in the midst of the earth.

48:17 And when Joseph saw that his father laid his right hand upon the head of Ephraim, it displeased him: and he held up his father's hand, to remove it from Ephraim's head unto Manasseh's head.

48:18 And Joseph said unto his father, Not so, my father: for this is the firstborn; put thy right hand upon his head.

48:19 And his father refused, and said, I know it, my son, I know it: he also shall become a people, and he also shall be great: but truly his younger brother shall be greater than he, and his seed shall become a multitude of nations.

48:20 And he blessed them, that day, saying, In thee shall Israel bless, saying, God make thee as Ephraim and as Manasseh: and he set Ephraim before Manasseh.

48:21 And Israel said unto Joseph, Behold, I die: but God shall be with you, and bring you again unto the land of your fathers.

48:22 Moreover I have given to thee one portion above thy brethren, which I took out of the hand of the Amorite with my sword and with my bow.

JACOB'S BLESSINGS AND PROPHECIES

49:1 And Jacob called unto his sons, and said, Gather yourselves together, that I may tell you that ~~which~~ ***what*** shall befall you in the last days.

49:2 Gather yourselves together, and hear, ye sons of Jacob; and hearken unto Israel your father.

49:3 Reuben, thou art my firstborn, my might, and the beginning of my strength,
the excellency of dignity, and the excellency of power:
49:4 Unstable as water, thou shalt not excel; because thou wentest up to thy
father's bed; then defiledst thou it: he went up to my couch.
49:5 Simeon and Levi are brethren; instruments of cruelty are in their
habitations.
49:6 O my soul, come not thou into their secret; unto their assembly, mine
honour, be not thou united: for in their anger they slew a man, and in their selfwill
they digged down a wall.
49:7 Cursed be their anger, for it was fierce; and their wrath, for it was cruel: I
will divide them in Jacob, and scatter them in Israel.
49:8 Judah, thou art he whom thy brethren shall praise: thy hand shall be in the
neck of thine enemies; thy father's children shall bow down before thee.
49:9 Judah is a lion's whelp: from the prey, my son, thou art gone up: he stooped
down, he couched as a lion, and as an old lion; who shall rouse him up?
49:10 The sceptre shall not depart from Judah, nor a lawgiver from between his
feet, until Shiloh come; and unto him shall the gathering of the people be.
49:11 Binding his foal unto the vine, and his ass's colt unto the choice vine; he
washed his garments in wine, and his clothes in the blood of grapes:
49:12 His eyes shall be red with wine, and his teeth white with milk.
49:13 Zebulun shall dwell at the haven of the sea; and ~~he~~ shall be for an haven of
ships; and his border shall be unto Zidon.
49:14 Issachar is a strong ass couching down between two burdens:
49:15 And he saw that rest was good, and the land that it was pleasant; and bowed
his shoulder to bear, and became a servant unto tribute.
49:16 Dan shall judge his people, as one of the tribes of Israel.
49:17 Dan shall be a serpent by the way, an adder in the path, that biteth the horse
heels, so that his rider shall fall backward.
49:18 I have waited for thy salvation, O Lord.
49:19 Gad, a troop shall overcome him: but he shall overcome at the last.
49:20 Out of Asher his bread shall be fat, and he shall yield royal dainties.
49:21 Naphtali is a hind let loose: he giveth goodly words.
49:22 Joseph is a fruitful bough, even a fruitful bough by a well; whose branches
run over the wall:
49:23 The archers have sorely grieved him, and shot at him, and hated him:
49:24 But his bow abode in strength, and the arms of his hands were made strong
by the hands of the mighty God of Jacob; (from thence is the shepherd, the stone
of Israel:)
49:25 Even by the God of thy father, who shall help thee; and by the Almighty,
who shall bless thee with blessings of heaven above, blessings of the deep that
lieth under, blessings of the breasts, and of the womb:
49:26 The blessings of thy father have prevailed above the blessings of my
progenitors unto the utmost bound of the everlasting hills: they shall be on the
head of Joseph, and on the crown of the head of him that was separate from his
brethren.
49:27 Benjamin shall ravin as a wolf: in the morning he shall devour the prey, and
at night he shall divide the spoil.
49:28 All these are the twelve tribes of Israel: and this is it that their father spake
unto them, and blessed them; every one according to his blessing he blessed them.

DEATH AND BURIAL OF JACOB

49:29 And he charged them, and said unto them, I am to be gathered unto my
people: bury me with my fathers in the cave that is in the field of Ephron the
Hittite,

49:30 In the cave that is in the field of Machpelah, which is before Mamre, in the land of Canaan, which Abraham bought with the field of Ephron the Hittite for a possession of a buryingplace.
49:31 There they buried Abraham and Sarah his wife; there they buried Isaac and Rebekah his wife; and there I buried Leah.
49:32 The purchase of the field and of the cave that is therein was from the children of Heth.
49:33 And when Jacob had made an end of commanding his sons, he gathered up his feet into the bed, and yielded up the ghost, and was gathered unto his people.
50:1 And Joseph fell upon his father's face, and wept upon him, and kissed him.
50:2 And Joseph commanded his servants the physicians to embalm his father: and the physicians embalmed Israel.
50:3 And forty days were fulfilled for him; for so are fulfilled the days of those which are embalmed: and the Egyptians mourned for him threescore and ten days.
50:4 And when the days of his mourning were past, Joseph spake unto the house of Pharaoh, saying, If now I have found grace in your eyes, speak, I pray you, in the ears of Pharaoh, saying,
50:5 My father made me swear, saying, Lo, I die: in my grave which I have digged for me in the land of Canaan, there shalt thou bury me. Now therefore let me go up, I pray thee, and bury my father, and I will come again.
50:6 And Pharaoh said, Go up, and bury thy father, according as he made thee swear.
50:7 And Joseph went up to bury his father: and with him went up all the servants of Pharaoh, the elders of his house, and all the elders of the land of Egypt,
50:8 And all the house of Joseph, and his brethren, and his father's house: only their little ones, and their flocks, and their herds, they left in the land of Goshen.
50:9 And there went up with him both chariots and horsemen: and it was a very great company.
50:10 And they came to the threshingfloor of Atad, which is beyond Jordan, and there they mourned with a great and very sore lamentation: and he made a mourning for his father seven days.
50:11 And when the inhabitants of the land, the Canaanites, saw the mourning in the floor of Atad, they said, This is a grievous mourning to the Egyptians: wherefore the name of it was called Abelmizraim, which is beyond Jordan.
50:12 And his sons did unto him according as he commanded them:
50:13 For his sons carried him into the land of Canaan, and buried him in the cave of the field of Machpelah, which Abraham bought with the field for a possession of a buryingplace of Ephron the Hittite, before Mamre.
50:14 And Joseph returned into Egypt, he, and his brethren, and all that went up with him to bury his father, after he had buried his father.

JOSEPH FORGIVES HIS BROTHERS

50:15 And when Joseph's brethren saw that their father was dead, they said, Joseph will peradventure hate us, and will certainly requite us all the evil which we did unto him.
50:16 And they sent a messenger unto Joseph, saying, Thy father did command before he died, saying,
50:17 So shall ye say unto Joseph, Forgive, I pray thee now, the trespass of thy brethren, and their sin; for they did unto thee evil: and now, we pray thee, forgive the trespass of the servants of the God of thy father. And Joseph wept when they spake unto him.
50:18 And his brethren also went and fell down before his face; and they said, Behold, we be thy servants.
50:19 And Joseph said unto them, Fear not: for am I in the place of God?

50:20 But as for you, ye thought evil against me; but God meant it unto good, to bring to pass, as it is this day, to save much people alive.
50:21 Now therefore fear ye not: I will nourish you, and your little ones. And he comforted them, and spake kindly unto them.
50:22 And Joseph dwelt in Egypt, he, and his father's house: and Joseph lived an hundred and ten years.
50:23 And Joseph saw Ephraim's children of the third generation: the children also of Machir the son of Manasseh were brought up upon Joseph's knees.

JOSEPH'S PROPHECY

50:24a And Joseph said unto his brethren, I die, and ***go unto my fathers; and I go down to my grave with joy. The God of my father Jacob be with you, to deliver you out of affliction in the days of your bondage; for the Lord hath visited me, and I have obtained a promise of the Lord, that out of the fruit of my loins, the Lord God will raise up a righteous branch out of my loins; and unto thee, whom my father Jacob hath named Israel, a prophet; (not the Messiah who is called Shilo;) and this prophet shall deliver my people out of Egypt in the days of thy bondage.***

And it shall come to pass that they shall be scattered again; and a branch shall be broken off, and shall be carried into a far country; nevertheless they shall be remembered in the covenants of the Lord, when the Messiah cometh; for he shall be made manifest unto them in the latter days, in the Spirit of power; and shall bring them out of darkness into light; out of hidden darkness, and out of captivity unto freedom.

A seer shall the Lord my God raise up, who shall be a choice seer unto the fruit of my loins.

Thus saith the Lord God of my fathers unto me, A choice seer will I raise up out of the fruit of thy loins, and he shall be esteemed highly among the fruit of thy loins, and unto him will I give commandment that he shall do a work for the fruit of thy loins, his brethren.

And he shall bring them to the knowledge of the covenants which I have made with thy fathers; and he shall do whatsoever work I shall command him.

And I will make him great in mine eyes, for he shall do my work; and he shall be great like unto him whom I have said I would raise up unto you, to deliver my people, O house of Israel, out of the land of Egypt; for a seer will I raise up to deliver my people out of the land of Egypt; and be shall be called Moses. And by this name he shall know that he is of thy house; for he shall be nursed by the king's daughter, and shall be called her son.

And again, a seer will I raise up out of the fruit of thy loins, and unto him will I give power to bring forth my word unto the seed of thy loins; and not to the bringing forth of my word only, saith the Lord, but to the convincing them of my word, which shall have already gone forth among them in the last days;

Wherefore the fruit of thy loins shall write, and the fruit of the loins of Judah shall write; and that which shall be written by the fruit of thy loins, and also that which shall be written by the fruit of the loins of Judah, shall grow together unto the confounding of false doctrines, and laying down of contentions, and establishing peace among the fruit of thy loins, and bringing them to a knowledge of their fathers in the latter days; and also to the knowledge of my covenants, saith the Lord.

And out of weakness shall he be made strong, in that day when my work shall go forth among all my people, which shall restore them, who are of the house of Israel, in the last days.

And that seer will I bless, and they that seek to destroy him shall be confounded; for this promise I give unto you; for I will remember you from generation to generation; and his name shall be called Joseph, and it shall be after the name of his father; and he shall be like unto you; for the thing which the Lord shall bring forth by his hand shall bring my people unto salvation.

50:24b And the Lord sware unto Joseph that he would preserve his seed for ever saying, I will raise up Moses, and a rod shall be in his hand, and he shall gather together my people, and he shall lead them as a flock, and he shall smite the waters of the Red Sea with his rod.

And he shall have judgment, and shall write the word of the Lord. And he shall not speak many words, for I will write unto him my law by the finger of mine own hand. And I will make a spokesman for him, and his name shall be called Aaron.

And it shall be done unto thee in the last days also, even as I have sworn. Therefore, Joseph said unto his brethren,

50:24c God will surely visit you, and bring you out of this land, unto the land which he sware ***un***to Abraham, ***and un***to Isaac, and to Jacob.

50:25 And Joseph ***confirmed many other things unto his brethren, and*** took an oath of the children of Israel, saying ***unto them***, God will surely visit you, and ye shall carry up my bones from hence.

DEATH OF JOSEPH

50:26 So Joseph died~~, being~~ ***when he was*** an hundred and ten years old: and they embalmed him, and he was put in a coffin in Egypt***; and he was kept from burial by the children of Israel, that he might be carried up and laid in the sepulchre with his father. And thus they remembered the oath which they sware unto him.***

THE BOOK OF ISAIAH

With the Joseph Smith Translation
in Parallel Harmony
with the Book of Mormon Isaiah Texts

ISAIAH, Introduction in the Book of Mormon

1st Nephi
19:22 Now it came to pass that I, Nephi, did teach my brethren these things; and it came to pass that I did read many things to them, which were engraven upon the plates of brass, that they might know concerning the doings of the Lord in other lands, among people of old.
19:23 And I did read many things unto them which were written in the books of Moses; but that I might more fully persuade them to believe in the Lord their Redeemer I did read unto them that which was written by the prophet Isaiah; for I did liken all scriptures unto us, that it might be for our profit and learning.
19:24 Wherefore I spake unto them, saying: Hear ye the words of the prophet, ye who are a remnant of the house of Israel, a branch who have been broken off; hear ye the words of the prophet, which were written unto all the house of Israel, and liken them unto yourselves, that ye may have hope as well as your brethren from whom ye have been broken off; for after this manner has the prophet written.

3rd Nephi
23:1 AND now, behold, I say unto you, that ye ought to search these things. Yea, a commandment I give unto you that ye search these things diligently; for great are the words of Isaiah.
23:2 For surely he spake as touching all things concerning my people which are of the house of Israel; therefore it must needs be that he must speak also to the Gentiles.
23:3 And all things that he spake have been and shall be, even according to the words which he spake.

ISAIAH, Chapter 1

1 Nephi
15:19 And it came to pass that I, Nephi, spake much unto them concerning these things; yea, I spake unto them concerning the restoration of the Jews in the latter days.
15:20 And I did rehearse unto them the words of Isaiah, who spake concerning the restoration of the Jews, or of the house of Israel; and after they were restored they should no more be confounded, neither should they be scattered again.

1:1 ¶ THE vision of Isaiah the son of Amoz, which he saw concerning Judah and Jerusalem in the days of Uzziah, Jotham, Ahaz, and Hezekiah, kings of Judah.
1:2 ¶ Hear, O heavens, and give ear, O earth: for the LORD hath spoken, I have nourished and brought up children, and they have rebelled against me.
1:3 The ox knoweth his owner, and the ass his master's crib: but Israel doth not know, my people doth not consider.
1:4 Ah sinful nation, a people laden with iniquity, a seed of evildoers, children that are corrupters: they have forsaken the LORD, they have provoked the Holy One of Israel unto anger, they are gone away backward.
1:5 Why should ye be stricken any more? ye will revolt more and more: the whole head is sick, and the whole heart faint.
1:6 From the sole of the foot even unto the head there is no soundness in it; but wounds, and bruises, and putrifying sores: they have not been closed, neither bound up, neither mollified with ointment.
1:7 Your country is desolate, your cities are burned with fire: your land, strangers devour it in your presence, and it is desolate, as overthrown by strangers.
1:8 And the daughter of Zion is left as a cottage in a vineyard, as a lodge in a garden of cucumbers, as a besieged city.
1:9 Except the LORD of hosts had left unto us a very small remnant, we should have been as Sodom, and we should have been like unto Gomorrah.

1:10 ¶ Hear the word of the LORD, ye rulers of Sodom; give ear unto the law of our God, ye people of Gomorrah.

1:11 To what purpose is the multitude of your sacrifices unto me? saith the LORD: I am full of the burnt offerings of rams, and the fat of fed beasts; and I delight not in the blood of bullocks, or of lambs, or of he goats.

1:12 When ye come to appear before me, who hath required this at your hand, to tread my courts?

1:13 Bring no more vain oblations; incense is an abomination unto me; the new moons and sabbaths, the calling of assemblies, I cannot away with; it is iniquity, even the solemn meeting.

1:14 Your new moons and your appointed feasts my soul hateth: they are a trouble unto me; I am weary to bear them.

1:15 And when ye spread forth your hands, I will hide mine eyes from you: yea, when ye make many prayers, I will not hear: your hands are full of blood.

1:16 ¶ Wash ***ye*** ~~you~~, make you clean; put away the evil of your doings from before mine eyes; cease to do evil;

1:17 Learn to do well; seek judgment, relieve the oppressed, judge the fatherless, plead for the widow.

1:18 Come now, and let us reason together, saith the LORD: though your sins be as scarlet, they shall be as white as snow; though they be red like crimson, they shall be as wool.

1:19 If ye be willing and obedient, ye shall eat the good of the land:

1:20 But if ye refuse and rebel, ye shall be devoured with the sword: for the mouth of the LORD hath spoken it.

1:21 ¶ How is the faithful city become an harlot! it was full of judgment; righteousness lodged in it; but now murderers.

1:22 Thy silver is become dross, thy wine mixed with water:

1:23 Thy princes are rebellious, and companions of thieves: every one loveth gifts, and followeth after rewards: they judge not the fatherless, neither doth the cause of the widow come unto them.

1:24 Therefore saith the Lord, the LORD of hosts, the mighty One of Israel, Ah, I will ease me of mine adversaries, and avenge me of mine enemies:

1:25 And I will turn my hand upon thee, and purely purge away thy dross, and take away all thy tin:
1:26 And I will restore thy judges as at the first, and thy counsellors as at the beginning: afterward thou shalt be called, The city of righteousness, the faithful city.
1:27 Zion shall be redeemed with judgment, and her converts with righteousness.
1:28 And the destruction of the transgressors and of the sinners shall be together, and they that forsake the LORD shall be consumed.
1:29 For they shall be ashamed of the oaks which ye have desired, and ye shall be confounded for the gardens that ye have chosen.
1:30 For ye shall be as an oak whose leaf fadeth, and as a garden that hath no water.
1:31 And the strong shall be as tow, and the maker of it as a spark, and they shall both burn together, and none shall quench them.

ISAIAH, Chapter 2

2:1 ¶ THE word that Isaiah the son of Amoz saw concerning Judah and Jerusalem.
2:2 And it shall come to pass in the last days, ***when*** ~~that~~ the mountain of the LORD'S house shall be established in the top of the mountains, and shall be exalted above the hills, ~~;~~ and all nations shall flow unto it.
2:3 And many people shall go and say, Come ye, and let us go up to the mountain of the LORD, to the house of the God of Jacob; and he will teach us of his ways, and we will walk in his paths: for out of Zion shall go forth the law, and the word of the LORD from Jerusalem.
2:4 And he shall judge among the nations, and shall rebuke many people: and they shall beat their swords into plowshares, and their spears into pruninghooks: nation shall not lift up sword against nation, neither shall they learn war any more.
2:5 O house of Jacob, come ye, and let us walk in the light of the LORD~~.~~ ***; yea, come, for ye have all gone astray, every one to his wicked ways.***

<u>2nd Nephi</u>
12:1 THE word that Isaiah, the son of Amoz, saw concerning Judah and Jerusalem:
12:2 And it shall come to pass in the last days, when the mountain of the Lord's house shall be established in the top of the mountains, and shall be exalted above the hills, and all nations shall flow unto it.
12:3 And many people shall go and say, Come ye, and let us go up to the mountain of the Lord, to the house of the God of Jacob; and he will teach us of his ways, and we will walk in his paths; for out of Zion shall go forth the law, and the word of the Lord from Jerusalem.
12:4 And he shall judge among the nations, and shall rebuke many people: and they shall beat their swords into plow-shares, and their spears into pruning-hooks--nation shall not lift up sword against nation, neither shall they learn war any more.
12:5 O house of Jacob, come ye and let us walk in the light of the Lord; yea, come, for ye have all gone astray, every one to his wicked ways.

Isaiah

2:6 ¶ Therefore, ***O Lord,*** thou hast forsaken thy people the house of Jacob, because they be replenished from the east, and ***hearken unto the*** ~~are~~ soothsayers like the Philistines, and they please themselves in the children of strangers.
2:7 Their land also is full of silver and gold, neither is there any end of their treasures; their land is also full of horses, neither is there any end of their chariots:
2:8 Their land also is full of idols; they worship the work of their own hands, that which their own fingers have made:
2:9 And the mean man boweth ***not*** down, and the great man humbleth himself ***not***: therefore forgive them not.
2:10 ¶ ***O ye wicked ones,*** ~~E~~*e*nter into the rock, and hide ***ye*** ~~thee~~ in the dust, for fear of the LORD, and ~~for the glory of~~ his majesty ***shall smite thee.***
2:11 ***And it shall come to pass that*** ~~T~~*t*he lofty looks of man shall be humbled, and the haughtiness of ***man*** ~~men~~ shall be bowed down, and the LORD alone shall be exalted in that day.
2:12 For the day of the LORD of hosts ***soon cometh*** ~~shall be~~ upon ***all nations; yea, upon*** every one*;* ***yea, upon the*** ~~that is~~ proud and lofty, and upon every one ***who*** ~~that~~ is lifted up***,*** ~~;~~ and he shall be brought low:
2:13 ***Yea,*** ~~A~~*a*nd ***the day of the Lord shall come*** upon all the cedars of Lebanon, ***for they*** ~~that~~ are high and lifted up***;*** ~~,~~ and upon all the oaks of Bashan,
2:14 And upon all the high mountains, and upon all the hills***, and upon all the nations which*** ~~that~~ are lifted up,
2:15 ***And upon every people,*** ~~A~~*a*nd upon every high tower, and upon every fenced wall,
2:16 And upon all the ships of ***the sea, and upon all the ships of*** Tarshish, and upon all pleasant pictures.
2:17 And the loftiness of man shall be bowed down, and the haughtiness of men shall be made low: and the LORD alone shall be exalted in that day.
2:18 And the idols he shall utterly abolish.
2:19 And they shall go into the holes of the rocks, and into the caves of the

The Book of Mormon

2nd Nephi (cont.)

12:6 Therefore, O Lord, thou hast forsaken thy people, the house of Jacob, because they be replenished from the east, and hearken unto (-) soothsayers like the Philistines, and they please themselves in the children of strangers.
12:7 Their land also is full of silver and gold, neither is there any end of their treasures; their land is also full of horses, neither is there any end of their chariots.
12:8 Their land is also full of idols; they worship the work of their own hands, that which their own fingers have made.
12:9 And the mean man boweth not down, and the great man humbleth himself not, therefore, forgive him not.
12:10 O ye wicked ones, enter into the rock, and hide thee in the dust, for the fear of the Lord and the glory of his majesty shall smite thee.
12:11 And it shall come to pass that the lofty looks of man shall be humbled, and the haughtiness of men shall be bowed down, and the Lord alone shall be exalted in that day.
12:12 For the day of the Lord of Hosts soon cometh upon all nations, yea, upon every one; yea, upon the proud and lofty, and upon every one who is lifted up, and he shall be brought low.
12:13 Yea, and the day of the Lord shall come upon all the cedars of Lebanon, for they are high and lifted up; and upon all the oaks of Bashan;
12:14 And upon all the high mountains, and upon all the hills, and upon all the nations which are lifted up,
and upon every people;
12:15 And upon every high tower, and upon every fenced wall;
12:16 And upon all the ships of the sea, and upon all the ships of Tarshish, and upon all pleasant pictures.
12:17 And the loftiness of man shall be bowed down, and the haughtiness of men shall be made low; and the Lord alone shall be exalted in that day.
12:18 And the idols he shall utterly abolish.
12:19 And they shall go into the holes of the rocks, and into the caves of the

earth, for ***the*** fear of the LORD ***shall come upon them***, and ~~for~~ the glory of his majesty ***shall smite them***, when he ariseth to shake terribly the earth.

2:20 In that day a man shall cast his idols of silver, and his idols of gold, which ***he hath*** ~~they~~ made ~~each one~~ for himself to worship, to the moles and to the bats;

2:21 To go into the clefts of the rocks, and into the tops of the ragged rocks, for fear of the LORD ***shall come upon them***, and ~~for~~ the ~~glory of his~~ majesty ***of the Lord shall smite them***, when he ariseth to shake terribly the earth.

2:22 Cease ye from man, whose breath is in his nostrils: for wherein is he to be accounted of?

2nd Nephi (cont.)

earth, for the fear of the Lord shall come upon them and (-) the glory of his majesty shall smite them, when he ariseth to shake terribly the earth.

12:20 In that day a man shall cast his idols of silver, and his idols of gold, which he hath made for himself to worship, to the moles and to the bats;

12:21 To go into the clefts of the rocks, and into the tops of the ragged rocks, for the fear of the Lord shall come upon them and the majesty of his glory (- -) shall smite them, when he ariseth to shake terribly the earth.

12:22 Cease ye from man, whose breath is in his nostrils; for wherein is he to be accounted of?

ISAIAH, Chapter 3

3:1 ¶ For, behold, the Lord, the LORD of hosts, doth take away from Jerusalem and from Judah the stay and the staff, the whole ***staff*** ~~stay~~ of bread, and the whole stay of water,

3:2 The mighty man, and the man of war, the judge, and the prophet, and the prudent, and the ancient,

3:3 The captain of fifty, and the honourable man, and the counsellor, and the cunning artificer, and the eloquent orator.

3:4 And I will give children ***unto them*** to be their princes, and babes shall rule over them.

3:5 And the people shall be oppressed, every one by another, and every one by his neighbour: the child shall behave himself proudly against the ancient, and the base against the honourable.

3: 6 When a man shall take hold of his brother of the house of his father, ***and shall say*** ~~saying~~, Thou hast clothing, be thou our ruler, and let ***not*** this ruin ***come*** ~~be~~ under thy hand:

3:7 In that day shall he swear, saying, I will not be ***a*** ~~an~~ healer; for in my house ***there*** is neither bread nor clothing: make me not a ruler of the people.

3:8 For Jerusalem is ruined, and Judah is fallen: because their tongue*s*

2nd Nephi

13:1 For behold, the Lord, the Lord of Hosts, doth take away from Jerusalem, and from Judah, the stay and the staff, the whole staff of bread, and the whole stay of water–

13:2 The mighty man, and the man of war, the judge, and the prophet, and the prudent, and the ancient;

13:3 The captain of fifty, and the honorable man, and the counselor, and the cunning artificer, and the eloquent orator.

13:4 And I will give children unto them to be their princes, and babes shall rule over them.

13:5 And the people shall be oppressed, every one by another, and every one by his neighbor; the child shall behave himself proudly against the ancient, and the base against the honorable.

13:6 When a man shall take hold of his brother of the house of his father, and shall say: Thou hast clothing, be thou our ruler, and let not this ruin come under thy hand–

13:7 In that day shall he swear, saying: I will not be a healer; for in my house there is neither bread nor clothing; make me not a ruler of the people.

13:8 For Jerusalem is ruined, and Judah is fallen, because their tongues

and their doings ***have been*** ~~are~~ against
the LORD, to provoke the eyes of his
glory.
3:9 The ***show*** ~~shew~~ of their
countenance doth witness against them;
and they declare their sin ***to be even*** as
Sodom, they ***cannot*** hide it ~~not~~. Woe
unto their soul*s*! for they have rewarded
evil unto themselves.
3:10 Say ~~ye~~ ***un***to the righteous, that it
is ~~shall be~~ well with ***them*** ~~him~~: for they
shall eat the fruit of their doings.
3:11 Woe unto the wicked! ***for they***
shall perish ~~it shall be ill with him~~: for
the reward of ***their*** ~~his~~ hands shall be
upon ~~given~~ him.
3:12 As for my people, children are
their oppressors, and women rule over
them. O my people, they ***who*** ~~which~~
lead thee cause thee to err, and destroy
the way of thy paths.
3:13 The LORD standeth up to plead,
and standeth to judge the people.
3:14 The LORD will enter into
judgment with the ancients of his
people, and the princes thereof: for ye
have eaten up the vineyard; the spoil of
the poor is in your houses.
3:15 What mean ye***?*** ~~that~~ ye beat my
people to pieces, and grind the faces of
the poor**,** ~~?~~ saith the Lord GOD of hosts.
3:16 ¶ Moreover the LORD saith,
Because the daughters of Zion are
haughty, and walk with stretched forth
necks and wanton eyes, walking and
mincing as they go, and making a
tinkling with their feet:
3:17 Therefore the Lord will smite
with a scab the crown of the head of the
daughters of Zion, and the LORD will
discover their secret parts.
3:18 In that day the Lord will take
away the bravery of their tinkling
ornaments ~~about their feet~~, and ~~their~~
cauls, and ~~their~~ round tires like the
moon,
3:19 The chains, and the bracelets ,
and the mufflers,
3:20 The bonnets, and the ornaments
of the legs, and the headbands, and the
tablets, and the earrings,
3:21 The rings, and nose jewels,
3:22 The changeable suits of apparel,
and the mantles, and the wimples, and
the crisping pins,
3:23 The glasses, and the fine linen,
and the hoods, and the vails.

2nd Nephi (cont.)
and their doings have been against the
Lord, to provoke the eyes of his glory.

13:9 The show of their countenance
doth witness against them, and doth
declare their sin to be even as Sodom,
and they cannot hide it. Wo unto their
souls, for they have rewarded evil unto
themselves !
13:10 Say unto the righteous that it is
well with them; for they shall eat the
fruit of their doings.
13:11 Wo unto the wicked,for they
shall perish; for the reward of their
hands shall be upon them!

13:12 And (- - -) my people, children
are their oppressors, and women rule
over them. O my people, they who lead
thee cause thee to err and destroy the
way of thy paths.
13:13 The Lord standeth up to plead,
and standeth to judge the people.
13:14 The Lord will enter into
judgment with the ancients of his people
and the princes thereof; for ye have
eaten up the vineyard and the spoil of
the poor in your houses.
13:15 What mean ye? Ye beat my
people to pieces, and grind the faces of
the poor, saith the Lord God of Hosts.
13:16 Moreover, the Lord saith:
Because the daughters of Zion are
haughty, and walk with stretched-forth
necks and wanton eyes, walking and
mincing as they go, and making a
tinkling with their feet–
13:17 Therefore the Lord will smite
with a scab the crown of the head of the
daughters of Zion, and the Lord will
discover their secret parts.
13:18 In that day the Lord will take
away the bravery of their tinkling
ornaments, and cauls, and round tires
like the moon;

13:19 The chains and the bracelets, and
the mufflers;
13:20 The bonnets, and the ornaments
of the legs, and the headbands, and the
tablets, and the ear-rings;
13:21 The rings, and nose jewels;
13:22 The changeable suits of apparel,
and the mantles, and the wimples, and
the crisping-pins ;
13:23 The glasses, and the fine linen,
and (-) hoods, and the veils.

3:24 And it shall come to pass, ~~that~~ instead of sweet smell there shall be stink; and instead of a girdle a rent; and instead of well-set hair, baldness; and instead of a stomacher a girding of sackcloth; ~~and~~ burning instead of beauty.
3:25 Thy men shall fall by the sword, and thy mighty in the war.
3:26 And her gates shall lament and mourn; and she ***shall be*** ~~being~~ desolate***, and*** shall sit upon the ground.

2nd Nephi (cont.)
13:24 And it shall come to pass, instead of sweet smell there shall be stink; and instead of a girdle, a rent; and instead of well_set hair, baldness; and instead of a stomacher, a girding of sackcloth; burning instead of beauty.

13:25 Thy men shall fall by the sword and thy mighty in the war.
13:26 And her gates shall lament and mourn; and she shall be desolate, and shall sit upon the ground.

ISAIAH, Chapter 4

4:1 AND in that day seven women shall take hold of one man, saying, We will eat our own bread, and wear our own apparel***;*** ~~:~~ only let us be called by thy name, to take away our reproach.
4:2 In that day shall the branch of the LORD be beautiful and glorious, and the fruit of the earth shall be excellent and comely for them that are escaped of Israel.
4:3 And it shall come to pass, ***they*** that ***are*** ~~he that is~~ left in Zion, and he that remaineth in Jerusalem, shall be called holy, even every one that is written among the living in Jerusalem:
4:4 When the Lord shall have washed away the filth of the daughters of Zion, and shall have purged the blood of Jerusalem from the midst thereof by the spirit of judgment, and by the spirit of burning.
4:5 And the LORD will create upon every dwelling-place of mount Zion, and upon her assemblies, a cloud and smoke by day, and the shining of a flaming fire by night: for upon all the glory shall be a defence.
4:6 And there shall be a tabernacle for a shadow in the daytime from the heat, and for a place of refuge, and for a covert from storm and from rain.

2nd Nephi
14:1 And in that day, seven women shall take hold of one man, saying: We will eat our own bread, and wear our own apparel; only let us be called by thy name_ to take away our reproach.
14:2 In that day shall the branch of the Lord be beautiful and glorious; the fruit of the earth (- -) excellent and comely to them that are escaped of Israel.
14:3 And it shall come to pass, they that are left in Zion and (- -) remain in Jerusalem shall be called holy, (-) every one that is written among the living in Jerusalem–
14:4 When the Lord shall have washed away the filth of the daughters of Zion, and shall have purged the blood of Jerusalem from the midst thereof by the spirit of judgment and by the spirit of burning.
14:5 And the Lord will create upon every dwelling-place of mount Zion, and upon her assemblies, a cloud and smoke by day and the shining of a flaming fire by night; for upon all the glory of Zion shall be a defence.
14:6 And there shall be a tabernacle for a shadow in the daytime from the heat, and for a place of refuge, and (-) a covert from storm and from rain.

ISAIAH, Chapter 5

5:1 ¶ ~~NOW~~ ***And then*** will I sing to my well-beloved a song of my beloved touching his vineyard. My well-beloved hath a vineyard in a very fruitful hill:

5:2 And he fenced it, and gathered out the stones thereof, and planted it with the choicest vine, and built a tower in the midst of it, and also made a winepress therein: and he looked that it should bring forth grapes, and it brought forth wild grapes.

5:3 And now, O inhabitants of Jerusalem, and men of Judah, judge, I pray you, betwixt me and my vineyard.

5:4 What could have been done more to my vineyard, that I have not done in it? wherefore, when I looked that it should bring forth grapes, brought it forth wild grapes***.*** ~~?~~

5:5 And now go to; I will tell you what I will do to my vineyard***;*** ~~:~~ I will take away the hedge thereof, and it shall be eaten up; and ***I will*** break down the wall thereof, and it shall be trodden down***;*** ~~:~~

5:6 And I will lay it waste: it shall not be pruned, nor digged; but there shall come up briers and thorns: I will also command the clouds that they rain no rain upon it.

5:7 For the vineyard of the LORD of hosts is the house of Israel, and the men of Judah his pleasant plant: and he looked for judgment, but behold oppression; for righteousness, but behold a cry.

5:8 Woe unto them that join house to house, that lay field to field, till there be no place, that they may be placed alone in the midst of the earth!

5:9 In mine ears said the LORD of hosts, Of a truth many houses shall be desolate, even great and fair ***cities***, without inhabitant.

5:10 Yea, ten acres of vineyard shall yield one bath, and the seed of an homer shall yield an ephah.

5:11 Woe unto them that rise up early in the morning, that they may follow strong drink; that continue until night, ***and*** ~~till~~ wine inflame them!

5:12 And the harp, and the viol, the tablet, and pipe, and wine, are in their feasts: but they regard not the work of

2nd Nephi

15:1 And then will I sing to my well-beloved a song of my beloved, touching his vineyard. My well-beloved hath a vineyard in a very fruitful hill.

15:2 And he fenced it, and gathered out the stones thereof, and planted it with the choicest vine, and built a tower in the midst of it, and also made a wine-press therein; and he looked that it should bring forth grapes, and it brought forth wild grapes.

15:3 And now, O inhabitants of Jerusalem, and men of Judah, judge, I pray you, betwixt me and my vineyard.

15:4 What could have been done more to my vineyard that I have not done in it? Wherefore, when I looked that it should bring forth grapes it brought forth wild grapes.

15:5 And now go to; I will tell you what I will do to my vineyard--I will take away the hedge thereof, and it shall be eaten up; and I will break down the wall thereof, and it shall be trodden down;

15:6 And I will lay it waste; it shall not be pruned nor digged; but there shall come up briers and thorns; I will also command the clouds that they rain no rain upon it.

15:7 For the vineyard of the Lord of Hosts is the house of Israel, and the men of Judah his pleasant plant; and he looked for judgment, and behold, oppression; for righteousness, but behold, a cry.

15:8 Wo unto them that join house to house, (- -) till there can be no place, that they may be placed alone in the midst of the earth!

15:9 In mine ears, said the Lord of Hosts, of a truth many houses shall be desolate, and (-) great and fair cities without inhabitant.

15:10 Yea, ten acres of vineyard shall yield one bath, and the seed of a homer shall yield an ephah.

15:11 Wo unto them that rise up early in the morning, that they may follow strong drink, that continue until night, and wine inflame them!

15:12 And the harp, and the viol, the tablet, and pipe, and wine are in their feasts; but they regard not the work of the LORD, neither consider the operation of his hands.

5:13 Therefore my people are gone into captivity, because they have no knowledge: and their honourable men are famished, and their multitude dried up with thirst.

5:14 Therefore hell hath enlarged herself, and opened her mouth without measure: and their glory, and their multitude, and their pomp, and he that rejoiceth, shall descend into it.

5:15 And the mean man shall be brought down, and the mighty man shall be humbled, and the eyes of the lofty shall be humbled:

5:16 But the LORD of hosts shall be exalted in judgment, and God that is holy shall be sanctified in righteousness.

5:17 Then shall the lambs feed after their manner, and the waste places of the fat ones shall strangers eat.

5:18 Woe unto them that draw iniquity with cords of vanity, and sin as it were with a cart rope:

5:19 That say, Let him make speed, and hasten his work, that we may see it: and let the counsel of the Holy One of Israel draw nigh and come, that we may know it !

5:20 Woe unto them that call evil good, and good evil; that put darkness for light, and light for darkness; that put bitter for sweet, and sweet for bitter!

5:21 Woe unto ***the*** ~~them that are~~ wise in their own eyes, and prudent in their own sight!

5:22 Woe unto ***the*** ~~them that are~~ mighty to drink wine, and men of strength to mingle strong drink***;*** ~~:~~

5:23 Which justify the wicked for reward, and take away the righteousness of the righteous from him!

5:24 Therefore as the fire devoureth the stubble, and the flame consumeth the chaff, so their root shall be as rottenness, and their blossom shall go up as dust: because they have cast away the law of the LORD of hosts, and despised the word of the Holy One of Israel.

5:25 Therefore is the anger of the LORD kindled against his people, and he hath stretched forth his hand against them, and hath smitten them: and the hills did tremble, and their carcasses were torn in the midst of the streets. For

2nd Nephi (cont).

the Lord, neither consider the operation of his hands.

15:13 Therefore, my people are gone into captivity, because they have no knowledge; and their honorable men are famished, and their multitude dried up with thirst.

15:14 Therefore, hell hath enlarged herself, and opened her mouth without measure; and their glory, and their multitude, and their pomp, and he that rejoiceth, shall descend into it.

15:15 And the mean man shall be brought down, and the mighty man shall be humbled, and the eyes of the lofty shall be humbled.

15:16 But the Lord of Hosts shall be exalted in judgment, and God that is holy shall be sanctified in righteousness.

15:17 Then shall the lambs feed after their manner, and the waste places of the fat ones shall strangers eat.

15:18 Wo unto them that draw iniquity with cords of vanity, and sin as it were with a cart rope;

15:19 That say: Let him make speed, hasten his work, that we may see it; and let the counsel of the Holy One of Israel draw nigh and come, that we may know it.

15:20 Wo unto them that call evil good, and good evil, that put darkness for light, and light for darkness, that put bitter for sweet, and sweet for bitter!

15:21 Wo unto the wise in their own eyes and prudent in their own sight!

15:22 Wo unto the mighty to drink wine, and men of strength to mingle strong drink;

15:23 Who justify the wicked for reward, and take away the righteousness of the righteous from him!

15:24 Therefore, as the fire devoureth the stubble, and the flame consumeth the chaff, their root shall be (-) rottenness, and their blossoms shall go up as dust; because they have cast away the law of the Lord of Hosts, and despised the word of the Holy One of Israel.

15:25 Therefore, is the anger of the Lord kindled against his people, and he hath stretched forth his hand against them, and hath smitten them; and the hills did tremble, and their carcasses were torn in the midst of the streets. For

all this his anger is not turned away, but his hand is stretched out still.
5:26 And he will lift up an ensign to the nations from far, and will hiss unto them from the end of the earth: and, behold, they shall come with speed swiftly:
5:27 None shall be weary nor stumble among them;
none shall slumber nor sleep; neither shall the girdle of their loins be loosed, nor the latchet of their shoes be broken:

5:28 Whose arrows ***shall be*** ~~are~~ sharp, and all their bows bent, ***and*** their horses' hoofs shall be counted like flint, and their wheels like a whirlwind:

5:29 Their roaring shall be like a lion**.** ~~;~~ ~~t~~***T***hey shall roar like young lions***;*** ~~:~~ yea, they shall roar, and lay hold of the prey, and shall carry ~~it~~ away safe, and none shall deliver ~~it.~~
5:30 And in that day they shall roar against them like the roaring of the sea: and if ***they*** ~~one~~ look unto the land, behold darkness and sorrow***;*** ~~;~~ and the light is darkened in the heavens thereof.

2nd Nephi (cont.)
all this his anger is not turned away, but his hand is stretched out still.
15:26 And he will lift up an ensign to the nations from far, and will hiss unto them from the end of the earth; and behold, they shall come with speed swiftly;
none shall be weary nor stumble among them.
15:27 None shall slumber nor sleep; neither shall the girdle of their loins be loosed, nor the latchet of their shoes be broken;
15:28 Whose arrows shall be sharp, and all their bows bent, and their horses' hoofs shall be counted like flint, and their wheels like a whirlwind,
their roaring (- -) like a lion.
15:29 They shall roar like young lions; yea, they shall roar, and lay hold of the prey, and shall carry away safe, and none shall deliver.

15:30 And in that day they shall roar against them like the roaring of the sea; and if they look unto the land, behold, darkness and sorrow, and the light is darkened in the heavens thereof.

ISAIAH, Chapter 6

6:1 In the year that king Uzziah died I saw also the Lord sitting upon a throne, high and lifted up, and his train filled the temple.
6:2 Above it stood the seraphims: each one had six wings; with twain he covered his face, and with twain he covered his feet, and with twain he did fly.
6:3 And one cried unto another, and said, Holy, holy, holy, is the LORD of hosts: the whole earth is full of his glory.
6:4 And the posts of the door moved at the voice of him that cried, and the house was filled with smoke.
6:5 ¶ Then said I, Woe is me! for I am undone; because I am a man of unclean lips, and I dwell in the midst of a people of unclean lips: for mine eyes have seen the King, the LORD of hosts.
6:6 Then flew one of the seraphims unto me, having a live coal in his hand,

2nd Nephi
16:1 In the year that king Uzziah died, I saw also the Lord sitting upon a throne, high and lifted up, and his train filled the temple.
16:2 Above it stood the seraphim; each one had six wings; with twain he covered his face, and with twain he covered his feet, and with twain he did fly.
16:3 And one cried unto another, and said: Holy, holy, holy, is the Lord of Hosts; the whole earth is full of his glory.
16:4 And the posts of the door moved at the voice of him that cried, and the house was filled with smoke.
16:5 Then said I: Wo is unto me! for I am undone; because I am a man of unclean lips; and I dwell in the midst of a people of unclean lips; for mine eyes have seen the King, the Lord of Hosts.
16:6 Then flew one of the seraphim unto me, having a live coal in his hand,

which he had taken with the tongs from off the altar:
6:7 And he laid it upon my mouth, and said, Lo, this hath touched thy lips; and thine iniquity is taken away, and thy sin purged.
6:8 Also I heard the voice of the Lord, saying, Whom shall I send, and who will go for us? Then said I, Here am I; send me.
6:9 And he said, Go, and tell this people, Hear ye indeed, but ***they understood*** ~~understand~~ not; and see ye indeed, but ***they*** perceive***d*** not.
6:10 Make the heart of this people fat, and make their ears heavy, and shut their eyes; lest they see with their eyes, and hear with their ears, and understand with their heart, and convert, and be healed.
6:11 Then said I, Lord, how long? And he ***said*** ~~answered~~, Until the cities be wasted without inhabitant, and the houses without man, and the land be utterly desolate**.** ~~;~~
6:12 And the LORD have removed men far away, ~~and~~ ***for*** there ***shall*** be a great forsaking in the midst of the land.
6:13 But yet in it ***there*** shall be a tenth, and ***they*** ~~it~~ shall return, and shall be eaten***;*** ~~:~~ as a teil tree, and as an oak, whose substance is in them, when they cast their leaves***;*** ~~:~~ so the holy seed shall be the substance thereof.

<u>2nd Nephi (cont.)</u>
which he had taken with the tongs from off the altar<u>;</u>
16:7 And he laid it upon my mouth, and said: Lo, this <u>has</u> touched thy lips; and thine iniquity is taken away, and thy sin purged.
16:8 Also I heard the voice of the Lord, saying: Whom shall I send, and who will go for us? Then I said<u>:</u> Here am I; send me.
16:9 And he said: Go_ and tell this people--Hear ye indeed, but <u>they</u> understood not; and see ye indeed, but <u>they perceived</u> not.
16:10 Make the heart of this people fat, and make their ears heavy, and shut their eyes--lest they see with their eyes, and hear with their ears, and understand with their heart, and <u>be converted</u> and be healed.
16:11 Then said I: Lord, how long? And he <u>said</u>: Until the cities be wasted without inhabitant, and the houses without man, and the land be utterly desolate<u>;</u>
16:12 And the Lord have removed men far away, for there shall be a great forsaking in the midst of the land.
16:13 But yet (- - -) <u>there</u> shall be a tenth, and they shall return, and shall be eaten<u>,</u> as a teil-tree, and as an oak<u>,</u> whose substance is in them_ when they cast their leaves; so the holy seed shall be the substance thereof.

ISAIAH, Chapter 7

7:1 And it came to pass in the days of Ahaz the son of Jotham, the son of Uzziah, king of Judah, that Rezin the king of Syria, and Pekah the son of Remaliah, king of Israel, went up toward Jerusalem to war against it, but could not prevail against it.
7:2 And it was told the house of David, saying, Syria is confederate with Ephraim. And his heart was moved, and the heart of his people, as the trees of the wood are moved with the wind.
7:3 Then said the LORD unto Isaiah, Go forth now to meet Ahaz, thou, and Shearjashub thy son, at the end of the conduit of the upper pool in the highway of the fuller's field;
7:4 And say unto him, Take heed, and be quiet; fear not, neither be

<u>2nd Nephi</u>
17:1 And it came to pass in the days of Ahaz the son of Jotham, the son of Uzziah, king of Judah, that Rezin, (-) king of Syria, and Pekah the son of Remaliah, king of Israel, went up toward Jerusalem to war against it, but could not prevail against it.
17:2 And it was told the house of David, saying<u>:</u> Syria is confederate with Ephraim. And his heart was moved, and the heart of his people, as the trees of the wood are moved with the wind.
17:3 Then said the Lord unto Isaiah<u>:</u> Go forth now to meet Ahaz, thou and Shearjashub thy son, at the end of the conduit of the upper pool in the highway of the fuller's field;
17:4 And say unto him<u>:</u> Take heed, and be quiet; fear not, neither be

fainthearted for the two tails of these smoking firebrands, for the fierce anger of Rezin with Syria, and of the son of Remaliah.
7:5 Because Syria, Ephraim, and the son of Remaliah, have taken evil counsel against thee, saying,
7:6 Let us go up against Judah, and vex it, and let us make a breach therein for us, and set a king in the midst of it, ***yea,*** even the son of Tabeal:
7:7 Thus saith the Lord GOD, It shall not stand, neither shall it come to pass.
7:8 For the head of Syria is Damascus, and the head of Damascus is Rezin; and within threescore and five years shall Ephraim be broken, that it be not a people.
7:9 And the head of Ephraim is Samaria, and the head of Samaria is Remaliah's son. If ye will not believe, surely ye shall not be established.
7:10 ¶ Moreover the LORD spake again unto Ahaz, saying,
7:11 Ask thee a sign of the LORD thy God; ask it either in the depth, or in the height above.
7:12 But Ahaz said, I will not ask, neither will I tempt the LORD.
7:13 And he said, Hear ye now, O house of David; Is it a small thing for you to weary men, but will ye weary my God also?
7:14 Therefore the Lord himself shall give you a sign; Behold, a virgin shall conceive, and ***shall*** bear a son, and shall call his name Immanuel.
7:15 Butter and honey shall he eat, that he may know to refuse the evil, and ***to*** choose the good.
7:16 For before the child shall know to refuse the evil, and choose the good, the land that thou abhorrest shall be forsaken of both her kings.
7:17 The LORD shall bring upon thee, and upon thy people, and upon thy father's house, days that have not come, from the day that Ephraim departed from Judah; even the king of Assyria.
7:18 And it shall come to pass in that day, that the LORD shall hiss for the fly that is in the uttermost part of the rivers of Egypt, and for the bee that is in the land of Assyria.
7:19 And they shall come, and shall rest all of them in the desolate valleys, and in the holes of the rocks, and upon all thorns, and upon all bushes.

2nd Nephi (cont.)
faint-hearted for the two tails of these smoking firebrands, for the fierce anger of Rezin with Syria, and of the son of Remaliah.
17:5 Because Syria, Ephraim, and the son of Remaliah, have taken evil counsel against thee, saying:
17:6 Let us go up against Judah and vex it, and let us make a breach therein for us, and set a king in the midst of it, yea, (-) the son of Tabeal.
17:7 Thus saith the Lord God: It shall not stand, neither shall it come to pass.
17:8 For the head of Syria is Damascus, and the head of Damascus, (-) Rezin; and within three score and five years shall Ephraim be broken, that it be not a people.
17:9 And the head of Ephraim is Samaria, and the head of Samaria is Remaliah's son. If ye will not believe surely ye shall not be established.
17:10 Moreover, the Lord spake again unto Ahaz, saying:
17:11 Ask thee a sign of the Lord thy God; ask it either in the depths, or in the heights above.
17:12 But Ahaz said: I will not ask, neither will I tempt the Lord.
17:13 And he said: Hear ye now, O house of David; Is it a small thing for you to weary men, but will ye weary my God also?
17:14 Therefore, the Lord himself shall give you a sign--Behold, a virgin shall conceive, and shall bear a son, and shall call his name Immanuel.
17:15 Butter and honey shall he eat, that he may know to refuse the evil and to choose the good.
17:16 For before the child shall know to refuse the evil and choose the good, the land that thou abhorrest shall be forsaken of both her kings.
17:17 The Lord shall bring upon thee, and upon thy people, and upon thy father's house, days that have not come from the day that Ephraim departed from Judah, (-) the king of Assyria.
17:18 And it shall come to pass in that day that the Lord shall hiss for the fly that is in the uttermost part (- - -) of Egypt, and for the bee that is in the land of Assyria.
17:19 And they shall come, and shall rest all of them in the desolate valleys, and in the holes of the rocks, and upon all thorns, and upon all bushes.

7:20 In the same day shall the Lord shave with a razor that is hired, namely, by them beyond the river, by the king of Assyria, the head, and the hair of the feet: and it shall also consume the beard.
7:21 And it shall come to pass in that day, that a man shall nourish a young cow, and two sheep;
7:22 And it shall come to pass, for the abundance of milk that they shall give he shall eat butter: for butter and honey shall every one eat that is left in the land.
7:23 And it shall come to pass in that day~~;~~ that every place shall be, where there were a thousand vines at a thousand silverlings, ***which*** ~~it~~ shall even be for briers and thorns.
7:24 With arrows and with bows shall men come thither; because all the land shall become briers and thorns.
7:25 And on all hills that shall be digged with the mattock, there shall not come thither the fear of briers and thorns: but it shall be for the sending forth of oxen, and for the treading of lesser cattle.

2nd Nephi (cont.)
17:20 In the same day shall the Lord shave with a razor that is hired, (-) by them beyond the river, by the king of Assyria, the head, and the hair of the feet; and it shall also consume the beard.
17:21 And it shall come to pass in that day, a man shall nourish a young cow and two sheep;
17:22 And it shall come to pass, for the abundance of milk (-) they shall give he shall eat butter; for butter and honey shall every one eat that is left in the land.
17:23 And it shall come to pass in that day, (-) every place shall be, where there were a thousand vines at a thousand silverlings, which (-) shall (-) be for briers and thorns.
17:24 With arrows and with bows shall men come thither, because all the land shall become briers and thorns.
17:25 And (-) all hills that shall be digged with the mattock, there shall not come thither the fear of briers and thorns; but it shall be for the sending forth of oxen, and the treading of lesser cattle.

ISAIAH, Chapter 8

8:1 Moreover ***the word of*** the LORD said unto me, Take thee a great roll, and write in it with a man's pen concerning Maher-shalal-hash-baz.
8:2 And I took unto me faithful witnesses to record, Uriah the priest, and Zechariah the son of Jeberechiah.
8:3 And I went unto the prophetess; and she conceived, and bare a son. Then said the LORD to me, Call his name Maher-shalal-hash-baz.
8:4 For ***behold,*** ~~before~~ the child shall ***not*** have knowledge to cry, My father, and my mother, ***before*** the riches of Damascus and the spoil of Samaria shall be taken away before the king of Assyria.
8:5 The LORD spake also unto me again, saying,
8:6 Forasmuch as this people refuseth the waters of Shiloah that go softly, and rejoice in Rezin and Remaliah's son;
8:7 Now therefore, behold, the Lord bringeth up upon them the waters of the river, strong and many, even the king of

2nd Nephi
18:1 Moreover, the word of the Lord said unto me: Take thee a great roll, and write in it with a man's pen, concerning Maher-shalal-hash-baz.
18:2 And I took unto me faithful witnesses to record, Uriah the priest, and Zechariah the son of Jeberechiah.
18:3 And I went unto the prophetess; and she conceived and bare a son. Then said the Lord to me: Call his name, Maher-shalal-hash-baz.
18:4 For behold, the child shall not have knowledge to cry, My father, and my mother, before the riches of Damascus and the spoil of Samaria shall be taken away before the king of Assyria.
18:5 The Lord spake also unto me again, saying:
18:6 Forasmuch as this people refuseth the waters of Shiloah that go softly, and rejoice in Rezin and Remaliah's son;
18:7 Now therefore, behold, the Lord bringeth up upon them the waters of the river, strong and many, even the king of

Assyria, and all his glory: and he shall come up over all his channels, and go over all his banks:

8:8 And he shall pass through Judah; he shall overflow and go over, he shall reach even to the neck; and the stretching out of his wings shall fill the breadth of thy land, O Immanuel.

8:9 Associate yourselves, O ye people, and ye shall be broken in pieces; and give ear, all ye of far countries: gird yourselves, and ye shall be broken in pieces; gird yourselves, and ye shall be broken in pieces.

8:10 Take counsel together, and it shall come to nought; speak the word, and it shall not stand: for God is with us.

8:11 For the LORD spake thus to me with a strong hand, and instructed me that I should not walk in the way of this people, saying,

8:12 Say ye not, A confederacy, to all them to whom this people shall say, A confederacy; neither fear ye their fear, nor be afraid.

8:13 Sanctify the LORD of hosts himself; and let him be your fear, and let him be your dread.

8:14 And he shall be for a sanctuary; but for a stone of stumbling and for a rock of offence to both the houses of Israel, for a gin and for a snare to the inhabitants of Jerusalem.

8:15 And many among them shall stumble, and fall, and be broken, and be snared, and be taken.

8:16 Bind up the testimony, seal the law among my disciples.

8:17 And I will wait upon the LORD, that hideth his face from the house of Jacob, and I will look for him.

8:18 Behold, I and the children whom the LORD hath given me are for signs and for wonders in Israel from the LORD of hosts, which dwelleth in mount Zion.

8:19 And when they shall say unto you, Seek unto them that have familiar spirits, and unto wizards that peep, and that mutter***;*** ~~:~~ should not a people seek unto their God? for the living to ***to hear from*** the dead?

8:20 To the law and to the testimony***;*** ~~:~~ ***and*** if they speak not according to this word, it is because there is no light in them.

2nd Nephi (cont.)

Assyria and all his glory; and he shall come up over all his channels, and go over all his banks.

18:8 And he shall pass through Judah; he shall overflow and go over, he shall reach even to the neck; and the stretching out of his wings shall fill the breadth of thy land, O Immanuel.

18:9 Associate yourselves, O ye people, and ye shall be broken in pieces; and give ear all ye of far countries; gird yourselves, and ye shall be broken in pieces; gird yourselves, and ye shall be broken in pieces.

18:10 Take counsel together, and it shall come to naught; speak the word, and it shall not stand; for God is with us.

18:11 For the Lord spake thus to me with a strong hand, and instructed me that I should not walk in the way of this people, saying:

18:12 Say ye not, A confederacy, to all to whom this people shall say, A confederacy; neither fear ye their fear, nor be afraid.

18:13 Sanctify the Lord of Hosts himself, and let him be your fear, and let him be your dread.

18:14 And he shall be for a sanctuary; but for a stone of stumbling, and for a rock of offense to both the houses of Israel, for a gin and a snare to the inhabitants of Jerusalem.

18:15 And many among them shall stumble and fall, and be broken, and be snared, and be taken.

18:16 Bind up the testimony, seal the law among my disciples.

18:17 And I will wait upon the Lord, that hideth his face from the house of Jacob, and I will look for him.

18:18 Behold, I and the children whom the Lord hath given me are for signs and for wonders in Israel from the Lord of Hosts, which dwelleth in Mount Zion.

18:19 And when they shall say unto you: Seek unto them that have familiar spirits, and unto wizards that peep and mutter--should not a people seek unto their God for the living to hear from the dead?

18:20 To the law and to the testimony; and if they speak not according to this word, it is because there is no light in them.

Isaiah (King James Version w/JST)	The Book of Mormon (With Comparison to JST)	Additional LDS Scripture
	2nd Nephi (cont.)	
8:21 And they shall pass through it, hardly bestead and hungry: and it shall come to pass, that when they shall be hungry, they shall fret themselves, and curse their king and their God, and look upward.	18:21 And they shall pass through it_ hardly bestead and hungry; and it shall come to pass_ that when they shall be hungry, they shall fret themselves, and curse their king and their God, and look upward.	
8:22 And they shall look unto the earth; and behold trouble and darkness, dimness of anguish; and they shall be driven to darkness.	18:22 And they shall look unto the earth_ and behold trouble, and darkness, dimness of anguish, and shall be driven to darkness.	

ISAIAH, Chapter 9

Isaiah (King James Version w/JST)	The Book of Mormon (With Comparison to JST)	Additional LDS Scripture
	2nd Nephi	
9:1 Nevertheless the dimness shall not be such as was in her vexation, when at the first he lightly afflicted the land of Zebulun, and the land of Naphtali, and afterward did more grievously afflict her by the way of the ***Red*** sea, beyond Jordan, in Galilee of the nations.	19:1 Nevertheless, the dimness shall not be such as was in her vexation, when at first he lightly afflicted the land of Zebulun, and the land of Naphtali, and afterwards did more grievously afflict (-) by the way of the Red Sea beyond Jordan_ in Galilee of the nations.	
9:2 The people that walked in darkness have seen a great light: they that dwell in the land of the shadow of death, upon them hath the light shined.	19:2 The people that walked in darkness have seen a great light; they that dwell in the land of the shadow of death, upon them hath the light shined.	
9:3 Thou hast multiplied the nation, and ~~not~~ increased the joy***;*** ~~:~~ they joy before thee, according to the joy in harvest, and as men rejoice when they divide the spoil.	19:3 Thou hast multiplied the nation, and increased the joy – they joy before thee_ according to the joy in harvest, and as men rejoice when they divide the spoil.	
9:4 For thou hast broken the yoke of his burden, and the staff of his shoulder, the rod of his oppressor, as in the day of Midian.	19:4 For thou hast broken the yoke of his burden, and the staff of his shoulder, the rod of his oppressor (- - -).	
9:5 For every battle of the warrior is with confused noise, and garments rolled in blood; but this shall be with burning and fuel of fire.	19:5 For every battle of the warrior is with confused noise, and garments rolled in blood; but this shall be with burning and fuel of fire.	
9:6 For unto us a child is born, unto us a son is given: and the government shall be upon his shoulder: and his name shall be called Wonderful, Counsellor, The mighty God , The everlasting Father, The Prince of Peace.	19:6 For unto us a child is born, unto us a son is given; and the government shall be upon his shoulder; and his name shall be called, Wonderful, Counselor, The Mighty God, The Everlasting Father, The Prince of Peace.	
9:7 Of the increase of his government and peace there ***is*** ~~shall~~ be no end, upon the throne of David, and upon his kingdom, to order it, and to establish it with judgment and with justice from henceforth even ***for ever*** ~~for ever~~. The zeal of the LORD of hosts will perform this.	19:7 Of the increase of (-) government and peace there is no end, upon the throne of David, and upon his kingdom_ to order it, and to establish it with judgment and with justice from henceforth, even forever. The zeal of the Lord of Hosts will perform this.	
9:8 The Lord sent ***his*** ~~a~~ word ***unto*** ~~into~~ Jacob, and it hath lighted upon Israel.	19:8 The Lord sent his word unto Jacob and it hath lighted upon Israel.	

9:9 And all the people shall know, even Ephraim and the inhabitant of Samaria, that say in the pride and stoutness of heart,

9:10 The bricks are fallen down, but we will build with hewn stones: the sycamores are cut down, but we will change them into cedars.

9:11 Therefore the LORD shall set up the adversaries of Rezin against him, and join his enemies together;

9:12 The Syrians before, and the Philistines behind; and they shall devour Israel with open mouth. For all this his anger is not turned away, but his hand is stretched out still.

9:13 For the people turneth not unto him that smiteth them, neither do they seek the LORD of hosts.

9:14 Therefore the LORD will cut off from Israel head and tail, branch and rush, in one day.

9:15 The ancient and honourable, he is the head; and the prophet that teacheth lies, he is the tail.

9:16 For the leaders of this people cause them to err; and they that are led of them are destroyed.

9:17 Therefore the Lord shall have no joy in their young men, neither shall have mercy on their fatherless and widows***;*** ~~:~~ for every one is ***a*** ~~an~~ hypocrite and an evildoer, and every mouth speaketh folly. For all this his anger is not turned away, but his hand is stretched out still.

9:18 For wickedness burneth as the fire: it shall devour the briers and thorns, and shall kindle in the thickets of the forest, and they shall mount up like the lifting up of smoke.

9:19 Through the wrath of the LORD of hosts is the land darkened, and the people shall be as the fuel of the fire: no man shall spare his brother.

9:20 And he shall snatch on the right hand, and be hungry; and he shall eat on the left hand, and they shall not be satisfied: they shall eat every man the flesh of his own arm:

9:21 Manasseh, Ephraim; and Ephraim, Manasseh: and they together shall be against Judah. For all this his anger is not turned away, but his hand is stretched out still.

2nd Nephi (cont.)

19:9 And all the people shall know, even Ephraim and the inhabitants of Samaria, that say in the pride and stoutness of heart:

19:10 The bricks are fallen down, but we will build with hewn stones; the sycamores are cut down, but we will change them into cedars.

19:11 Therefore the Lord shall set up the adversaries of Rezin against him, and join his enemies together;

19:12 The Syrians before_ and the Philistines behind; and they shall devour Israel with open mouth. For all this his anger is not turned away, but his hand is stretched out still.

19:13 For the people turneth not unto him that smiteth them, neither do they seek the Lord of Hosts.

19:14 Therefore will the Lord cut off from Israel head and tail, branch and rush_ in one day.

19:15 The ancient (- -), he is the head; and the prophet that teacheth lies, he is the tail.

19:16 For the leaders of this people cause them to err; and they that are led of them are destroyed.

19:17 Therefore the Lord shall have no joy in their young men, neither shall have mercy on their fatherless and widows; for every one of them is a hypocrite and an evildoer, and every mouth speaketh folly. For all this his anger is not turned away, but his hand is stretched out still.

19:18 For wickedness burneth as the fire; it shall devour the briers and thorns, and shall kindle in the thickets of the forests, and they shall mount up like the lifting up of smoke.

19:19 Through the wrath of the Lord of Hosts is the land darkened, and the people shall be as the fuel of the fire; no man shall spare his brother.

19:20 And he shall snatch on the right hand_ and be hungry; and he shall eat on the left hand_ and they shall not be satisfied; they shall eat every man the flesh of his own arm–

19:21 Manasseh, Ephraim; and Ephraim, Manasseh; they together shall be against Judah. For all this his anger is not turned away, but his hand is stretched out still.

ISAIAH, Chapter 10

10:1 WOE unto them that decree unrighteous decrees, and that write grievousness which they have prescribed;
10:2 To turn aside the needy from judgment, and to take away the right from the poor of my people, that widows may be their prey, and that they may rob the fatherless!
10:3 And what will ye do in the day of visitation, and in the desolation which shall come from far? to whom will ye flee for help? and where will ye leave your glory?
10:4 Without me they shall bow down under the prisoners, and they shall fall under the slain. For all this his anger is not turned away, but his hand is stretched out still.
10:5 O Assyrian, the rod of mine anger, and the staff in their hand is mine indignation.
10:6 I will send him against an hypocritical nation, and against the people of my wrath will I give him a charge, to take the spoil, and to take the prey, and to tread them down like the mire of the streets.
10:7 Howbeit he meaneth not so, neither doth his heart think so; but ~~it is~~ in his heart ***it is*** to destroy and cut off nations not a few.
10:8 For he saith, Are not my princes altogether kings?
10:9 Is not Calno as Carchemish? is not Hamath as Arpad? is not Samaria as Damascus?
10:10 As my hand hath found***ed*** the kingdoms of the idols, and whose graven images did excel them of Jerusalem and of Samaria;
10:11 Shall I not, as I have done unto Samaria and her idols, so do to Jerusalem and ***to*** her idols?
10:12 Wherefore it shall come to pass, that**,** when the Lord hath performed his whole work upon ~~m~~***M***ount Zion and on Jerusalem, I will punish the fruit of the stout heart of the king of Assyria, and the glory of his high looks.
10:13 For he saith, By the strength of my hand**,** ~~I have done it~~, and by my wisdom ***I have done these things***;
for I am prudent, ~~:~~ and I have ~~re~~moved the *borders* ~~bounds~~ of the people, and

2nd Nephi

20:1 Wo unto them that decree unrighteous decrees, and that write grievousness which they have prescribed;
20:2 To turn away the needy from judgment, and to take away the right from the poor of my people, that widows may be their prey, and that they may rob the fatherless!
20:3 And what will ye do in the day of visitation, and in the desolation which shall come from far? to whom will ye flee for help? and where will ye leave your glory?
20:4 Without me they shall bow down under the prisoners, and they shall fall under the slain. For all this his anger is not turned away, but his hand is stretched out still.
20:5 O Assyrian, the rod of mine anger, and the staff in their hand is their indignation.
20:6 I will send him against a hypocritical nation, and against the people of my wrath will I give him a charge to take the spoil, and to take the prey, and to tread them down like the mire of the streets.
20:7 Howbeit he meaneth not so, neither doth his heart think so; but in his heart it is to destroy and cut off nations not a few.
20:8 For he saith: Are not my princes altogether kings?
20:9 Is not Calno as Carchemish? Is not Hamath as Arpad? Is not Samaria as Damascus?
20:10 As my hand hath founded the kingdoms of the idols, and whose graven images did excel them of Jerusalem and of Samaria;
20:11 Shall I not, as I have done unto Samaria and her idols, so do to Jerusalem and to her idols?
20:12 Wherefore it shall come to pass that_ when the Lord hath performed his whole work upon Mount Zion and upon Jerusalem, I will punish the fruit of the stout heart of the king of Assyria, and the glory of his high looks.
20:13 For he saith: By the strength of my hand_ and by my wisdom I have done these things;
for I am prudent; and I have moved the borders of the people, and

have robbed their treasures, and I have
put down the inhabitants like a valiant
man:
10:14 And my hand hath found as a
nest the riches of the people: and as one
gathereth eggs that are left, have I
gathered all the earth; and there was
none that moved the wing, or opened
the mouth, or peeped.
10:15 Shall the axe boast itself against
him that heweth therewith? or shall the
saw magnify itself against him that
shaketh it? as if the rod should shake
itself against them that lift it up, or as if
the staff should lift up itself, as if it were
no wood.
10:16 Therefore shall the Lord, the
Lord of hosts, send among his fat ones
leanness; and under his glory he shall
kindle a burning like the burning of a
fire.
10:17 And the light of Israel shall be
for a fire, and his Holy One for a flame:
and it shall burn and devour his thorns
and his briers in one day;
10:18 And shall consume the glory of
his forest, and of his fruitful field, both
soul and body: and they shall be as
when a standardbearer fainteth.
10:19 And the rest of the trees of his
forest shall be few, that a child may
write them.
10:20 And it shall come to pass in that
day, that the remnant of Israel, and such
as are escaped of the house of Jacob,
shall no more again stay upon him that
smote them; but shall stay upon the
LORD, the Holy One of Israel, in truth.
10:21 The remnant shall return, ***yea,***
even the remnant of Jacob, unto the
mighty God.
10:22 For though thy people Israel be
as the sand of the sea, yet a remnant of
them shall return: the consumption
decreed shall overflow with
righteousness.
10:23 For the Lord GOD of hosts shall
make a consumption, even determined,
in ~~the midst of~~ all the land.
10:24 Therefore thus saith the Lord
GOD of hosts, O my people that
dwellest in Zion, be not afraid of the
Assyrian: he shall smite thee with a rod,
and shall lift up his staff against thee,
after the manner of Egypt.
10:25 For yet a very little while, and
the indignation shall cease, and mine
anger in their destruction.

2nd Nephi (cont.)
have robbed their treasures, and I have
put down the inhabitants like a valiant
man;
20:14 And my hand hath found as a
nest the riches of the people; and as one
gathereth eggs that are left_ have I
gathered all the earth; and there was
none that moved the wing, or opened
the mouth, or peeped.
20:15 Shall the ax boast itself against
him that heweth therewith? Shall the
saw magnify itself against him that
shaketh it? As if the rod should shake
itself against them that lift it up, or as if
the staff should lift up itself_ as if it were
no wood!
20:16 Therefore shall the Lord, the
Lord of Hosts, send among his fat ones,
leanness; and under his glory he shall
kindle a burning like the burning of a
fire.
20:17 And the light of Israel shall be
for a fire, and his Holy One for a flame,
and (-) shall burn and shall devour his
thorns and his briers in one day;
20:18 And shall consume the glory of
his forest, and of his fruitful field, both
soul and body; and they shall be as
when a standard-bearer fainteth.
20:19 And the rest of the trees of his
forest shall be few, that a child may
write them.
20:20 And it shall come to pass in that
day, that the remnant of Israel, and such
as are escaped of the house of Jacob,
shall no more again stay upon him that
smote them, but shall stay upon the
Lord, the Holy One of Israel, in truth.
20:21 The remnant shall return, yea,
even the remnant of Jacob, unto the
mighty God.
20:22 For though thy people Israel be
as the sand of the sea, yet a remnant of
them shall return; the consumption
decreed shall overflow with
righteousness.
20:23 For the Lord God of Hosts shall
make a consumption, even determined
in all the land.
20:24 Therefore, thus saith the Lord
God of Hosts: O my people that
dwellest in Zion, be not afraid of the
Assyrian; he shall smite thee with a rod,
and shall lift up his staff against thee,
after the manner of Egypt.
20:25 For yet a very little while, and
the indignation shall cease, and mine
anger in their destruction.

10:26 And the LORD of hosts shall stir up a scourge for him according to the slaughter of Midian at the rock of Oreb: and as his rod was upon the sea, so shall he lift it up after the manner of Egypt.

10:27 And it shall come to pass in that day, that his burden shall be taken away from off thy shoulder, and his yoke from off thy neck, and the yoke shall be destroyed because of the anointing.

10:28 He is come to Aiath, he is passed to Migron; at Michmash he hath laid up his carriages:

10:29 They are gone over the passage: they have taken up their lodging at Geba; Ramah is afraid; Gibeah of Saul is fled.

10:30 Lift up thy voice, O daughter of Gallim: cause it to be heard unto Laish, O poor Anathoth.

10:31 Madmenah is removed; the inhabitants of Gebim gather themselves to flee.

10:32 As yet shall he remain at Nob that day: he shall shake his hand against the mount of the daughter of Zion, the hill of Jerusalem.

10:33 Behold, the Lord, the LORD of hosts, shall lop the bough with terror: and the high ones of stature shall be hewn down, and the haughty shall be humbled.

10:34 And he shall cut down the thickets of the forest with iron, and Lebanon shall fall by a mighty one.

2nd Nephi (cont.)

20:26 And the Lord of Hosts shall stir up a scourge for him according to the slaughter of Midian at the rock of Oreb; and as his rod was upon the sea so shall he lift it up after the manner of Egypt.

20:27 And it shall come to pass in that day that his burden shall be taken away from off thy shoulder, and his yoke from off thy neck, and the yoke shall be destroyed because of the anointing.

20:28 He is come to Aiath, he is passed to Migron; at Michmash he hath laid up his carriages.

20:29 They are gone over the passage; they have taken up their lodging at Geba; Ramath is afraid; Gibeah of Saul is fled.

20:30 Lift up the voice, O daughter of Gallim; cause it to be heard unto Laish, O poor Anathoth.

20:31 Madmenah is removed; the inhabitants of Gebim gather themselves to flee.

20:32 As yet shall he remain at Nob that day; he shall shake his hand against the mount of the daughter of Zion, the hill of Jerusalem.

20:33 Behold, the Lord, the Lord of Hosts shall lop the bough with terror; and the high ones of stature shall be hewn down; and the haughty shall be humbled.

20:34 And he shall cut down the thickets of the forests with iron, and Lebanon shall fall by a mighty one.

ISAIAH, Chapter 11

11:1 And there shall come forth a rod out of the stem of Jesse, and a Branch shall grow out of his roots:

2nd Nephi

21:1 And there shall come forth a rod out of the stem of Jesse, and a branch shall grow out of his roots.

History of Joseph Smith

1:40 In addition to these, he [Moroni] quoted the eleventh chapter of Isaiah, saying that it was about to be fulfilled.

D&C 113

113:3 What is the rod spoken of in the first verse of the 11th chapter of Isaiah, that should come of the Stem of Jesse?

113:4 Behold, thus saith the Lord: It is a servant in the hands of Christ, who is partly a descendant of Jesse as well as of Ephraim, or of the house of Joseph, on whom there is laid much power.

Isaiah

11:2 And the spirit of the LORD shall rest upon him, the spirit of wisdom and understanding, the spirit of counsel and might, the spirit of knowledge and of the fear of the LORD;
11:3 And shall make him of quick understanding in the fear of the LORD: and he shall not judge after the sight of his eyes, neither reprove after the hearing of his ears:

2nd Nephi (cont.)

21:2 And the Spirit of the Lord shall rest upon him, the spirit of wisdom and understanding, the spirit of counsel and might, the spirit of knowledge and of the fear of the Lord;
21:3 And shall make him of quick understanding in the fear of the Lord; and he shall not judge after the sight of his eyes, neither reprove after the hearing of his ears.

Isaiah

11:4 But with righteousness shall he judge the poor, and reprove with equity for the meek of the earth: and he shall smite the earth with the rod of his mouth, and with the breath of his lips shall he slay the wicked.

2nd Nephi

21:4 But with righteousness shall he judge the poor, and reprove with equity for the meek of the earth; and he shall smite the earth with the rod of his mouth, and with the breath of his lips shall he slay the wicked.

2nd Nephi

30:9 And with righteousness shall the Lord God judge the poor, and reprove with equity for the meek of the earth. And he shall smite the earth with the rod of his mouth; and with the breath of his lips shall he slay the wicked.

30:10 For the time speedily cometh that the Lord God shall cause a great division among the people, and the wicked will he destroy; and he will spare his people, yea, even if it so be that he must destroy the wicked by fire.

Isaiah

11:5 And righteousness shall be the girdle of his loins, and faithfulness the girdle of his reins.

2nd Nephi

21:5 And righteousness shall be the girdle of his loins, and faithfulness the girdle of his reins.

2nd Nephi

30:11 And righteousness shall be the girdle of his loins, and faithfulness the girdle of his reins.

D&C

113:1 Who is the stem of Jesse spoken of in the 1st, 2d, 3d, 4th, and 5th verses of the 11th chapter of Isaiah?
113:2 Verily thus saith the Lord: It is Christ.

Isaiah

11:6 The wolf also shall dwell with the lamb, and the leopard shall lie down with the kid; and the calf and the young lion and the fatling together;

and a little child shall lead them.
11:7 And the cow and the bear shall feed; their young ones shall lie down together: and the lion shall eat straw like the ox.
11:8 And the sucking child shall play on the hole of the asp, and the weaned child shall put his hand on the cockatrice' den.
11:9 They shall not hurt nor destroy in all my holy mountain: for the earth shall be full of the knowledge of the LORD, as the waters cover the sea.

2nd Nephi

21:6 The wolf also shall dwell with the lamb, and the leopard shall lie down with the kid, and the calf and the young lion and fatling together;

and a little child shall lead them.
21:7 And the cow and the bear shall feed; their young ones shall lie down together; and the lion shall eat straw like the ox.
21:8 And the sucking child shall play on the hole of the asp, and the weaned child shall put his hand on the cockatrice's den.
21:9 They shall not hurt nor destroy in all my holy mountain, for the earth shall be full of the knowledge of the Lord, as the waters cover the sea.

2nd Nephi

30:12 And then shall the wolf (- -) dwell with the lamb; and the leopard shall lie down with the kid, and the calf, and the young lion, and the fatling, together;
and a little child shall lead them.
30:13 And the cow and the bear shall feed; their young ones shall lie down together; and the lion shall eat straw like the ox.
30:14 And the sucking child shall play on the hole of the asp, and the weaned child shall put his hand on the cockatrice's den.
30:15 They shall not hurt nor destroy in all my holy mountain; for the earth shall be full of the knowledge of the Lord as the waters cover the sea.

11:10 ¶ And in that day there shall be a root of Jesse, which shall stand for an ensign of the people; to it shall the Gentiles seek: and his rest shall be glorious.

11:11 And it shall come to pass in that day, that the Lord shall set his hand again the second time to recover the remnant of his people, which shall be left, from Assyria, and from Egypt, and from Pathros, and from Cush, and from Elam, and from Shinar, and from Hamath, and from the islands of the sea.
11:12 And he shall set up an ensign for the nations, and shall assemble the outcasts of Israel, and gather together the dispersed of Judah from the four corners of the earth.
11:13 The envy also of Ephraim shall depart, and the adversaries of Judah shall be cut off: Ephraim shall not envy Judah, and Judah shall not vex Ephraim.

11:14 But they shall fly upon the shoulders of the Philistines toward the west; they shall spoil them of the east together: they shall lay their hand upon Edom and Moab; and the children of Ammon shall obey them.
11:15 And the LORD shall utterly destroy the tongue of the Egyptian sea; and with his mighty wind shall he shake his hand over the river, and shall smite it in the seven streams, and make men go over dryshod.
11:16 And there shall be an highway for the remnant of his people, which shall be left, from Assyria; like as it was to Israel in the day that he came up out of the land of Egypt.

2nd Nephi (cont.)
21:10 And in that day there shall be a root of Jesse, which shall stand for an ensign of the people; to it shall the Gentiles seek; and his rest shall be glorious.

21:11 And it shall come to pass in that day_ that the Lord shall set his hand again the second time to recover the remnant of his people_ which shall be left, from Assyria, and from Egypt, and from Pathros, and from Cush, and from Elam, and from Shinar, and from Hamath, and from the islands of the sea.
21:12 And he shall set up an ensign for the nations, and shall assemble the outcasts of Israel, and gather together the dispersed of Judah from the four corners of the earth.
21:13 The envy (-) of Ephraim also shall depart, and the adversaries of Judah shall be cut off; Ephraim shall not envy Judah, and Judah shall not vex Ephraim.
21:14 But they shall fly upon the shoulders of the Philistines towards the west; they shall spoil them of the east together; they shall lay their hand upon Edom and Moab; and the children of Ammon shall obey them.
21:15 And the Lord shall utterly destroy the tongue of the Egyptian sea; and with his mighty wind he shall shake his hand over the river, and shall smite it in the seven streams, and make men go over dry shod.
21:16 And there shall be a highway for the remnant of his people which shall be left, from Assyria, like as it was to Israel in the day that he came up out of the land of Egypt.

D&C 113
113:5 What is the root of Jesse spoken of in the 10th verse of the 11th chapter?
113:6 Behold, thus saith the Lord, it is a descendant of Jesse, as well as of Joseph, unto whom rightly belongs the priesthood, and the keys of the kingdom, for an ensign, and for the gathering of my people in the last days.

ISAIAH, Chapter 12

Isaiah	2nd Nephi
12:1 And in that day thou shalt say, O LORD, I will praise thee: though thou wast angry with me, thine anger is turned away, and thou comfortedst me.	22:1 And in that day thou shalt say: O Lord, I will praise thee; though thou wast angry with me thine anger is turned away, and thou comfortedst me.
12:2 Behold, God is my salvation; I will trust, and not be afraid: for the LORD JEHOVAH is my strength and my song; he also is become my salvation.	22:2 Behold, God is my salvation; I will trust, and not be afraid; for the Lord JEHOVAH is my strength and my song; he also has become my salvation.
12:3 Therefore with joy shall ye draw water out of the wells of salvation.	22:3 Therefore, with joy shall ye draw water out of the wells of salvation.
12:4 And in that day shall ye say, Praise the LORD, call upon his name, declare his doings among the people, make mention that his name is exalted.	22:4 And in that day shall ye say: Praise the Lord, call upon his name, declare his doings among the people, make mention that his name is exalted.
12:5 Sing unto the LORD; for he hath done excellent things: this is known in all the earth.	22:5 Sing unto the Lord; for he hath done excellent things; this is known in all the earth.
12:6 Cry out and shout, thou inhabitant of Zion: for great is the Holy One of Israel in the midst of thee.	22:6 Cry out and shout, thou inhabitant of Zion; for great is the Holy One of Israel in the midst of thee.

ISAIAH, Chapter 13

Isaiah	2nd Nephi
13:1 The burden of Babylon, which Isaiah the son of Amoz did see.	23:1 The burden of Babylon, which Isaiah the son of Amoz did see.
13:2 Lift ye up ~~a~~ ***my*** banner upon the high mountain, exalt the voice unto them, shake the hand, that they may go into the gates of the nobles.	23:2 Lift ye up a banner upon the high mountain, exalt the voice unto them, shake the hand, that they may go into the gates of the nobles.
13:3 I have commanded my sanctified ones, I have also called my mighty ones for mine anger ***is not upon*** ~~, even~~ them that rejoice in my highness.	23:3 I have commanded my sanctified ones, I have also called my mighty ones, for mine anger is not upon them that rejoice in my highness.
13:4 The noise of ***the*** ~~a~~ multitude in the mountains, like as of a great people; a tumultuous noise of the kingdoms of nations gathered together: the LORD of hosts mustereth the host of the battle.	23:4 The noise of the multitude in the mountains_ like as of a great people, a tumultuous noise of the kingdoms of nations gathered together, the Lord of Hosts mustereth the hosts of the battle.
13:5 They come from a far country, from the end of heaven, ***yea,*** ~~even~~ the LORD, and the weapons of his indignation, to destroy the whole land.	23:5 They come from a far country, from the end of heaven, yea, the Lord, and the weapons of his indignation, to destroy the whole land.
13:6 Howl ye; for the day of the LORD is at hand; it shall come as a destruction from the Almighty.	23:6 Howl ye, for the day of the Lord is at hand; it shall come as a destruction from the Almighty.
13:7 Therefore shall all hands be faint, and every man's heart shall melt:	23:7 Therefore shall all hands be faint, every man's heart shall melt;
13:8 And they shall be afraid: pangs and sorrows shall take hold of them; they shall be in pain as a woman that travaileth: they shall be amazed one at another; their faces shall be as flames.	23:8 And they shall be afraid; pangs and sorrows shall take hold of them; (- - -) they shall be amazed one at another; their faces shall be as flames.

Isaiah	The Book of Mormon	Additional LDS Scripture
	2nd Nephi (cont.)	
13:9 Behold, the day of the LORD cometh, cruel both with wrath and fierce anger, to lay the land desolate: and he shall destroy the sinners thereof out of it.	23:9 Behold, the day of the Lord cometh, cruel both with wrath and fierce anger, to lay the land desolate; and he shall destroy the sinners thereof out of it.	
13:10 For the stars of heaven and the constellations thereof shall not give their light: the sun shall be darkened in his going forth, and the moon shall not cause her light to shine.	23:10 For the stars of heaven and the constellations thereof shall not give their light; the sun shall be darkened in his going forth, and the moon shall not cause her light to shine.	
13:11 And I will punish the world for their evil, and the wicked for their iniquity; and I will cause the arrogancy of the proud to cease, and will lay low the haughtiness of the terrible.	23:11 And I will punish the world for (-) evil, and the wicked for their iniquity; (-) I will cause the arrogancy of the proud to cease, and will lay <u>down</u> the haughtiness of the terrible.	
13:12 I will make a man more precious than fine gold; even a man than the golden wedge of Ophir.	23:12 I will make a man more precious than fine gold; even a man than the golden wedge of Ophir.	
13:13 Therefore I will shake the heavens, and the earth shall remove out of her place, in the wrath of the LORD of hosts, and in the day of his fierce anger.	23:13 Therefore, I will shake the heavens, and the earth shall remove out of her place, in the wrath of the Lord of <u>H</u>osts, and in the day of his fierce anger.	
13:14 And it shall be as the chased roe, and as a sheep that no man taketh up: they shall every man turn to his own people, and flee every one into his own land.	23:14 And it shall be as the chased roe, and as a sheep that no man taketh up; and they shall every man turn to his own people, and flee every one into his own land.	
13:15 Every one that is found shall be thrust through; and every one that is joined ***to the wicked*** ~~unto them~~ shall fall by the sword.	24:15 Every one that is <u>proud</u> shall be thrust through; yea, and every one that is joined to the wicked shall fall by the sword.	
13:16 Their children also shall be dashed to pieces before their eyes; their houses shall be spoiled, and their wives ravished.	23:16 Their children also shall be dashed to pieces before their eyes; their houses shall be spoiled_ and their wives ravished.	
13:17 Behold, I will stir up the Medes against them, which shall not regard silver; and as for gold, they shall not delight in it.	23:17 Behold, I will stir up the Medes against them, which shall not regard silver_ and (- -) gold, <u>nor shall they</u> delight in it.	
13:18 Their bows also shall dash the young men to pieces; and they shall have no pity on the fruit of the womb; their eye shall not spare children.	23:18 Their bows shall also dash the young men to pieces; and they shall have no pity on the fruit of the womb; their eyes shall not spare children.	
13:19 And Babylon, the glory of kingdoms, the beauty of the Chaldees' excellency, shall be as when God overthrew Sodom and Gomorrah.	23:19 And Babylon, the glory of kingdoms, the beauty of the Chaldees' excellency, shall be as when God overthrew Sodom and Gomorrah.	
13:20 It shall never be inhabited, neither shall it be dwelt in from generation to generation: neither shall the Arabian pitch tent there; neither shall the shepherds make their fold there.	23:20 It shall never be inhabited, neither shall it be dwelt in from generation to generation: neither shall the Arabian pitch tent there; neither shall the shepherds make their fold there.	
13:21 But wild beasts of the desert shall lie there; and their houses shall be full of doleful creatures; and owls shall dwell there, and satyrs shall dance there.	23:21 But wild beasts of the desert shall lie there; and their houses shall be full of doleful creatures; and owls shall dwell there, and satyrs shall dance there.	

13:22 And the wild beasts of the islands shall cry in their desolate houses, and dragons in their pleasant palaces: and her time is near to come, and her days shall not be prolonged***; for I will destroy her speedily; yeah, for I will be merciful unto my people, but the wicked shall perish.***

2nd Nephi (cont.)

23:22 And the wild beasts of the islands shall cry in their desolate houses, and dragons in their pleasant palaces; and her time is near to come, and her day shall not be prolonged. For I will destroy her speedily; yea, for I will be merciful unto my people, but the wicked shall perish.

ISAIAH, Chapter 14

14:1 ¶ For the LORD will have mercy on Jacob, and will yet choose Israel, and set them in their own land: and the strangers shall be joined with them, and they shall cleave to the house of Jacob.

14:2 And the people shall take them, and bring them to their place: ***yeah, from far, unto the end of the earth, and they shall return to their land of promise,*** and the house of Israel shall possess them in the land of the LORD for servants and handmaids***;*** ~~:~~ and they shall take them captives, whose captives they were; and they shall rule over their oppressors.

14:3 And it shall come to pass in ***that*** ~~the~~ day that the LORD shall give thee rest from thy sorrow~~,~~ and from thy fear, and from the hard bondage wherein thou wast made to serve,

14:4 ***And it shall come to pass in that day*** ~~T~~*t*hat thou shalt take up this proverb against the king of Babylon, and say, How hath the oppressor ceased! the golden city ceased!

14:5 The LORD hath broken the staff of the wicked, and the sceptre of the rulers.

14:6 He who smote the people in wrath with a continual stroke, he that ruled the nations in anger, is persecuted, and none hindereth.

14:7 The whole earth is at rest, and is quiet: they break forth into singing.

14:8 Yea, the fir trees rejoice at thee, and ***also*** the cedars of Lebanon, saying, Since thou art laid down, no feller is come up against us.

14:9 Hell from beneath is moved for thee to meet thee at thy coming: it stirreth up the dead for thee, even all the chief ones of the earth; it hath raised up from their thrones all the kings of the nations.

2nd Nephi

24:1 For the Lord will have mercy on Jacob, and will yet choose Israel, and set them in their own land; and the strangers shall be joined with them, and they shall cleave to the house of Jacob.

24:2 And the people shall take them and bring them to their place; yea, from far unto the ends of the earth; and they shall return to their lands of promise. And the house of Israel shall possess them, and (-) the land of the Lord shall be for servants and handmaids; and they shall take them captives unto whom they were captives; and they shall rule over their oppressors.

24:3 And it shall come to pass in that day that the Lord shall give thee rest, from thy sorrow, and from thy fear, and from the hard bondage wherein thou wast made to serve.

24:4 And it shall come to pass in that day, that thou shalt take up this proverb against the king of Babylon, and say: How hath the oppressor ceased, the golden city ceased!

24:5 The Lord hath broken the staff of the wicked, (-) the scepters of the rulers.

24:6 He who smote the people in wrath with a continual stroke, he that ruled the nations in anger, is persecuted, and none hindereth.

24:7 The whole earth is at rest, and is quiet; they break forth into singing.

24:8 Yea, the fir-trees rejoice at thee, and also the cedars of Lebanon, saying: Since thou art laid down_ no feller is come up against us.

24:9 Hell from beneath is moved for thee to meet thee at thy coming; it stirreth up the dead for thee, even all the chief ones of the earth; it hath raised up from their thrones all the kings of the nations.

14:10 All they shall speak and say unto thee, Art thou also become weak as we? art thou become like unto us?
14:11 Thy pomp is brought down to the grave, and the noise of thy viols: the worm is spread under thee, and the worms cover thee.
14:12 How art thou fallen from heaven, O Lucifer, son of the morning! how art thou cut down to the ground, which didst weaken the nations!
14:13 For thou hast said in thine heart, I will ascend into heaven, I will exalt my throne above the stars of God: I will sit also upon the mount of the congregation, in the sides of the north:
14:14 I will ascend above the heights of the clouds; I will be like the most High.
14:15 Yet thou shalt be brought down to hell, to the sides of the pit.
14:16 They that see thee shall narrowly look upon thee, and consider thee, ***and shall say*** ~~saying~~, Is this the man that made the earth to tremble, that did shake kingdoms;
14:17 ***And*** ~~That~~ made the world as a wilderness, and destroyed the cities thereof; ~~that~~ ***and*** opened not the house of his prisoners?
14:18 All the kings of the nations, ***yea,*** even all of them, lie in glory, every one in his own house.
14:19 But thou art cast out of thy grave like an abominable branch, and as the ***remnant*** ~~raiment~~ of those that are slain, thrust through with a sword, that go down to the stones of the pit; as a carcase trodden under feet.
14:20 Thou shalt not be joined with them in burial, because thou hast destroyed thy land, and slain thy people: the seed of evildoers shall never be renowned.
14:21 Prepare slaughter for his children for the iniquity of their fathers; that they do not rise, nor possess the land, nor fill the face of the world with cities.
14:22 For I will rise up against them, saith the LORD of hosts, and cut off from Babylon the name, and remnant, and son, and nephew, saith the LORD.
14:23 I will also make it a possession for the bittern, and pools of water: and I will sweep it with the besom of destruction, saith the LORD of hosts.

2nd Nephi (cont.)
24:10 All they shall speak and say unto thee: Art thou also become weak as we? Art thou become like unto us?
24:11 Thy pomp is brought down to the grave; the noise of thy viols is not heard; the worm is spread under thee, and the worms cover thee.
24:12 How art thou fallen from heaven, O Lucifer, son of the morning! (-) Art thou cut down to the ground, which did weaken the nations!
24:13 For thou hast said in thy heart: I will ascend into heaven, I will exalt my throne above the stars of God; I will sit also upon the mount of the congregation, in the sides of the north;
24:14 I will ascend above the heights of the clouds; I will be like the Most High.
24:15 Yet thou shalt be brought down to hell, to the sides of the pit.
24:16 They that see thee shall narrowly look upon thee, and shall consider thee, and shall say: Is this the man that made the earth to tremble, that did shake kingdoms?
24:17 And made the world as a wilderness, and destroyed the cities thereof, and opened not the house of his prisoners?
24:18 All the kings of the nations, yea, (-) all of them, lie in glory, every one of them in his own house.
24:19 But thou art cast out of thy grave like an abominable branch, and the remnant of those that are slain, thrust through with a sword, that go down to the stones of the pit; as a carcass trodden under feet.
24:20 Thou shalt not be joined with them in burial, because thou hast destroyed thy land and slain thy people; the seed of evil-doers shall never be renowned.
24:21 Prepare slaughter for his children for the iniquities of their fathers, that they do not rise, nor possess the land, nor fill the face of the world with cities.
24:22 For I will rise up against them, saith the Lord of Hosts, and cut off from Babylon the name, and remnant, and son, and nephew, saith the Lord.
24:23 I will also make it a possession for the bittern, and pools of water; and I will sweep it with the besom of destruction, saith the Lord of Hosts.

14:24 The LORD of hosts hath sworn, saying, Surely as I have thought, so shall it come to pass; and as I have purposed, so shall it stand:
14:25 That I will break the Assyrian in my land, and upon my mountains tread him under foot: then shall his yoke depart from off them, and his burden depart from off their shoulders.
14:26 This is the purpose that is purposed upon the whole earth: and this is the hand that is stretched out upon all the nations.
14:27 For the LORD of hosts hath purposed, and who shall disannul it? and his hand is stretched out, and who shall turn it back?
14:28 In the year that king Ahaz died was this burden.
14:29 Rejoice not thou, whole Palestina, because the rod of him that smote thee is broken: for out of the serpent's root shall come forth a cockatrice, and his fruit shall be a fiery flying serpent.
14:30 And the firstborn of the poor shall feed, and the needy shall lie down in safety: and I will kill thy root with famine, and he shall slay thy remnant.
14:31 Howl, O gate; cry, O city; thou, whole Palestina, art dissolved: for there shall come from the north a smoke, and none shall be alone in his appointed times.
14:32 What shall ~~one~~ then answer the messengers of the nation? That the LORD hath founded Zion, and the poor of his people shall trust in it.

2nd Nephi (cont.)
24:24 The Lord of Hosts hath sworn, saying: Surely as I have thought, so shall it come to pass; and as I have purposed, so shall it stand–
24:25 That I will bring the Assyrian in my land, and upon my mountains tread him under foot; then shall his yoke depart from off them, and his burden depart from off their shoulders.
24:26 This is the purpose that is purposed upon the whole earth; and this is the hand that is stretched out upon all (-) nations.
24:27 For the Lord of Hosts hath purposed, and who shall disannul (-)? And his hand is stretched out, and who shall turn it back?
24:28 In the year that king Ahaz died was this burden.
24:29 Rejoice not thou, whole Palestina, because the rod of him that smote thee is broken; for out of the serpent's root shall come forth a cockatrice, and his fruit shall be a fiery flying serpent.
24:30 And the first-born of the poor shall feed, and the needy shall lie down in safety; and I will kill thy root with famine, and he shall slay thy remnant.
24:31 Howl, O gate; cry, O city; thou, whole Palestina, art dissolved; for there shall come from the north a smoke, and none shall be alone in his appointed times.
24:32 What shall then answer the messengers of the nations? That the Lord hath founded Zion, and the poor of his people shall trust in it.

ISAIAH, Chapter 15

15:1 The burden of Moab. Because in the night Ar of Moab is laid waste, and brought to silence; because in the night Kir of Moab is laid waste, and brought to silence;
15:2 He is gone up to Bajith, and to Dibon, the high places, to weep: Moab shall howl over Nebo, and over Medeba: on all their heads shall be baldness, and every beard cut off.
15:3 In their streets they shall gird themselves with sackcloth: on the tops of their houses, and in their streets, every one shall howl, weeping abundantly.
15:4 And Heshbon shall cry, and Elealeh: their voice shall be heard even

unto Jahaz: therefore the armed soldiers of Moab shall cry out; his life shall be grievous unto him.
15:5 My heart shall cry out for Moab; his fugitives shall flee unto Zoar, an heifer of three years old: for by the mounting up of Luhith with weeping shall they go it up; for in the way of Horonaim they shall raise up a cry of destruction.
15:6 For the waters of Nimrim shall be desolate: for the hay is withered away, the grass faileth, there is no green thing.
15:7 Therefore the abundance they have gotten, and that which they have laid up, shall they carry away to the brook of the willows.
15:8 For the cry is gone round about the borders of Moab; the howling thereof unto Eglaim, and the howling thereof unto Beerelim.
15:9 For the waters of Dimon shall be full of blood: for I will bring more upon Dimon, lions upon him that escapeth of Moab, and upon the remnant of the land.

ISAIAH, Chapter 16

16:1 Send ye the lamb to the ruler of the land from Sela to the wilderness, unto the mount of the daughter of Zion.
16:2 For it shall be, that, as a wandering bird cast out of the nest, so the daughters of Moab shall be at the fords of Arnon.
16:3 Take counsel, execute judgment; make thy shadow as the night in the midst of the noonday; hide the outcasts; bewray not him that wandereth.
16:4 Let mine outcasts dwell with thee, Moab; be thou a covert to them from the face of the spoiler: for the extortioner is at an end, the spoiler ceaseth, the oppressors are consumed out of the land.
16:5 And in mercy shall the throne be established: and he shall sit upon it in truth in the tabernacle of David, judging, and seeking judgment, and hasting righteousness.
16:6 We have heard of the pride of Moab; ~~he is very proud: even~~ of his haughtiness, and his pride,***for he is very proud;*** and his wrath**,** ~~: but~~ his lies ~~shall not be so~~***, and his evil works.***
16:7 Therefore shall Moab howl for Moab, every one shall howl: for the

foundations of Kirhareseth shall ye mourn; surely they are stricken.
16:8 For the fields of Heshbon languish, and the vine of Sibmah: the lords of the heathen have broken down the principal plants thereof, they are come even unto Jazer, they wandered through the wilderness: her branches are stretched out, they are gone over the sea.
16:9 Therefore I will bewail with the weeping of Jazer the vine of Sibmah: I will water thee with my tears, O Heshbon, and Elealeh: for the shouting for thy summer fruits and for thy harvest is fallen.
16:10 And gladness is taken away, and joy out of the plentiful field; and in the vineyards there shall be no singing, neither shall there be shouting: the treaders shall tread out no wine in their presses; I have made their vintage shouting to cease.
16:11 Wherefore my bowels shall sound like an harp for Moab, and mine inward parts for Kirharesh.
16:12 And it shall come to pass, when it is seen that Moab is weary on the high place, that he shall come to his sanctuary to pray; but he shall not prevail.
16:13 This is the word that the LORD hath spoken concerning Moab since that time.
16:14 But now the LORD hath spoken, saying, Within three years, as the years of an hireling, and the glory of Moab shall be contemned, with all that great multitude; and the remnant shall be very small and feeble.

ISAIAH, Chapter 17

17:1 The burden of Damascus. Behold, Damascus is taken away from being a city, and it shall be a ruinous heap.
17:2 The cities of Aroer are forsaken: they shall be for flocks, which shall lie down, and none shall make them afraid.
17:3 The fortress also shall cease from Ephraim, and the kingdom from Damascus, and the remnant of Syria: they shall be as the glory of the children of Israel, saith the LORD of hosts.
17:4 And in that day it shall come to pass, that the glory of Jacob shall be made thin, and the fatness of his flesh shall wax lean.

17:5 And it shall be as when the harvestman gathereth the corn, and reapeth the ears with his arm; and it shall be as he that gathereth ears in the valley of Rephaim.
17:6 Yet gleaning grapes shall be left in it, as the shaking of an olive tree, two or three berries in the top of the uppermost bough, four or five in the outmost fruitful branches thereof, saith the LORD God of Israel.
17:7 At that day shall a man look to his Maker, and his eyes shall have respect to the Holy One of Israel.
17:8 And he shall not look to the altars, the work of his hands, neither shall respect that which his fingers have made, either the groves, or the images.
17:9 In that day shall his strong cities be as a forsaken bough, and an uppermost branch, which they left because of the children of Israel: and there shall be desolation.
17:10 Because thou hast forgotten the God of thy salvation, and hast not been mindful of the rock of thy strength, therefore shalt thou plant pleasant plants, and shalt set it with strange slips:
17:11 In the day shalt thou make thy plant to grow, and in the morning shalt thou make thy seed to flourish: but the harvest shall be a heap in the day of grief and of desperate sorrow.
17:12 Woe to the multitude of many people, which make a noise like the noise of the seas; and to the rushing of nations, that make a rushing like the rushing of mighty waters!
17:13 The nations shall rush like the rushing of many waters: but God shall rebuke them, and they shall flee far off, and shall be chased as the chaff of the mountains before the wind, and like a rolling thing before the whirlwind.
17:14 And behold at eveningtide trouble; and before the morning he is not. This is the portion of them that spoil us, and the lot of them that rob us.

ISAIAH, Chapter 18

18:1 WOE to the land shadowing with wings, which is beyond the rivers of Ethiopia:
18:2 That sendeth ambassadors by the sea, even in vessels of bulrushes upon the waters, saying, Go, ye swift messengers, to a nation scattered and

peeled, to a people terrible from their beginning hitherto; a nation meted out and trodden down, whose land the rivers have spoiled!
18:3 All ye inhabitants of the world, and dwellers on the earth, see ye, when he lifteth up an ensign on the mountains; and when he bloweth a trumpet, hear ye.
18:4 For so the LORD said unto me, I will take my rest, and I will consider in my dwelling place like a clear heat upon herbs, and like a cloud of dew in the heat of harvest.
18:5 For afore the harvest, when the bud is perfect, and the sour grape is ripening in the flower, he shall both cut off the sprigs with pruning hooks, and take away and cut down the branches.
18:6 They shall be left together unto the fowls of the mountains, and to the beasts of the earth: and the fowls shall summer upon them, and all the beasts of the earth shall winter upon them.
18:7 In that time shall the present be brought unto the LORD of hosts of a people scattered and peeled, and from a people terrible from their beginning hitherto; a nation meted out and trodden under foot, whose land the rivers have spoiled, to the place of the name of the LORD of hosts, the mount Zion.

ISAIAH, Chapter 19

19:1 The burden of Egypt. Behold, the LORD rideth upon a swift cloud, and shall come into Egypt: and the idols of Egypt shall be moved at his presence, and the heart of Egypt shall melt in the midst of it.
19:2 And I will set the Egyptians against the Egyptians: and they shall fight every one against his brother, and every one against his neighbour; city against city, and kingdom against kingdom.
19:3 And the spirit of Egypt shall fail in the midst thereof; and I will destroy the counsel thereof: and they shall seek to the idols, and to the charmers, and to them that have familiar spirits, and to the wizards.
19:4 And the Egyptians will I give over into the hand of a cruel lord; and a fierce king shall rule over them, saith the Lord, the LORD of hosts.

19:5 And the waters shall fail from the sea, and the river shall be wasted and dried up.

19:6 And they shall turn the rivers far away; and the brooks of defence shall be emptied and dried up: the reeds and flags shall wither.

19:7 The paper reeds by the brooks, by the mouth of the brooks, and every thing sown by the brooks, shall wither, be driven away, and be no more.

19:8 The fishers also shall mourn, and all they that cast angle into the brooks shall lament, and they that spread nets upon the waters shall languish.

19:9 Moreover they that work in fine flax, and they that weave networks, shall be confounded.

19:10 And they shall be broken in the purposes thereof, all that make sluices and ponds for fish.

19:11 Surely the princes of Zoan are fools, the counsel of the wise counsellors of Pharaoh is become brutish: how say ye unto Pharaoh, I am the son of the wise, the son of ancient kings?

19:12 Where are they? where are thy wise men? and let them tell thee now, and let them know what the LORD of hosts hath purposed upon Egypt.

19:13 The princes of Zoan are become fools, the princes of Noph are deceived; they have also seduced Egypt, even they that are the stay of the tribes thereof.

19:14 The LORD hath mingled a perverse spirit in the midst thereof: and they have caused Egypt to err in every work thereof, as a drunken man staggereth in his vomit.

19:15 Neither shall there be any work for Egypt, which the head or tail, branch or rush, may do.

19:1 In that day shall Egypt be like unto women: and it shall be afraid and fear because of the shaking of the hand of the LORD of hosts, which he shaketh over it.

19:17 And the land of Judah shall be a terror unto Egypt, every one that maketh mention thereof shall be afraid in himself, because of the counsel of the LORD of hosts, which he hath determined against it.

19:18 In that day shall five cities in the land of Egypt speak the language of Canaan, and swear to the LORD of hosts; one shall be called, The city of destruction.

19:19 In that day shall there be an altar to the LORD in the midst of the land of Egypt, and a pillar at the border thereof to the LORD.
19:20 And it shall be for a sign and for a witness unto the LORD of hosts in the land of Egypt: for they shall cry unto the LORD because of the oppressors, and he shall send them a saviour, and a great one, and he shall deliver them.
19:21 And the LORD shall be known to Egypt, and the Egyptians shall know the LORD in that day, and shall do sacrifice and oblation; yea, they shall vow a vow unto the LORD, and perform it.
19:22 And the LORD shall smite Egypt: he shall smite and heal it: and they shall return even to the LORD, and he shall be intreated of them, and shall heal them.
19:23 In that day shall there be a highway out of Egypt to Assyria, and the Assyrian shall come into Egypt, and the Egyptian into Assyria, and the Egyptians shall serve with the Assyrians.
19:24 In that day shall Israel be the third with Egypt and with Assyria, even a blessing in the midst of the land:
19:25 Whom the LORD of hosts shall bless, saying, Blessed be Egypt my people, and Assyria the work of my hands, and Israel mine inheritance.

ISAIAH, Chapter 20

20:1 In the year that Tartan came unto Ashdod, (when Sargon the king of Assyria sent him,) and fought against Ashdod, and took it;
20:2 At the same time spake the LORD by Isaiah the son of Amoz, saying, Go and loose the sackcloth from off thy loins, and put off thy shoe from thy foot. And he did so, walking naked and barefoot.
20:3 And the LORD said, Like as my servant Isaiah hath walked naked and barefoot three years for a sign and wonder upon Egypt and upon Ethiopia;
20:4 So shall the king of Assyria lead away the Egyptians prisoners, and the Ethiopians captives, young and old, naked and barefoot, even with their buttocks uncovered, to the shame of Egypt.

20:5 And they shall be afraid and ashamed of Ethiopia their expectation, and of Egypt their glory.
20:6 And the inhabitant of this isle shall say in that day, Behold, such is our expectation, whither we flee for help to be delivered from the king of Assyria: and how shall we escape?

ISAIAH, Chapter 21

21:1 The burden of the desert of the sea. As whirlwinds in the south pass through; so it cometh from the desert, from ***the*** ~~a~~ terrible land.
21:2 A grievous vision is declared unto me; the treacherous dealer dealeth treacherously, and the spoiler spoileth. Go up, O Elam: besiege, O Media; all the sighing thereof have I made to cease.
21:3 Therefore are my loins filled with pain: pangs have taken hold upon me, as the pangs of a woman that travaileth: I was bowed down at the hearing of it; I was dismayed at the seeing of it.
21:4 My heart panted, fearfulness affrighted me: the night of my pleasure hath he turned into fear unto me.
21:5 Prepare the table, watch in the watchtower, eat, drink: arise, ye princes, and anoint the shield.
21:6 For thus hath the Lord said unto me, Go, set a watchman, let him declare what he seeth.
21:7 And he saw a chariot with a couple of horsemen, a chariot of asses, and a chariot of camels; and he hearkened diligently with much heed:
21:8 And he cried, A lion: My lord, I stand continually upon the watchtower in the daytime, and I am set in my ward whole nights:
21:9 And, behold, here cometh a chariot of men, with a couple of horsemen. And he answered and said, Babylon is fallen, is fallen; and all the graven images of her gods he hath broken unto the ground.
21:10 O my threshing, and the corn of my floor: that which I have heard of the LORD of hosts, the God of Israel, have I declared unto you.
21:11 The burden of Dumah. He calleth to me out of Seir, Watchman, what of the night? Watchman, what of the night?

21:12 The watchman said, The morning cometh, and also the night: if ye will enquire, enquire ye: return, come.
21:13 The burden upon Arabia. In the forest in Arabia shall ye lodge, O ye travelling companies of Dedanim.
21:14 The inhabitants of the land of Tema brought water to him that was thirsty, they prevented with their bread him that fled.
21:15 For they fled from the swords, from the drawn sword, and from the bent bow, and from the grievousness of war.
21:16 For thus hath the Lord said unto me, Within a year, according to the years of an hireling, and all the glory of Kedar shall fail:
21:17 And the residue of the number of archers, the mighty men of the children of Kedar, shall be diminished: for the LORD God of Israel hath spoken it.

ISAIAH, Chapter 22

22:1 The burden of the valley of vision. What aileth thee now, that thou art wholly gone up to the housetops?
22:2 Thou that art full of stirs, a tumultuous city, a joyous city: thy slain men are not slain with the sword, nor dead in battle.
22:3 All thy rulers are fled together, they are bound by the archers: all that are found in thee are bound together, which have fled from far.
22:4 Therefore said I, Look away from me; I will weep bitterly, labour not to comfort me, because of the spoiling of the daughter of my people.
22:5 For it is a day of trouble, and of treading down, and of perplexity by the Lord GOD of hosts in the valley of vision, breaking down the walls, and of crying to the mountains.
22:6 And Elam bare the quiver with chariots of men and horsemen, and Kir uncovered the shield.
22:7 And it shall come to pass, that thy choicest valleys shall be full of chariots, and the horsemen shall set themselves in array at the gate.
22:8 ¶And he discovered the covering of Judah, and thou didst look in that day to the armour of the house of the forest.

22:9 Ye have seen also the breaches of the city of David, that they are many: and ye gathered together the waters of the lower pool.
22:10 And ye have numbered the houses of Jerusalem, and the houses have ye broken down to fortify the wall.
22:11 Ye made also a ditch between the two walls for the water of the old pool: but ye have not looked unto the maker thereof, neither had respect unto him that fashioned it long ago.
22:12 And in that day did the Lord GOD of hosts call to weeping, and to mourning, and to baldness, and to girding with sackcloth:
22:13 And behold joy and gladness, slaying oxen, and killing sheep, eating flesh, and drinking wine: let us eat and drink; for to morrow we shall die.
22:14 And it was revealed in mine ears by the LORD of hosts, Surely this iniquity shall not be purged from you till ye die, saith the Lord GOD of hosts.
22:15 Thus saith the Lord GOD of hosts, Go, get thee unto this treasurer, even unto Shebna, which is over the house, and say,
22:16 What hast thou here? and whom hast thou here, that thou hast hewed thee out a sepulchre here, as he that heweth him out a sepulchre on high, and that graveth an habitation for himself in a rock?
22:17 Behold, the LORD will carry thee away with a mighty captivity, and will surely cover thee.
22:18 He will surely violently turn and toss thee like a ball into a large country: there shalt thou die, and there the chariots of thy glory shall be the shame of thy lord's house.
22:19 And I will drive thee from thy station, and from thy state shall he pull thee down.
22:20 And it shall come to pass in that day, that I will call my servant Eliakim the son of Hilkiah:
22:21 And I will clothe him with thy robe, and strengthen him with thy girdle, and I will commit thy government into his hand: and he shall be a father to the inhabitants of Jerusalem, and to the house of Judah.
22:22 And the key of the house of David will I lay upon his shoulder; so he shall open, and none shall shut; and he shall shut, and none shall open.

22:23 And I will fasten him as a nail in a sure place; and he shall be for a glorious throne to his father's house.
22:24 And they shall hang upon him all the glory of his father's house, the offspring and the issue, all vessels of small quantity, from the vessels of cups, even to all the vessels of flagons.
22:25 In that day, saith the LORD of hosts, shall the nail that is fastened in the sure place be removed, and be cut down, and fall; and the burden that was upon it shall be cut off: for the LORD hath spoken it.

ISAIAH, Chapter 23

23:1 The burden of Tyre. Howl, ye ships of Tarshish; for it is laid waste, so that there is no house, no entering in: from the land of Chittim it is revealed to them.
23:2 Be still, ye inhabitants of the isle; thou whom the merchants of Zidon, that pass over the sea, have replenished.
23:3 And by great waters the seed of Sihor, the harvest of the river, is her revenue; and she is a mart of nations.
23:4 Be thou ashamed, O Zidon: for the sea hath spoken, even the strength of the sea, saying, I travail not, nor bring forth children, neither do I nourish up young men, nor bring up virgins.
23:5 As at the report concerning Egypt, so shall they be sorely pained at the report of Tyre.
23:6 Pass ye over to Tarshish; howl, ye inhabitants of the isle.
23:7 Is this your joyous city, whose antiquity is of ancient days? her own feet shall carry her afar off to sojourn.
23:8 Who hath taken this counsel against Tyre, the crowning city, whose merchants are princes, whose traffickers are the honourable of the earth?
23:9 The LORD of hosts hath purposed it, to stain the pride of all glory, and to bring into contempt all the honourable of the earth.
23:10 Pass through thy land as a river, O daughter of Tarshish: there is no more strength ***in thee***.
23:11 He stretched out his hand over the sea, he shook the kingdoms: the LORD hath given a commandment against the merchant city, to destroy the strong holds thereof.

23:12 And he said, Thou shalt no more rejoice, O thou oppressed virgin, daughter of Zidon: arise, pass over to Chittim; there also shalt thou have no rest.
23:13 Behold the land of the Chaldeans; this people was not, till the Assyrian founded it for them that dwell in the wilderness: they set up the towers thereof, they raised up the palaces thereof; and he brought it to ruin.
23:14 Howl, ye ships of Tarshish: for your strength is laid waste.
23:15 And it shall come to pass in that day, that Tyre shall be forgotten seventy years, according to the days of one king: after the end of seventy years shall Tyre sing as an harlot.
23:16 Take an harp, go about the city, thou harlot that hast been forgotten; make sweet melody, sing many songs, that thou mayest be remembered.
23:17 And it shall come to pass after the end of seventy years, that the LORD will visit Tyre, and she shall turn to her hire, and shall commit fornication with all the kingdoms of the world upon the face of the earth.
23:18 And her merchandise and her hire shall be holiness to the LORD: it shall not be treasured nor laid up; for her merchandise shall be for them that dwell before the LORD, to eat sufficiently, and for durable clothing.

ISAIAH, Chapter 24

24:1 BEHOLD, the LORD maketh the earth empty, and maketh it waste, and turneth it upside down, and scattereth abroad the inhabitants thereof.
24:2 And it shall be, as with the people, so with the priest; as with the servant, so with his master; as with the maid, so with her mistress; as with the buyer, so with the seller; as with the lender, so with the borrower; as with the taker of usury, so with the giver of usury to him.
24:3 The land shall be utterly emptied, and utterly spoiled: for the LORD hath spoken this word.
24:4 The earth mourneth and fadeth away, the world languisheth and fadeth away, the haughty people of the earth do languish.
24:5 The earth also is defiled under the inhabitants thereof; because they

have transgressed the laws, changed the ordinance, broken the everlasting covenant.
24:6 Therefore hath the curse devoured the earth, and they that dwell therein are desolate: therefore the inhabitants of the earth are burned, and few men left.
24:7 The new wine mourneth, the vine languisheth, all the merryhearted do sigh.
24:8 The mirth of tabrets ceaseth, the noise of them that rejoice endeth, the joy of the harp ceaseth.
24:9 They shall not drink wine with a song; strong drink shall be bitter to them that drink it.
24:10 The city of confusion is broken down: every house is shut up, that no man may come in.
24:11 There is a crying for wine in the streets; all joy is darkened, the mirth of the land is gone.
24:12 In the city is left desolation, and the gate is smitten with destruction.
24:13 When thus it shall be in the midst of the land among the people, there shall be as the shaking of an olive tree, and as the gleaning grapes when the vintage is done.
24:14 They shall lift up their voice, they shall sing for the majesty of the LORD, they shall cry aloud from the sea.
24:15 Wherefore glorify ye the LORD in the fires, even the name of the LORD God of Israel in the isles of the sea.
24:16 From the uttermost part of the earth have we heard songs, even glory to the righteous. But I said, My leanness, my leanness, woe unto me! the treacherous dealers have dealt treacherously; yea, the treacherous dealers have dealt very treacherously.
24:17 Fear, and the pit, and the snare, are upon thee, O inhabitant of the earth.
24:18 And it shall come to pass, that he who fleeth from the noise of the fear shall fall into the pit; and he that cometh up out of the midst of the pit shall be taken in the snare: for the windows from on high are open, and the foundations of the earth do shake.
24:19 The earth is utterly broken down, the earth is clean dissolved, the earth is moved exceedingly.
24:20 The earth shall reel to and fro like a drunkard, and shall be removed like a cottage; and the transgression

thereof shall be heavy upon it; and it shall fall, and not rise again.
24:21 And it shall come to pass in that day, that the LORD shall punish the host of the high ones that are on high, and the kings of the earth upon the earth.
24:22 And they shall be gathered together, as prisoners are gathered in the pit, and shall be shut up in the prison, and after many days shall they be visited.
24:23 Then the moon shall be confounded, and the sun ashamed, when the LORD of hosts shall reign in mount Zion, and in Jerusalem, and before his ancients gloriously.

ISAIAH, Chapter 25

25:1 O LORD, thou art my God; I will exalt thee, I will praise thy name; for thou hast done wonderful things; thy counsels of old are faithfulness and truth.
25:2 For thou hast made of a city an heap; of a defenced city a ruin: a palace of strangers to be no city; it shall never be built.
25:3 Therefore shall the strong people glorify thee, the city of the terrible nations shall fear thee.
25:4 For thou hast been a strength to the poor, a strength to the needy in his distress, a refuge from the storm, a shadow from the heat, when the blast of the terrible ones is as a storm against the wall.
25:5 Thou shalt bring down the noise of strangers, as the heat in a dry place; even the heat with the shadow of a cloud: the branch of the terrible ones shall be brought low.
25:6 And in this mountain shall the LORD of hosts make unto all people a feast of fat things, a feast of wines on the lees, of fat things full of marrow, of wines on the lees well refined.
25:7 And he will destroy in this mountain the face of the covering cast over all people, and the vail that is spread over all nations.
25:8 He will swallow up death in victory; and the Lord GOD will wipe away tears from off all faces; and the rebuke of his people shall he take away from off all the earth: for the LORD hath spoken it.

25:9 ¶ And it shall be said in that day, Lo, this is our God; we have waited for him, and he will save us: this is the LORD; we have waited for him, we will be glad and rejoice in his salvation.
25:10 For in this mountain shall the hand of the LORD rest, and Moab shall be trodden down under him, even as straw is trodden down for the dunghill.
25:11 And he shall spread forth his hands in the midst of them, as he that swimmeth spreadeth forth his hands to swim: and he shall bring down their pride together with the spoils of their hands.
25:12 And the fortress of the high fort of thy walls shall he bring down, lay low, and bring to the ground, even to the dust.

ISAIAH, Chapter 26

26:1 In that day shall this song be sung in the land of Judah; We have a strong city; salvation will God appoint for walls and bulwarks.
26:2 Open ye the gates, that the righteous nation which keepeth the truth may enter in.
26:3 Thou wilt keep him in perfect peace, whose mind is stayed on thee: because he trusteth in thee.
26:4 Trust ye in the LORD for ever: for in the LORD JEHOVAH is everlasting strength:
26:5 For he bringeth down them that dwell on high; the lofty city, he layeth it low; he layeth it low, even to the ground; he bringeth it even to the dust.
26:6 The foot shall tread it down, even the feet of the poor, and the steps of the needy.
26:7 The way of the just is uprightness: thou, most upright, dost weigh the path of the just.
26:8 Yea, in the way of thy judgments, O LORD, have we waited for thee; the desire of our soul is to thy name, and to the remembrance of thee.
26:9 With my soul have I desired thee in the night; yea, with my spirit within me will I seek thee early: for when thy judgments are in the earth, the inhabitants of the world will learn righteousness.
26:10 Let favour be shewed to the wicked, yet will he not learn righteousness: in the land of uprightness will he

deal unjustly, and will not behold the majesty of the LORD.
26:11 LORD, when thy hand is lifted up, they will not see: but they shall see, and be ashamed for their envy at the people; yea, the fire of thine enemies shall devour them.
26:12 LORD, thou wilt ordain peace for us: for thou also hast wrought all our works in us.
26:13 O LORD our God, other lords beside thee have had dominion over us: but by thee only will we make mention of thy name.
26:14 They are dead, they shall not live; they are deceased, they shall not rise: therefore hast thou visited and destroyed them, and made all their memory to perish.
26:15 Thou hast increased the nation, O LORD, thou hast increased the nation: thou art glorified: thou hadst removed it far unto all the ends of the earth.
26:16 LORD, in trouble have they visited thee, they poured out a prayer when thy chastening was upon them.
26:17 Like as a woman with child, that draweth near the time of her delivery, is in pain, and crieth out in her pangs; so have we been in thy sight, O LORD.
26:18 We have been with child, we have been in pain, we have as it were brought forth wind; we have not wrought any deliverance in the earth; neither have the inhabitants of the world fallen.
26:19 Thy dead men shall live, together with my dead body shall they arise. Awake and sing, ye that dwell in dust: for thy dew is as the dew of herbs, and the earth shall cast out the dead.
26:20 Come, my people, enter thou into thy chambers, and shut thy doors about thee: hide thyself as it were for a little moment, until the indignation be overpast.
26:21 For, behold, the LORD cometh out of his place to punish the inhabitants of the earth for their iniquity: the earth also shall disclose her blood, and shall no more cover her slain.

ISAIAH, Chapter 27

27:1 In that day the LORD with his
sore and great and strong sword shall
punish leviathan the piercing serpent,
even leviathan that crooked serpent; and
he shall slay the dragon that is in the
sea.
27:2 In that day sing ye unto her, A
vineyard of red wine.
27:3 I the LORD do keep it; I will
water it every moment: lest any hurt it,
I will keep it night and day.
27:4 Fury is not in me: who would set
the briers and thorns against me in
battle? I would go through them, I
would burn them together.
27:5 Or let him take hold of my
strength, that he may make peace with
me; and he shall make peace with me.
27:6 He shall cause them that come of
Jacob to take root: Israel shall blossom
and bud, and fill the face of the world
with fruit.
27:7 Hath he smitten him, as he smote
those that smote him? or is he slain
according to the slaughter of them that
are slain by him?
27:8 In measure, when it shooteth
forth, thou wilt debate with it: he stayeth
his rough wind in the day of the east
wind.
27:9 By this therefore shall the
iniquity of Jacob be purged; and this is
all the fruit to take away his sin; when
he maketh all the stones of the altar as
chalkstones that are beaten in sunder,
the groves and images shall not stand
up.
27:10 Yet the defenced city shall be
desolate, and the habitation forsaken,
and left like a wilderness: there shall the
calf feed, and there shall he lie down,
and consume the branches thereof.
27:11 When the boughs thereof are
withered, they shall be broken off: the
women come, and set them on fire: for it
is a people of no understanding:
therefore he that made them will not
have mercy on them, and he that formed
them will shew them no favour.
27:12 And it shall come to pass in that
day, that the LORD shall beat off from
the channel of the river unto the stream
of Egypt, and ye shall be gathered one
by one, O ye children of Israel.
27:13 And it shall come to pass in
that day, that the great trumpet shall be
blown, and they shall come which

were ready to perish in the land of Assyria, and the outcasts in the land of Egypt, and shall worship the LORD in the holy mount at Jerusalem.

ISAIAH, Chapter 28

28:1 WOE to the crown of pride, to the drunkards of Ephraim, whose glorious beauty is a fading flower, which are on the head of the fat valleys of them that are overcome with wine!
28:2 Behold, the Lord hath a mighty and strong one, which as a tempest of hail and a destroying storm, as a flood of mighty waters overflowing, shall cast down to the earth with the hand.
28:3 The crown of pride, the drunkards of Ephraim, shall be trodden under feet:
28:4 And the glorious beauty, which is on the head of the fat valley, shall be a fading flower, and as the hasty fruit before the summer; which when he that looketh upon it seeth, while it is yet in his hand he eateth it up.
28:5 In that day shall the LORD of hosts be for a crown of glory, and for a diadem of beauty, unto the residue of his people,
28:6 And for a spirit of judgment to him that sitteth in judgment, and for strength to them that turn the battle to the gate.
28:7 But they also have erred through wine, and through strong drink are out of the way; the priest and the prophet have erred through strong drink, they are swallowed up of wine, they are out of the way through strong drink; they err in vision, they stumble in judgment.
28:8 For all tables are full of vomit and filthiness, so that there is no place clean.
28:9 Whom shall he teach knowledge? and whom shall he make to understand doctrine? them that are weaned from the milk, and drawn from the breasts.
28:10 For precept must be upon precept, precept upon precept; line upon line, line upon line; here a little, and there a little:
28:11 For with stammering lips and another tongue will he speak to this people.
28:12 To whom he said, This is the rest wherewith ye may cause the weary to

rest; and this is the refreshing: yet they
would not hear.
28:13 But the word of the LORD was
unto them precept upon precept, precept
upon precept; line upon line, line upon
line; here a little, and there a little; that
they might go, and fall backward, and
be broken, and snared, and taken.
28:14 Wherefore hear the word of the
LORD, ye scornful men, that rule this
people which is in Jerusalem.
28:15 Because ye have said, We have
made a covenant with death, and with
hell are we at agreement; when the
overflowing scourge shall pass through,
it shall not come unto us: for we have
made lies our refuge, and under
falsehood have we hid ourselves:
28:16 Therefore thus saith the Lord
GOD, Behold, I lay in Zion for a
foundation a stone, a tried stone, a
precious corner stone, a sure
foundation: he that believeth shall not
make haste.
28:17 Judgment also will I lay to the
line, and righteousness to the plummet:
and the hail shall sweep away the refuge
of lies, and the waters shall overflow the
hiding place.
28:18 And your covenant with death
shall be disannulled, and your
agreement with hell shall not stand;
when the overflowing scourge shall pass
through, then ye shall be trodden down
by it.
28:19 From the time that it goeth forth
it shall take you: for morning by
morning shall it pass over, by day and
by night: and it shall be a vexation only
to understand the report.
28:20 For the bed is shorter than that a
man can stretch himself on it: and the
covering narrower than that he can wrap
himself in it.
28:21 For the LORD shall rise up as in
mount Perazim, he shall be wroth as in
the valley of Gibeon, that he may do his
work, his strange work; and bring to
pass his act, his strange act.
28:22 Now therefore be ye not
mockers, lest your bands be made
strong: for I have heard from the Lord
GOD of hosts a consumption, even
determined upon the whole earth.
28:23 Give ye ear, and hear my voice;
hearken, and hear my speech.
28:24 Doth the plowman plow all day
to sow? doth he open and break the
clods of his ground?

28:25 When he hath made plain the face thereof, doth he not cast abroad the fitches, and scatter the cummin, and cast in the principal wheat and the appointed barley and the rie in their place?
28:26 For his God doth instruct him to discretion, and doth teach him.
28:27 For the fitches are not threshed with a threshing instrument, neither is a cart wheel turned about upon the cummin; but the fitches are beaten out with a staff, and the cummin with a rod.
28:28 Bread corn is bruised; because he will not ever be threshing it, nor break it with the wheel of his cart, nor bruise it with his horsemen.
28:29 This also cometh forth from the LORD of hosts, which is wonderful in counsel, and excellent in working.

ISAIAH, Chapter 29

29:1 WOE to Ariel, to Ariel, the city where David dwelt! add ye year to year; let them kill sacrifices.
29:2 Yet I will distress Ariel, and there shall be heaviness and sorrow: ***for thus hath the Lord said unto me,*** ~~and~~ it shall be unto me as Ariel.

2 Nephi
26:15 After my seed and the seed of my brethren shall have dwindled in unbelief, and shall have been smitten by the Gentiles;

29:3 And I ***the Lord*** will camp against ***her*** ~~thee~~ round about, and will lay siege against ***her*** ~~thee~~ with a mount, and I will raise forts against ***her*** ~~thee~~.

yea, after the Lord God shall have camped against them round about, and shall have laid siege against them with a mount, and (- -) raised forts against them;

29:4 And ***she*** ~~thou~~ shalt be brought down,

and after they shall have been brought down low in the dust, even that they are not, yet the words of the righteous shall be written, and the prayers of the faithful shall be heard, and all those who have dwindled in unbelief shall not be forgotten.

Mormon
8:23a Search the prophesies of Isaiah. Behold, I cannot write them. Yeah, behold I say unto you, that those saints who have gone before me, who have possessed this land, shall cry, yea, even from the dust will they cry unto the Lord;

and ***shall*** ~~shalt~~ speak out of the ground,

26:16 For those who shall be destroyed shall speak unto them out of the ground, and ***her*** ~~thy~~ speech shall be low out of the dust , and her ~~thy~~ voice shall be~~;~~ as of one that hath a familiar spirit,

out of the ground, and ***her*** ~~thy~~ speech shall whisper out of the dust.

29:5 Moreover the multitude of ***her*** ~~thy~~ strangers shall be like small dust, and the multitude of the terrible ones shall be as chaff that passeth away: yea, it shall be at an instant suddenly.

29:6 ~~Thou shalt~~ ***For they shall*** be visited of the LORD of hosts with thunder, and with earthquake, and great noise, with storm and tempest, and the flame of devouring fire.
29:7 And the multitude of all the nations that fight against Ariel, even all that fight against her and her munition, and that distress her, shall be as a dream of a night vision.
29:8 ***Yea,*** ~~I~~it shall ~~even~~ be ***unto them even*** as ***unto a*** ~~when an~~ hungry man ***who*** dreameth, and, behold, he eateth; but he awaketh, and his soul is empty: or ***like unto*** ~~as when~~ a thirsty man ***who*** dreameth, and, behold, he drinketh; but he awaketh, and, behold, he is faint, and his soul hath appetite: ***Yea, even*** so shall the multitude of all the nations be~~;~~ that fight against mount Zion.
29:9 ***For, behold, all ye that do iniquity,*** ~~S~~stay yourselves, and wonder;

2nd Nephi (cont.)
and their speech shall be low out of the dust, and their voice shall be as one that hath a familiar spirit;
for the Lord God will give unto him power, that he may whisper concerning them, even as it were out of the ground; and their speech shall whisper out of the dust.

26:17 For thus saith the Lord God: They shall write the things which shall be done among them, and they shall be written and sealed up in a book, and those who have dwindled in unbelief shall not have them, for they seek to destroy the things of God.
26:18 Wherefore, as those who have been destroyed have been destroyed speedily;

and the multitude of their terrible ones shall be as chaff that passeth away--
yea, thus saith the Lord God: It shall be at an instant, suddenly–
27:1 But, behold, in the last days, or in the days of the Gentiles--yea, behold all the nations of the Gentiles and also the Jews, both those who shall come upon this land and those who shall be upon other lands, yea, even upon all the lands of the earth, behold, they will be drunken with iniquity and all manner of abominations–
27:2 (- -) And when that day shall come they shall be visited of the Lord of Hosts, with thunder and with earthquake, and with a great noise, and with storm, and with tempest, and with the flame of devouring fire.
27:3 And (- - -) all the nations that fight against Zion,(- - -)

and that distress her, shall be as a dream of a night vision;
yea, it shall be unto them, even as unto a hungry man which dreameth, and behold_ he eateth_ but he awaketh and his soul is empty;
or like unto a thirsty man which dreameth, and_ behold_ he drinketh_ but he awaketh_ and_ behold_ he is faint, and his soul hath appetite; Yea, even so shall the multitude of all the nations be that fight against Mount Zion.
27:4 For behold, all ye that doeth iniquity, stay yourselves and wonder, for

Mormon (cont.)
8:23b and as the Lord liveth he will remember the covenant which he had made with them.

for ye shall cry ~~ye~~ out, and cry: ***yea, ye shall be*** ~~they are~~ drunken, but not with wine; ***ye shall*** ~~they~~ stagger, but not with strong drink.

29:10a For, ***behold,*** the LORD hath poured out upon you the spirit of deep sleep. ~~;~~ ***For behold, ye have*** ~~and hath~~ closed your eyes: ***and ye have rejected*** the prophets and your rulers, ***and*** the seers hath he covered ***because of your iniquities***.

And it shall come to pass, that the Lord God shall bring forth unto you the words of a book; and they shall be the words of them which have slumbered.

And behold, the book shall be sealed; and in the book shall be a revelation from God, from the beginning of the world to the ending thereof.

Wherefore because of the things which are sealed up, the things which are sealed shall not be delivered in the day of wickedness and abominations of the people. Wherefore, the book shall be kept from them.

But the book shall be delivered unto a man,

and he shall deliver the words of the book, which are the words of those who have slumbered in the dust; and he shall deliver these words unto another,

but the words that are sealed he shall not deliver, neither shall he deliver the book.

For the book shall be sealed by the power of God, and the revelation

2nd Nephi (cont.)

ye shall cry out, and cry; yea, ye shall be drunken_ but not with wine, ye shall stagger but not with strong drink.

27:5 For behold, the Lord hath poured out upon you the spirit of deep sleep. For behold, ye have closed your eyes, and ye have rejected the prophets; and your rulers, and the seers hath he covered because of your iniquity.

27:6 And it shall come to pass_ that the Lord God shall bring forth unto you the words of a book, and they shall be the words of them which have slumbered.

27:7 And behold_ the book shall be sealed; and in the book shall be a revelation from God, from the beginning of the world to the ending thereof.

27:8 Wherefore, because of the things which are sealed up, the things which are sealed shall not be delivered in the day of the wickedness and abominations of the people.
Wherefore the book shall be kept from them.

27:9 But the book shall be delivered unto a man,

and he shall deliver the words of the book, which are the words of those who have slumbered in the dust, and he shall deliver these words unto another;

27:10 But the words which are sealed he shall not deliver, neither shall he deliver the book.
For the book shall be sealed by the power of God, and the revelation which

Joseph Smith History

1:59 At length the time arrived for obtaining the plates, the Urim and Thummim, and the breastplate. On the twenty-second day of September, one thousand eight hundred and twenty-seven, having gone as usual at the end of another year to the place where they were deposited, the same heavenly messenger delivered them up to me with this charge: that I should be responsible for them; that if I should let them go carelessly, or through any neglect of mine, I should be cut off; but that if I would use all my endeavors to preserve them, until he, the messenger, should call for them, they should be protected.

which was sealed shall be kept in the book until the own due time of the Lord, that they may come forth; for, behold, they reveal all things from the foundation of the world unto the end thereof.

10:29b ***And the day cometh, that the words of the book which were sealed shall be read upon the house tops; and they shall be read by the power of Christ; and all things shall be revealed unto the children of men which ever have been among the children of men, and which ever will be, even unto the end of the earth.***

Wherefore, at that day when the book shall be delivered unto the man of whom I have spoken, the book shall be hid from the eyes of the world, that the eyes of none shall behold it, save it be that three witnesses shall behold it, by the power of God, besides him to whom the book shall be delivered: and they shall testify to the truth of the book and the things therein.

And there is none other which shall view it, save it be a few according to the will of God, to bear testimony of his word unto the children of men; for the Lord God hath said, that the words of the faithful should speak as if it were from the dead.

Wherefore, the Lord God will proceed to bring forth the words of the book; and in the mouth of as many witnesses as seemeth him good will he establish his word; and woe be unto him that rejecteth the word of God.

29:11a ***But, behold, it shall come to pass, that the Lord God shall say unto him to whom he shall deliver the book, Take these words which are not sealed and***

~~And the vision of all is become unto you as the words of a book that is sealed, which men~~ deliver them to ~~one~~ ***another, that he may show them unto the*** ~~that is~~ learned, saying, Read this, I pray thee.

2nd Nephi (cont.)

was sealed shall be kept in the book until the own due time of the Lord, that they may come forth; for behold, they reveal all things from the foundation of the world unto the end thereof.

27:11 And the day cometh, that the words of the book which were sealed shall be read upon the house tops; and they shall be read by the power of Christ; and all things shall be revealed unto the children of men which ever have been among the children of men, and which ever will be, even unto the end of the earth.

27:12 Wherefore, at that day when the book shall be delivered unto the man of whom I have spoken, the book shall be hid from the eyes of the world, that the eyes of none shall behold it_ save it be that three witnesses shall behold it, by the power of God, besides him to whom the book shall be delivered; and they shall testify to the truth of the book and the things therein.

27:13 And there is none other which shall view it, save it be a few according to the will of God, to bear testimony of his word unto the children of men; for the Lord God hath said, that the words of the faithful should speak as if it were from the dead.

27:14 Wherefore, the Lord God will proceed to bring forth the words of the book; and in the mouth of as many witnesses as seemeth him good will he establish his word; and wo be unto him that rejecteth the word of God!

27:15 But_ behold, it shall come to pass_ that the Lord God shall say unto him to whom he shall deliver the book: Take these words which are not sealed and

(- -)

deliver them to another, that he may show them unto the learned, saying: Read this, I pray thee.

Joseph Smith History

1:63 Sometime in this month of February, the aforementioned Mr. Martin Harris came to our place, got the characters which I had drawn off the plates, and started with them to the city of New York. For what took place relative to him and the characters, I refer to his own account of the circumstances,

11:29b And the learned shall say, Bring hither the book and I will read them;
and now because of the glory of the world, and to get gain will they say this, and not for the glory of God.

And the man shall say, I cannot bring the book for it is sealed.
Then shall the learned say ~~and he saith~~, I cannot ***read it.*** ~~; for it is sealed~~:

29:12 ***Wherefore it shall come to pass, that the Lord God will deliver again*** ~~And~~ the book ~~is delivered~~ to him that is not learned; ***and the man that is not learned shall say***, ~~saying, Read this, I pray thee: and he saith~~, I am not learned.

And the learned shall say: Bring hither the book, and I will read them;

27:16 And now, because of the glory of the world_ and to get gain will they say this, and not for the glory of God.

27:17 And the man shall say: I cannot bring the book, for it is sealed.
27:18 Then shall the learned say:
I cannot read it.

27:19 Wherefore it shall come to pass, that the Lord God will deliver again the book (- -) and the words thereof to him that is not learned; and the man that is not learned shall say: I am not learned.

History of Joseph Smith (cont.)
as he related them to me after his return, which was as follows:
1:64 "I went to the city of New York, and presented the characters which had been translated, with the translation thereof, to Professor Charles Anthon, a gentleman celebrated for his literary attainments. Professor Anthon stated that the translation was correct, more so than any he had before seen translated from the Egyptian. I then showed him those which were not yet translated, and he said that they were Egyptian, Chaldaid, Assyriac, and Arabic; and he said they were true characters. He gave me a certificate, certifying to the people of Palmyra that they were true characters, and that the translation of such of them as had been translated was also correct. I took the certificate and put it into my pocket, and was just leaving the house, when Mr. Anthon called me back, and asked me how the young man found out that there were gold plates in the place where he found them. I answered that an angel of God had revealed it unto him.
1:65 "He then said to me, `Let me see that certificate.' I accordingly took it out of my pocket and gave it to him, when he took it and tore it to pieces, saying that there was no such thing now as ministering of angels, and that if I would bring the plates to him he would translate them.

I informed him that part of the plates were sealed, and that I was forbidden to bring them.

He replied, `I cannot read a sealed book.'
I left him and went to Dr. Mitchell, who sanctioned what Professor Anthon had said respecting both the characters and the translation."

Then shall the Lord God say unto him, The learned shall not read them, for they have rejected them, and I am able to do mine own work; wherefore thou shalt read the words which I shall give unto thee.

Touch not the things which are sealed, for I will bring them forth in mine own due time; for I will show unto the children of men that I am able to do mine own work.

Wherefore, when thou hast read the words which I have commanded thee, and obtained the witnesses which I have promised unto thee, then shalt thou seal up the book again, and hide it up unto me, that I may preserve the words which thou hast not read until I shall see fit in mine own wisdom to reveal all things unto the children of men.

For behold, I am God; and I am a God of miracles; and I will show unto the world that I am the same, yesterday, to-day, and for ever; and I work not among the children of men, save it be according to their faith.

29:13 ***And again it shall come to pass, that the Lord shall say unto him that shall read the words that shall be delivered him,*** ~~Wherefore the Lord said~~,

2nd Nephi (cont.)

27:20 Then shall the Lord God say unto him: The learned shall not read them, for they have rejected them, and I am able to do mine own work; wherefore thou shalt read the words which I shall give unto thee.

27:21 Touch not the things which are sealed, for I will bring them forth in mine own due time; for I will show unto the children of men that I am able to do mine own work.

27:22 Wherefore, when thou hast read the words which I have commanded thee, and obtained the witnesses which I have promised unto thee, then shalt thou seal up the book again, and hide it up unto me, that I may preserve the words which thou hast not read, until I shall see fit in mine own wisdom to reveal all things unto the children of men.

27:23 For behold, I am God; and I am a God of miracles; and I will show unto the world that I am the same_ yesterday, today, and forever; and I work not among the children of men_ save it be according to their faith.

27:24 And again it shall come to pass that the Lord shall say unto him that shall read the words that shall be delivered him:

Joseph Smith History

1:19 I was answered that I must join none of them, for they were all wrong; and the Personage who addressed me said that all their creeds were an abomination in his sight; that those professors were all corrupt;

that: "they draw near to me with their lips, but (- -) their hearts are far from me, they teach for doctrines the commandments of men, having a form of godliness, but they deny the power thereof."

Forasmuch as this people draw near ***unto*** me with their mouth, and with their lips do ***honor*** ~~honour~~ me, but have removed their heart*s* far from me, and their fear toward me is taught by the precept of ***men***, ~~:~~

29:14 Therefore~~,~~ behold, I will proceed to do a marvellous work among this people***;*** ~~;~~ ***yea,*** ~~even~~ a marvellous work and a wonder: for the wisdom of their wise ***and learned*** ~~men~~ shall perish, and the understanding of their prudent men shall be hid.

29:15 ***And*** ~~W~~*w*oe unto them that seek deep to hide their counsel from the LORD. ~~, a~~*A*nd their works are in the dark***;*** ~~;~~ and they say, Who seeth us~~?~~ and who knoweth us? ***And they also say,***

27:25 Forasmuch as this people draw near unto me with their mouth, and with their lips do honor me, but have removed their hearts far from me, and their fear towards me is taught by the precepts of men–

27:26 Therefore, I will proceed to do a marvelous work among this people, yea, a marvelous work and a wonder, for the wisdom of their wise and learned shall perish, and the understanding of their prudent (-) shall be hid.

27:27 And wo unto them that seek deep to hide their counsel from the Lord! And their works are in the dark; and they say: Who seeth us, and who knoweth us? And they also say:

29:16 Surely your turning of things upside down shall be esteemed as the potter's clay:
But behold, I will show unto them, saith the Lord of hosts, that I know all their works. ~~f~~*F*or shall the work say of him that made it, He made me not? or shall the thing framed say of him that framed it, He had no understanding?
29:17 ***But behold, saith the Lord of hosts, I will show unto the children of men, that it*** ~~I~~*i*s ~~it~~ not yet a very little while, and Lebanon shall be turned into a fruitful field*;* ~~,~~ and the fruitful field shall be esteemed as a forest?
29:18 And in that day shall the deaf hear the words of the book*;* ~~,~~ and the eyes of the blind shall see out of obscurity~~,~~ and out of darkness.
29:19 The meek also shall increase, ***and*** their joy ***shall be*** in the LORD, and the poor among men shall rejoice in the Holy One of Israel.
29:20 ***For, assuredly as the Lord liveth, they shall see that*** ~~For~~ the terrible one is brought to nought, and the scorner is consumed, and all that watch for iniquity are cut off:
29:21 ***And they*** ~~T~~*t*hat make a man an offender for a word, and lay a snare for him that reproveth in the gate, and turn aside the just for a thing of nought.
29:22 Therefore, thus saith the LORD, who redeemed Abraham~~,~~ concerning the house of Jacob, Jacob shall not now be ashamed, neither shall his face now wax pale*;* ~~,~~
29:23 ~~B~~***but*** when he seeth his children, the work of ~~mine~~ ***my*** hands, in the midst of him, they shall sanctify my name, and sanctify the Holy One of Jacob, and shall fear the God of Israel.
29:24 They also that erred in spirit shall come to understanding, and they that murmured shall learn doctrine.

2nd Nephi (cont.)
Surely, your turning of things upside down shall be esteemed as the potter's clay.
But behold, I will show unto them, saith the Lord of Hosts, that I know all their works. For shall the work say of him that made it, he made me not? Or shall the thing framed say of him that framed it, he had no understanding?
27:28 But behold, saith the Lord of Hosts: I will show unto the children of men_ that it is(-) yet a very little while and Lebanon shall be turned into a fruitful field; and the fruitful field shall be esteemed as a forest.
27:29 And in that day shall the deaf hear the words of the book, and the eyes of the blind shall see out of obscurity and out of darkness.
27:30 And the meek also shall increase, and their joy shall be in the Lord, and the poor among men shall rejoice in the Holy One of Israel.
27:31 For_ assuredly as the Lord liveth they shall see that the terrible one is brought to naught, and the scorner is consumed, and all that watch for iniquity are cut off;
27:32 And they that make a man an offender for a word, and lay a snare for him that reproveth in the gate, and turn aside the just for a thing of naught.
27:33 Therefore, thus saith the Lord, who redeemed Abraham, concerning the house of Jacob: Jacob shall not now be ashamed, neither shall his face now wax pale.
27:34 But when he seeth his children, the work of my hands, in the midst of him, they shall sanctify my name, and sanctify the Holy One of Jacob, and shall fear the God of Israel.
27:35 They also that erred in spirit shall come to understanding, and they that murmured shall learn doctrine.

ISAIAH, Chapter 30

30:1 Woe to the rebellious children, saith the LORD, that take counsel, but not
of me; and that cover with a covering, but not of my spirit, that they may add sin
to sin:
30:2 That walk to go down into Egypt, and have not asked at my mouth; to
strengthen themselves in the strength of Pharaoh, and to trust in the shadow of
Egypt!
30:3 Therefore shall the strength of Pharaoh be your shame, and the trust in the
shadow of Egypt your confusion.
30:4 For his princes were at Zoan, and his ambassadors came to Hanes.
30:5 They were all ashamed of a people that could not profit them, nor be an
help nor profit, but a shame, and also a reproach.
30:6 The burden of the beasts of the south: into the land of trouble and anguish,
from whence come the young and old lion, the viper and fiery flying serpent, they
will carry their riches upon the shoulders of young asses, and their treasures upon
the bunches of camels, to a people that shall not profit them.
30:7 For the Egyptians shall help in vain, and to no purpose: therefore have I
cried concerning this, Their strength is to sit still.
30:8 Now go, write it before them in a table, and note it in a book, that it may
be for the time to come for ever and ever:
30:9 That this is a rebellious people, lying children, children that will not hear
the law of the LORD:
30:10 Which say to the seers, See not; and to the prophets, Prophesy not unto us
right things, speak unto us smooth things, prophesy deceits:
30:11 Get you out of the way, turn aside out of the path, cause the Holy One of
Israel to cease from before us.
30:12 Wherefore thus saith the Holy One of Israel, Because ye despise this word,
and trust in oppression and perverseness, and stay thereon:
30:13 Therefore this iniquity shall be to you as a breach ready to fall, swelling
out in a high wall, whose breaking cometh suddenly at an instant.
30:14 And he shall break it as the breaking of the potters' vessel that is broken
in pieces; he shall not spare: so that there shall not be found in the bursting of it
a sherd to take fire from the hearth, or to take water withal out of the pit.
30:15 For thus saith the Lord GOD, the Holy One of Israel; In returning and rest
shall ye be saved; in quietness and in confidence shall be your strength: and ye
would not.
30:16 But ye said, No; for we will flee upon horses; therefore shall ye flee: and,
We will ride upon the swift; therefore shall they that pursue you be swift.
30:17 One thousand shall flee at the rebuke of one; at the rebuke of five shall ye
flee: till ye be left as a beacon upon the top of a mountain, and as an ensign on an
hill.
30:18 And therefore will the LORD wait, that he may be gracious unto you, and
therefore will he be exalted, that he may have mercy upon you: for the LORD is
a God of judgment: blessed are all they that wait for him.
30:19 For the people shall dwell in Zion at Jerusalem: thou shalt weep no more:
he will be very gracious unto thee at the voice of thy cry; when he shall hear it, he
will answer thee.
30:20 And though the Lord give you the bread of adversity, and the water of
affliction, yet shall not thy teachers be removed into a corner any more, but thine
eyes shall see thy teachers:
30:21 And thine ears shall hear a word behind thee, saying, This is the way, walk
ye in it, when ye turn to the right hand, and when ye turn to the left.
30:22 Ye shall defile also the covering of thy graven images of silver, and the
ornament of thy molten images of gold: thou shalt cast them away as a menstruous
cloth; thou shalt say unto it, Get thee hence.

30:23 Then shall he give the rain of thy seed, that thou shalt sow the ground withal; and bread of the increase of the earth, and it shall be fat and plenteous: in that day shall thy cattle feed in large pastures.
30:24 The oxen likewise and the young asses that ear the ground shall eat clean provender, which hath been winnowed with the shovel and with the fan.
30:25 And there shall be upon every high mountain, and upon every high hill, rivers and streams of waters in the day of the great slaughter, when the towers fall.
30:26 Moreover the light of the moon shall be as the light of the sun, and the light of the sun shall be sevenfold, as the light of seven days, in the day that the LORD bindeth up the breach of his people, and healeth the stroke of their wound.
30:27 Behold, the name of the LORD cometh from far, burning with his anger, and the burden thereof is heavy: his lips are full of indignation, and his tongue as a devouring fire:
30:28 And his breath, as an over-flowing stream, shall reach to the midst of the neck, to sift the nations with the sieve of vanity: and there shall be a bridle in the jaws of the people, causing them to err.
30:29 Ye shall have a song, as in the night when a holy solemnity is kept; and gladness of heart, as when one goeth with a pipe to come into the mountain of the LORD, to the mighty One of Israel.
30:30 And the LORD shall cause his glorious voice to be heard, and shall shew the lighting down of his arm, with the indignation of his anger, and with the flame of a devouring fire, with scattering, and tempest, and hailstones.
30:31 For through the voice of the LORD shall the Assyrian be beaten down, which smote with a rod.
30:32 And in every place where the grounded staff shall pass, which the LORD shall lay upon him, it shall be with tabrets and harps: and in battles of shaking will he fight with it.
30:33 For Tophet is ordained of old; yea, for the king it is prepared; he hath made it deep and large: the pile thereof is fire and much wood; the breath of the LORD, like a stream of brimstone, doth kindle it.

ISAIAH, Chapter 31

31:1 Woe to them that go down to Egypt for help; and stay on horses, and trust in chariots, because they are many; and in horsemen, because they are very strong; but they look not unto the Holy One of Israel, neither seek the LORD!
31:2 Yet he also is wise, and will bring evil, and will not call back his words: but will arise against the house of the evildoers, and against the help of them that work iniquity.
31:3 Now the Egyptians are men, and not God; and their horses flesh, and not spirit. When the LORD shall stretch out his hand, both he that helpeth shall fall, and he that is holpen shall fall down, and they all shall fail together.
31:4 For thus hath the LORD spoken unto me, Like as the lion and the young lion roaring on his prey, when a multitude of shepherds is called forth against him, he will not be afraid of their voice, nor abase himself for the noise of them: so shall the LORD of hosts come down to fight for mount Zion, and for the hill thereof.
31:5 As birds flying, so will the LORD of hosts defend Jerusalem; defending also he will deliver it; and passing over he will preserve it.
31:6 Turn ye unto him from whom the children of Israel have deeply revolted.
31:7 For in that day every man shall cast away his idols of silver, and his idols of gold, which your own hands have made unto you for a sin.
31:8 Then shall the Assyrian fall with the sword, not of a mighty man; and the sword, not of a mean man, shall devour him: but he shall flee from the sword, and his young men shall be discomfited.

31:9 And he shall pass over to his strong hold for fear, and his princes shall be afraid of the ensign, saith the LORD, whose fire is in Zion, and his furnace in Jerusalem.

ISAIAH, Chapter 32

32:1 Behold, a king shall reign in righteousness, and princes shall rule in judgment.
32:2 And a man shall be as an hiding place from the wind, and a covert from the tempest; as rivers of water in a dry place, as the shadow of a great rock in a weary land.
32:3 And the eyes of them that see shall not be dim, and the ears of them that hear shall hearken.
32:4 The heart also of the rash shall understand knowledge, and the tongue of the stammerers shall be ready to speak plainly.
32:5 The vile person shall be no more called liberal, nor the churl said to be bountiful.
32:6 For the vile person will speak villany, and his heart will work iniquity, to practise hypocrisy, and to utter error against the LORD, to make empty the soul of the hungry, and he will cause the drink of the thirsty to fail.
32:7 The instruments also of the churl are evil: he deviseth wicked devices to destroy the poor with lying words, even when the needy speaketh right.
32:8 But the liberal deviseth liberal things; and by liberal things shall he stand.
32:9 Rise up, ye women that are at ease; hear my voice, ye careless daughters; give ear unto my speech.
32:10 Many days and years shall ye be troubled, ye careless women: for the vintage shall fail, the gathering shall not come.
32:11 Tremble, ye women that are at ease; be troubled, ye careless ones: strip you, and make you bare, and gird sackcloth upon your loins.
32:12 They shall lament for the teats, for the pleasant fields, for the fruitful vine.
32:13 Upon the land of my people shall come up thorns and briers; yea, upon all the houses of joy in the joyous city:
32:14 Because the palaces shall be forsaken; the multitude of the city shall be left; the forts and towers shall be for dens for ever, a joy of wild asses, a pasture of flocks;
32:15 Until the spirit be poured upon us from on high, and the wilderness be a fruitful field, and the fruitful field be counted for a forest.
32:16 Then judgment shall dwell in the wilderness, and righteousness remain in the fruitful field.
32:17 And the work of righteousness shall be peace; and the effect of righteousness quietness and assurance for ever.
32:18 And my people shall dwell in a peaceable habitation, and in sure dwellings, and in quiet resting places;
32:19 When it shall hail, coming down on the forest; and the city shall be low in a low place.
32:20 Blessed are ye that sow beside all waters, that send forth thither the feet of the ox and the ass.

ISAIAH, Chapter 33

33:1 Woe to thee that spoilest, and thou wast not spoiled; and dealest treacherously, and they dealt not treacherously with thee! when thou shalt cease to spoil, thou shalt be spoiled; and when thou shalt make an end to deal treacherously, they shall deal treacherously with thee.
33:2 O LORD, be gracious unto us; we have waited for thee: be thou their arm every morning, ***their*** ~~our~~ salvation also in the time of trouble.

33:3 At the noise of the tumult the people fled; at the lifting up of thyself the nations were scattered.
33:4 And your spoil shall be gathered like the gathering of the caterpiller: as the running to and fro of locusts shall he run upon them.
33:5 The LORD is exalted; for he dwelleth on high: he hath filled Zion with judgment and righteousness.
33:6 And wisdom and knowledge shall be the stability of thy times, and strength of salvation: the fear of the LORD is his treasure.
33:7 Behold, their valiant ones shall cry without: the ambassadors of peace shall weep bitterly.
33:8 The highways lie waste, the wayfaring man ceaseth: he hath broken the covenant, he hath despised the cities, he regardeth no man.
33:9 The earth mourneth and languisheth: Lebanon is ashamed and hewn down: Sharon is like a wilderness; and Bashan and Carmel shake off their fruits.
33:10 Now will I rise, saith the LORD; now will I be exalted; now will I lift up myself.
33:11 Ye shall conceive chaff, ye shall bring forth stubble: your breath, as fire, shall devour you.
33:12 And the people shall be as the burnings of lime: as thorns cut up shall they be burned in the fire.
33:13 Hear, ye that are far off, what I have done; and, ye that are near, acknowledge my might.
33:14 The sinners in Zion are afraid; fearfulness hath surprised the hypocrites. Who among us shall dwell with the devouring fire? who among us shall dwell with everlasting burnings?
33:15 He that walketh righteously, and speaketh uprightly; he that despiseth the gain of oppressions, that shaketh his hands from holding of bribes, that stoppeth his ears from hearing of blood, and shutteth his eyes from seeing evil;
33:16 He shall dwell on high: his place of defence shall be the munitions of rocks: bread shall be given him; his waters shall be sure.
33:17 Thine eyes shall see the king in his beauty: they shall behold the land that is very far off.
33:18 Thine heart shall meditate ***in*** terror. Where is the scribe? where is the receiver? where is he that counted the towers?
33:19 Thou shalt not see a fierce people, a people of a deeper speech than thou canst perceive; of a stammering tongue, that thou canst not understand.
33:20 Look upon Zion, the city of our solemnities: thine eyes shall see Jerusalem a quiet habitation, a tabernacle that shall not be taken down; not one of the stakes thereof shall ever be removed, neither shall any of the cords thereof be broken.
33:21 But there the glorious LORD will be unto us a place of broad rivers and streams; wherein shall go no galley with oars, neither shall gallant ship pass thereby.
33:22 For the LORD is our judge, the LORD is our lawgiver, the LORD is our king; he will save us.
33:23 Thy tacklings are loosed; they could not well strengthen their mast, they could not spread the sail: then is the prey of a great spoil divided; the lame take the prey.
33: 24 And the inhabitant shall not say, I am sick: the people that dwell therein shall be forgiven their iniquity.

ISAIAH, Chapter 34

34:1 Come near, ye nations, to hear; and hearken, ye people: let the earth hear, and all that is therein; the world, and all things that come forth of it.
34:2 For the indignation of the LORD is upon all nations, and his fury upon all their armies: he hath utterly destroyed them, he hath delivered them to the slaughter.

34:3 Their slain also shall be cast out, and their stink shall come up out of their carcases, and the mountains shall be melted with their blood.
34:4 And all the host of heaven shall be dissolved, and the heavens shall be rolled together as a scroll: and all their host shall fall down, as the leaf falleth off from the vine, and as a falling fig from the fig tree.
34:5 For my sword shall be bathed in heaven: behold, it shall come down upon Idumea, and upon the people of my curse, to judgment.
34:6 The sword of the LORD is filled with blood, it is made fat with fatness, and with the blood of lambs and goats, with the fat of the kidneys of rams: for the LORD hath a sacrifice in Bozrah, and a great slaughter in the land of Idumea.
34:7 And the ***reem*** ~~unicorns~~ shall come down with them, and the bullocks with the bulls; and their land shall be soaked with blood, and their dust made fat with fatness.
34:8 For it is the day of the LORD'S vengeance, and the year of recompences for the controversy of Zion.
34:9 And the streams thereof shall be turned into pitch, and the dust thereof into brimstone, and the land thereof shall become burning pitch.
34:10 It shall not be quenched night nor day; the smoke thereof shall go up for ever: from generation to generation it shall lie waste; none shall pass through it for ever and ever.
34:11 But the cormorant and the bittern shall possess it; the owl also and the raven shall dwell in it: and he shall stretch out upon it the line of confusion, and the stones of emptiness.
34:12 They shall call the nobles thereof to the kingdom, but none shall be there, and all her princes shall be nothing.
34:13 And thorns shall come up in her palaces, nettles and brambles in the fortresses thereof: and it shall be an habitation of dragons, and a court for owls.
34:14 The wild beasts of the desert shall also meet with the wild beasts of the island, and the satyr shall cry to his fellow; the screech owl also shall rest there, and find for herself a place of rest.
34:15 There shall the great owl make her nest, and lay, and hatch, and gather under her shadow: there shall the vultures also be gathered, every one with her mate.
34:16 Seek ye out of the book of the LORD, and read ***the names written therein;*** ~~:~~ no one of these shall fail***;*** ~~,~~ none shall want ~~her~~ ***their*** mate***;*** ~~:~~ for my mouth it hath commanded, and ***my*** ~~his~~ ~~s~~***S***pirit it hath gathered them.
34:17 And ***I have*** ~~he hath~~ cast the lot for them, and ***I have*** ~~his hand hath~~ divided it unto them by line***;*** ~~:~~ they shall possess it for ever***;*** ~~,~~ from generation to generation ~~shall~~ they ***shall*** dwell therein.

ISAIAH, Chapter 35

35:1 The wilderness and the solitary place shall be glad for them; and the desert shall rejoice, and blossom as the rose.
35:2 It shall blossom abundantly, and rejoice even with joy and singing: the glory of Lebanon shall be given unto it, the excellency of Carmel and Sharon, they shall see the glory of the LORD, and the excellency of our God.
35:3 Strengthen ye the weak hands, and confirm the feeble knees.
35:4 Say to them that are of a fearful heart, Be strong, fear not: behold, your God will come with vengeance, even God with a recompence; he will come and save you.
35:5 Then the eyes of the blind shall be opened, and the ears of the deaf shall be unstopped.
35:6 Then shall the lame man leap as an hart, and the tongue of the dumb sing: for in the wilderness shall waters break out, and streams in the desert.

35:7 And the parched ground shall become a pool, and the thirsty land springs
of water: in the habitation of dragons, where each lay, shall be grass with reeds
and rushes.
35:8 And a~~n~~ highway shall be there***;*** ~~, and~~ ***for*** a way ***shall be cast up***, and it
shall be called ~~T~~***t*** he way of holiness~~.~~ ~~: t~~***T***he unclean shall not pass over ***upon*** it;
but it shall be ***cast up*** for those ***who are clean,***~~:~~ ***and*** the wayfaring men, though
they are accounted fools, shall not err therein.
35:9 No lion shall be there, nor any ravenous beast shall go up thereon, it shall
not be found there; but the redeemed shall walk there:
35:10 And the ransomed of the LORD shall return, and come to Zion with songs
and everlasting joy upon their heads: they shall obtain joy and gladness, and
sorrow and sighing shall flee away.

ISAIAH, Chapter 36

36:1 ¶ NOW it came to pass in the fourteenth year of king Hezekiah, that
Sennacherib king of Assyria came up against all the defenced cities of Judah, and
took them.
36:2 And the king of Assyria sent Rabshakeh from Lachish to Jerusalem unto
king Hezekiah with a great army. And he stood by the conduit of the upper pool
in the highway of the fuller's field.
36:3 Then came forth unto him Eliakim, Hilkiah's son, which was over the
house, and Shebna the scribe, and Joah, Asaph's son, the recorder.
36:4 And Rabshakeh said unto them, Say ye now to Hezekiah, Thus saith the
great king, the king of Assyria, What confidence is this wherein thou trustest?
36:5 I say ~~, sayest thou, (but they~~ ***thy words*** are but vain ~~words)~~ ***when thou***
sayest, I have counsel and strength for war***.*** ~~: n~~***Now,*** on whom dost thou trust~~;~~ that
thou rebellest against me?
36:6 Lo, thou trustest in the staff of this broken reed, on Egypt; whereon if a
man lean, it will go into his hand, and pierce it: so is Pharaoh king of Egypt to all
that trust in him.
36:7 But if thou say to me, We trust in the LORD our God: is it not he, whose
high places and whose altars Hezekiah hath taken away, and said to Judah and to
Jerusalem, Ye shall worship before this altar?
36:8 Now therefore give pledges, I pray thee, to my master the king of Assyria,
and I will give thee two thousand horses, if thou be able on thy part to set riders
upon them.
36:9 How then wilt thou turn away the face of one captain of the least of my
master's servants, and put thy trust on Egypt for chariots and for horsemen?
36:10 And am I now come up without the LORD against this land to destroy it?
the LORD said unto me, Go up against this land, and destroy it.
36:11 ¶ Then said Eliakim and Shebna and Joah unto Rabshakeh, Speak, I pray
thee, unto thy servants in the Syrian language; for we understand it: and speak not
to us in the Jews' language, in the ears of the people that are on the wall.
36:12 But Rabshakeh said, Hath my master sent me to thy master and to thee to
speak these words? hath he not sent me to the men that sit upon the wall, that they
may eat their own dung, and drink their own piss with you?
36:13 Then Rabshakeh stood, and cried with a loud voice in the Jews' language,
and said, Hear ye the words of the great king, the king of Assyria.
36:14 Thus saith the king, Let not Hezekiah deceive you: for he shall not be able
to deliver you.
36:15 Neither let Hezekiah make you trust in the LORD, saying, The LORD will
surely deliver us: this city shall not be delivered into the hand of the king of
Assyria.
36:16 Hearken not to Hezekiah: for thus saith the king of Assyria, Make an
agreement with me by a present, and come out to me: and eat ye every one of his

vine, and every one of his fig tree, and drink ye every one the waters of his own cistern;
36:17 Until I come and take you away to a land like your own land, a land of corn and wine, a land of bread and vineyards.
36:18 Beware lest Hezekiah persuade you, saying, The LORD will deliver us. Hath any of the gods of the nations delivered his land out of the hand of the king of Assyria?
36:19 Where are the gods of Hamath and Arphad? where are the gods of Sepharvaim? and have they delivered Samaria out of my hand?
36:20 Who are they among all the gods of these lands, that have delivered their land out of my hand, that the LORD should deliver Jerusalem out of my hand?
36:21 But they held their peace, and answered him not a word: for the king's commandment was, saying, Answer him not.
36:22 Then came Eliakim, the son of Hilkiah, that was over the household, and Shebna the scribe, and Joah, the son of Asaph, the recorder, to Hezekiah with their clothes rent, and told him the words of Rabshakeh.

ISAIAH, Chapter 37

37:1 ¶ AND it came to pass, when king Hezekiah heard it, that he rent his clothes, and covered himself with sackcloth, and went into the house of the LORD.
37:2 And he sent Eliakim, who was over the household, and Shebna the scribe, and the elders of the priests covered with sackcloth, unto Isaiah the prophet the son of Amoz.
37:3 And they said unto him, Thus saith Hezekiah, This day is a day of trouble, and of rebuke, and of blasphemy: for the children are come to the birth, and there is not strength to bring forth.
37:4 It may be the LORD thy God will hear the words of Rabshakeh, whom the king of Assyria his master hath sent to reproach the living God, and will reprove the words which the LORD thy God hath heard: wherefore lift up thy prayer for the remnant that is left.
37:5 So the servants of king Hezekiah came to Isaiah.
37:6 And Isaiah said unto them, Thus shall ye say unto your master, Thus saith the LORD, Be not afraid of the words that thou hast heard, wherewith the servants of the king of Assyria have blasphemed me.
37:7 Behold, I will send a blast upon him, and he shall hear a rumour, and return to his own land; and I will cause him to fall by the sword in his own land.
37:8 ¶ So Rabshakeh returned, and found the king of Assyria warring against Libnah: for he had heard that he was departed from Lachish.
37:9 And he heard say concerning Tirhakah king of Ethiopia, He is come forth to make war with thee. And when he heard it, he sent messengers to Hezekiah, saying,
37:10 Thus shall ye speak to Hezekiah king of Judah, saying, Let not thy God, in whom thou trustest, deceive thee, saying, Jerusalem shall not be given into the hand of the king of Assyria.
37:11 Behold, thou hast heard what the kings of Assyria have done to all lands by destroying them utterly; and shalt thou be delivered?
37:12 Have the gods of the nations delivered them which my fathers have destroyed, as Gozan, and Haran, and Rezeph, and the children of Eden which were in Telassar?
37:13 Where is the king of Hamath, and the king of Arphad, and the king of the city of Sepharvaim, Hena, and Ivah?
37:14 And Hezekiah received the letter from the hand of the messengers, and read it: and Hezekiah went up unto the house of the LORD, and spread it before the LORD.
37:15 And Hezekiah prayed unto the LORD, saying,

37:16 O LORD of hosts, God of Israel, that dwellest between the cherubims, thou art the God, even thou alone, of all the kingdoms of the earth: thou hast made heaven and earth.

37:17 Incline thine ear, O LORD, and hear; open thine eyes, O LORD, and see***;*** ~~:~~ and hear all the words of Sennacherib, which ***he*** hath sent to reproach the living God.

37:18 Of a truth, LORD, the kings of Assyria have laid waste all the nations, and their countries,

37:19 And have cast their gods into the fire: for they were no gods, but the work of men's hands, wood and stone: therefore they have destroyed them.

37:20 Now therefore, O LORD our God, save us from his hand, that all the kingdoms of the earth may know that thou art the LORD, even thou only.

37:21 ¶ Then Isaiah the son of Amoz sent unto Hezekiah, saying, Thus saith the LORD God of Israel, Whereas thou hast prayed to me against Sennacherib king of Assyria:

37:22 This is the word which the LORD hath spoken concerning him; The virgin, the daughter of Zion, hath despised thee and laughed thee to scorn; the daughter of Jerusalem hath shaken her head at thee.

37:23 Whom hast thou reproached and blasphemed? and against whom hast thou exalted thy voice, and lifted up thine eyes on high? even against the Holy One of Israel.

37:24 By thy servants hast thou reproached the Lord, and hast said, By the multitude of my chariots am I come up to the height of the mountains, to the sides of Lebanon; and I will cut down the tall cedars thereof, and the choice fir trees thereof: and I will enter into the height of his border, and the forest of his Carmel.

37:25 I have digged, and drunk water; and with the sole of my feet have I dried up all the rivers of the besieged places.

37:26 Hast thou not heard long ago, how I have done it; and of ancient times, that I have formed it? now have I brought ~~it~~ to pass, that thou shouldest be to lay waste defenced cities into ruinous heaps.

37:27 Therefore their inhabitants were of small power, they were dismayed and confounded: they were as the grass of the field, and as the green herb, as the grass on the housetops, and as corn blasted before it be grown up.

37:28 But I know thy abode, and thy going out, and thy coming in, and thy rage against me.

37:29 Because thy rage against me, and thy tumult, is come up into mine ears, therefore will I put my hook in thy nose, and my bridle in thy lips, and I will turn thee back by the way by which thou camest.

37:30 And this shall be a sign unto thee, Ye shall eat this year such as groweth of itself; and the second year that which springeth of the same: and in the third year sow ye, and reap, and plant vineyards, and eat the fruit thereof.

37:31 And the remnant that is escaped of the house of Judah shall again take root downward, and bear fruit upward:

37:32 For out of Jerusalem shall go forth a remnant ***;*** ~~,~~ and they that escape out of ***Jerusalem shall come upon*** mount Zion: the zeal of the LORD of hosts shall do this.

37:33 Therefore thus saith the LORD concerning the king of Assyria, He shall not come into this city, nor shoot an arrow there, nor come before it with shields, nor cast a bank against it.

37:34 By the way that he came, by the same shall he return, and shall not come into this city, saith the LORD.

37:35 For I will defend this city to save it for mine own sake, and for my servant David's sake.

37:36 Then the angel of the LORD went forth, and smote in the camp of the Assyrians a hundred and four-score and five thousand: and when they ***who were left*** arose***,*** early in the morning, behold, they were all dead corpses.

37:37 So Sennacherib king of Assyria departed, and went and returned, and dwelt at Nineveh.

37:38 And it came to pass, as he was worshipping in the house of Nisroch his god, that Adrammelech and Sharezer his sons smote him with the sword; and they escaped into the land of Armenia: and Esar-haddon his son reigned in his stead.

ISAIAH, Chapter 38

38:1 ¶ IN those days was Hezekiah sick unto death. And Isaiah the prophet the son of Amoz came unto him, and said unto him, Thus saith the LORD, Set thine house in order: for thou shalt die, and not live.
38:2 Then Hezekiah turned his face toward the wall, and prayed unto the LORD,
38:3 And said, Remember now, O LORD, I beseech thee, how I have walked before thee in truth and with a perfect heart, and have done that which is good in thy sight. And Hezekiah wept sore.
38:4 Then came the word of the LORD to Isaiah, saying,
38:5 Go, and say to Hezekiah, Thus saith the LORD, the God of David thy father, I have heard thy prayer, I have seen thy tears: behold, I will add unto thy days fifteen years.
38:6 And I will deliver thee and this city out of the hand of the king of Assyria: and I will defend this city.
38:7 And this shall be a sign unto thee from the LORD, that the LORD will do this thing that he hath spoken;
38:8 Behold, I will bring again the shadow of the degrees, which is gone down in the sun dial of Ahaz, ten degrees backward. So the sun returned ten degrees, by which degrees it was gone down.
38:9 ¶ The writing of Hezekiah king of Judah, when he had been sick, and was recovered of his sickness:
38:10 I said in the cutting off of my days, I shall go to the gates of the grave: I am deprived of the residue of my years.
38:11 I said, I shall not see the LORD, even the LORD, in the land of the living: I shall behold man no more with the inhabitants of the world.
38:12 Mine age is departed, and is removed from me as a shepherd's tent: I have cut off like a weaver my life: he will cut me off with pining sickness: from day even to night wilt thou make an end of me.
38:13 I reckoned till morning, that, as a lion, so will he break all my bones: from day even to night wilt thou make an end of me.
38:14 Like a crane or a swallow, so did I chatter***;*** ~~:~~ I did mourn as a dove***;*** ~~:~~ mine eyes fail with looking upward***;*** ~~:~~ O LORD, I am oppressed; undertake for me.
38:15 What shall I say? he hath both spoken unto me, and himself hath ***healed me.*** ~~done it:~~ I shall go softly all my years***, that I may not walk*** in the bitterness of my soul.
38:16 O Lord, ~~by these things men live, and in all these things is~~ ***thou art*** the life of my spirit***, in whom I live; and in all these things I will praise thee.*** ~~: so wilt thou recover me, and make me to live.~~
38:17 Behold, ~~for peace~~ I had great bitterness~~:~~ ***instead of peace,*** but thou hast in love to my soul***, saved me*** ~~delivered it~~ from the pit of corruption**,** : for thou hast cast all my sins behind thy back.
38:18 For the grave cannot praise thee, death can not celebrate thee: they that go down into the pit cannot hope for thy truth.
38:19 The living, the living, he shall praise thee, as I do this day: the father to the children shall make known thy truth.
38:20 The LORD was ready to save me: therefore we will sing my songs to the stringed instruments all the days of our life in the house of the LORD.
38:21 For Isaiah had said, Let them take a lump of figs, and lay it for a plaister upon the boil, and he shall recover.
38:22 Hezekiah also had said, What is the sign that I shall go up to the house of the LORD?

ISAIAH, Chapter 39

39:1 ¶ At that time Merodach-baladan, the son of Baladan, king of Babylon,
sent letters and a present to Hezekiah: for he had heard that he had been sick, and
was recovered.
39:2 And Hezekiah was glad of them, and shewed them the house of his
precious things, the silver, and the gold, and the spices, and the precious ointment,
and all the house of his ***armor*** ~~armour~~, and all that was found in his treasures***;*** ~~:~~
there was nothing in his house, nor in all his dominion, that Hezekiah shewed ***him***
~~them~~ not.
39:3 Then came Isaiah the prophet unto king Hezekiah, and said unto him,
What said these men? and from whence came they unto thee? And Hezekiah said,
They are come from a far country unto me, even from Babylon.
39:4 Then said he, What have they seen in thine house? And Hezekiah
answered, All that is in mine house have they seen: there is nothing among my
treasures that I have not shewed them.
39:5 ¶ Then said Isaiah to Hezekiah, Hear the word of the LORD of hosts:
39:6 Behold, the days come, that all that is in thine house, and that which thy
fathers have laid up in store until this day, shall be carried to Babylon: nothing
shall be left, saith the LORD.
39:7 And of thy sons that shall issue from thee, which thou shalt beget, shall
they take away; and they shall be eunuchs in the palace of the king of Babylon.
39:8 Then said Hezekiah to Isaiah, Good is the word of the LORD which thou
hast spoken. He said moreover, For there shall be peace and truth in my days.

ISAIAH, Chapter 40

40:1 ¶ COMFORT ye, comfort ye my people, saith your God.
40:2 Speak ye comfortably to Jerusalem, and cry unto her, that her warfare is
accomplished, that her iniquity is pardoned: for she hath received of the LORD'S
hand double for all her sins.
40:3 ¶ The voice of him that crieth in the wilderness, Prepare ye the way of the
LORD, make straight in the desert a highway for our God.
40:4 Every valley shall be exalted, and every mountain and hill shall be made
low: and the crooked shall be made straight, and the rough places plain:
40:5 And the glory of the LORD shall be revealed, and all flesh shall see it
together: for the mouth of the LORD hath spoken it.
40:6 The voice said, Cry. And he said, What shall I cry? All flesh is grass, and
all the goodliness thereof is as the flower of the field:
40:7 The grass withereth, the flower fadeth: because the spirit of the LORD
bloweth upon it: surely the people is grass.
40:8 The grass withereth, the flower fadeth: but the word of our God shall stand
for ever.
40:9 ¶ O Zion, that bringest good tidings, get thee up into the high mountain;
O Jerusalem, that bringest good tidings, lift up thy voice with strength; lift it up,
be not afraid; say unto the cities of Judah, Behold your God!
40:10 Behold, the Lord GOD will come with strong hand, and his arm shall rule
for him: behold, his reward is with him, and his work before him.
40:11 He shall feed his flock like a shepherd: he shall gather the lambs with his
arm, and carry them in his bosom, and shall gently lead those that are with young.
40:12 ¶ Who hath measured the waters in the hollow of his hand, and meted out
heaven with the span, and comprehended the dust of the earth in a measure, and
weighed the mountains in scales, and the hills in a balance?
40:13 Who hath directed the Spirit of the LORD, or being his counsellor hath
taught him?

40:14 With whom took he counsel, and who instructed him, and taught him in
the path of judgment , and taught him knowledge, and shewed to him the way of
understanding?
40:15 Behold, the nations are as a drop of a bucket, and are counted as the small
dust of the balance: behold, he taketh up the isles as a very little thing.
40:16 And Lebanon is not sufficient to burn, nor the beasts thereof sufficient for
a burnt offering.
40:17 All nations before him are as nothing; and they are counted to him less
than nothing, and vanity.
40:18 ¶ To whom then will ye liken God? or what likeness will ye compare unto
him?
40:19 The workman melteth a graven image, and the goldsmith spreadeth it over
with gold, and casteth silver chains.
40:20 He that is so impoverished that he hath no oblation chooseth a tree that
will not rot; he seeketh unto him a cunning workman to prepare a graven image,
that shall not be moved.
40:21 Have ye not known? have ye not heard? hath it not been told you from the
beginning? have ye not understood from the foundations of the earth?
40:22 It is he that sitteth upon the circle of the earth, and the inhabitants thereof
are as grasshoppers; that stretcheth out the heavens as a curtain, and spreadeth
them out as a tent to dwell in:
40:23 That bringeth the princes to nothing; he maketh the judges of the earth as
vanity.
40:24 Yea, they shall not be planted; yea, they shall not be sown: yea, their stock
shall not take root in the earth: and he shall also blow upon them, and they shall
wither, and the whirlwind shall take them away as stubble.
40:25 To whom then will ye liken me, or shall I be equal? saith the Holy One.
40:26 Lift up your eyes on high, and behold who hath created these things, that
bringeth out their host by number: he calleth them all by names by the greatness
of his might, for that he is strong in power; not one faileth.
40:27 ¶ Why sayest thou, O Jacob, and speakest, O Israel, My way is hid from
the LORD, and my judgment is passed over from my God?
40:28 Hast thou not known? hast thou not heard, that the everlasting God, the
LORD, the Creator of the ends of the earth, fainteth not, neither is weary? there
is no searching of his understanding.
40:29 He giveth power to the faint; and to them that have no might he increaseth
strength.
40:30 Even the youths shall faint and be weary, and the young men shall utterly
fall:
40:31 But they that wait upon the LORD shall renew their strength; they shall
mount up with wings as eagles; they shall run, and not be weary; and they shall
walk, and not faint.

ISAIAH, Chapter 41

41:1 ¶ KEEP silence before me, O islands; and let the people renew their
strength: let them come near; then let them speak: let us come near together to
judgment.
41:2 Who raised up the righteous man from the east, called him to his foot, gave
the nations before him, and made him rule over kings? he gave them as the dust
to his sword, and as driven stubble to his bow.
41:3 He pursued them, and passed safely; even by the way that he had not gone
with his feet.
41:4 Who hath wrought and done it, calling the generations from the beginning?
I the LORD, the first, and with the last; I am he.
41:5 The isles saw it, and feared; the ends of the earth were afraid, drew near,
and came.

41:6 They helped every one his neighbour; and every one said to his brother, Be of good courage.
41:7 So the carpenter encouraged the goldsmith, and he that smootheth with the hammer him that smote the anvil, saying, It is ready for the sodering: and he fastened it with nails, that it should not be moved.
41:8 But thou, Israel, art my servant, Jacob whom I have chosen, the seed of Abraham my friend.
41:9 Thou whom I have taken from the ends of the earth, and called thee from the chief men thereof, and said unto thee, Thou art my servant; I have chosen thee, and not cast thee away.
41:10 ¶ Fear thou not; for I am with thee: be not dismayed; for I am thy God: I will strengthen thee; yea, I will help thee; yea, I will uphold thee with the right hand of my righteousness.
41:11 Behold, all they that were incensed against thee shall be ashamed and confounded: they shall be as nothing; and they that strive with thee shall perish.
41:12 Thou shalt seek them, and shalt not find them, even them that contended with thee: they that war against thee shall be as nothing, and as a thing of nought.
41:13 For I the LORD thy God will hold thy right hand, saying unto thee, Fear not; I will help thee.
41:14 Fear not, thou worm Jacob, and ye men of Israel; I will help thee, saith the LORD, and thy redeemer, the Holy One of Israel.
41:15 Behold, I will make thee a new sharp threshing instrument having teeth: thou shalt thresh the mountains, and beat them small, and shalt make the hills as chaff.
41:16 Thou shalt fan them, and the wind shall carry them away, and the whirlwind shall scatter them: and thou shalt rejoice in the LORD, and shalt glory in the Holy One of Israel.
41:17 When the poor and needy seek water, and there is none, and their tongue faileth for thirst, I the LORD will hear them, I the God of Israel will not forsake them.
41:18 I will open rivers in high places, and fountains in the midst of the valleys: I will make the wilderness a pool of water, and the dry land springs of water.
41:19 I will plant in the wilderness the cedar, the shittah tree, and the myrtle, and the oil tree; I will set in the desert the fir tree, and the pine, and the box tree together:
41:20 That they may see, and know, and consider, and understand together, that the hand of the LORD hath done this, and the Holy One of Israel hath created it.
41:21 ¶ Produce your cause, saith the LORD; bring forth your strong reasons, saith the King of Jacob.
41:22 Let them bring them forth, and shew us what shall happen: let them shew the former things, what they be, that we may consider them, and know the latter end of them; or declare us things for to come.
41:23 Shew the things that are to come hereafter, that we may know that ye are gods: yea, do good, or do evil, that we may be dismayed, and behold it together.
41:24 Behold, ye are of nothing, and your work of nought: an abomination is he that chooseth you.
41:25 I have raised up one from the north, and he shall come: from the rising of the sun shall he call upon my name: and he shall come upon princes as upon molter, and as the potter treadeth clay.
41:26 Who hath declared from the beginning, that we may know? and beforetime, that we may say, He is righteous? yea, there is none that sheweth, yea, there is none that declareth, yea, there is none that heareth your words.
41:27 The first shall say to Zion, Behold, behold them: and I will give to Jerusalem one that bringeth good tidings.
41:28 For I beheld, and there was no man; even among ***men*** ~~them~~, and there was no counsellor, that, when I asked of them, could answer a word.
41:29 Behold, they are all vanity; their works are nothing: their molten images are wind and confusion.

ISAIAH, Chapter 42

42:1 ¶ BEHOLD my servant, whom I uphold; mine elect, in whom my soul delighteth; I have put my spirit upon him: he shall bring forth judgment to the Gentiles.

42:2 He shall not cry, nor lift up, nor cause his voice to be heard in the street.

42:3 A bruised reed shall he not break, and the smoking flax shall he not quench: he shall bring forth judgment unto truth.

42:4 He shall not fail nor be discouraged, till he have set judgment in the earth: and the isles shall wait for his law.

42:5 ¶ Thus saith God the LORD, he that created the heavens, and stretched them out; he that spread forth the earth, and that which cometh out of it; he that giveth breath unto the people upon it, and spirit to them that walk therein:

42:6 I the LORD have called thee in righteousness, and will hold thine hand, and will keep thee, and give thee for a covenant of the people, for a light of the Gentiles;

42:7 To open the blind eyes, to bring out the prisoners from the prison, and them that sit in darkness out of the prison house.

42:8 I am the LORD: that is my name: and my glory will I not give to another, neither my praise to graven images.

42:9 Behold, the former things are come to pass, and new things do I declare: before they spring forth I tell you of them.

42:10 Sing unto the LORD a new song, and his praise from the end of the earth, ye that go down to the sea, and all that is therein; the isles, and the inhabitants thereof.

42:11 Let the wilderness and the cities thereof lift up their voice, the villages that Kedar doth inhabit: let the inhabitants of the rock sing, let them shout from the top of the mountains.

42:12 Let them give glory unto the LORD, and declare his praise in the islands.

42:13 ¶ The LORD shall go forth as a mighty man, he shall stir up jealousy like a man of war: he shall cry, yea, roar; he shall prevail against his enemies.

42:14 I have long time holden my peace; I have been still, and refrained myself: now will I cry like a travailing woman; I will destroy and devour at once.

42:15 I will make waste mountains and hills, and dry up all their herbs; and I will make the rivers islands, and I will dry up the pools.

42:16 And I will bring the blind by a way that they knew not; I will lead them in paths that they have not known: I will make darkness light before them, and crooked things straight. These things will I do unto them, and not forsake them.

42:17 They shall be turned back, they shall be greatly ashamed, that trust in graven images, that say to the molten images, Ye are our gods.

42:18 ¶ Hear, ye deaf; and look, ye blind, that ye may see.

42:19 ***For I will send my servant unto you who are blind; yea, a messenger to open the eyes of the blind, and uunstop the ears of the deaf;*** ~~Who is blind, but my servant? or deaf, as my messenger that I sent? who is blind as he that is perfect, and blind as the LORD'S servant?~~

And they shall be made perfect not withstanding their blindness, if they will hearken unto the messenger, the Lord's servant.

42:20 ***Thou are a people,*** ~~S~~seeing many things, but thou observest not; opening the ears ***to hear***, but ***thou hearest*** ~~he heareth~~ not.

42:21 The LORD is ***not*** well pleased ***with such a people, but*** for his righteousness' sake ~~;~~ he will magnify the law~~;~~ and make it honourable.

42:22 But ***thou art***t ~~this is~~ a people robbed and spoiled; ~~they are~~ ***thine enemies,*** all of them snared ***thee*** in holes, and they ~~are~~ ***have*** hid ***thee*** in prison houses***;*** ~~:~~ they ~~are~~ ***have taken thee*** for a prey, and none delivereth; for a spoil, and none saith, Restore.

42:23 Who among ***them*** ~~you~~ will give ear ~~to this? who will~~ ***unto thee, or*** hearken and hear ***thee*** for the time to come?

42:24 ***and*** ~~W~~who gave Jacob for a spoil, and Israel to the robbers? did not the LORD, he against whom ***they*** ~~we~~ have sinned? for they would not walk in his ways, neither were they obedient unto his law.

42:25 Therefore he hath poured upon ***them*** ~~him~~ the fury of his anger, and the strength of battle: and ***they have*** ~~it hath~~ set ***them*** ~~him~~ on fire round about, yet ***they*** ~~he~~ knew not; and it burned ***them*** ~~him~~, yet ***they*** ~~he~~ laid it not to heart.

ISAIAH, Chapter 43

43:1 ¶ BUT now thus saith the LORD that created thee, O Jacob, and he that formed thee, O Israel, Fear not: for I have redeemed thee, I have called thee by thy name; thou art mine.

43:2 When thou passest through the waters, I will be with thee; and through the rivers, they shall not overflow thee: when thou walkest through the fire, thou shalt not be burned; neither shall the flame kindle upon thee.

43:3 For I am the LORD thy God, the Holy One of Israel, thy Saviour: I gave Egypt for thy ransom, Ethiopia and Seba for thee.

43:4 Since thou wast precious in my sight, thou hast been honourable, and I have loved thee: therefore will I give men for thee, and people for thy life.

43:5 Fear not: for I am with thee: I will bring thy seed from the east, and gather thee from the west;

43:6 I will say to the north, Give up; and to the south, Keep not back: bring my sons from far, and my daughters from the ends of the earth;

43:7 Even every one that is called by my name: for I have created him for my glory, I have formed him; yea, I have made him.

43:8 ¶ Bring forth the blind people that have eyes, and the deaf that have ears.

43:9 Let all the nations be gathered together, and let the people be assembled: who among them can declare this, and shew us former things? let them bring forth their witnesses, that they may be justified: or let them hear, and say, It is truth.

43:10 Ye are my witnesses, saith the LORD, and my servant whom I have chosen: that ye may know and believe me, and understand that I am he: before me there was no God formed, neither shall there be after me.

43:11 I, even I, am the LORD; and beside me there is no saviour.

43:12 I have declared, and have saved, and I have shewed, when there was no strange god among you: therefore ye are my witnesses, saith the LORD, that I am God.

43:13 Yea, before the day was I am he; and there is none that can deliver out of my hand: I will work, and who shall let it?

43:14 ¶ Thus saith the LORD, your redeemer, the Holy One of Israel; For your sake I have sent to Babylon, and have brought down all their nobles, and the Chaldeans, whose cry is in the ships.

43:15 I am the LORD, your Holy One, the creator of Israel, your King.

43:16 Thus saith the LORD, which maketh a way in the sea, and a path in the mighty waters;

43:17 Which bringeth forth the chariot and horse, the army and the power; they shall lie down together, they shall not rise: they are extinct, they are quenched as tow.

43:18 Remember ye not the former things, neither consider the things of old.

43:19 Behold, I will do a new thing; now it shall spring forth; shall ye not know it? I will even make a way in the wilderness, and rivers in the desert.

43:20 The beast of the field shall honour me, the dragons and the owls: because I give waters in the wilderness, and rivers in the desert, to give drink to my people, my chosen.

43:21 This people have I formed for myself; they shall shew forth my praise.

43:22 ¶ But thou hast not called upon me, O Jacob; but thou hast been weary of me, O Israel.

43:23 Thou hast not brought me the small cattle of thy burnt offerings; neither hast thou honoured me with thy sacrifices. I have not caused thee to serve with an offering, nor wearied thee with incense.
43:24 Thou hast bought me no sweet cane with money, neither hast thou filled me with the fat of thy sacrifices: but thou hast made me to serve with thy sins, thou hast wearied me with thine iniquities.
43:25 I, even I, am he that blotteth out thy transgressions for mine own sake, and will not remember thy sins.
43:26 Put me in remembrance: let us plead together: declare thou, that thou mayest be justified.
43:27 Thy first father hath sinned, and thy teachers have transgressed against me.
43:28 Therefore I have profaned the princes of the sanctuary, and have given Jacob to the curse, and Israel to reproaches.

ISAIAH, Chapter 44

44:1 ¶ YET now hear, O Jacob my servant; and Israel, whom I have chosen:
44:2 Thus saith the LORD that made thee, and formed thee from the womb, which will help thee; Fear not, O Jacob, my servant; and thou, Jesurun, whom I have chosen.
44:3 For I will pour water upon him that is thirsty, and floods upon the dry ground: I will pour my spirit upon thy seed, and my blessing upon thine offspring:
44:4 And they shall spring up as among the grass, as willows by the water courses.
44:5 One shall say, I am the LORD'S; and another shall call himself by the name of Jacob; and another shall subscribe with his hand unto the LORD, and surname himself by the name of Israel.
44:6 Thus saith the LORD the King of Israel, and his redeemer the LORD of hosts; I am the first, and I am the last; and beside me there is no God.
44:7 And who, as I, shall call, and shall declare it, and set it in order for me, since I appointed the ancient people? and the things that are coming, and shall come, let them shew unto them.
44:8 Fear ye not, neither be afraid: have not I told thee from that time, and have declared it? ye are even my witnesses. Is there a God beside me? yea, there is no God ; I know not any.
44:9 ¶ They that make a graven image are all of them vanity; and their delectable things shall not profit; and they are their own witnesses; they see not, nor know; that they may be ashamed.
44:10 Who hath formed a god, or molten a graven image that is profitable for nothing?
44:11 Behold, all his fellows shall be ashamed: and the workmen, they are of men: let them all be gathered together, let them stand up; yet they shall fear, and they shall be ashamed together.
44:12 The smith with the tongs both worketh in the coals, and fashioneth it with hammers, and worketh it with the strength of his arms: yea, he is hungry, and his strength faileth: he drinketh no water, and is faint.
44:13 The carpenter stretcheth out his rule; he marketh it out with a line; he fitteth it with planes, and he marketh it out with the compass, and maketh it after the figure of a man, according to the beauty of a man; that it may remain in the house.
44:14 He heweth him down cedars, and taketh the cypress and the oak, which he strengtheneth for himself among the trees of the forest: he planteth an ash, and the rain doth nourish it.
44:15 Then shall it be for a man to burn: for he will take thereof, and warm himself; yea, he kindleth it, and baketh bread; yea, he maketh a god, and worshippeth it; he maketh it a graven image, and falleth down thereto.

44:16 He burneth part thereof in the fire; with part thereof he eateth flesh; he roasteth roast, and is satisfied: yea, he warmeth himself, and saith, Aha, I am warm, I have seen the fire:
44:17 And the residue thereof he maketh a god, even his graven image: he falleth down unto it, and worshippeth it, and prayeth unto it, and saith, Deliver me; for thou art my god.
44:18 They have not known nor understood: for he hath shut their eyes, that they cannot see; and their hearts, that they cannot understand.
44:19 And none considereth in his heart, neither is there knowledge nor understanding to say, I have burned part of it in the fire; yea, also I have baked bread upon the coals thereof; I have roasted flesh, and eaten it: and shall I make the residue thereof an abomination? shall I fall down to the stock of a tree?
44:20 He feedeth on ashes: a deceived heart hath turned him aside, that he cannot deliver his soul, nor say, Is there not a lie in my right hand?
44:21 ¶ Remember these, O Jacob and Israel; for thou art my servant*;* : I have formed thee; thou art my servant*;* : O Israel, thou shalt not be forgotten of me.
44:22 I have blotted out, as a thick cloud, thy transgressions, and, as a cloud, thy sins: return unto me; for I have redeemed thee.
44:23 Sing, O ye heavens; for the LORD hath done it: shout, ye lower parts of the earth: break forth into singing, ye mountains, O forest, and every tree therein: for the LORD hath redeemed Jacob, and glorified himself in Israel.
44:24 Thus saith the LORD, thy redeemer, and he that formed thee from the womb, I am the LORD that maketh all things; that stretcheth forth the heavens alone; that spreadeth abroad the earth by myself;
44:25 That frustrateth the tokens of the liars, and maketh diviners mad; that turneth wise men backward, and maketh their knowledge foolish;
44:26 That confirmeth the word of his servant, and performeth the counsel of his messengers; that saith to Jerusalem, Thou shalt be inhabited; and to the cities of Judah, Ye shall be built, and I will raise up the decayed places thereof:
44:27 That saith to the deep, Be dry, and I will dry up thy rivers:
44:28 That saith of Cyrus, He is my shepherd, and shall perform all my pleasure: even saying to Jerusalem, Thou shalt be built; and to the temple, Thy foundation shall be laid.

ISAIAH, Chapter 45

45:1 ¶ THUS saith the LORD to his anointed, to Cyrus, whose right hand I have holden, to subdue nations before him; and I will loose the loins of kings, to open before him the two leaved gates; and the gates shall not be shut;
45:2 I will go before thee, and make the crooked places straight: I will break in pieces the gates of brass, and cut in sunder the bars of iron:
45:3 And I will give thee the treasures of darkness, and hidden riches of secret places, that thou mayest know that I, the LORD, which call thee by thy name, am the God of Israel.
45:4 For Jacob my servant's sake, and Israel mine elect, I have even called thee by thy name: I have surnamed thee, though thou hast not known me.
45:5 ¶ I am the LORD, and there is none else, there is no God beside me: I girded thee, though thou hast not known me:
45:6 That they may know from the rising of the sun, and from the west, that there is none beside me. I am the LORD, and there is none else.
45:7 I form the light, and create darkness: I make peace, and create evil: I the LORD do all these things.
45:8 Drop down, ye heavens, from above, and let the skies pour down righteousness: let the earth open, and let them bring forth salvation, and let righteousness spring up together; I the LORD have created it.
45:9 Woe unto him that striveth with his Maker! Let the potsherd strive with the potsherds of the earth. Shall the clay say to him that fashioneth it, What makest thou? or thy work, He hath no hands?

45:10 Woe unto him that saith unto his father, What begettest thou? or to the
woman, What hast thou brought forth?
45:11 ¶ Thus saith the LORD, the Holy One of Israel, and his Maker, Ask me of
things to come concerning my sons, and concerning the work of my hands command
ye me.
45:12 I have made the earth, and created man upon it: I, even my hands, have
stretched out the heavens, and all their host have I commanded.
45:13 I have raised him up in righteousness, and I will direct all his ways: he shall
build my city, and he shall let go my captives, not for price nor reward, saith the
LORD of hosts.
45:14 Thus saith the LORD, The labour of Egypt, and merchandise of Ethiopia and
of the Sabeans, men of stature, shall come over unto thee, and they shall be thine:
they shall come after thee; in chains they shall come over, and they shall fall down
unto thee, they shall make supplication unto thee, saying, Surely God is in thee; and
there is none else, there is no God.
45:15 Verily thou art a God that hidest thyself, O God of Israel, the Saviour.
45:16 They shall be ashamed, and also confounded, all of them: they shall go to
confusion together that are makers of idols.
45:17 But Israel shall be saved in the LORD with an everlasting salvation: ye shall
not be ashamed nor confounded world without end.
45:18 For thus saith the LORD that created the heavens; God himself that formed
the earth and made it; he hath established it, he created it not in vain, he formed it
to be inhabited: I am the LORD; and there is none else.
45:19 I have not spoken in secret, in a dark place of the earth: I said not unto the
seed of Jacob, Seek ye me in vain: I the LORD speak righteousness, I declare things
that are right.
45:20 ¶ Assemble yourselves and come; draw near together, ye that are escaped of
the nations: they have no knowledge that set up the wood of their graven image, and
pray unto a god that cannot save.
45:21 Tell ye, and bring them near; yea, let them take counsel together: who hath
declared this from ancient time? who hath told it from that time? have not I the
LORD? and there is no God else beside me; a just God and a Saviour; there is none
beside me.
45:22 Look unto me, and be ye saved, all the ends of the earth: for I am God, and
there is none else.
45:23 I have sworn by myself, the word is gone out of my mouth in righteousness,
and shall not return, That unto me every knee shall bow, every tongue shall swear.
45:24 Surely, shall one say, in the LORD have I righteousness and strength : even
to him shall men come; and all that are incensed against him shall be ashamed.
45:25 In the LORD shall all the seed of Israel be justified, and shall glory.

ISAIAH, Chapter 46

46:1 BEL boweth down, Nebo stoopeth, their idols were upon the beasts, and
upon the cattle: your carriages were heavy loaden; they are a burden to the weary
beast.
46:2 They stoop, they bow down together; they could not deliver the burden, but
themselves are gone into captivity.
46:3 Hearken unto me, O house of Jacob, and all the remnant of the house of
Israel, which are borne by me from the belly, which are carried from the womb:
46:4 And even to your old age I am he; and even to hoar hairs will I carry you: I
have made, and I will bear; even I will carry, and will deliver you.
46:5 ¶ To whom will ye liken me, and make me equal, and compare me, that we
may be like?
46:6 They lavish gold out of the bag, and weigh silver in the balance, and hire a
goldsmith; and he maketh it a god: they fall down, yea, they worship.

46:7 They bear him upon the shoulder, they carry him, and set him in his place,
and he standeth; from his place shall he not remove: yea, one shall cry unto him, yet
can he not answer, nor save him out of his trouble.
46:8 Remember this, and shew yourselves men: bring it again to mind, O ye
transgressors.
46:9 Remember the former things of old: for I am God, and there is none else; I
am God, and there is none like me,
46:10 Declaring the end from the beginning, and from ancient times the things that
are not yet done, saying, My counsel shall stand, and I will do all my pleasure:
46:11 Calling a ravenous bird from the east, the man that executeth my counsel
from a far country: yea, I have spoken it, I will also bring it to pass; I have purposed
it, I will also do it.
46:12 Hearken unto me, ye stouthearted, that are far from righteousness:
46:13 I bring near my righteousness; it shall not be far off, and my salvation shall
not tarry: and I will place salvation in Zion for Israel my glory.

ISAIAH, Chapter 47

47:1 ¶ COME down, and sit in the dust, O virgin daughter of Babylon, sit on the
ground: there is no throne, O daughter of the Chaldeans: for thou shalt no more be
called tender and delicate.
47:2 Take the millstones, and grind meal: uncover thy locks, make bare the leg,
uncover the thigh, pass over the rivers.
47:3 Thy nakedness shall be uncovered, yea, thy shame shall be seen: I will take
vengeance, and I will not meet thee as a man.
47:4 As for our redeemer, the LORD of hosts is his name, the Holy One of
Israel.
47:5 Sit thou silent, and get thee into darkness, O daughter of the Chaldeans: for
thou shalt no more be called, The lady of kingdoms.
47:6 I was wroth with my people, I have polluted mine inheritance, and given
them into thine hand: thou didst shew them no mercy; upon the ancient hast thou
very heavily laid thy yoke.
47:7 ¶ And thou saidst, I shall be a lady for ever: so that thou didst not lay these
things to thy heart, neither didst remember the latter end of it.
47:8 Therefore hear now this, thou that art given to pleasures, that dwellest
carelessly, that sayest in thine heart, I am, and none else beside me; I shall not sit
as a widow, neither shall I know the loss of children:
47:9 But these two things shall come to thee in a moment in one day, the loss of
children, and widowhood: they shall come upon thee in their perfection for the
multitude of thy sorceries, and for the great abundance of thine enchantments.
47:10 For thou hast trusted in thy wickedness: thou hast said, None seeth me. Thy
wisdom and thy knowledge, it hath perverted thee; and thou hast said in thine heart,
I am, and none else beside me.
47:11 Therefore shall evil come upon thee; thou shalt not know from whence it
riseth: and mischief shall fall upon thee; thou shalt not be able to put it off: and
desolation shall come upon thee suddenly, which thou shalt not know.
47:12 Stand now with thine enchantments, and with the multitude of thy sorceries,
wherein thou hast laboured from thy youth; if so be thou shalt be able to profit, if so
be thou mayest prevail.
47:13 Thou art wearied in the multitude of thy counsels. Let now the astrologers,
the stargazers, the monthly prognosticators, stand up, and save thee from these
things that shall come upon thee.
47:14 Behold, they shall be as stubble; the fire shall burn them; they shall not
deliver themselves from the power of the flame: there shall not be a coal to warm
at, nor fire to sit before it.
47:15 Thus shall they be unto thee with whom thou hast laboured, even thy
merchants, from thy youth: they shall wander every one to his quarter; none shall
save thee.

ISAIAH, Chapter 48

Isaiah	1st Nephi
48:1 ¶ HEAR ye this, O house of Jacob, which are called by the name of Israel, and are come forth out of the waters of Judah,	20:1 HEARKEN and hear this, O house of Jacob, who are called by the name of Israel, and are come forth out of the waters of Judah, or out of the waters of baptism,
which swear by the name of the LORD, and make mention of the God of Israel, but not in truth, nor in righteousness.	who swear by the name of the Lord, and make mention of the God of Israel, yet they swear not in truth nor in righteousness.
48:2 For they call themselves of the holy city, and stay themselves upon the God of Israel;	20:2 Nevertheless, they call themselves of the holy city, but they do not stay themselves upon the God of Israel, who is the Lord of Hosts; yea, the Lord of Hosts is his name.
The LORD of hosts is his name.	
48:3 I have declared the former things from the beginning; and they went forth out of my mouth, and I shewed them; I did them suddenly, and they came to pass.	20:3 Behold, I have declared the former things from the beginning; and they went forth out of my mouth, and I showed them. I did show them suddenly (- -).
48:4 Because I knew that thou art obstinate, and thy neck is an iron sinew, and thy brow brass;	20:4 And I did it because I knew that thou art obstinate, and thy neck is an iron sinew, and thy brow brass;
48:5 I have even from the beginning declared it to thee; before it came to pass I shewed it thee: lest thou shouldest say, Mine idol hath done them, and my graven image, and my molten image, hath commanded them.	20:5 And I have even from the beginning declared (-) to thee; before it came to pass I showed them thee; and I showed them for fear lest thou shouldst say–mine idol hath done them, and my graven image, and my molten image hath commanded them.
48:6 Thou hast heard, see all this; and will not ye declare it? I have shewed thee new things from this time, even hidden things, and thou didst not know them.	20:6 Thou hast seen and heard (-) all this; and will ye not declare them? And that I have showed thee new things from this time, even hidden things, and thou didst not know them.
48:7 They are created now, and not from the beginning; even before the day when thou heardest them not; lest thou shouldest say, Behold, I knew them.	20:7 They are created now, and not from the beginning, even before the day when thou heardest them not they were declared unto thee; lest thou shouldst say--Behold, I knew them.
48:8 Yea, thou heardest not; yea, thou knewest not; yea, from that time that thine ear was not opened: for I knew that thou wouldest deal very treacherously, and wast called a transgressor from the womb.	20:8 Yea, and thou heardest not; yea, thou knewest not; yea, from that time thine ear was not opened; for I knew that thou wouldst deal very treacherously, and wast called a transgressor from the womb.
49:9 ¶ For my name's sake will I defer mine anger, and for my praise will I refrain for thee, that I cut thee not off.	20:9 Nevertheless, for my name's sake will I defer mine anger, and for my praise will I refrain from thee, that I cut thee not off.
48:10 Behold, I have refined thee, but not with silver; I have chosen thee in the furnace of affliction.	20:10 For, behold, I have refined thee, (- -) I have chosen thee in the furnace of affliction.

Isaiah	The Book of Mormon	Additional LDS Scripture
	1st Nephi (cont.)	
48:11 For mine own sake, even for mine own sake, will I do it: for how should my name be polluted? and I will not give my glory unto another.	20:11 For mine own sake, yea, for mine own sake will I do this, for I will not suffer (- -) my name to be polluted, and I will not give my glory unto another.	
48:12 Hearken unto me, O Jacob and Israel, my called; I am he; I am the first, I also am the last.	20:12 Hearken unto me, O Jacob, and Israel my called, for I am he; I am the first, and I am also the last.	
48:13 Mine hand also hath laid the foundation of the earth, and my right hand hath spanned the heavens: when I call unto them, they stand up together.	20:13 Mine hand hath also laid the foundation of the earth, and my right hand hath spanned the heavens. (-) I call unto them and they stand up together.	
48:14 All ye, assemble yourselves, and hear; which among them hath declared these things? The LORD hath loved him:	20:14 All ye, assemble yourselves, and hear; who among them hath declared these things unto them? The Lord hath loved him;;	
	yea, and he will fulfil his word which he hath declared by them; and	
he will do his pleasure on Babylon and his arm shall be on the Chaldeans.	he will do his pleasure on Babylon, and his arm shall come upon the Chaldeans.	
48:15 I, even I, have spoken; yea, I have called him: I have brought him, and he shall make his way prosperous.	20:15 Also, saith the Lord; I the Lord, yea, (-) I have spoken; yea, I have called him to declare, I have brought him, and he shall make his way prosperous.	
48:16 ¶ Come ye near unto me, hear ye this; I have not spoken in secret from the beginning; from the time that it was, there am I: and now the Lord GOD, and his Spirit, hath sent me.	20:16 Come ye near unto me (- -); I have not spoken in secret; from the beginning, from the time that it was (- -) declared have I spoken; and (-) the Lord God, and his Spirit, hath sent me.	
48:17 Thus saith the LORD, thy Redeemer, the Holy One of Israel; I am the LORD thy God which teacheth thee to profit, which leadeth thee by the way that thou shouldest go.	20:17 And thus saith the Lord, thy Redeemer, the Holy One of Israel; I (-) have sent him, the Lord thy God who teacheth thee to profit, who leadeth thee by the way thou shouldst go, hath done it.	
48:18 O that thou hadst hearkened to my commandments! then had thy peace been as a river, and thy righteousness as the waves of the sea:	20:18 O that thou hadst hearkened to my commandments--then had thy peace been as a river, and thy righteousness as the waves of the sea.	
48:19 Thy seed also had been as the sand, and the offspring of thy bowels like the gravel thereof; his name should not have been cut off nor destroyed from before me.	20:19 Thy seed also had been as the sand; the offspring of thy bowels like the gravel thereof; his name should not have been cut off nor destroyed from before me.	
48:20 Go ye forth of Babylon, flee ye from the Chaldeans, with a voice of singing declare ye, tell this, utter it even to the end of the earth; say ye, The LORD hath redeemed his servant Jacob.	20:20 Go ye forth of Babylon, flee ye from the Chaldeans, with a voice of singing declare ye, tell this, utter (- -) to the end of the earth; say ye: The Lord hath redeemed his servant Jacob.	
48:21 And they thirsted not when he led them through the deserts: he caused the waters to flow out of the rock for them: he clave the rock also, and the waters gushed out.	20:21 And they thirsted not; (-) he led them through the deserts; he caused the waters to flow out of the rock for them; he clave the rock also_ and the waters gushed out.	
48:22 There is no peace, saith the LORD, unto the wicked.	20:22 And notwithstanding he hath done all this, and greater also, there is no peace, saith the Lord, unto the wicked.	

ISAIAH, Chapter 49

49:1 ¶ LISTEN, O isles, unto me; and
hearken, ye people, from far; The LORD
hath called me from the womb; from the
bowels of my mother hath he made
mention of my name.
49:2 And he hath made my mouth
like a sharp sword; in the shadow of his
hand hath he hid me, and made me a
polished shaft; in his quiver hath he hid
me;
49:3 And said unto me, Thou art my
servant, O Israel, in whom I will be
glorified.
49:4 Then I said, I have laboured in
vain, I have spent my strength for
nought, and in vain: yet surely my
judgment is with the LORD, and my
work with my God.
49:5 And now, saith the LORD that
formed me from the womb to be his
servant, to bring Jacob again to him,
Though Israel be not gathered, yet shall
I be glorious in the eyes of the LORD,
and my God shall be my strength.
49:6 And he said, It is a light thing
that thou shouldest be my servant to
raise up the tribes of Jacob, and to
restore the preserved of Israel: I will
also give thee for a light to the Gentiles,
that thou mayest be my salvation unto
the end of the earth.
49:7 ¶Thus saith the LORD, the
Redeemer of Israel, and his Holy One,
to him whom man despiseth, to him
whom the nation abhorreth, to a servant
of rulers, Kings shall see and arise,
princes also shall worship, because of
the LORD that is faithful, and the Holy
One of Israel, and he shall choose thee.
49:8 Thus saith the LORD, In an
acceptable time have I heard thee, and
in a day of salvation have I helped thee:
and I will preserve thee, and give thee
for a covenant of the people, to establish
the earth, to cause to inherit the desolate
heritages;

1st Nephi
21:1 AND again: Hearken, O ye
house of Israel, all ye that are broken off
and are driven out because of the
wickedness of the pastors of my people;
yea, all ye that are broken off, that are
scattered abroad, who are of my people,
O house of Israel.
Listen, O isles, unto me, and hearken_
ye people_ from far; the Lord hath called
me from the womb; from the bowels of
my mother hath he made mention of my
name.
21:2 And he hath made my mouth
like a sharp sword; in the shadow of his
hand hath he hid me, and made me a
polished shaft; in his quiver hath he hid
me;
21:3 And said unto me: Thou art my
servant, O Israel, in whom I will be
glorified.
21:4 Then I said, I have labored in
vain, I have spent my strength for
naught__ and in vain; (-) surely my
judgment is with the Lord, and my work
with my God.
21:5 And now, saith the Lord--that
formed me from the womb that I should
be his servant, to bring Jacob again to
him--though Israel be not gathered, yet
shall I be glorious in the eyes of the
Lord, and my God shall be my strength.
21:6 And he said: It is a light thing
that thou shouldst be my servant to raise
up the tribes of Jacob, and to restore the
preserved of Israel. I will also give thee
for a light to the Gentiles, that thou
mayest be my salvation unto the ends of
the earth.
21:7 Thus saith the Lord, the
Redeemer of Israel, his Holy One, to
him whom man despiseth, to him whom
the nations abhorreth, to (-) servant of
rulers: Kings shall see and arise,
princes also shall worship, because of
the Lord that is faithful (- - -).

21:8 Thus saith the Lord: In an
acceptable time have I heard thee, O
isles of the sea, and in a day of salvation
have I helped thee; and I will preserve
thee, and give thee my servant for a
covenant of the people, to establish the
earth, to cause to inherit the desolate
heritages;

49:9 That thou mayest say to the prisoners, Go forth; to them that are in darkness, Shew yourselves. They shall feed in the ways, and their pastures shall be in all high places.
49:10 They shall not hunger nor thirst; neither shall the heat nor sun smite them: for he that hath mercy on them shall lead them, even by the springs of water shall he guide them.
49:11 And I will make all my mountains a way, and my highways shall be exalted.

49:12 Behold, these shall come from far: and, lo, these from the north and from the west; and these from the land of Sinim.
49:13 ¶ Sing, O heavens; and be joyful, O earth;
and break forth into singing, O mountains:
for the LORD hath comforted his people, and will have mercy upon his afflicted.
49:14 But Zion said, The LORD hath forsaken me, and my Lord hath forgotten me.

49:15 Can a woman forget her sucking child, that she should not have compassion on the son of her womb? yea, they may forget, yet will I not forget thee.
49:16 Behold, I have graven thee upon the palms of my hands; thy walls are continually before me.
49:17 Thy children shall make haste; thy destroyers and they that made thee waste shall go forth of thee.
49:18 ¶ Lift up thine eyes round about, and behold: all these gather themselves together, and come to thee.
As I live, saith the LORD, thou shalt surely clothe thee with them all, as with an ornament, and bind them on thee, as a bride doeth.
49:19 For thy waste and thy desolate places, and the land of thy destruction, shall even now be too narrow by reason of the inhabitants, and they that swallowed thee up shall be far away.
49:20 The children which thou shalt have, after thou hast lost the other, shall say again in thine ears, The place is too strait for me: give place to me that I may dwell.

1st Nephi (cont.)
21:9 That thou mayest say to the prisoners: Go forth; to them that sit in darkness: Show yourselves. They shall feed in the ways, and their pastures shall be in all high places.
21:10 They shall not hunger nor thirst, neither shall the heat nor the sun smite them; for he that hath mercy on them shall lead them, even by the springs of water shall he guide them.
21:11 And I will make all my mountains a way, and my highways shall be exalted.
21:12 And then, O house of Israel, behold, these shall come from far; and lo, these from the north and from the west; and these from the land of Sinim.

21:13 Sing, O heavens; and be joyful, O earth; for the feet of those who are in the east shall be established; and break forth into singing, O mountains; for they shall be smitten no more; for the Lord hath comforted his people, and will have mercy upon his afflicted.
21:14 But, behold, Zion hath said: The Lord hath forsaken me, and my Lord hath forgotten me– but he will show that he hath not.
21:15 For can a woman forget her sucking child, that she should not have compassion on the son of her womb? Yea, they may forget, yet will I not forget thee, O house of Israel.
21:16 Behold, I have graven thee upon the palms of my hands; thy walls are continually before me.
21:17 Thy children shall make haste against thy destroyers; and they that made thee waste shall go forth of thee.
21:18 Lift up thine eyes round about and behold; all these gather themselves together, and they shall come to thee. And as I live, saith the Lord, thou shalt surely clothe thee with them all, as with an ornament, and bind them on (-) even as a bride (-).
21:19 For thy waste and thy desolate places, and the land of thy destruction, shall even now be too narrow by reason of the inhabitants; and they that swallowed thee up shall be far away.
21:20 The children whom thou shalt have, after thou hast lost the first, shall (-) again in thine ears say: The place is too strait for me; give place to me that I may dwell.

49:21 Then shalt thou say in thine heart, Who hath begotten me these, seeing I have lost my children, and am desolate, a captive, and removing to and fro? and who hath brought up these? Behold, I was left alone; these, where had they been?

49:22 Thus saith the Lord GOD, Behold, I will lift up mine hand to the Gentiles, and set up my standard to the people: and they shall bring thy sons in their arms, and thy daughters shall be carried upon their shoulders.
49:23 And kings shall be thy nursing fathers, and their queens thy nursing mothers: they shall bow down to thee with their face toward the earth, and lick up the dust of thy feet; and thou shalt know that I am the LORD: for they shall not be ashamed that wait for me.
49:24 ¶ Shall the prey be taken from the mighty, or the lawful captive delivered?
49:25 But thus saith the LORD***;*** ~~,~~ ~~E~~even the captives of the mighty shall be taken away, and the prey of the terrible shall be delivered***;*** ~~:~~
for the might God shall deliver his covenant people. ~~f~~***F***or ***thus saith the Lord***, I will contend with ***them*** ~~him~~ that contend~~eth~~ with thee,
and I will save thy children.
49:26 And I will feed them that oppress thee with their own flesh; and they shall be drunken with their own blood, as with sweet wine:
and all flesh shall know that I the LORD am thy Saviour and thy Redeemer, the mighty One of Jacob.

1st Nephi (cont.)
21:21 Then shalt thou say in thine heart: Who hath begotten me these, seeing I have lost my children, and am desolate, a captive, and removing to and fro? And who hath brought up these? Behold, I was left alone; these, where have they been?

21:22 Thus saith the Lord God: Behold, I will lift up mine hand to the Gentiles, and set up my standard to the people; and they shall bring thy sons in their arms, and thy daughters shall be carried upon their shoulders.
21:23 And kings shall be thy nursing fathers, and their queens thy nursing mothers; they shall bow down to thee with their face towards the earth, and lick up the dust of thy feet; and thou shalt know that I am the Lord; for they shall not be ashamed that wait for me.
21:24 For shall the prey be taken from the mighty, or the lawful captives delivered?
21:25 But thus saith the Lord, even the captives of the mighty shall be taken away, and the prey of the terrible shall be delivered;
(- -)

for (- -) I will contend with him that contendeth with thee,
and I will save thy children.
21:26 And I will feed them that oppress thee with their own flesh; (-) they shall be drunken with their own blood as with sweet wine;
and all flesh shall know that I, the Lord, am thy Savior and thy Redeemer, the Mighty One of Jacob.

2nd Nephi
6:6 And now, these are the words: Thus saith the Lord God: Behold, I will lift up mine hand to the Gentiles, and set up my standard to the people; and they shall bring thy sons in their arms, and thy daughters shall be carried upon their shoulders.
6:7 And kings shall be thy nursing fathers, and their queens thy nursing mothers; they shall bow down to thee with their faces towards the earth, and lick up the dust of thy feet; and thou shalt know that I am the Lord; for they shall not be ashamed that wait for me.
6:16 For shall the prey be taken from the mighty, or the lawful captive delivered?
6:17 But thus saith the Lord: Even the captives of the mighty shall be taken away, and the prey of the terrible shall be delivered;
for the Mighty God shall deliver his covenant people. For thus saith the Lord: I will contend with them that contendeth with thee--
(- -)
6:18 And I will feed them that oppress thee, with their own flesh; and they shall be drunken with their own blood as with sweet wine;
and all flesh shall know that I the Lord am thy Savior and thy Redeemer, the Mighty One of Jacob.

ISAIAH, Chapter 50

50:1 ¶ ***Yea, for thus saith the Lord, Have I put thee away, or have I cast thee off for ever?*** THUS saith the LORD, Where is the bill of your mother's divorcement~~.~~ ~~,~~ ***To*** whom ***have*** I ~~have~~ put ***thee*** away ~~?~~ or ***to*** which of my creditors ~~is it to whom I~~ have ***I*** sold you***;*** ~~?~~
Yea, to whom have I sold you? Behold, for your iniquities have ye sold

2nd Nephi
7:1 Yea, for thus saith the Lord: Have I put thee away, or have I cast thee off forever? For thus saith the Lord: Where is the bill of your mother's divorcement? To whom have I put thee away, or to which of my creditors have I sold you?

Yea, to whom have I sold you? Behold, for your iniquities have ye sold

yourselves, and for your transgressions is your mother put away.
50:2 Wherefore, when I came, ***there*** was ~~there~~ no man***.*** ~~?~~ when I called, ~~was~~ there ***was*** none to answer***.*** ~~?~~ ***Oh, house of Israel,*** ~~I~~ ***i***s my hand shortened at all, that it cannot redeem***;*** ~~?~~ or have I no power to deliver?
~~b~~***B***ehold, at my rebuke I dry up the sea, I make the rivers a wilderness~~:~~ ***; and*** their fish ***to*** stink~~eth~~, because ***the waters are dried up, and they die because of*** ~~there is no water, and dieth for~~ thirst.
50:3 I clothe the heavens with blackness, and I make sackcloth their covering.
50:4 ¶ The Lord GOD hath given me the tongue of the learned, that I should know how to speak a word in season ***un***to ***thee , O house of Israel, when ye are*** ~~him that is~~ weary***.*** ~~:~~ ~~h~~***H***e ***waketh*** ~~wakeneth~~ morning by morning, he wakeneth mine ear to hear as the learned.
50:5 The Lord GOD hath ***appointed*** ~~opened~~ mine ear***s***, and I was not rebellious, neither turned away back.
50:6 I gave my back to the smiters, and my cheeks to them that plucked off the hair***.*** ~~:~~ I hid not my face from shame and spitting***,*** ~~.~~
50:7 For the Lord GOD will help me; therefore shall I not be confounded***;*** ~~:~~ therefore have I set my face like a flint, and I know that I shall not be ashamed.
50:8 ~~He is~~ ***and the Lord is*** near ***and he*** ~~that~~ justifieth me***.*** ~~; w~~ ***W***ho will contend with me? let us stand together***.*** ~~:~~ ~~w~~***Who*** is mine adversary? let him come near ~~to~~ me ***and I will smite him with the strength of my mouth;***
50:9 ~~Behold~~, ***for*** the Lord GOD will help me; ***and all they which*** ~~who is he that~~ shall condemn me***,*** ~~?~~ ~~lo~~, ***behold all*** they ~~all~~ shall wax old as a garment; ***and*** the moth shall eat them up.
50:10 ¶ Who is among you that feareth the LORD, that obeyeth the voice of his servant, that walketh in darkness, and hath no light? ~~l~~Let him trust in the name of the LORD, and stay upon his God.
50:11 Behold~~;~~ all ye that kindle ~~a~~ fire, that compass yourselves about with sparks***;*** ~~:~~ walk in the light of your fire, and in the sparks ***which*** ~~that~~ ye have kindled***;*** ~~. T~~ ***t***his shall ye have of mine hand***,*** ~~;~~ ye shall lie down in sorrow.

2nd Nephi (cont.)
yourselves, and for your transgressions is your mother put away.
7:2 Wherefore, when I came, there was no man; when I called, yea, there was none to answer. O house of Israel, is my hand shortened at all_ that it cannot redeem, or have I no power to deliver?
Behold, at my rebuke I dry up the sea, I make their rivers a wilderness, and their fish to stink because the waters are dried up, and they die because of (- -) thirst.

7:3 I clothe the heavens with blackness, and I make sackcloth their covering.
7:4 The Lord God hath given me the tongue of the learned, that I should know how to speak a word in season unto thee, O house of Israel. When ye are weary he waketh morning by morning. He waketh mine ear to hear as the learned.

7:5 The Lord God hath opened mine ear, and I was not rebellious, neither turned away back.
7:6 I gave my back to the smiter, and my cheeks to them that plucked off the hair. I hid not my face from shame and spitting.
7:7 For the Lord God will help me, therefore shall I not be confounded. Therefore have I set my face like a flint, and I know that I shall not be ashamed.
7:8 And the Lord is near, and he justifieth me. Who will contend with me? Let us stand together. Who is mine adversary? Let him come near me, and I will smite him with the strength of my mouth.
7:9 For the Lord God will help me. And all they who shall condemn me, behold, all they shall wax old as a garment; and the moth shall eat them up.

7:10 Who is among you that feareth the Lord, that obeyeth the voice of his servant, that walketh in darkness and hath no light? (- - -)

7:11 Behold all ye that kindle fire, that compass yourselves about with sparks; walk in the light of your fire_ and in the sparks which ye have kindled. This shall ye have of mine hand--ye shall lie down in sorrow.

ISAIAH, Chapter 51

51:1 ¶ HEARKEN ***un***to me, ye that follow after righteousness, ~~;~~ ye that seek the LORD: look unto the rock ***from*** whence ye ***were*** ~~are~~ hewn, and to the hole of the pit ***from*** whence ye are digged.

51:2 Look unto Abraham your father, and unto Sarah that bare you: for I called him alone, and blessed him, and increased him.

51:3 For the LORD shall comfort Zion: he will comfort all her waste places; and he will make her wilderness like Eden, and her desert like the garden of the LORD; joy and gladness shall be found therein, thanksgiving, and the voice of melody.

51:4 ¶Hearken unto me, my people; and give ear unto me, O my nation: for a law shall proceed from me, and I will make my judgment to rest for a light of the people.

51:5 My righteousness is near; my salvation is gone forth, and mine arms shall judge the people; the isles shall wait upon me, and on mine arm shall they trust.

51:6 Lift up your eyes to the heavens, and look upon the earth beneath: for the heavens shall vanish away like smoke, and the earth shall wax old like a garment, and they that dwell therein shall die in like manner: but my salvation shall be for ever, and my righteousness shall not be abolished.

51:7 Hearken unto me, ye that know righteousness, the people in whose heart ***I have written*** ~~is~~ my law; fear ye not the reproach of men, neither be ye afraid of their revilings.

51:8 For the moth shall eat them up like a garment, and the worm shall eat them like wool: but my righteousness shall be for ever, and my salvation from generation to generation.

51:9 ¶Awake, awake, put on strength, O arm of the LORD; awake, as in the ancient days, in the generations of old. Art thou not it that hath cut Rahab, and wounded the dragon?

51:10 Art thou not it which hath dried the sea, the waters of the great deep; that hath made the depths of the sea a way for the ransomed to pass over?

2nd Nephi

8:1 HEARKEN unto me, ye that follow after righteousness. (- -) Look unto the rock from whence ye were hewn, and to the hole of the pit from whence ye are digged.

8:2 Look unto Abraham, your father, and unto Sarah, she that bare you; for I called him alone, and blessed him (- -).

8:3 For the Lord shall comfort Zion, he will comfort all her waste places; and he will make her wilderness like Eden, and her desert like the garden of the Lord. Joy and gladness shall be found therein, thanksgiving and the voice of melody.

8:4 Hearken unto me, my people; and give ear unto me, O my nation; for a law shall proceed from me, and I will make my judgment to rest for a light for the people.

8:5 My righteousness is near; my salvation is gone forth, and mine arm shall judge the people. The isles shall wait upon me, and on mine arm shall they trust.

8:6 Lift up your eyes to the heavens, and look upon the earth beneath; for the heavens shall vanish away like smoke, and the earth shall wax old like a garment; and they that dwell therein shall die in like manner. But my salvation shall be forever, and my righteousness shall not be abolished.

8:7 Hearken unto me, ye that know righteousness, the people in whose heart I have written my law, fear ye not the reproach of men, neither be ye afraid of their revilings.

8:8 For the moth shall eat them up like a garment, and the worm shall eat them like wool. But my righteousness shall be forever, and my salvation from generation to generation.

8:9 Awake, awake! Put on strength, O arm of the Lord; awake as in the ancient days (- -). Art thou not he that hath cut Rahab, and wounded the dragon?

8:10 Art thou not he who hath dried the sea, the waters of the great deep; that hath made the depths of the sea a way for the ransomed to pass over?

Isaiah	The Book of Mormon	Additional LDS Scripture
	2nd Nephi (cont.)	
51:11 Therefore the redeemed of the LORD shall return, and come with singing unto Zion; and everlasting joy ***and holiness*** shall be upon their heads***;*** ~~:~~ they shall obtain gladness and joy; and sorrow and mourning shall flee away.	8:11 Therefore, the redeemed of the Lord shall return, and come with singing unto Zion; and everlasting joy and holiness shall be upon their heads; and they shall obtain gladness and joy; sorrow and mourning shall flee away.	
51:12 I ***am he, yea,*** ~~even I,~~ ***I*** am he that comforteth you***;*** ~~:~~ ***behold,*** who art thou, that thou shouldest be afraid of a man that shall die, and of the son of man which shall be made as grass;	8:12 I am he; yea, I am he that comforteth you. Behold, who art thou, that thou shouldst be afraid of (-) man, who shall die, and of the son of man, who shall be made like unto grass?	
51:13 And forgettest the LORD thy maker, that hath stretched forth the heavens, and laid the foundations of the earth; and hast feared continually every day because of the fury of the oppressor, as if he were ready to destroy? and where is the fury of the oppressor?	8:13 And forgettest the Lord thy maker, that hath stretched forth the heavens, and laid the foundations of the earth, and hast feared continually every day, because of the fury of the oppressor, as if he were ready to destroy? And where is the fury of the oppressor?	
51:14 The captive exile hasteneth that he may be loosed, and that he should not die in the pit, nor that his bread should fail.	8:14 The captive exile hasteneth, that he may be loosed, and that he should not die in the pit, nor that his bread should fail.	
51:15 But I am the LORD thy God, that divided the sea, whose waves roared: The LORD of hosts is his name.	8:15 But I am the Lord thy God, (- -) whose waves roared; the Lord of Hosts is my name.	
51:16 And I have put my words in thy mouth, and I have covered thee in the shadow of mine hand, that I may plant the heavens, and lay the foundations of the earth, and say unto Zion, ***Behold,*** ~~T~~*t*hou art my people.	8:16 And I have put my words in thy mouth, and have covered thee in the shadow of mine hand, that I may plant the heavens and lay the foundations of the earth, and say unto Zion: Behold, thou art my people.	
51:17 ¶Awake, awake, stand up, O Jerusalem, which hast drunk at the hand of the LORD the cup of his fury; thou hast drunken the dregs of the cup of trembling, and wrung them out.	8:17 Awake, awake, stand up, O Jerusalem, which hast drunk at the hand of the Lord the cup of his fury--thou hast drunken the dregs of the cup of trembling_ (-) wrung (-) out--	
51:18 ***And*** ~~T~~*t*here is none to guide her among all the sons whom she hath brought forth; neither is there any that taketh her by the hand of all the sons that she hath brought up.	8:18 And (- -) none to guide her among all the sons (-) she hath brought forth; neither (- -) that taketh her by the hand, of all the sons (-) she hath brought up.	
51:19 These two ***sons*** ~~things~~ are come unto thee; ~~who~~ ***they*** shall be sorry for thee***,*** ~~?~~ ***thy*** desolation, and destruction, and the famine, and the sword***;*** ~~:~~ by whom shall I comfort thee?	8:19 These two sons are come unto thee, who shall be sorry for thee--thy desolation_ and destruction, and the famine_ and the sword--and by whom shall I comfort thee?	
51:20 Thy sons have fainted ***save these two***, they lie at the head of all the streets, as a wild bull in a net***;*** ~~:~~ they are full of the fury of the LORD, the rebuke of thy God.	8:20 Thy sons have fainted, save these two; they lie at the head of all the streets; as a wild bull in a net, they are full of the fury of the Lord, the rebuke of thy God.	
51:21 Therefore hear now this, thou afflicted, and drunken, but not with wine:	8:21 Therefore hear now this, thou afflicted, and drunken, and not with wine:	

Isaiah	The Book of Mormon	Additional LDS Scripture
51:22 Thus saith thy Lord the LORD, and thy God that pleadeth the cause of his people, Behold, I have taken out of thine hand the cup of trembling, even the dregs of the cup of my fury; thou shalt no more drink it again: 51:23 But I will put it into the hand of them that afflict thee; which have said to thy soul, Bow down, that we may go over: and thou hast laid thy body as the ground, and as the street, to them that went over.	2nd Nephi (cont.) 8:22 Thus saith thy Lord, the Lord and thy God (-) pleadeth the cause of his people; Behold, I have taken out of thine hand the cup of trembling, the dregs of the cup of my fury; thou shalt no more drink it again. 8:23 But I will put it into the hand of them that afflict thee; who have said to thy soul: Bow down, that we may go over--and thou hast laid thy body as the ground_ and as the street_ to them that went over.	

ISAIAH, Chapter 52

Isaiah	The Book of Mormon	Additional LDS Scripture
52:1 ¶AWAKE, awake; put on thy strength, O Zion; put on thy beautiful garments, O Jerusalem, the holy city: for henceforth there shall no more come into thee the uncircumcised and the unclean.	3rd Nephi 20:36 And then shall be brought to pass that which is written: Awake, awake again, and put on thy strength, O Zion; put on thy beautiful garments, O Jerusalem, the holy city, for henceforth there shall no more come into thee the uncircumcised and the unclean.	2nd Nephi 8:24 Awake, awake, put on thy strength, O Zion; put on thy beautiful garments, O Jerusalem, the holy city; for henceforth there shall no more come into thee the uncircumcised and the unclean. D&C 113:7 Questions by Elias Higbee: What is meant by the command in Isaiah, 52d chapter, 1st verse, which saith: Put on thy strength, O Zion–and what people had Isaiah reference to? 113:8 He had reference to those whom God should call in the last days, who should hold the power of priesthood to bring again Zion, and the redemption of Israel; and to put on her strength is to put on the authority of the priesthood, which she, Zion, has a right to by lineage; also to return to that power which she had lost.
52:2 Shake thyself from the dust; arise, and sit down, O Jerusalem: loose thyself from the bands of thy neck, O captive daughter of Zion.	20:37 Shake thyself from the dust; arise, sit down, O Jerusalem; loose thyself from the bands of thy neck, O captive daughter of Zion.	2nd Nephi 8:25 Shake thyself from the dust; arise, sit down, O Jerusalem; loose thyself from the bands of thy neck, O captive daughter of Zion. D&C 113:9 What are we to understand by Zion loosing herself from the bands of her neck; 2d verse? 113:10 We are to understand that the scattered remnants are exhorted to return to the Lord from whence they have fallen; which if they do, the promise of the Lord is that he will speak to them, or give them revelation. See

Isaiah

52:3 For thus saith the LORD, Ye have sold yourselves for nought; and ye shall be redeemed without money.
52:4 For thus saith the Lord GOD, My people went down aforetime into Egypt to sojourn there; and the Assyrian oppressed them without cause.
52:5 Now therefore, what have I here, saith the LORD, that my people is taken away for nought? they that rule over them make them to howl, saith the LORD; and my name continually every day is blasphemed.

52:6 Therefore my people shall know my name***;*** ~~:~~ ~~therefore~~ ***yeah in that day,*** they shall know ~~in that day~~ that I am he that doth speak***;*** ~~:~~ behold, it is I.

52:7 ¶ ***And then they shall say,***
How beautiful upon the mountains are the feet of him that bringeth good tidings ***unto them***, that publisheth peace; that bringeth good tidings ***unto them*** of good, that publisheth salvation; that saith unto Zion, Thy God reigneth!

The Book of Mormon

3rd Nephi (cont.)

20:38 For thus saith the Lord: Ye have sold yourselves for naught, and ye shall be redeemed without money.

20:39 Verily, verily, I say unto you, that my people shall know my name; yea, in that day_ they shall know that I am he that doth speak_ (- -).

20:40 And then shall they say:
How beautiful upon the mountains are the feet of him that bringeth good tidings unto them, that publisheth peace; that bringeth good tidings unto them of good, that publisheth salvation; that saith unto Zion: Thy God reigneth!

Additional LDS Scripture

D&C (cont.)
the 6th, 7th and 8th verses. The bands of her neck are the curses of God upon her, or the remnants of Israel in their scattered condition among the Gentiles.

Mosiah
12:20 And it came to pass that one of them said unto him [Abinidi]: What meaneth the words which are written, and which have been taught by our fathers, saying:
12:21 How beautiful upon the mountains are the feet of him that bringeth good tidings (- -); that publisheth peace; that bringeth good tidings (- -) of good; that publisheth salvation; that saith unto Zion, Thy God reigneth;
15:13 Yea, and are not the prophets, every one that has opened his mouth to prophesy, that has not fallen into transgression, I mean all the holy prophets ever since the world began? I say unto you that they are his seed.
15:14 And these are they who hve published peace, who have brought good tidings of good, who have published slavation; and said unto Zion: Thy God reigneth!
15:15 And O how beautiful upon the mountains were their feet!
15:16 And again, how beautiful upon the mountains are the feet of those that are still publishing peace!
15:17 And again, how beautiful upon the mountains are the feet of those who shall hereafter publish peace, yea, from this time henceforth and forever!

Isaiah	The Book of Mormon	Additional LDS Scripture
	3rd Nephi (cont.)	Mosiah (cont.) 15:18 And behold, I say unto you, this is not all. For O how beautiful upon the mountains are the feet of him that bringeth good tidings, that is the founder of peace, yea, even the Lord, who has redeemed his people; yea, him who has granted salvation untio his people;
52:8 Thy watchmen shall lift up the voice; with the voice together shall they sing: for they shall see eye to eye, when the LORD shall bring again Zion.	20:31 And they shall believe in me, that I am Jesus Christ, the Son of God, and shall pray unto the Father in my name. 20:32 Then shall their watchmen lift up their voice, and with the voice together shall they sing; for they shall see eye to eye_ (- -).	12:22 Thy watchman shall lift up the voice; with the voice together shall they sing; for they shall see eye to eye_ when the Lord shall bring again Zion; 15:29 Yea, Lord, thy watchmen shall lift up their voice; with the voice together shall they sing; for they shall see eye to eye, when the Lord shall bring again Zion.
52:9 Break forth into joy, sing together, ye waste places of Jerusalem: for the LORD hath comforted his people, he hath redeemed Jerusalem.	20:33 Then will the Father gather them together again, and give unto them Jerusalem for the land of their inheritance. 20:34 Then shall they break forth into joy--Sing together, ye waste places of Jerusalem; for the Father hath comforted his people, he hath redeemed Jerusalem.	12:23 Break forth into joy; sing together_ ye waste places of Jerusalem; for the Lord hath comforted his people, he hath redeemed Jerusalem; 15:30 Break forth into joy, sing together, ye waste places of Jerusalem; for the Lord hath comforted his people, he hath redeemed Jerusalem.
52:10 The LORD hath made bare his holy arm in the eyes of all the nations; and all the ends of the earth shall see the salvation of our God.	20:35 The Father hath made bare his holy arm in the eyes of all the nations; and all the ends of the earth shall see the salvation of (- -) the Father; and the Father and I are one.	12:24 The Lord had made bare his holy arm in the eyes of all the nations, and all the ends of the earth shall see the salvation of our God? 15:31 The Lord hath made bare his holy arm in the eyes of all the nations; and all the ends of the earth shall see the salvation of our God.
52:11 Depart ye, depart ye, go ye out from thence, touch no unclean thing; go ye out of the midst of her; be ye clean, that bear the vessels of the LORD. 52:12 For ye shall not go out with haste, nor go by flight: for the LORD will go before you; and the God of Israel will be your rereward. 52:13 ¶ Behold, my servant shall deal prudently, he shall be exalted and extolled, and be very high.	20:41 And then shall a cry go forth: Depart ye, depart ye, go ye out from thence, touch not that which is unclean; go ye out of the midst of her; be ye clean that bear the vessels of the Lord. 20:42 For ye shall not go out with haste_ nor go by flight; for the Lord will go before you, and the God of Israel shall be your rearward. 20:43 Behold, my servant shall deal prudently; he shall be exalted and extolled_ and be very high.	

52:14 As many were astonied at thee; his visage was so marred more than any man, and his form more than the sons of men:
52:15 So shall he ***gather*** ~~sprinkle~~ many nations; the kings shall shut their mouths at him ***;*** ~~:~~ for that which had not been told them shall they see; and that which they had not heard shall they consider.

3rd Nephi (cont.)
20:44 As many were astonished at thee--his visage was so marred, more than any man, and his form more than the sons of men--
20:45 So shall he sprinkle many nations; the kings shall shut their mouths at him for that which had not been told them shall they see; and that which they had not heard shall they consider.

1st Nephi
13:37 And blessed are they who shall seek to bring forth my Zion at that day, for they shall have the gift and the power of the Holy Ghost; and if they endure unto the end they shall be lifted up at the last day, and shall be saved in the everlasting kingdom of the Lamb; and whoso shall publish peace, yea, tidings of great joy, how beautiful upon the mountains shall they be.

ISAIAH, Chapter 53

53:1 ¶ WHO hath believed our report? and to whom is the arm of the LORD revealed?
53:2 For he shall grow up before him as a tender plant, and as a root out of a dry ground: he hath no form nor comeliness; and when we shall see him, there is no beauty that we should desire him.
53:3 He is despised and rejected of men; a man of sorrows, and acquainted with grief: and we hid as it were our faces from him; he was despised, and we esteemed him not.
53:4 ¶ Surely he hath borne our griefs, and carried our sorrows: yet we did esteem him stricken, smitten of God, and afflicted.
53:5 But he was wounded for our transgressions, he was bruised for our iniquities: the chastisement of our peace was upon him; and with his stripes we are healed.
53:6 All we like sheep have gone astray; we have turned every one to his own way; and the LORD hath laid on him the iniquity of us all.
53:7 He was oppressed, and he was afflicted, yet he opened not his mouth: he is brought as a lamb to the slaughter, and as a sheep before her shearers is dumb, so he openeth not his mouth.

Mosiah
14:1 Yea, even doth not Isaiah say: Who hath believed our report, and to whom is the arm of the Lord revealed?

14:2 For he shall grow up before him as a tender plant, and as a root out of dry ground; he hath no form nor comeliness; and when we shall see him there is no beauty that we should desire him.
14:3 He is despised and rejected of men; a man of sorrows, and acquainted with grief; and we hid as it were our faces from him; he was despised, and we esteemed him not.
14:4 Surely he has borne our griefs, and carried our sorrows; yet we did esteem him stricken, smitten of God, and afflicted.
14:5 But he was wounded for our transgressions, he was bruised for our iniquities; the chastisement of our peace was upon him; and with his stripes we are healed.
14:6 All we, like sheep, have gone astray; we have turned every one to his own way; and the Lord hath laid on him the iniquities of us all.
14:7 He was oppressed, and he was afflicted, yet he opened not his mouth; he is brought as a lamb to the slaughter, and as a sheep before her shearers is dumb so he opened not his mouth.

53:8 He was taken from prison and from judgment: and who shall declare his generation? for he was cut off out of the land of the living: for the transgression of my people was he stricken.
53:9 And he made his grave with the wicked, and with the rich in his death; because he had done no violence, neither was any deceit in his mouth.
53:10 ¶ Yet it pleased the LORD to bruise him; he hath put him to grief: when thou shalt make his soul an offering for sin, he shall see his seed, he shall prolong his days, and the pleasure of the LORD shall prosper in his hand.
53:11 He shall see of the travail of his soul, and shall be satisfied: by his knowledge shall my righteous servant justify many; for he shall bear their iniquities.
53:12 Therefore will I divide him a portion with the great, and he shall divide the spoil with the strong; because he hath poured out his soul unto death: and he was numbered with the transgressors; and he bare the sin of many, and made intercession for the transgressors.

Mosiah (cont.)
14:8 He was taken from prison and from judgment; and who shall declare his generation? For he was cut off out of the land of the living; for the transgressions of my people was he stricken.
14:9 And he made his grave with the wicked, and with the rich in his death; because he had done no evil, neither was any deceit in his mouth.
14:10 Yet it pleased the Lord to bruise him; he hath put him to grief; when thou shalt make his soul an offering for sin he shall see his seed, he shall prolong his days, and the pleasure of the Lord shall prosper in his hand.
14:11 He shall see the travail of his soul, and shall be satisfied; by his knowledge shall my righteous servant justify many; for he shall bear their iniquities.
14:12 Therefore will I divide him a portion with the great, and he shall divide the spoil with the strong; because he hath poured out his soul unto death; and he was numbered with the transgressors; and he bore the sins of many, and made intercession for the transgressors.

ISAIAH, Chapter 54

54:1 ¶ SING, O barren, thou that didst not bear; break forth into singing, and cry aloud, thou that didst not travail with child: for more are the children of the desolate than the children of the married wife, saith the LORD.
54:2 Enlarge the place of thy tent, and let them stretch forth the curtains of thine habitations: spare not, lengthen thy cords, and strengthen thy stakes;
54:3 For thou shalt break forth on the right hand and on the left; and thy seed shall inherit the Gentiles, and make the desolate cities to be inhabited.
54:4 Fear not; for thou shalt not be ashamed: neither be thou confounded; for thou shalt not be put to shame: for thou shalt forget the shame of thy youth, and shalt not remember the reproach of thy widowhood any more.

3rd Nephi
22:1 AND then shall that which is written come to pass: Sing, O barren, thou that didst not bear; break forth into singing, and cry aloud, thou that didst not travail with child; for more are the children of the desolate than the children of the married wife, saith the Lord.
22:2 Enlarge the place of thy tent, and let them stretch forth the curtains of thy habitations; spare not, lengthen thy cords and strengthen thy stakes;
22:3 For thou shalt break forth on the right hand and on the left, and thy seed shall inherit the Gentiles and make the desolate cities to be inhabited.
22:4 Fear not, for thou shalt not be ashamed; neither be thou confounded, for thou shalt not be put to shame; for thou shalt forget the shame of thy youth, and shalt not remember the reproach of thy youth, and shalt not remember the reproach of thy widowhood any more.

54:5 For thy Maker is thine husband; the LORD of hosts is his name; and thy Redeemer the Holy One of Israel; The God of the whole earth shall he be called.

54:6 ¶ For the LORD hath called thee as a woman forsaken and grieved in spirit, and a wife of youth, when thou wast refused, saith thy God.

54:7 For a small moment have I forsaken thee; but with great mercies will I gather thee.

54:8 In a little wrath I hid my face from thee for a moment; but with everlasting kindness will I have mercy on thee, saith the LORD thy Redeemer.

54:9 For this is as the waters of Noah unto me: for as I have sworn that the waters of Noah should no more go over the earth; so have I sworn that I would not be wroth with thee, nor rebuke thee.

54:10 For the mountains shall depart, and the hills be removed; but my kindness shall not depart from thee, neither shall the covenant of my ***people*** ~~peace~~ be removed, saith the LORD that hath mercy on thee.

54:11 ¶ O thou afflicted, tossed with tempest, and not comforted, behold, I will lay thy stones with fair colours, and lay thy foundations with sapphires.

54:12 And I will make thy windows of agates, and thy gates of carbuncles, and all thy borders of pleasant stones.

54:13 And all thy children shall be taught of the LORD; and great shall be the peace of thy children.

54:14 In righteousness shalt thou be established: thou shalt be far from oppression; for thou shalt not fear: and from terror; for it shall not come near thee.

54:15 Behold, they shall surely gather together ***against thee***, but not by me: whosoever shall gather together against thee shall fall for thy sake.

54:16 Behold, I have created the smith that bloweth the coals in the fire, and that bringeth forth an instrument for his work; and I have created the waster to destroy.

54:17 No weapon that is formed against thee shall prosper; and every tongue that shall rise against thee in judgment thou shalt condemn. This is the heritage of the servants of the LORD, and their righteousness is of me, saith the LORD.

3rd Nephi (cont.)

22:5 For thy maker, thy husband, the Lord of Hosts is his name; and thy Redeemer, the Holy One of Israel--the God of the whole earth shall he be called.

22:6 For the Lord hath called thee as a woman forsaken and grieved in spirit, and a wife of youth, when thou wast refused, saith thy God.

22:7 For a small moment have I forsaken thee, but with great mercies will I gather thee.

22:8 In a little wrath I hid my face from thee for a moment, but with everlasting kindness will I have mercy on thee, saith the Lord thy Redeemer.

22:9 For this, (- -) the waters of Noah unto me, for as I have sworn that the waters of Noah should no more go over the earth, so have I sworn that I would not be wroth with thee (- -).

22:10 For the mountains shall depart and the hills be removed, but my kindness shall not depart from thee, neither shall the covenant of my peace be removed, saith the Lord that hath mercy on thee.

22:11 O thou afflicted, tossed with tempest, and not comforted! Behold, I will lay thy stones with fair colors, and lay thy foundations with sapphires.

22:12 And I will make thy windows of agates, and thy gates of carbuncles, and all thy borders of pleasant stones.

22:13 And all thy children shall be taught of the Lord; and great shall be the peace of thy children.

22:14 In righteousness shalt thou be established; thou shalt be far from oppression for thou shalt not fear, and from terror for it shall not come near thee.

22:15 Behold, they shall surely gather together against thee, (-) not by me; whosoever shall gather together against thee shall fall for thy sake.

22:16 Behold, I have created the smith that bloweth the coals in the fire, and that bringeth forth an instrument for his work; and I have created the waster to destroy.

22:17 No weapon that is formed against thee shall prosper; and every tongue that shall revile against thee in judgment thou shalt condemn. This is the heritage of the servants of the Lord, and their righteousness is of me, saith the Lord.

ISAIAH, Chapter 55

55:1 ¶ HO, every one that thirsteth,
come ye to the waters, and he that hath
no money; come ye, buy, and eat; yea,
come, buy wine and milk without
money and without price.
55:2 Wherefore do ye spend money
for that which is not bread? and your
labour for that which satisfieth not?
hearken diligently unto me, and eat ye
that which is good, and let your soul
delight itself in fatness.
55:3 Incline your ear, and come unto
me: hear, and your soul shall live; and I
will make an everlasting covenant with
you, even the sure mercies of David.
55:4 Behold, I have given him for a
witness to the people, a leader and
commander to the people.
55:5 Behold, thou shalt call a nation
that thou knowest not, and nations that
knew not thee shall run unto thee
because of the LORD thy God, and for
the Holy One of Israel; for he hath
glorified thee.
55:6 ¶ Seek ye the LORD while he may
be found, call ye upon him while he is
near:
55:7 Let the wicked forsake his way,
and the unrighteous man his thoughts:
and let him return unto the LORD, and
he will have mercy upon him; and to our
God, for he will abundantly pardon.
55:8 For my thoughts are not your
thoughts, neither are your ways my
ways, saith the LORD.
55:9 For as the heavens are higher
than the earth, so are my ways higher
than your ways, and my thoughts than
your thoughts.
55:10 For as the rain cometh down,
and the snow from heaven, and
returneth not thither, but watereth the
earth, and maketh it bring forth and bud,
that it may give seed to the sower, and
bread to the eater:
55:11 So shall my word be that goeth
forth out of my mouth: it shall not return
unto me void, but it shall accomplish
that which I please, and it shall prosper
in the thing whereto I sent it.
55:12 For ye shall go out with joy, and
be led forth with peace: the mountains
and the hills shall break forth before you
into singing, and all the trees of the field
shall clap their hands.

55:13 Instead of the thorn shall come
up the fir tree, and instead of the brier
shall come up the myrtle tree: and it
shall be to the LORD for a name, for an
everlasting sign that shall not be cut off.

ISAIAH, Chapter 56

56:1 ¶ THUS saith the LORD, Keep ye
judgment, and do justice: for my
salvation is near to come, and my
righteousness to be revealed.
56:2 Blessed is the man that doeth
this, and the son of man that layeth hold
on it; that keepeth the sabbath from
polluting it, and keepeth his hand from
doing any evil.
56:3 ¶ Neither let the son of the
stranger, that hath joined himself to the
LORD, speak, saying, The LORD hath
utterly separated me from his people:
neither let the eunuch say, Behold, I am
a dry tree.
56:4 For thus saith the LORD unto
the eunuchs that keep my sabbaths, and
choose the things that please me, and
take hold of my covenant;
56:5 Even unto them will I give in
mine house and within my walls a place
and a name better than of sons and of
daughters: I will give them an
everlasting name, that shall not be cut
off.
56:6 Also the sons of the stranger,
that join themselves to the LORD, to
serve him, and to love the name of the
LORD, to be his servants, every one that
keepeth the sabbath from polluting it,
and taketh hold of my covenant;
56:7 Even them will I bring to my
holy mountain, and make them joyful in
my house of prayer: their burnt offerings
and their sacrifices shall be accepted
upon mine altar; for mine house shall be
called an house of prayer for all people.
56:8 The Lord GOD which gathereth
the outcasts of Israel saith, Yet will I
gather others to him, beside those that
are gathered unto him.
56:9 ¶ All ye beasts of the field, come to
devour, yea, all ye beasts in the forest.
56:10 His watchmen are blind: they are
all ignorant, they are all dumb dogs,
they cannot bark; sleeping, lying down,
loving to slumber.
56:11 Yea, they are greedy dogs which
can never have enough, and they

are shepherds that cannot understand:
they all look to their own way, every
one for his gain, from his quarter.
56:12 Come ye, say they, I will fetch
wine, and we will fill ourselves with
strong drink; and to morrow shall be as
this day, and much more abundant.

ISAIAH, Chapter 57

57:1 ¶ The righteous perisheth, and no
man layeth it to heart: and merciful men
are taken away, none considering that
the righteous is taken away from the evil
to come.
57:2 He shall enter into peace: they
shall rest in their beds, each one walking
in his uprightness.
57:3 ¶ But draw near hither, ye sons of
the sorceress, the seed of the adulterer
and the whore.
57:4 Against whom do ye sport
yourselves? against whom make ye a
wide mouth, and draw out the tongue?
are ye not children of transgression, a
seed of falsehood,
57:5 Enflaming yourselves with idols
under every green tree, slaying the
children in the valleys under the clifts of
the rocks?
57:6 Among the smooth stones of the
stream is thy portion; they, they are thy
lot: even to them hast thou poured a
drink offering, thou hast offered a meat
offering. Should I receive comfort in
these?
57:7 Upon a lofty and high mountain
hast thou set thy bed: even thither
wentest thou up to offer sacrifice.
57:8 Behind the doors also and the
posts hast thou set up thy remembrance:
for thou hast discovered thyself to
another than me, and art gone up; thou
hast enlarged thy bed, and made thee a
covenant with them; thou lovedst their
bed where thou sawest it.
57:9 And thou wentest to the king
with ointment, and didst increase thy
perfumes, and didst send thy messengers
far off, and didst debase thyself even
unto hell.
57:10 Thou art wearied in the greatness
of thy way; yet saidst thou not, There is
no hope: thou hast found the life of
thine hand; therefore thou wast not
grieved.

57:11 And of whom hast thou been
afraid or feared, that thou hast lied, and
hast not remembered me, nor laid it to
thy heart? have not I held my peace
even of old, and thou fearest me not?
57:12 I will declare thy righteousness,
and thy works; for they shall not profit
thee.
57:13 ¶ When thou criest, let thy
companies deliver thee; but the wind
shall carry them all away; vanity shall
take them: but he that putteth his trust in
me shall possess the land, and shall
inherit my holy mountain;
57:14 And shall say, Cast ye up, cast
ye up, prepare the way, take up the
stumblingblock out of the way of my
people.
57:15 For thus saith the high and lofty
One that inhabiteth eternity, whose
name is Holy; I dwell in the high and
holy place, with him also that is of a
contrite and humble spirit, to revive the
spirit of the humble, and to revive the
heart of the contrite ones.
57:16 For I will not contend for ever,
neither will I be always wroth: for the
spirit should fail before me, and the
souls which I have made.
57:17 ¶ For the iniquity of his
covetousness was I wroth, and smote
him: I hid me, and was wroth, and he
went on frowardly in the way of his
heart.
57:18 I have seen his ways, and will
heal him: I will lead him also, and
restore comforts unto him and to his
mourners.
57:19 I create the fruit of the lips;
Peace, peace to him that is far off, and
to him that is near, saith the LORD; and
I will heal him.
57:20 But the wicked are like the
troubled sea, when it cannot rest, whose
waters cast up mire and dirt.
57:21 There is no peace, saith my God,
to the wicked.

ISAIAH, Chapter 58

58:1 ¶ CRY aloud, spare not, lift up
thy voice like a trumpet, and shew my
people their transgression, and the
house of Jacob their sins.
58:2 Yet they seek me daily, and
delight to know my ways, as a nation
that did righteousness, and forsook not

the ordinance of their God: they ask of me the ordinances of justice; they take delight in approaching to God.
58:3 ¶ Wherefore have we fasted, say they, and thou seest not? wherefore have we afflicted our soul, and thou takest no knowledge? Behold, in the day of your fast ye find pleasure, and exact all your labours.
58:4 Behold, ye fast for strife and debate, and to smite with the fist of wickedness: ye shall not fast as ye do this day, to make your voice to be heard on high.
58:5 Is it such a fast that I have chosen? a day for a man to afflict his soul? is it to bow down his head as a bulrush, and to spread sackcloth and ashes under him? wilt thou call this a fast, and an acceptable day to the LORD?
58:6 Is not this the fast that I have chosen? to loose the bands of wickedness, to undo the heavy burdens, and to let the oppressed go free, and that ye break every yoke?
58:7 Is it not to deal thy bread to the hungry, and that thou bring the poor that are cast out to thy house? when thou seest the naked, that thou cover him; and that thou hide not thyself from thine own flesh?
58:8 ¶ Then shall thy light break forth as the morning, and thine health shall spring forth speedily: and thy righteousness shall go before thee; the glory of the LORD shall be thy reward.
58:9 Then shalt thou call, and the LORD shall answer; thou shalt cry, and he shall say, Here I am. If thou take away from the midst of thee the yoke, the putting forth of the finger, and speaking vanity;
58:10 And if thou draw out thy soul to the hungry, and satisfy the afflicted soul; then shall thy light rise in obscurity, and thy darkness be as the noonday:
58:11 And the LORD shall guide thee continually, and satisfy thy soul in drought, and make fat thy bones: and thou shalt be like a watered garden, and like a spring of water, whose waters fail not.
58:12 And they that shall be of thee shall build the old waste places: thou shalt raise up the foundations of many generations; and thou shalt be called,

The repairer of the breach, The restorer of paths to dwell in.
58:13 ¶ If thou turn away thy foot from the sabbath, from doing thy pleasure on my holy day; and call the sabbath a delight, the holy of the LORD, honourable; and shalt honour him, not doing thine own ways, nor finding thine own pleasure, nor speaking thine own words:
58:14 Then shalt thou delight thyself in the LORD; and I will cause thee to ride upon the high places of the earth, and feed thee with the heritage of Jacob thy father: for the mouth of the LORD hath spoken it.

ISAIAH, Chapter 59

59:1 ¶ BEHOLD, the LORD'S hand is not shortened, that it cannot save; neither his ear heavy, that it cannot hear:
59:2 But your iniquities have separated between you and your God, and your sins have hid his face from you, that he will not hear.
59:3 For your hands are defiled with blood, and your fingers with iniquity; your lips have spoken lies, your tongue hath muttered perverseness.
59:4 None calleth for justice, nor any pleadeth for truth: they trust in vanity, and speak lies; they conceive mischief, and bring forth iniquity.
59:5 They hatch cockatrice' eggs, and weave the spider's web: he that eateth of their eggs dieth, and that which is crushed breaketh out into a viper.
59:6 Their webs shall not become garments, neither shall they cover themselves with their works: their works are works of iniquity, and the act of violence is in their hands.
59:7 Their feet run to evil, and they make haste to shed innocent blood: their thoughts are thoughts of iniquity; wasting and destruction are in their paths.
59:8 The way of peace they know not; and there is no judgment in their goings: they have made them crooked paths: whosoever goeth therein shall not know peace.
59:9 ¶ Therefore is judgment far from us, neither doth justice overtake us: we wait for light, but behold obscurity; for brightness, but we walk in darkness.

59:10 We grope for the wall like the blind, and we grope as if we had no eyes: we stumble at noonday as in the night; we are in desolate places as dead men.
59:11 We roar all like bears, and mourn sore like doves: we look for judgment, but there is none; for salvation, but it is far off from us.
59:12 For our transgressions are multiplied before thee, and our sins testify against us: for our transgressions are with us; and as for our iniquities, we know them;
59:13 In transgressing and lying against the LORD, and departing away from our God, speaking oppression and revolt, conceiving and uttering from the heart words of falsehood.
59:14 And judgment is turned away backward, and justice standeth afar off: for truth is fallen in the street, and equity cannot enter.
59:15 Yea, truth faileth; and he that departeth from evil maketh himself a prey: and the LORD saw it, and it displeased him that there was no judgment.
59:16 ¶ And he saw that there was no man, and wondered that there was no intercessor: therefore his arm brought salvation unto him; and his righteousness, it sustained him.
59:17 For he put on righteousness as a breastplate, and an helmet of salvation upon his head; and he put on the garments of vengeance for clothing, and was clad with zeal as a cloke.
59:18 According to their deeds, accordingly he will repay, fury to his adversaries, recompence to his enemies; to the islands he will repay recompence.
59:19 So shall they fear the name of the LORD from the west, and his glory from the rising of the sun. When the enemy shall come in like a flood, the Spirit of the LORD shall lift up a standard against him.
59:20 And the Redeemer shall come to Zion, and unto them that turn from transgression in Jacob, saith the LORD.
59:21 As for me, this is my covenant with them, saith the LORD; My spirit that is upon thee, and my words which I have put in thy mouth, shall not depart out of thy mouth, nor out of the mouth of thy seed, nor out of the mouth of thy seed's seed, saith the LORD, from henceforth and for ever.

ISAIAH, Chapter 60

60:1 ¶ ARISE, shine; for thy light is
come, and the glory of the LORD is
risen upon thee.
60:2 For, behold, the darkness shall
cover the earth, and gross darkness the
people: but the LORD shall arise upon
thee, and his glory shall be seen upon
thee.
60:3 And the Gentiles shall come to
thy light, and kings to the brightness of
thy rising.
60:4 Lift up thine eyes round about,
and see: all they gather themselves
together, they come to thee: thy sons
shall come from far, and thy daughters
shall be nursed at thy side.
60:5 Then thou shalt see, and flow
together, and thine heart shall fear, and
be enlarged; because the abundance of
the sea shall be converted unto thee, the
forces of the Gentiles shall come unto
thee.
60:6 The multitude of camels shall
cover thee, the dromedaries of Midian
and Ephah; all they from Sheba shall
come: they shall bring gold and incense;
and they shall shew forth the praises of
the LORD.
60:7 All the flocks of Kedar shall be
gathered together unto thee, the rams of
Nebaioth shall minister unto thee: they
shall come up with acceptance on mine
altar, and I will glorify the house of my
glory.
60:8 Who are these that fly as a cloud,
and as the doves to their windows?
60:9 ¶ Surely the isles shall wait for
me, and the ships of Tarshish first, to
bring thy sons from far, their silver and
their gold with them, unto the name of
the LORD thy God, and to the Holy One
of Israel, because he hath glorified thee.
60:10 And the sons of strangers shall
build up thy walls, and their kings shall
minister unto thee: for in my wrath I
smote thee, but in my favour have I had
mercy on thee.
60:11 Therefore thy gates shall be open
continually; they shall not be shut day
nor night; that men may bring unto thee
the forces of the Gentiles, and that their
kings may be brought.
60:12 For the nation and kingdom that
will not serve thee shall perish; yea,
those nations shall be utterly wasted.

60:13 The glory of Lebanon shall come unto thee, the fir tree, the pine tree, and the box together, to beautify the place of my sanctuary; and I will make the place of my feet glorious.
60:14 The sons also of them that afflicted thee shall come bending unto thee; and all they that despised thee shall bow themselves down at the soles of thy feet; and they shall call thee, The city of the LORD, The Zion of the Holy One of Israel.
60:15 ¶Whereas thou hast been forsaken and hated, so that no man went through thee, I will make thee an eternal excellency, a joy of many generations.
60:16 Thou shalt also suck the milk of the Gentiles, and shalt suck the breast of kings: and thou shalt know that I the LORD am thy Saviour and thy Redeemer, the mighty One of Jacob.
60:17 For brass I will bring gold, and for iron I will bring silver, and for wood brass, and for stones iron: I will also make thy officers peace, and thine exactors righteousness.
60:18 Violence shall no more be heard in thy land, wasting nor destruction within thy borders; but thou shalt call thy walls Salvation, and thy gates Praise.
60:19 The sun shall be no more thy light by day; neither for brightness shall the moon give light unto thee: but the LORD shall be unto thee an everlasting light, and thy God thy glory.
60:20 Thy sun shall no more go down; neither shall thy moon withdraw itself: for the LORD shall be thine everlasting light, and the days of thy mourning shall be ended.
60:21 Thy people also shall be all righteous: they shall inherit the land for ever, the branch of my planting, the work of my hands, that I may be glorified.
60:22 A little one shall become a thousand, and a small one a strong nation;: I the LORD will hasten it in his time.

ISAIAH, Chapter 61

61:1 ¶THE Spirit of the Lord GOD is upon me; because the LORD hath anointed me to preach good tidings unto the meek; he hath sent me to bind up the

brokenhearted, to proclaim liberty to the captives, and the opening of the prison to them that are bound;
61:2 To proclaim the acceptable year of the LORD, and the day of vengeance of our God; to comfort all that mourn;
61:3 To appoint unto them that mourn in Zion, to give unto them beauty for ashes, the oil of joy for mourning, the garment of praise for the spirit of heaviness; that they might be called trees of righteousness, the planting of the LORD, that he might be glorified.
61:4 ¶ And they shall build the old wastes, they shall raise up the former desolations, and they shall repair the waste cities, the desolations of many generations.
61:5 And strangers shall stand and feed your flocks, and the sons of the alien shall be your plowmen and your vinedressers.
61:6 But ye shall be named the Priests of the LORD: men shall call you the Ministers of our God: ye shall eat the riches of the Gentiles, and in their glory shall ye boast yourselves.
61:7 For your shame ye shall have double; and for confusion they shall rejoice in their portion: therefore in their land they shall possess the double: everlasting joy shall be unto them.
61:8 For I the LORD love judgment, I hate robbery for burnt offering; and I will direct their work in truth, and I will make an everlasting covenant with them.
61:9 And their seed shall be known among the Gentiles, and their offspring among the people: all that see them shall acknowledge them, that they are the seed which the LORD hath blessed.
61:10 ¶ I will greatly rejoice in the LORD, my soul shall be joyful in my God; for he hath clothed me with the garments of salvation, he hath covered me with the robe of righteousness, as a bridegroom decketh himself with ornaments, and as a bride adorneth herself with her jewels.
61:11 For as the earth bringeth forth her bud, and as the garden causeth the things that are sown in it to spring forth; so the Lord GOD will cause righteousness and praise to spring forth before all the nations.

ISAIAH, Chapter 62

62:1 ¶ FOR Zion's sake will I not
hold my peace, and for Jerusalem's sake
I will not rest, until the righteousness
thereof go forth as brightness, and the
salvation thereof as a lamp that burneth.
62:2 And the Gentiles shall see thy
righteousness, and all kings thy glory:
and thou shalt be called by a new name,
which the mouth of the LORD shall
name.
62:3 Thou shalt also be a crown of
glory in the hand of the LORD, and a
royal diadem in the hand of thy God.
62:4 Thou shalt no more be termed
Forsaken; neither shall thy land any
more be termed Desolate***;*** ~~:~~ but thou
shalt be called ***Delightful*** ~~Hephzibah~~,
and thy land ***Union*** ~~Beulah~~ ***;*** ~~:~~ for the
LORD delighteth in thee, and thy land
shall be married.
62:5 ¶ For as a young man marrieth a
virgin, so shall thy ***God*** ~~sons~~ marry thee***;***
~~:~~ and as the bridegroom rejoiceth over
the bride, so shall thy God rejoice over
thee.
62:6 I have set watchmen upon thy
walls, O Jerusalem, which shall never
hold their peace day nor night: ye that
make mention of the LORD, keep not
silence,
62:7 And give him no rest, till he
establish, and till he make Jerusalem a
praise in the earth.
62:8 The LORD hath sworn by his
right hand, and by the arm of his
strength, Surely I will no more give thy
corn to be meat for thine enemies; and
the sons of the stranger shall not drink
thy wine, for the which thou hast
laboured:
62:9 But they that have gathered it
shall eat it, and praise the LORD; and
they that have brought it together shall
drink it in the courts of my holiness.
62:10 ¶ Go through, go through the
gates; prepare ye the way of the people;
cast up, cast up the highway; gather out
the stones; lift up a standard for the
people.
62:11 Behold, the LORD hath
proclaimed unto the end of the world,
Say ye to the daughter of Zion, Behold,
thy salvation cometh; behold, his reward
is with him, and his work before him.
62:12 And they shall call them, The
holy people, The redeemed of the
LORD: and thou shalt be called, Sought
out, A city not forsaken.

ISAIAH, Chapter 63

Isaiah	The Book of Mormon	Additional LDS Scripture
63:1 ¶ WHO is this that cometh from Edom, with dyed garments from Bozrah? this that is glorious in his apparel, travelling in the greatness of his strength? I that speak in righteousness, mighty to save.		D&C 133:46 And it shall be said: Who is this that cometh down from God in heaven with dyed garments (-); yea, from the regions which are not known, clothed in his glorious apparel, traveling in the greatness of his strength? 133:47 And he shall say: I am he who spake in righteousness, mighty to save.
63:2 Wherefore art thou red in thine apparel, and thy garments like him that treadeth in the winefat?		133:48 (- -) And the Lord shall be red in his apparel, and his garments like him that treadeth in the wine-vat. 133:49 And so great shall be the glory of his presence that the sun shall hide his face in shame, and the moon shall withhold its light, and the stars shall be hurled from their places.
63:3 I have trodden the winepress alone; and of the people there was none with me: for I will tread them in mine anger, and trample them in my fury; and their blood shall be sprinkled upon my garments, and I will stain all my raiment. 63:4 For the day of vengeance is in mine heart, and the year of my redeemed is come. 63:5 And I looked, and there was none to help; and I wondered that there was none to uphold: therefore mine own arm brought salvation unto me; and my fury, it upheld me. 63:6 And I will tread down the people in mine anger, and make them drunk in my fury, and I will bring down their strength to the earth.		133:50 And his voice shall be heard: I have trodden the wine-press alone, and (- -) have brought judgment upon all people; and (- -) none were with me; 133:51 And I have trampled them in my fury, and (-) I did tread upon them in mine anger, (- -) and their blood have I (- -) sprinkled upon my garments, and stained (- -) all my raiment; for this was the day of vengeance which was in my (- -) heart (- -).
63:7 ¶I will mention the loving kindnesses of the LORD, and the praises of the LORD, according to all that the LORD hath bestowed on us, and the great goodness toward the house of Israel, which he hath bestowed on them according to his mercies, and according to the multitude of his lovingkindnesses. 63:8 For he said, Surely they are my people, children that will not lie: so he was their Saviour.		133:52 And now the year of my redeemed is come; and they shall (- -) mention the loving kindness of their Lord, (- -) and all that he has bestowed upon them according to his (-) goodness (- -), and according to (- -) his loving kindness, forever and ever.
63:9 In all their affliction he was afflicted, and the angel of his presence saved them: in his love and in his pity he redeemed them; and he bare them, and carried them all the days of old.		133:53 In all their afflictions he was afflicted. And the angel of his presence saved them; and in his love, and in his pity, he redeemed them, and bore them, and carried them all the days of old;

63:10 But they rebelled , and vexed his holy Spirit: therefore he was turned to be their enemy, and he fought against them.

63:11 Then he remembered the days of old, Moses, and his people, saying, Where is he that brought them up out of the sea with the shepherd of his flock? where is he that put his holy Spirit within him?

63:12 That led them by the right hand of Moses with his glorious arm, dividing the water before them, to make himself an everlasting name?

63:13 That led them through the deep, as an horse in the wilderness, that they should not stumble?

63:14 As a beast goeth down into the valley, the Spirit of the LORD caused him to rest: so didst thou lead thy people, to make thyself a glorious name.

63:15 ¶ Look down from heaven, and behold from the habitation of thy holiness and of thy glory: where is thy zeal and thy strength, the sounding of thy bowels and of thy mercies toward me? are they restrained?

63:16 Doubtless thou art our father, though Abraham be ignorant of us, and Israel acknowledge us not: thou, O LORD, art our father, our redeemer; thy name is from everlasting.

63:17 O LORD, why hast thou ***suffered*** ~~made~~ us to err from thy ways, and ***to*** harden~~ed~~ our heart from thy fear? Return for thy servants' sake, the tribes of thine inheritance.

63:18 The people of thy holiness have possessed it but a little while: our adversaries have trodden down thy sanctuary.

63:19 We are thine: thou never barest rule over them; they were not called by thy name.

ISAIAH, Chapter 64

64:1 ¶ OH that thou wouldest rend the heavens, that thou wouldest come down, that the mountains might flow down at thy presence,

64:2 As when the melting fire burneth, the fire causeth the waters to boil, to make thy name known to thine adversaries, that the nations may tremble at thy presence!

64:3 When thou didst terrible things which we looked not for, thou camest down, the mountains flowed down at thy presence.

64:4 For since the beginning of the world men have not heard, nor perceived by the ear, neither hath the eye seen, O God, beside thee, what he hath prepared for him that waiteth for him.

64:5 Thou meetest him that ~~rejoiceth and~~ worketh righteousness, ~~those~~ ***and rejoiceth him*** that remember thee in thy ways***;*** ~~: behold, thou art wroth; for we have sinned: in those~~ ***in righteousness there*** is continuance, and ~~we~~ ***such*** shall be saved.

64:6 ¶ But ***we have sinned;*** we are all as an unclean thing, and all our righteousnesses are as filthy rags; and we all do fade as a leaf; and our iniquities, like the wind, have taken us away.

64:7 And there is none that calleth upon thy name, that stirreth up himself to take hold of thee: for thou hast hid thy face from us, and hast consumed us, because of our iniquities.

64:8 But now, O LORD, thou art our father; we are the clay, and thou our potter; and we all are the work of thy hand.

64:9 Be not wroth very sore, O LORD, neither remember iniquity for ever: behold, see, we beseech thee, we are all thy people.

64:10 Thy holy cities are a wilderness, Zion is a wilderness, Jerusalem a desolation.

64:11 Our holy and our beautiful house, where our fathers praised thee, is burned up with fire: and all our pleasant things are laid waste.

64:12 Wilt thou refrain thyself for these things, O LORD? wilt thou hold thy peace, and afflict us very sore?

ISAIAH, Chapter 65

65:1 ¶ ***I am found of them who seek after me, I give unto all them that ask of me;*** ~~I am sought of them that asked not for me;~~ I am ***not*** found of them that sought me not***, or that inquireth not after me.*** I said ***unto my servant***, Behold me, ~~behold~~ ***look upon*** me***;*** ~~,~~ ***I***

will send you unto a nation that ***is*** ~~was~~
not called ***after*** ~~by~~ my name**,** ~~.~~
65:2 ***for*** I have spread out my hands all
the day ~~un~~to a ~~rebellious~~ people,*who*
~~which~~ walketh ***not*** in ***my*** ~~a~~ way*s*, ~~that~~
~~was~~ ***and their works are evil and*** not
good, ***and they walk*** after their own
thoughts**.** ~~;~~
65:3 A people that provoketh me to
anger continually to my face; that
sacrificeth in gardens, and burneth
incense upon altars of brick;
65:4 Which remain among the graves,
and lodge in the monuments**;** ~~,~~ which eat
swine's flesh, and broth of abominable
beasts, ~~things is in~~ ***and pollute*** their
vessels;
65:5 Which say, Stand by thyself,
come not near to me; for I am holier
than thou. These are a smoke in my
nose, a fire that burneth all the day.
65:6 Behold, it is written before me:
I will not keep silence, but will
recompense, even recompense into their
bosom,
65:7 Your iniquities, and the
iniquities of your fathers together, saith
the LORD, which have burned incense
upon the mountains, and blasphemed
me upon the hills: therefore will I
measure their former work into their
bosom.
65:8 ¶ Thus saith the LORD, As the new
wine is found in the cluster, and one
saith, Destroy it not; for a blessing is in
it: so will I do for my servants' sakes,
that I may not destroy them all.
65:9 And I will bring forth a seed out
of Jacob, and out of Judah an inheritor
of my mountains: and mine elect shall
inherit it, and my servants shall dwell
there.
65:10 And Sharon shall be a fold of
flocks, and the valley of Achor a place
for the herds to lie down in, for my
people that have sought me.
65:11 ¶ But ye are they that forsake the
LORD, that forget my holy mountain,
that prepare a table for that troop, and
that furnish the drink offering unto that
number.
65:12 Therefore will I number you to
the sword, and ye shall all bow down to
the slaughter: because when I called, ye
did not answer; when I spake, ye did not
hear; but did evil before mine eyes, and
did choose that wherein I delighted not.

65:13 Therefore thus saith the Lord GOD, Behold, my servants shall eat, but ye shall be hungry: behold, my servants shall drink, but ye shall be thirsty: behold, my servants shall rejoice, but ye shall be ashamed:

65:14 Behold, my servants shall sing for joy of heart, but ye shall cry for sorrow of heart, and shall howl for vexation of spirit.

65:15 And ye shall leave your name for a curse unto my chosen: for the Lord GOD shall slay thee, and call his servants by another name:

65:16 That he who blesseth himself in the earth shall bless himself in the God of truth; and he that sweareth in the earth shall swear by the God of truth; because the former troubles are forgotten, and because they are hid from mine eyes.

65:17 ¶ For, behold, I create new heavens and a new earth: and the former shall not be remembered, nor come into mind.

65:18 But be ye glad and rejoice for ever in that which I create: for, behold, I create Jerusalem a rejoicing, and her people a joy.

65:19 And I will rejoice in Jerusalem, and joy in my people: and the voice of weeping shall be no more heard in her, nor the voice of crying.

65:20 ***In those days,*** ~~T~~ *t*here shall be no more thence an infant of days, nor an old man that hath not filled his days***;*** ~~:~~ for the child [g] shall ***not*** die***, but shall live to be*** an hundred years old; but the sinner***, living to be*** ~~being~~ an hundred years old***,*** shall be accursed.

65:21 And they shall build houses, and inhabit them; and they shall plant vineyards, and eat the fruit of them.

65:22 They shall not build, and another inhabit; they shall not plant, and another eat: for as the days of a tree are the days of my people, and mine elect shall long enjoy the work of their hands.

65:23 They shall not labour in vain, nor bring forth for trouble; for they are the seed of the blessed of the LORD, and their offspring with them.

65:24 And it shall come to pass, that before they call, I will answer; and while they are yet speaking, I will hear.

65:25 The wolf and the lamb shall feed together, and the lion shall eat straw like the bullock: and dust shall be the serpent's meat. They shall not hurt nor destroy in all my holy mountain, saith the LORD.

ISAIAH, Chapter 66

66:1 ¶ THUS saith the LORD, The heaven is my throne, and the earth is my footstool: where is the house that ye build unto me? and where is the place of my rest?
66:2 For all those things hath mine hand made, and all those things have been, saith the LORD: but to this man will I look, even to him that is poor and of a contrite spirit, and trembleth at my word.
66:3 He that killeth an ox is as if he slew a man; he that sacrificeth a lamb, as if he cut off a dog's neck; he that offereth an oblation, as if he offered swine's blood; he that burneth incense, as if he blessed an idol. Yea, they have chosen their own ways, and their soul delighteth in their abominations.
66:4 I also will choose their delusions, and will bring their fears upon them; because when I called, none did answer; when I spake, they did not hear: but they did evil before mine eyes, and chose that in which I delighted not.
66:5 ¶ Hear the word of the LORD, ye that tremble at his word; Your brethren that hated you, that cast you out for my name's sake, said, Let the LORD be glorified: but he shall appear to your joy, and they shall be ashamed.
66:6 A voice of noise from the city, a voice from the temple, a voice of the LORD that rendereth recompence to his enemies.
66:7 Before she travailed, she brought forth; before her pain came, she was delivered of a man child.
66:8 Who hath heard such a thing? who hath seen such things? Shall the earth be made to bring forth in one day? or shall a nation be born at once? for as soon as Zion travailed, she brought forth her children.
66:9 Shall I bring to the birth, and not cause to bring forth? saith the LORD: shall I cause to bring forth, and shut the womb? saith thy God.

66:10 Rejoice ye with Jerusalem, and be glad with her, all ye that love her: rejoice for joy with her, all ye that mourn for her:
66:11 That ye may suck, and be satisfied with the breasts of her consolations; that ye may milk out, and be delighted with the abundance of her glory.
66:12 For thus saith the LORD, Behold, I will extend peace to her like a river, and the glory of the Gentiles[a] like a flowing stream: then shall ye suck, ye shall be borne upon her sides, and be dandled upon her knees.
66:13 As one whom his mother comforteth, so will I comfort you; and ye shall be comforted in Jerusalem.
66:14 And when ye see this, your heart shall rejoice, and your bones shall flourish like an herb: and the hand of the LORD shall be known toward his servants, and his indignation toward his enemies.
66:15 ¶ For, behold, the LORD will come with fire , and with his chariots like a whirlwind, to render his anger with fury, and his rebuke with flames of fire.
66:16 For by fire and by his sword will the LORD plead with all flesh: and the slain of the LORD shall be many.
66:17 They that sanctify themselves, and purify themselves in the gardens behind one tree in the midst, eating swine's flesh, and the abomination, and the mouse, shall be consumed together, saith the LORD.
66:18 For I know their works and their thoughts: it shall come, that I will gather all nations and tongues; and they shall come, and see my glory.
66:19 And I will set a sign among them, and I will send those that escape of them unto the nations, to Tarshish, Pul, and Lud, that draw the bow, to Tubal, and Javan, to the isles afar off, that have not heard my fame, neither have seen my glory; and they shall declare my glory among the Gentiles.
66:20 And they shall bring all your brethren for an offering unto the LORD out of all nations upon horses, and in chariots, and in litters, and upon mules, and upon swift beasts, to my holy mountain Jerusalem, saith the LORD, as the children of Israel bring an offering in a clean vessel into the house of the LORD.

66:21 And I will also take of them for
priests and for Levites, saith the LORD.
66:22 For as the new heavens and the
new earth, which I will make, shall
remain before me, saith the LORD, so
shall your seed and your name remain.
66:23 And it shall come to pass, that
from one new moon to another, and
from one sabbath to another, shall all
flesh come to worship before me, saith
the LORD.
66:24 And they shall go forth, and look
upon the carcases of the men that have
transgressed against me: for their worm
shall not die, neither shall their fire be
quenched; and they shall be an
abhorring unto all flesh.

THE BOOK OF MALACHI

With the Joseph Smith Translation
in Parallel Harmony
with LDS Scripture

MALACHI, Chapter 1

1:1 ¶ THE burden of the word of the
LORD to Israel by Malachi.
1:2 I have loved you, saith the
LORD. Yet ye say, Wherein hast thou
loved us? Was not Esau Jacob's brother?
saith the LORD: yet I loved Jacob,
1:3 And I hated Esau, and laid his
mountains and his heritage waste for the
dragons of the wilderness.
1:4 Whereas Edom saith, We are
impoverished, but we will return and
build the desolate places; thus saith the
LORD of hosts, They shall build, but I
will throw down; and they shall call
them, The border of wickedness, and,
The people against whom the LORD
hath indignation for ever.
1:5 And your eyes shall see, and ye
shall say, The LORD will be magnified
from the border of Israel.
1:6 ¶ A son honoureth his father,
and a servant his master: if then I be a
father, where is mine honour? and if I be
a master, where is my fear? saith the
LORD of hosts unto you, O priests, that
despise my name. And ye say, Wherein
have we despised thy name?
1:7 Ye offer polluted bread upon
mine altar; and ye say, Wherein have we
polluted thee? In that ye say, The table
of the LORD is contemptible.
1:8 And if ye offer the blind for
sacrifice, is it not evil? and if ye offer
the lame and sick, is it not evil? offer it
now unto thy governor; will he be
pleased with thee, or accept thy person?
saith the LORD of hosts.
1:9 And now, I pray you, beseech
God that he will be gracious unto us:
this hath been by your means: will he
regard your persons? saith the LORD of
hosts.
1:10 Who is there even among you
that would shut the doors for nought?
neither do ye kindle fire on mine altar
for nought. I have no pleasure in you,
saith the LORD of hosts, neither will I
accept an offering at your hand.
1:11 For from the rising of the sun
even unto the going down of the same
my name shall be great among the
Gentiles; and in every place incense
shall be offered unto my name, and a
pure offering: for my name shall be
great among the heathen, saith the
LORD of hosts.
1:12 But ye have profaned it, in that
ye say, The table of the LORD is

polluted; and the fruit thereof, even his
meat, is contemptible.
1:13 Ye said also, Behold, what a
weariness is it! and ye have snuffed at it,
saith the LORD of hosts; and ye brought
that which was torn, and the lame, and
the sick; thus ye brought an offering:
should I accept this of your hand? saith
the LORD.
1:14 But cursed be the deceiver,
which hath in his flock a male, and
voweth, and sacrificeth unto the Lord a
corrupt thing: for I am a great King,
saith the LORD of hosts, and my name
is dreadful among the heathen.

MALACHI, Chapter 2

2:1 ¶ AND now, O ye priests, this
commandment is for you.
2:2 If ye will not hear, and if ye will
not lay it to heart, to give glory unto my
name, saith the LORD of hosts, I will
even send a curse upon you, and I will
curse your blessings: yea, I have cursed
them already, because ye do not lay it to
heart.
2:3 Behold, I will corrupt your seed,
and spread dung upon your faces, even
the dung of your solemn feasts; and one
shall take you away with it.
2:4 And ye shall know that I have
sent this commandment unto you, that
my covenant might be with Levi, saith
the LORD of hosts.
2:5 My covenant was with him of
life and peace; and I gave them to him
for the fear wherewith he feared me, and
was afraid before my name.
2:6 The law of truth was in his
mouth, and iniquity was not found in his
lips: he walked with me in peace and
equity, and did turn many away from
iniquity.
2:7 For the priest's lips should keep
knowledge , and they should seek the
law at his mouth: for he is the
messenger of the LORD of hosts.
2:8 But ye are departed out of the
way; ye have caused many to stumble at
the law; ye have corrupted the covenant
of Levi, saith the LORD of hosts.
2:9 Therefore have I also made you
contemptible and base before all the
people, according as ye have not kept
my ways, but have been partial in the
law.
2:10 ¶ Have we not all one father?
hath not one God created us? why do we
deal treacherously every man against his

brother, by profaning the covenant of
our fathers?
2:11 Judah hath dealt treacherously,
and an abomination is committed in
Israel and in Jerusalem; for Judah hath
profaned the holiness of the LORD
which he loved, and hath married the
daughter of a strange god.
2:12 The LORD will cut off the man
that doeth this, the master and the
scholar, out of the tabernacles of Jacob,
and him that offereth an offering unto
the LORD of hosts.
2:13 And this have ye done again,
covering the altar of the LORD with
tears, with weeping, and with crying
out, insomuch that he regardeth not the
offering any more, or receiveth it with
good will at your hand.
2:14 Yet ye say, Wherefore? Because
the LORD hath been witness between
thee and the wife of thy youth, against
whom thou hast dealt treacherously: yet
is she thy companion, and the wife of
thy covenant.
2:15 And did not he make one? Yet
had he the residue of the spirit. And
wherefore one? That he might seek a
godly seed. Therefore take heed to your
spirit, and let none deal treacherously
against the wife of his youth.
2:16 For the LORD, the God of
Israel, saith that he hateth putting away:
for one covereth violence with his
garment, saith the LORD of hosts:
therefore take heed to your spirit, that ye
deal not treacherously.
2:17 Ye have wearied the LORD with
your words. Yet ye say, Wherein have
we wearied him? When ye say, Every
one that doeth evil is good in the sight
of the LORD, and he delighteth in them;
or, Where is the God of judgment?

MALACHI, Chapter 3

3:1 ¶ BEHOLD, I will send my
messenger , and he shall prepare the
way before me: and the Lord, whom ye
seek, shall suddenly come to his temple,
even the messenger of the covenant,

3 Nephi
24:1 AND it came to pass that he
commanded them that they should write
the words which the Father had given
unto Malachi, which he should tell unto
them. And it came to pass that after they
were written he expounded them. And
these are the words which he did tell
unto them, saying: Thus said the Father
unto Malachi--
Behold, I will send my messenger, and
he shall prepare the way before me, and
the Lord whom ye seek shall suddenly
come to his temple, even the messenger
of the covenant, whom ye delight in;

whom ye delight in: behold, he shall come, saith the LORD of hosts.

3:2 But who may abide the day of his coming? and who shall stand when he appeareth? for he is like a refiner's fire, and like fullers' soap:

3:3 And he shall sit as a refiner and purifier of silver: and he shall purify the sons of Levi, and purge them as gold and silver, that they may offer unto the LORD an offering in righteousness.

3:4 Then shall the offering of Judah and Jerusalem be pleasant unto the LORD, as in the days of old, and as in former years.

3:5 And I will come near to you to judgment; and I will be a swift witness against the sorcerers, and against the adulterers, and against false swearers, and against those that oppress the hireling in his wages, the widow[1], and the fatherless, and that turn aside the stranger from his right, and fear not me, saith the LORD of hosts.

3:6 For I am the LORD, I change not; therefore ye sons of Jacob are not consumed.

3:7 ¶ Even from the days of your fathers ye are gone away from mine ordinances, and have not kept them. Return unto me, and I will return unto you, saith the LORD of hosts. But ye said, Wherein shall we return?

3:8 Will a man rob God? Yet ye have robbed me. But ye say, Wherein have we robbed thee? In tithes and offerings.

3:9 Ye are cursed with a curse: for ye have robbed me, even this whole nation.

3:10 Bring ye all the tithes into the storehouse, that there may be meat in mine house, and prove me now herewith, saith the LORD of hosts, if I will not open you the windows of heaven, and pour you out a blessing, that there shall not be room enough to receive it.

3:11 And I will rebuke the devourer for your sakes, and he shall not destroy the fruits of your ground; neither shall your vine cast her fruit before the time in the field, saith the LORD of hosts.

3:12 And all nations shall call you blessed: for ye shall be a delightsome land, saith the LORD of hosts.

3:13 ¶ Your words have been stout against me, saith the LORD. Yet ye say, What have we spoken so much against thee?

3rd Nephi (cont.)

behold, he shall come, saith the Lord of Hosts.

24:2 But who may abide the day of his coming, and who shall stand when he appeareth? For he is like a refiner's fire, and like fuller's soap.

24:3 And he shall sit as a refiner and purifier of silver; and he shall purify the sons of Levi, and purge them as gold and silver, that they may offer unto the Lord an offering in righteousness.

24:4 Then shall the offering of Judah and Jerusalem be pleasant unto the Lord, as in the days of old, and as in former years.

24:5 And I will come near to you to judgment; and I will be a swift witness against the sorcerers, and against the adulterers, and against false swearers, and against those that oppress the hireling in his wages, the widow and the fatherless, and that turn aside the stranger, and fear not me, saith the Lord of Hosts.

24:6 For I am the Lord, I change not; therefore ye sons of Jacob are not consumed.

24:7 Even from the days of your fathers ye are gone away from mine ordinances, and have not kept them. Return unto me and I will return unto you, saith the Lord of Hosts. But ye say: Wherein shall we return?

24:8 Will a man rob God? Yet ye have robbed me. But ye say: Wherein have we robbed thee? In tithes and offerings.

24:9 Ye are cursed with a curse, for ye have robbed me, even this whole nation.

24:10 Bring ye all the tithes into the storehouse, that there may be meat in my house; and prove me now herewith, saith the Lord of Hosts, if I will not open you the windows of heaven, and pour you out a blessing that there shall not be room enough to receive it.

24:11 And I will rebuke the devourer for your sakes, and he shall not destroy the fruits of your ground; neither shall your vine cast her fruit before the time in the fields, saith the Lord of Hosts.

24:12 And all nations shall call you blessed, for ye shall be a delightsome land, saith the Lord of Hosts.

24:13 Your words have been stout against me, saith the Lord. Yet ye say: What have we spoken [- -] against thee?

3:14 Ye have said, It is vain to serve God: and what profit is it that we have kept his ordinance, and that we have walked mournfully before the LORD of hosts?
3:15 And now we call the proud happy; yea, they that work wickedness are set up; yea, they that tempt God are even delivered.
3:16 Then they that feared the LORD spake often one to another: and the LORD hearkened, and heard it, and a book of remembrance was written before him for them that feared the LORD, and that thought upon his name.
3:17 And they shall be mine, saith the LORD of hosts, in that day when I make up my jewels; and I will spare them, as a man spareth his own son that serveth him.
3:18 Then shall ye return, and discern between the righteous and the wicked, between him that serveth God and him that serveth him not.

3rd Nephi (cont.)
24:14 Ye have said: It is vain to serve God, and what doth it profit that we have kept his ordinances and that we have walked mournfully before the Lord of Hosts?
24:15 And now we call the proud happy; yea, they that work wickedness are set up; yea, they that tempt God are even delivered.
24:16 Then they that feared the Lord spake often one to another, and the Lord hearkened and heard [-]; and a book of remembrance was written before him for them that feared the Lord, and that thought upon his name.
24:17 And they shall be mine, saith the Lord of Hosts, in that day when I make up my jewels; and I will spare them as a man spareth his own son that serveth him.
24:18 Then shall ye return and discern between the righteous and the wicked, between him that serveth God and him that serveth him not.

MALACHI, Chapter 4

4:1 ¶ For , behold, the day cometh, that shall burn as an oven; and all the proud, yea, and all that do wickedly, shall be stubble: and the day that cometh shall burn them up, saith the LORD of hosts, that it shall leave them neither root nor branch.
4:2 But unto you that fear my name shall the Sun of righteousness arise with healing in his wings; and ye shall go forth, and grow up as calves of the stall.
4:3 And ye shall tread down the wicked; for they shall be ashes under the soles of your feet in the day that I shall do this, saith the LORD of hosts.
4:4 ¶ Remember ye the law of Moses my servant, which I commanded unto him in Horeb for all Israel, with the statutes and judgments.

3rd Nephi
25:1 FOR behold, the day cometh that shall burn as an oven; and all the proud, yea, and all that do wickedly, shall be stubble; and the day that cometh shall burn them up, saith the Lord of Hosts, that it shall leave them neither root nor branch.
25:2 But unto you that fear my name, shall the Son of Righteousness arise with healing in his wings; and ye shall go forth and grow up as calves in the stall.
25:3 And ye shall tread down the wicked; for they shall be ashes under the soles of your feet in the day that I shall do this, saith the Lord of Hosts.
25:4 Remember ye the law of Moses, my servant, which I commanded unto him in Horeb for all Israel, with the statutes and judgments.

Joseph Smith History
1:36 After telling me these things, he commenced quoting the prophecies of the Old Testament. He first quoted part of the third chapter of Malachi; and he quoted also the fourth or last chapter of the same prophecy, though with a little variation from the way it reads in our Bibles. Instead of quoting the first verse as it reads in our books, he quoted it thus:

1:37 For behold, the day cometh that shall burn as an oven, and all the proud, yea, and all that do wickedly shall (-) burn as stubble; (- -) for they that come shall burn them (-), saith the Lord of Hosts, that it shall leave them neither root nor branch.

4:5 Behold , I will send you

Elijah the prophet before the coming of the great and dreadful day of the LORD:

4:6 And he shall turn the heart of the fathers to the children, and the heart of the children to their fathers, lest I come and smite the earth with a curse.

Doctrine and Covenants

2:1 Behold, I will (-) reveal unto you the Priesthood, by the hand of Elijah the prophet, before the coming of the great and dreadful day of the Lord.

2:2 And he shall (-) plant in the hearts of the (- -) children the promises made to the fathers, and the hearts of the children shall turn to their fathers (- -).
2:3 If it were not so, the whole earth would be utterly wasted at his coming.

Joseph Smith History (cont.)
1:38 And again, he quoted the fifth verse thus: Behold, I will reveal unto you the Priesthood, by the hand of Elijah the prophet, before the coming of the great and dreadful day of the Lord.
1:39 He also quoted the next verse differently: And he shall (-) plant in the hearts of the (- -) children the promises made to the fathers, and the hearts of the children shall turn to their fathers. (- -). If it were not so, the whole earth would be utterly wasted at his coming.

Doctrine & Covenants
110:13 After this vision had closed, another great and glorious vision burst upon us; for Elijah the prophet, who was taken to heaven without tasting death, stood before us, and said:
110:14 Behold, the time has fully come, which was spoken of by the mouth of Malachi--testifying that he [Elijah] should be sent, before the great and dreadful day of the Lord come--
110:15 To turn the hearts of the fathers to the children, and the children to the fathers, lest the whole earth be smitten with a curse--
110:16 Therefore, the keys of this dispensation are committed into your hands; and by this ye may know that the great and dreadful day of the Lord is near, even at the doors.

APPENDIX

Joseph Smith Translation
changes in Other Books of
the Old Testament

EXODUS

1:1 Now these are the names of the children of Israel, which came into Egypt; every man ~~and~~ ***according to*** his household ***who*** came with Jacob.

1:11 And it came to pass in those days, when Moses was grown, that he went out unto his brethren, and looked on their burdens***;*** ~~:~~ and he spied an Egyptian smiting an Hebrew, one of his brethren.

3:1 Now Moses kept the flock of Jethro his father in law, the priest of Midian***;*** ~~:~~
and he led the flock to the ~~backside~~ ***back side*** of the desert, and came to the mountain of God~~,~~ even to Horeb.
3:2 And***, again,*** the ~~angel~~ ***presence*** of the LORD appeared unto him~~,~~ in a flame of fire ~~out of~~ ***in*** the midst of a bush***,*** ~~:~~ and he looked, and, behold, the bush burned with fire, and the bush was not consumed.
3:3 And Moses said, I will now turn aside, and see this great sight, why the bush is not ~~burnt~~ ***consumed***.

3:21 And I will give this people ~~favour~~ ***favor*** in the sight of the Egyptians***;*** ~~:~~ and it shall come to pass, that, when ye go, ye shall not go empty***;*** ~~:~~
3:22 But every woman shall borrow of her ~~neighbour~~ ***neighbor***, and of her that sojourneth in her house, jewels of silver, and jewels of gold, and raiment***;*** ~~:~~ and ye shall put them upon your sons, and upon your daughters; and ye shall spoil the Egyptians.

4:7 And he said, Put ~~thine~~ ***thy*** hand into thy bosom again. And he put his hand into his bosom again; and plucked it out of his bosom, and, behold, it was turned again as his other flesh.

4:21 And the LORD said unto Moses, When thou goest to return into Egypt, see that thou do all those wonders before Pharaoh, which I have put in thine hand***,*** ~~:~~ ***and I will prosper thee;*** but ~~I~~ ***Pharoah*** will harden his heart, that he ~~shall~~ ***will*** not let the people go.

4:24 And it came to pass ~~by the way in the inn~~, that the LORD ~~met~~ ***appeared unto*** him~~,~~ ***as he was in the way, by the inn. The Lord was angry with Moses, and his hand was about to fall upon him,*** ~~and sought~~ ***to kill him; for he had not circumcised his son.***
4:25 Then Zipporah took a sharp stone~~,~~ and ~~cut off the foreskin of~~ ***circumcised*** her son, and cast ~~it~~ ***the stone*** at his feet, and said, Surely ***thou art*** a bloody husband ~~art thou~~ to me.
4:26 ***And the Lord spared Moses and*** ~~So he~~ let him go***,*** ~~:~~ ***because Zipporah, his wife, circumcised the child. And*** ~~then~~ she said, ***Thou art*** ~~A~~***a*** bloody husband ~~thou art, because of the circumcision~~. ***And Moses was ashamed, and hid his face from the Lord, and said, I have sinned before the Lord.***
4:27 And the LORD said ***un***to Aaron, Go into the wilderness to meet Moses***,*** ~~:~~ ~~A~~***a***nd he went~~,~~ and met him***, in the mount of God;*** in the mount ~~of~~ ***where*** God ***appeared unto him***, and ***Aaron*** kissed him.

5:4 And the king of Egypt said unto them, Wherefore do ye, Moses and Aaron, ~~let~~ ***lead*** the people from their works? get you unto your burdens.

5:11 Go ye, get ~~you~~ *your* straw where ye can find it***;*** ~~:~~ yet not ~~ought~~ ***aught*** of your work shall be diminished.

6:3 And I appeared unto Abraham, unto Isaac, and unto Jacob***.*** ~~,~~ ***I am the Lord*** ~~by the name of~~ God Almighty***;*** ~~, but by my name~~ ***the Lord*** JEHOVAH. ***And*** was ***not*** ~~I not~~ ***my name*** known ***un***to them***?*** ~~.~~

EXODUS

6:8 And I will bring you in unto the land, concerning the which I did swear to give it to Abraham, to Isaac, and to Jacob; and I will give it you for ~~an~~ ***a*** heritage***;*** ~~:~~ I ~~am~~ the LORD ***will do it***.

6:12 And Moses spake before the LORD, saying, Behold, the children of Israel have not hearkened unto me; how then shall Pharaoh hear me, who ~~am~~ ***is*** of uncircumcised lips?

6:14 These be the heads of their fathers' houses**;** ~~:~~: ***tThe*** sons of Reuben the firstborn of Israel; Hanoch, and Pallu, Hezron, and Carmi***;*** ~~:~~ these ***are*** ~~be~~ the families of Reuben.

6:18 And the sons of Kohath; Amram, and Izhar, and Hebron, and Uzziel***;*** ~~:~~ and the years of the life of Kohath were ***a*** ~~an~~ hundred thirty and three years.

6:20 And Amram took him Jochebed his father's sister to wife; and she bare him Aaron and Moses***;*** ~~:~~ and the years of the life of Amram were ***a*** ~~an~~ hundred and thirty and seven years.

6:24 And the sons of Korah; Assir, and Elkanah, and Abiasaph**;** ~~:~~ these are the families of the Korhites.

6:26 These are ***the sons of Aaron, according to their families. And all these are the names of the children of Israel according to the heads of their families, that the Lord said unto*** ~~that~~ Aaron and Moses, ~~to whom the LORD said,~~ *they should* ***~~B~~bring up*** out ~~the children of Israel from~~ ***of*** the land of Egypt, according to their armies.

6:27 These are they ***concerning whom the Lord*** ~~which~~ spake to Pharaoh, king of Egypt, ***that he should let them go. And he sent Moses and Aaron*** to bring out the children of Israel from Egypt~~: these are that Moses and Aaron~~.

6:28 And it came to pass, on the day ~~when~~ the LORD spake unto Moses, in the land of Egypt,

6:29 ~~T~~*t*hat the LORD ~~spake unto~~ ***commanded*** Moses ~~saying, I am the LORD~~: ***that he should*** speak thou unto Pharaoh king of Egypt***, saying, I the Lord, will do unto Pharaoh, king of Egypt,*** all that I say unto thee.

6:30 And Moses said, before the Lord,~~:~~ Behold, I am of ~~uncircumcised~~ ***stammering*** lips, ***and slow of speech;*** ~~and~~ how shall Pharaoh hearken unto me?

7:1 And the LORD said unto Moses, See, I have made thee a ~~god~~ ***prophet*** to Pharaoh: and Aaron thy brother shall be thy ~~prophet~~ ***spokesman***.

7:2 Thou shalt speak ***unto thy brother*** all that I command thee***;*** ~~:~~ and Aaron thy brother shall speak unto Pharaoh, that he send the children of Israel out of his land.

7:3 And ~~I~~ ***Pharaoh*** will harden ~~Pharaoh's~~ ***his*** heart, ***as I said unto thee; and thou shalt*** ~~and~~ multiply my signs, and my wonders, in the land of Egypt.

7:4 But Pharaoh ~~shall~~ ***will*** not hearken unto you, ~~that~~ ***therefore*** I ~~may~~ *will* lay my hand upon Egypt, and bring forth mine armies, ~~and~~ my people, the children of Israel, out of the land of Egypt by great judgments.

7:9 When Pharaoh shall speak unto you, saying, ~~Shew~~ ***Show*** a miracle ~~for~~ ***that I may know*** you; ~~:~~ then thou shalt say unto Aaron, Take thy rod, and cast it before Pharaoh, and it shall become a serpent.

7:13 And ~~he~~ ***Pharaoh*** hardened ~~Pharaoh's~~ ***his*** heart, that he hearkened not unto them; as the LORD had said.

8:29 And Moses said, Behold, I go out from thee, and I will ~~intreat~~ ***entreat*** the LORD that the swarms of flies may depart from Pharaoh, from his servants, and from his people, ~~to morrow:~~ ***tomorrow;*** but let not Pharaoh deal deceitfully any more in not letting the people go to sacrifice to the LORD.

EXODUS

9:12 And ~~the LORD~~ ***Pharaoh*** hardened ~~the~~ ***his*** heart ~~of Pharaoh~~, and he hearkened not unto them; as the LORD had spoken unto Moses.

9:17 ***Therefore speak unto Pharaoh the thing which I command thee, who*** ~~A~~as yet exaltest ~~thou thyself against my people,~~ ***himself*** that ~~thou wilt~~ ***he will*** not let them go?

10:1 And the LORD said unto Moses, Go in unto Pharaoh***;*** ~~:~~ for ~~I have~~ ***he hath*** hardened his heart, and the heart*s* of his servants, ~~that I might shew~~ ***therefore I will show*** these my signs before him***;*** ~~:~~

10:20 But ~~the LORD~~ ***Pharaoh*** hardened ~~Pharaoh's~~ ***his*** heart, so that he would not let the children of Israel go.

10:27 But ~~the LORD~~ ***Pharaoh*** hardened ~~Pharaoh's~~ ***his*** heart, and he would not let them go.

11:8 And all these ~~thy~~ ***the*** servants ***of Pharaoh*** shall come down unto me, and bow ~~down~~ themselves ***down*** unto me, saying, Get thee out, and all the people that follow thee***;*** ~~:~~ and after that I will go out. ~~And he went out from Pharaoh in a great anger~~.
11:9 And the LORD said unto Moses, Pharaoh ~~shall~~ ***will*** not hearken unto you; ~~that~~ ***therefore*** my wonders ~~may~~ ***shall*** be multiplied in the land of Egypt.
11:10 And Moses and Aaron did all these wonders before Pharaoh***,*** ~~:~~ ***and they went out from Pharaoh, and he was in great anger.*** ~~a~~*A*nd ~~the LORD~~ ***Pharaoh*** hardened ~~Pharaoh's~~ ***his*** heart, so that he would not let the children of Israel go out of his land.

12:3 Speak ye unto all the congregation of Israel, saying, In the tenth day of this month they shall take to them every man a lamb, according to the house of their fathers, a lamb for an house***;*** ~~:~~

12:16 And in the first day there shall be ~~an~~ ***a*** holy convocation, and in the seventh day there shall be ~~an~~ ***a*** holy convocation to you; no manner of work shall be done in them, save that which every man must eat, that only may be done of you.

12:33 And the Egyptians were urgent upon the people, that they might send them out of the land in haste; for they said, ~~We be all dead men~~ ***We have found our first-born all dead; therefore get ye out of the land lest we die also***.

12:37 And the children of Israel journeyed from Rameses to Succoth, about six hundred thousand ***men*** on foot ~~that were men, beside~~ ***besides women and*** children.

12:45 A foreigner and ~~an~~ ***a*** hired servant shall not eat thereof.

13:11 And it shall be when the LORD shall bring thee into the land of the Canaanites, as he sware unto thee and ~~to~~ thy fathers, and shall give it thee,

---

14:4 And ~~I~~ ***Pharaoh*** will harden ~~Pharaoh's~~ ***his*** heart***,*** that he shall follow after them; and I will be ~~honoured~~ ***honored*** upon Pharaoh, and upon all his host; that the Egyptians may know that I am the LORD. And they did so.

EXODUS

14: 8 And ~~the LORD~~ ***Pharaoh*** hardened ~~the~~ ***his*** heart ~~of Pharaoh king of Egypt~~, and he pursued after the children of Israel***;*** ~~:~~ and the children of Israel went out with ~~an~~ ***a*** high hand.

14:17 And I ***say unto thee***~~, behold, I will harden~~ the hearts of the Egyptians ***shall be hardened***, and they shall follow them***;*** ~~:~~ and I will get me ~~honour~~ ***honor*** upon Pharaoh, and upon all his host, upon his chariots, and upon his horsemen.

14: 20 And it came between the camp of the Egyptians and the camp of Israel; and it was a cloud and darkness to ~~them~~ ***the Egyptians***, but it gave light by night to ~~these:~~ ***the Israelites,*** so that the one came not near the other all the night.

15: 2 The LORD is my strength and song, and he is become my salvation***;*** ~~:~~ he is my God, and I will prepare him ~~an~~ ***a*** habitation; my father's God, and I will exalt him.

15:8 And with the blast of thy nostrils the waters were gathered together, the floods stood upright as ~~an~~ ***a*** heap, and the depths were congealed in the heart of the sea.

15:16 Fear and dread shall fall upon them; by the greatness of thine arm they shall be as still as a stone; till ~~thy~~ ***the*** people pass over, O LORD, till the people pass over, which thou hast purchased.

18:1 When Jethro, the ***high*** priest of Midian, Moses' father in law, heard of all that God had done for Moses, and for Israel his people, and that the LORD had brought Israel out of Egypt;

19:6 And ye shall be unto me a kingdom of priests, and ~~an~~ ***a*** holy nation. These are the words which thou shalt speak unto the children of Israel.

19:13 There shall not ~~an~~ ***a*** hand touch it, but he shall surely be stoned, or shot through; whether it be beast or man, it shall not live***;*** ~~:~~ when the trumpet soundeth long, they shall come up to the mount.

20:23 Ye shall not make ~~with me~~ ***unto you*** gods of silver, neither shall ye make unto you gods of gold.

21:2 If thou buy ~~an~~ ***a*** Hebrew servant, six years he shall serve***;*** ~~:~~ and in the seventh he shall go out free for nothing.

21:6 Then his master shall bring him unto the judges; he shall also bring him to ~~the~~ ***his*** door, or unto the door post; and his master shall bore his ear through with an ~~aul~~ ***awl***; and he shall serve him for ever.

21:8 If she please not her master, who hath betrothed her to himself, then shall he let her be redeemed: ***not*** to sell her unto a strange nation***;*** he shall have no power ***to do this***, seeing he hath dealt deceitfully with her.

21:20 And if a man smite his servant, or his maid, with a rod, and he die under his hand; he shall ***surely*** be ~~surely punished~~ ***put to death***.
21:21 Notwithstanding, if he continue a day or two, ***and recover,*** he shall not be ~~punished~~ ***put to death,*** ~~:~~ for he is his ~~money~~ ***servant***.

EXODUS

22:15 But if the owner thereof be with it, he shall not make it good***;*** ~~:~~ if it be ~~an~~ ***a*** hired thing, it came for his hire.

22:18 Thou shalt not suffer a ~~witch~~ ***murderer*** to live.

22:25 If thou lend money to any of my people that is poor by thee, thou shalt not be to him as ~~an~~ ***a*** usurer, neither shalt thou lay upon him usury.

22:28 Thou shalt not revile ~~the gods~~ ***against God***, nor curse the ruler of thy people.

23:33 Neither shalt thou countenance a ~~poor~~ ***wicked*** man in his cause.

23:27 I will send my fear before thee, and ***I*** will destroy all the people to whom thou shalt come***;*** ~~,~~ and I will make all thine enemies turn their backs unto thee.

25:36 Their knops and their branches shall be of the same***;*** ~~:~~ all ***of*** it shall be one beaten work of pure gold.

26:36 And thou shalt make ~~an~~ ***a*** hanging for the door of the tent, of blue, and purple, and scarlet, and fine twined linen, wrought with needlework.

27:3 And thou shalt make his pans to receive his ashes, and his shovels, and his ~~basons~~ ***basins***, and his fleshhooks, and his firepans***;*** ~~:~~ ***and*** all the vessels thereof thou shalt make of brass.

27:8 Hollow with boards shalt thou make it***;*** ~~:~~ as it was ~~shewed~~ ***showed*** thee in the mount, so shall ~~they~~ ***thou*** make it.
27:9 And thou shalt make the court of the tabernacle***;*** ~~:~~ for the south side southward there shall be hangings for the court of fine twined linen of ~~an~~ ***a*** hundred cubits long for one side***;*** ~~:~~

27:11 And likewise for the north side in length there shall be hangings of ~~an~~ ***a*** hundred cubits long, and his twenty pillars and their twenty sockets of brass; the hooks of the pillars and their fillets of silver.

27:16 And for the gate of the court shall be an hanging of twenty cubits, of blue, and purple, and scarlet, and fine twined linen, wrought with needlework***;*** ~~:~~ and their pillars shall be four, and their sockets four.

27:18 The length of the court shall be ~~an~~ ***a*** hundred cubits, and the breadth fifty ~~every where~~ ***everywhere***, and the height five cubits of fine twined linen, and their sockets of brass.

28:32 And there shall be ~~an~~ ***a*** hole in the top of it, in the midst thereof***;*** ~~:~~ it shall have a binding of woven work round about the hole of it, as it were the hole of an habergeon, that it be not rent.

29:28 And it shall be Aaron's and his sons' by a statute for ever from the children of Israel***;*** ~~:~~ for it is ~~an~~ ***a*** heave offering***;*** ~~:~~ and it shall be an heave offering from the children of Israel of the sacrifice of their peace offerings, even their heave offering unto the LORD.

EXODUS

29:40 And with the one lamb a tenth deal of flour mingled with the fourth part of ~~an~~ ***a*** hin of beaten oil; and the fourth part of ~~an~~ ***a*** hin of wine for a drink offering.

30:13 This they shall give, every one that passeth among them that are numbered, half a shekel after the shekel of the sanctuary***;*** ~~:~~ (a shekel is twenty gerahs; ~~:~~) ~~an~~ ***a*** half shekel shall be the offering of the LORD.

30:24 And of cassia five hundred shekels, after the shekel of the sanctuary, and of oil olive ~~an~~ ***a*** hin:
30:25 And thou shalt make it an oil of holy ointment, an ointment compound after the art of the apothecary***;*** ~~:~~ it shall be ~~an~~ ***a*** holy anointing oil.

30:31 And thou shalt speak unto the children of Israel, saying, This shall be ~~an~~ ***a*** holy anointing oil unto me throughout your generations.

31:10 And the cloths of service, and the holy garments ~~for~~ ***of*** Aaron the priest, and the garments of his sons, to minister in the priest's office,

---

32:1 And when the people saw that Moses delayed to come down out of the mount, the people gathered themselves together unto Aaron, and said unto him, Up, make us gods, which shall go before us; for as for this Moses, the man that brought us up out of the land of Egypt, we ~~wot~~ ***know*** not what is become of him.

32:12 Wherefore should the Egyptians speak, and say, For mischief did he bring them out, to slay them in the mountains, and to consume them from the face of the earth? Turn from thy fierce wrath***.*** ~~;~~ ***Thy people will*** ~~and~~ repent of this evil***; therefore come thou not out*** against ~~thy people~~ ***them***.

32:14 And the LORD ***said unto Moses, If they will repent*** ~~repented~~ of the evil which ***they have done, I will spare them, and turn away my fierce wrath; but, behold, thou shalt execute judgement upon all that will not repent of this evil this day. Therefore, see thou do this thing that I have commanded thee, or I will execute all that which I had*** ~~he~~ thought to do unto ~~his~~ ***my*** people.

32:23 For they said unto me, Make us gods, which shall go before us***;*** ~~:~~ for as for this Moses, the man that brought us up out of the land of Egypt, we ~~wot~~ ***know*** not what is become of him.

32:35 And the LORD plagued the people, because they ~~made~~ ***worshipped*** the calf, which Aaron made.

33:1 And the LORD said unto Moses, Depart, and go up hence, thou and the people which thou hast brought up out of the land of Egypt, unto ***a land flowing with milk and honey,*** the land which I sware unto Abraham, to Isaac, and to Jacob, saying, Unto thy seed will I give it***;*** ~~:~~

33:20 And he said ***unto Moses***, Thou canst not see my face~~:~~ ***at this time, lest mine anger be kindled against thee also, and I destroy thee, and thy people;*** for there shall no man ***among them*** see me ***at this time***, and live***, for they are exceeding sinful. And no sinful man hath at any time, neither shall there be any sinful man at any time, that shall see my face and live***.
33:21 And the LORD said, Behold, ~~there is a place by me, and~~ thou shalt stand upon a rock***,*** ~~:~~ ***and I will prepare a place by me for thee.***
33:22 And it shall come to pass, while my glory passeth by, that I will put thee in a ~~clift~~ ***cleft*** of ~~the~~ ***a*** rock, and ~~will~~ cover thee with my hand while I pass by:

EXODUS

33:23 And I will take away mine hand, and thou shalt see my back parts***;*** ~~:~~ but my face shall not be seen***, as at other times; for I am angry with my people Israel.***.

34:1 And the LORD said unto Moses, Hew thee two tables of stone, like unto the first, ~~:~~ and I will write upon ~~these tables the words that were in the first~~ ***them also, the words of the law, according as they were written at the first on the*** tables, which thou brakest***; but it shall not be according to the first, for I will take way the priesthood out of their midst; therefore my holy order, and the ordinances thereof, shall not go before them; for my presence shall not go up in their midst, lest I destroy them***.
34:2 ***but I will give unto them the law as at the first, but it shall be after the law of a carnal commandment; for I have sworn in my wrath, that they shall not enter into my presence, into my rest, in the days of their pilgrimage. Therefore do as I have commanded thee,*** ~~A~~***a***nd be ready in the morning, and come up in the morning unto mount Sinai, and present thyself there to me, in the top of the mount.

34:4 And ~~he~~ ***Moses*** hewed two tables of stone like unto the first***;*** ~~;~~ and ~~Moses~~ ***he*** rose up early in the morning, and went up unto mount Sinai, as the LORD had commanded him, and took in his hand the two tables of stone.

34:7 Keeping mercy for thousands, forgiving iniquity and transgression and sin, and that will by no means clear the ~~guilty~~ ***rebellious***; visiting the iniquity of the fathers upon the children, and upon the children's children, unto the third and to the fourth generation.

34:14 For thou shalt worship no other god***;*** ~~:~~ for the LORD, whose name is ~~Jealous~~ ***Jehovah***, is a jealous God***.*** ~~:~~

34:35 And the children of Israel saw the face of Moses, that the skin of Moses' face shone***;*** ~~:~~ and Moses put the ~~vail~~ ***veil*** upon his face again, until he went in to speak with ~~him~~ ***the Lord***.

35:2 Six days shall work be done, but on the seventh day there shall be to you ~~an~~ ***a*** holy day, a sabbath of rest to the LORD***;*** ~~:~~ whosoever doeth work therein shall be put to death.

36:37 And he made ~~an~~ ***a*** hanging for the tabernacle door of blue, and purple, and scarlet, and fine twined linen, of needlework;

37:12 Also he made thereunto a border of ~~an~~ ***a*** hand-breadth round about; and made a crown of gold for the border thereof round about.

38:9 And he made the court***;*** ~~:~~ on the south side southward the hangings of the court were of fine twined linen, an hundred cubits:

38:11 And for the north side the hangings were ~~an~~ ***a*** hundred cubits, their pillars were twenty, and their sockets of brass twenty; the hooks of the pillars, and their fillets of silver.

38:25 And the silver of them that were numbered of the congregation was ~~an~~ ***a*** hundred talents, and a thousand seven hundred and threescore and fifteen shekels, after the shekel of the sanctuary***;*** ~~:~~

EXODUS

38:27 And of the hundred talents of silver were cast the sockets of the sanctuary, and the sockets of the ~~vail~~ ***veil***; ~~an~~ ***a*** hundred sockets of the hundred talents, a talent for a socket.

39:23 And there was ~~an~~ ***a*** hole in the midst of the robe, as the hole of an habergeon, with a band round about the hole, that it should not rend.

LEVITICUS

7:14 And of it he shall offer one out of the whole oblation for ~~an~~ ***a*** heave offering unto the LORD, and it shall be the priest's that sprinkleth the blood of the peace offerings.

7:32 And the right shoulder shall ye give unto the priest for ~~an~~ ***a*** heave offering of the sacrifices of your peace offerings.

8:14 And he brought the bullock for the sin offering***;*** ~~:~~ and Aaron and his sons laid their hands upon the head of the bullock for the sin offering.

9:17 And he brought the meat offering, and took ~~an~~ ***a*** handful thereof, and burnt it upon the altar, beside the burnt sacrifice of the morning.

12:3 And in the eighth day***,*** the ~~flesh of his foreskin~~ ***man child*** shall be circumcised.
12:4 And she shall then continue in the ~~blood~~ ***time*** of her purifying ***which shall be*** three and thirty days; she shall touch no hallowed thing, nor come into the sanctuary, until the days of her purifying be fulfilled.
12:5 But if she bear a maid child, ~~then~~ she shall be unclean two weeks, as in her separation***;*** ~~:~~ and she shall continue in the ~~blood~~ ***time*** of her purifying threescore and six days.

15:16 And if any man's seed of copulation go out ~~from~~ ***of*** him, then he shall wash all his flesh in water, and be unclean until the even.

17:4 And bringeth it not ~~unto~~ ***into*** the door of the tabernacle of the congregation, to offer an offering unto the LORD before the tabernacle of the LORD; blood shall be imputed unto that man; he hath shed blood; and that man shall be cut off from among his people***;*** ~~:~~

19:20 And whosoever lieth carnally with a woman, that is a bondmaid, betrothed to ~~an~~ ***a*** husband, and not at all redeemed, nor freedom given her; she shall be scourged; they shall not be put to death, because she was not free.

21:1 And the LORD said unto Moses, Speak unto the priests the sons of Aaron, and say unto them, There shall none be defiled ~~for~~ ***with*** the dead among his people:
21:11 Neither shall he go in to ***touch*** any dead body, nor defile himself for his father, or ~~for~~ his mother;

22:9 They shall therefore keep mine ordinance, lest they bear sin for it, and die***;*** therefore, if they profane ~~it:~~ ***not mine ordinances,*** I the LORD do sanctify them.
22:10 There shall no stranger eat of the holy thing***;*** ~~:~~ a sojourner of the priest, or an hired servant, shall not eat of the holy thing.

23:3 Six days shall work be done***;*** ~~:~~ but the seventh day is the sabbath of rest, ~~an~~ ***a*** holy convocation; ye shall do no work therein***;*** ~~:~~ it is the sabbath of the LORD in all your dwellings.

LEVITICUS

23:7 In the first day ye shall have ~~an~~ ***a*** holy convocation: ye shall do no servile work therein.
23:8 But ye shall offer an offering made by fire unto the LORD seven days***;*** ~~:~~ in the seventh day is ~~an~~ ***a*** holy convocation***;*** ~~:~~ ye shall do no servile work therein.

23:12 And ye shall offer that day when ye wave the sheaf ~~an~~ ***a*** he lamb without blemish of the first year for a burnt offering unto the LORD.
23:13 And the meat offering thereof shall be two tenth deals of fine flour mingled with oil, an offering made by fire unto the LORD for a sweet savour***;*** ~~:~~ and the drink offering thereof shall be of wine, the fourth part of ~~an~~ ***a*** hin.

23:21 And ye shall proclaim on the selfsame day, that it may be ~~an~~ ***a*** holy convocation unto you***;*** ~~:~~ ye shall do no servile work therein***;*** ~~:~~ it shall be a statute for ever in all your dwellings throughout your generations.

23:24 Speak unto the children of Israel, saying, In the seventh month, in the first day of the month, shall ye have a sabbath, a memorial of blowing of trumpets, ~~an~~ ***a*** holy convocation.

23:27 Also on the tenth day of this seventh month there shall be a day of atonement***;*** ~~:~~ it shall be ~~an~~ ***a*** holy convocation unto you; and ye shall afflict your souls, and offer an offering made by fire unto the LORD.

23:35 On the first day shall be ~~an~~ ***a*** holy convocation***;*** ~~:~~ ye shall do no servile work therein.
23:36 Seven days ye shall offer an offering made by fire unto the LORD***;*** ~~:~~ on the eighth day shall be ~~an~~ ***a*** holy convocation unto you***,*** ~~;~~ and ye shall offer an offering made by fire unto the LORD***;*** ~~:~~ it is a solemn assembly; and ye shall do no servile work therein.

25:29 And if a man sell ~~a~~ ***his*** dwelling house in a walled city, then he may redeem it within a whole year after it is sold; within a full year may he redeem it.

25:40 But as ~~an~~ ***a*** hired servant, and as a sojourner, he shall be with thee, and shall serve thee unto the year of ~~jubile:~~ ***jubilee;***

22:50 And he shall reckon with him that bought him from the year that he was sold to him unto the year of ~~jubile:~~ ***jubilee;*** and the price of his sale shall be according unto the number of years, according to the time of ~~an~~ ***a*** hired servant shall it be with him.

26:8 And five of you shall chase ~~an~~ ***a*** hundred, and ~~an~~ ***a*** hundred of you shall put ten thousand to flight***;*** ~~:~~ and your enemies shall fall before you by the sword.

27:16 And if a man shall sanctify unto the LORD some part of a field of his possession, then thy estimation shall be according to the seed thereof***;*** ~~:~~ ~~an~~ ***a*** homer of barley seed shall be valued at fifty shekels of silver.

NUMBERS

2:9 All that were numbered in the camp of Judah were ~~an~~ ***a*** hundred thousand and four-score thousand and six thousand and four hundred, throughout their armies***;*** ~~:~~ ~~T~~***t***hese shall first set forth.

2:24 All that were numbered of the camp of Ephraim were ~~an~~ ***a*** hundred thousand and eight thousand and ~~an~~ ***a*** hundred, throughout their armies***;*** ~~:~~ ~~A~~***a***nd they shall go forward in the third rank. an hundred thousand and fifty and seven thousand and six hundred. They shall go hindmost with their standards.

2:31 All they that were numbered in the camp of Dan were ~~an~~ ***a*** hundred thousand and fifty and seven thousand and six hundred***;*** ~~:~~ ~~T~~***t***hey shall go hindmost with their standards.

3:9 And thou shalt give the Levites unto Aaron and to his sons: they are wholly given ~~unto~~ ***to*** him out of the children of Israel.

5:26 And the priest shall take ~~an~~ ***a*** handful of the offering, even the memorial thereof, and burn it upon the altar, and afterward shall cause the woman to drink the water.

7:1 And his offering was one silver charger, the weight ~~thereof~~ ***whereof*** was ~~an~~ ***a*** hundred and thirty shekels, one silver bowl of seventy shekels, after the shekel of the sanctuary; both of them were full of fine flour mingled with oil for a meat offering***;*** ~~:~~

14:2 And all the children of Israel murmured against Moses and against Aaron***;*** ~~:~~ and the whole congregation said unto them, Would God that we had died in the land of Egypt! or would God we had died in this wilderness!

14:10 ***And*** ~~But~~ all the congregation bade stone them with stones. And the glory of the LORD appeared in the tabernacle of the congregation before all the children of Israel.

15:15 One ordinance shall be both for you of the congregation, and also for ~~the~~ ***a*** stranger that sojourneth with you, an ordinance for ever in your generations***;*** ~~:~~ as ye are, so shall the stranger be before the LORD.

16:10 And he hath brought thee near to him, and all thy brethren the sons of Levi with thee***;*** ~~:~~ and seek ye the priesthood also?

22:6 Come now therefore, I pray thee, curse me this people; for they are too mighty for me***;*** ~~:~~ peradventure I shall prevail, that we may smite them, and that I may drive them out of the land***;*** ~~:~~ for I ~~wot~~ ***know*** that he whom thou blessest is blessed, and he whom thou cursest is cursed.

22:20 And God came unto Balaam at night, and said unto him, If the men come to call thee, rise up, ~~and~~ ***if thou wilt*** go with them; but yet the word which I shall say unto thee, that shalt thou ~~do~~ ***speak***.

33:39 And Aaron was ~~an~~ ***a*** hundred and twenty and three years old when he died in mount Hor.

34:10 And ye shall point out your east border from Hazar-enan to Shepham***;*** ~~:~~

DEUTERONOMY

2:30 But Sihon king of Heshbon would not let us pass by him***;*** ~~:~~ for ~~the LORD thy God~~ ***he*** hardened his spirit, and made his heart obstinate, that ~~he~~ ***the Lord thy God*** might deliver him into thy hand, as ~~appeareth~~ ***he hath done*** this day.

10:1 At that time the LORD said unto me, Hew thee two tables of stone like unto the first, and come up unto me ~~into~~ ***upon*** the mount, and make thee an ark of wood.
10:2 And I will write on the tables***,*** the words that were in the first tables which thou ~~brakest~~ ***breakest, save the words of the everlasting covenant of the holy priesthood***, and thou shalt put them in the ark.

14:21 Ye shall not eat of ~~any thing~~ ***anything*** that dieth of itself***;*** ~~:~~ thou shalt give it unto the stranger that is in thy gates, that he may eat it; or thou mayest ***not*** sell it unto an alien***;*** ~~:~~ for thou art ~~an~~ ***a*** holy people unto the LORD thy God. Thou shalt not seethe a kid in his mother's milk.

16:2 Thou shalt therefore sacrifice the passover unto the LORD thy God, of the flock and the herd, in the place ~~which~~ ***where*** the LORD shall choose to place his name there.

16:4 And there shall be no leavened bread seen with thee in all thy coast seven days; neither shall there any thing of the flesh, which thou sacrificedst the first day at even, remain all night until ~~the~~ morning.

16:22 Neither shalt thou set thee up any ***graven*** image; which the LORD thy God hateth.

18:4 The ~~firstfruit~~ ***first fruit*** also of thy corn, of thy wine, and of thine oil, and the first of the fleece of thy sheep, shalt thou give him.

34:6 ~~And he buried him~~ ***For the Lord took him unto his fathers,*** in a valley in the land of Moab, over against Beth-peor***;*** ~~:~~ ~~but~~ ***therefore*** no man knoweth of his sepulchre unto this day.

JOSHUA

2:5 And it came to pass about the time of shutting of the gate, when it was dark, that the men went out***;*** : whither the men went I ~~wot~~ ***know*** not***;*** ~~:~~ pursue after them quickly; for ye shall overtake them.

3:14 And it came to pass, when the people removed from their tents, to pass over ***the*** Jordan, and the priests bearing the ark of the covenant before the people;

8:31 As Moses the servant of the LORD commanded the children of Israel, as it is written in the book of the law of Moses, an altar of whole stones, over which no man hath lift up any iron***;*** ~~:~~ and they offered thereon burnt offerings unto the LORD, and sacrificed peace offerings.

11:6 And the LORD said unto Joshua, Be not afraid because of them***;*** ~~:~~ for ~~to-morrow~~ ***tomorrow*** about this time will I deliver them up all slain before Israel***;*** ~~:~~ thou shalt hough their horses, and burn their chariots with fire.

11:9 And Joshua did unto them as the LORD bade him***;*** ~~:~~ he houghed their horses, and burnt their chariots with fire.

11:20 For it was of the Lord to ***destroy them utterly, because they*** ~~harden~~ ***hardened*** their hearts, that they should come against Israel in battle***;*** ~~, that he might destroy the utterly, and~~ that they might have no ~~favour~~ ***favor***, ~~but~~ that ~~he~~ ***they*** might destroy them ***in battle***, as the Lord commanded Moses.

13:6 All the inhabitants of the hill country from Lebanon unto Misrephoth-maim, and all the Sidonians, them will I drive out from before the children of Israel***;*** ~~:~~ only divide thou it by lot unto the Israelites for an inheritance, as I have commanded thee.

17:5 And there fell ten portions to Manasseh, beside the land of Gilead and Bashan, which were on the other side ***of*** Jordan;

18:16 And the border came down to the end of the mountain that lieth before the valley of the son of Hinnom, and which is ~~in~~ the valley of the giants on the north, and descended to the valley of Hinnom, to the side of Jebusi on the south, and descended to En-rogel,

---

19:2 And they had in their inheritance Beer-sheba, ~~and~~ ***or*** Sheba, and Moladah,

---

22:31 And Phinehas the son of Eleazar the priest said unto the children of Reuben, and to the children of Gad, and to the children of Manasseh, This day we perceive that the LORD *is* among us, because ~~ye~~ ***we*** have not committed this trespass against the LORD***;*** ~~:~~ now ye have delivered the children of Israel out of the hand of the LORD.

JUDGES

2:18 And when the LORD raised them up judges, then the LORD was with the judge, and delivered them out of the hand of their enemies all the days of the judge***;*** ~~:~~ for ~~it repented~~ the LORD ***hearkened*** because of their groanings by reason of them that oppressed them and vexed them.

8:1 And the men of Ephraim said unto him, Why hast thou served us thus, that thou calledst ~~us~~not, when thou wentest to fight with the Midianites? And they did chide with him sharply.

9:29 And would to God ~~this~~ ***these*** people were under my hand! then would I remove Abimelech. And he said to Abimelech, Increase thine army, and come out.

9:54 Then he called hastily unto the young man his ~~armourbearer~~ ***armor-bearer***, and said unto him, Draw thy sword, and slay me, that ***the*** men say not of me, A woman slew him. And his young man thrust him through, and he died.

10:6 And the children of Israel did evil again in the sight of the LORD, and served Baalim, and Ashtaroth, and the gods of Syria, and the gods of Zidon, and the gods of Moab, and the gods of the children of Ammon, and the gods of the Philistines, and forsook the LORD, and served ***him*** not ~~him~~.

20:47 But six hundred men turned and fled to the wilderness unto the rock ***of*** Rimmon, and abode in the rock Rimmon four months.

RUTH

No JST changes to the Book of Ruth.

1st SAMUEL

1:17 Then Eli answered and said, Go in peace***;*** ~~:~~ and the God of Israel grant thee thy petition that thou hast asked of him.

7:9 And Samuel took a sucking lamb, and offered it for a burnt offering wholly unto the LORD***;*** ~~:~~ and Samuel cried unto the LORD for Israel; and the LORD heard him.

9:16 To-morrow about this time I will send thee a man out of the land of Benjamin, and thou shalt anoint him to be ***a*** captain over my people Israel, that he may save my people out of the hand of the Philistines***;*** ~~:~~ for I have looked upon my people, because their cry is come unto me.

11:2 And Nahash the Ammonite answered them, On this condition will I make a covenant with you, that I may thrust out all your right eyes, and lay it for a reproach ~~upon~~ ***in*** all Israel.

14:7 And his armourbearer said unto him, Do all that is in thine heart***;*** ~~:~~ turn thee; behold, I am with thee according to thy heart.

14:14 And that first slaughter, which Jonathan and his ~~armourbearer~~ ***armor-bearer*** made, was about twenty men, within as it were ~~an~~ ***a*** half acre of land, which a yoke of oxen might plow.

14:27 But Jonathan heard not when his father charged the people with the oath***;*** ~~:~~ wherefore he put forth the end of the rod that was in his hand, and dipped it in an honey-comb, and put his hand to his mouth; and his eyes were enlightened.

14:48 And he gathered ~~an~~ ***a*** host, and smote the Amalekites, and delivered Israel out of the hands of them that spoiled them.

15:11 ~~It repenteth me that~~ I have set up Saul to be ***a*** king, ~~:~~ ***and he repenteth not that he hath sinned,*** for he is turned back from following me, and hath not performed my commandments. And it grieved Samuel; and he cried unto the LORD all night.

15:35 And Samuel came no more to see Saul until the day of his death***;*** ~~:~~ nevertheless, Samuel mourned for Saul***;*** ~~:~~ and the LORD ~~repented that~~ ***rent the kingdom from Saul whom*** he had made ~~Saul~~ king over Israel.

16:2 And Samuel said, How can I go? if Saul hear it, he will kill me. And the LORD said, Take ~~an~~ ***a*** heifer with thee, and say, I am come to sacrifice to the LORD.

16:14 But the Spirit of the LORD departed from Saul, and an evil spirit ***which was not of*** ~~from~~ the LORD troubled him.
16:15 And Saul's servants said unto him, Behold now, an evil spirit ***which is not of*** ~~from~~ God troubleth thee.
16:16 Let our lord now command thy servants, which are before thee, to seek out a man, who is a cunning player on an harp***;*** ~~:~~ and it shall come to pass, when the evil spirit***, which is not of*** ~~from~~ God is upon thee, that he shall play with his hand, and thou shalt be well.

1st SAMUEL

16:23 And it came to pass, when the evil spirit***, which was not of*** ~~from~~ God was upon Saul, that David took an harp, and played with his hand***;*** ~~:~~ so Saul was refreshed, and was well, and the evil spirit departed from him.

17:5 And he had ~~an~~ ***a*** helmet of brass upon his head, and he was armed with a coat of mail; and the weight of the coat was five thousand shekels of brass.

17:38 And Saul armed David with his ~~armour~~ ***armor***, and he put ~~an~~ ***a*** helmet of brass upon his head; also he armed him with a coat of mail.

17:50 So David prevailed over the ~~Philistine~~ ***Philistines*** with a sling and with a stone, and smote the Philistine, and slew him; but there was no sword in the hand of David.

18:10 And it came to pass on the morrow, that the evil spirit ***which was not of*** ~~from~~ God came upon Saul, and he prophesied in the midst of the house***;*** ~~:~~ and David played with his hand, as at other times***;*** ~~:~~ and there was a javelin in Saul's hand.

18:25 And Saul said, Thus shall ye say to David, The king desireth not any dowry, but ~~an~~ ***a*** hundred foreskins of the Philistines, to be avenged of the king's enemies. But Saul thought to make David fall by the hand of the Philistines.

19:9 And the evil spirit ***which was not of*** ~~from~~ the LORD was upon Saul, as he sat in his house with his javelin in his hand***;*** ~~:~~ and David played with his hand.

24:18 And thou hast shewed this day how that thou hast dealt well with me***;*** ~~:~~ forasmuch as when the LORD had delivered me into ~~thine~~ ***thy*** hand, thou killedst me not.

25:18 Then Abigail made haste, and took two hundred loaves, and two bottles of wine, and five sheep ready dressed***,*** and five measures of parched corn, and ~~an~~ ***a*** hundred clusters of raisins, and two hundred cakes of figs, and laid them on asses.

28:9 And the woman said unto him, Behold, thou knowest what Saul hath done, how he hath cut off those that have familiar spirits, and the wizards, out of the land***;*** ~~:~~ wherefore then layest thou a snare for my life, to cause me to die ***also, who hath not a familiar spirit***?

28:11 Then said the woman, ***The word of*** ~~W~~***w***hom shall I bring up unto thee? And he said, Bring me up ***the word of*** Samuel
28:12 And when the woman saw ***the words of*** Samuel, she cried with a loud voice***;*** ~~:~~ and the woman spake to Saul, saying, Why hast thou deceived me? for thou art Saul.
28:13 And the king said unto her, Be not afraid***;*** ~~:~~ for what sawest thou? And the woman said unto Saul, I saw ~~gods~~ ***the words of Samuel*** ascending out of the earth. ***And she said, I saw Samuel also.***
28:14 And he said unto her, What form is he of? And she said, ***I saw*** ~~A~~n old man ~~cometh~~ ***coming*** up, ~~; and he is~~ covered with a mantle. And Saul perceived that it was Samuel, and he stooped***,*** ~~with~~ his face to the ground, and bowed himself.
28:15 And ***these are the words of*** Samuel ~~said~~ ***un***to Saul, Why hast thou disquieted me, to bring me up? And Saul answered, I am sore distressed; for the Philistines make war against me, and God is departed from me, and answereth me

1st SAMUEL

no more, neither by prophets, nor by dreams***;*** ~~:~~ therefore I have called thee, that thou mayest make known unto me what I shall do.

28:23 But he refused, and said, I will not eat. But his servants, together with the woman, compelled him; and he hearkened unto their voice. So he ~~arose~~ ***rose*** from the earth, and sat upon the bed.

30:12 And they gave him a piece of a cake of figs, and two clusters of raisins***;*** ~~:~~ and when he had eaten, his spirit came again to him***;*** ~~:~~ for he had eaten no bread, nor ~~drunk~~ ***drank*** any water, three days and three nights.

2nd SAMUEL

2:25 And the children of Benjamin gathered themselves together after Abner, and became one troop, and stood on the top of ~~an~~ ***a*** hill.
2:26 Then Abner called to Joab, and said, Shall the sword devour for ever? knowest thou not that it will be ***a*** bitterness in the latter end? how long shall it be then, ere thou bid the people return from following their brethren?

3:14 And David sent messengers to Ish-bosheth Saul's son, saying, Deliver me my wife Michal, which I espoused to me for ~~an~~ ***a*** hundred foreskins of the Philistines.

3:20 So Abner came to David to Hebron, and twenty men with him. And David made Abner and ~~the~~ ***his*** men that were with him a feast.

5:11 And Hiram king of Tyre sent messengers to David, and cedar trees, and carpenters, and masons***;*** ~~:~~ and they built David ~~an~~ ***a*** house.

5:16 And Elishama, and Eliada, ~~and~~ Eliphalet.

7:2 That the king said unto Nathan the prophet, See**,** now~~;~~ I dwell in ~~an~~ ***a*** house of cedar, but the ark of God dwelleth within curtains.

7:5 Go and tell my servant David, Thus saith the LORD, Shalt thou build me ~~an~~ ***a*** house for me to dwell in?

7:7 In all the places wherein I have walked with all the children of Israel spake I a word with any of the tribes of Israel, whom I commanded to feed my people Israel, saying, Why build ye not me ~~an~~ ***a*** house of cedar?

7:11 And as since the time that I commanded judges to be over my people Israel, and have caused thee to rest from all thine enemies. Also the LORD telleth thee that he will make thee ~~an~~ ***a*** house.

7:13 He shall build ~~an~~ ***a*** house for my name, and I will ~~establish~~ ***stablish*** the throne of his kingdom for ever.

7:27 For thou, O LORD of ~~h~~***H***osts, God of Israel, hast revealed to thy servant, saying, I will build thee ~~an~~ ***a*** house***;*** ~~:~~ therefore hath thy servant found in his heart to pray this prayer unto thee.

8:2 And he smote Moab, and measured them with a line, casting them down to the ground; even with two lines measured he to put to death, and ~~with~~ one full line to keep alive. And so the Moabites became David's servants, and brought gifts.

8:4 And David took from him a thousand chariots, and seven hundred horsemen, and twenty thousand footmen***;*** ~~:~~ and David houghed all the chariot horses, but reserved of them for ~~an~~ ***a*** hundred chariots.

11:11 And Uriah said unto David, The ark, and Israel, and Judah, abide in tents; and my lord Joab, and the servants of my lord, are encamped in the open fields; shall I then go into mine house, to eat and ~~to~~ drink, and to lie with my wife? as thou livest, and as thy soul liveth, I will not do this thing.

2nd SAMUEL

12:13 And David said unto Nathan, I have sinned against the LORD. And Nathan said unto David, The LORD also hath ***not*** put away thy sin~~;~~ ***that*** thou shalt not die.

13:15 Then Amnon hated her exceedingly; so that the hatred wherewith he hated her was greater than the love wherewith he had loved her. And Amnon said unto her, Arise, ~~be gone~~ ***begone***.

14:7 And, behold, the whole family is risen against thine handmaid, and they said, Deliver him that smote his brother, that we may kill him, for the life of his brother whom he slew; and we will destroy the heir also: and so they ~~shall~~ ***will*** quench my coal which is left, and shall not leave to my husband neither name nor remainder upon the earth.

16:1 And when David was a little past the top of the hill, behold, Ziba the servant of Mephibosheth met him, with a couple of asses saddled, and upon them two hundred loaves of bread, and ~~an~~ ***a*** hundred bunches of raisins, and ~~an~~ ***a*** hundred of summer fruits, and a bottle of wine.

20:18 Then she spake, saying, They ~~were~~ ***are*** wont to speak in old time, saying, They shall surely ask counsel at Abel: and so they ended the matter.

22:48 It is God that avengeth me, and that bringeth down the people ~~under~~ ***unto*** me,

---

23:14 And David was then in ~~an~~ ***a*** hold, and the garrison of the Philistines was then in Bethlehem.

24:3 And Joab said unto the king, Now the LORD thy ~~G~~***g***od add unto the people, how many soever they be, ~~an~~ ***a*** hundred-fold, and that the eyes of my lord the king may see it***;*** ~~:~~ but why doth my lord the king delight in this thing?

24:16 And when the angel stretched out his hand upon Jerusalem to destroy it, the LORD ***said unto*** ~~repented~~ him, ~~of the evil, and said to the angel that destroyed the people, It is enough:~~ ~~s~~***Stay*** now thine hand***, it is enough;*** ~~:~~ ***for the people repented, and the Lord stayed the hand of the angel, that he destroyed not the people.*** And the angel of the LORD was by the ~~threshingplace~~ ***threshing floor*** of Araunah***,*** the Jebusite.
24:17 And David spake unto the LORD when he saw the angel that smote the people, and said, Lo, I have sinned, and I have done wickedly***;*** ~~:~~ but these sheep, what have they done? let thine hand, I pray thee, be against me, and against my father's house.

1st KINGS

1:39 And Zadok the priest took ~~an~~ ***a*** horn of oil out of the tabernacle, and anointed Solomon. And they blew the trumpet; and all the people said, God save king Solomon.

2:24 Now therefore, as the LORD liveth, which hath established me, and set me on the throne of David my father, and who hath made me ~~an~~ ***a*** house, as he promised, Adonijah shall be put to death this day.

2:36 And the king sent and called for Shimei, and said unto him, Build thee ~~an~~ ***a*** house in Jerusalem, and dwell there, and go not forth thence any whither.

3:1 And ***the Lord was not pleased with*** Solomon***, for he*** made affinity with Pharaoh, king of Egypt, and took Pharaoh's daughter ***to wife***, and brought her into the ~~city~~ ***house*** of David~~,~~ until he had made an end of building his own house, and the house of the LORD, and the wall of Jerusalem round about. ***And the Lord blessed Solomon for the people's sake only.***

3:2 ***And*** ~~Only~~ the people sacrificed in high places, because there was no house built unto the name of the LORD, until those days.

3:3 And ***because the Lord blessed*** Solomon ~~loved the LORD,~~ ***as he was*** walking in the statutes of David, his father, ~~:~~ ***he began to love the Lord and*** ~~only~~ he sacrificed and burnt incense in high places***, and he called on the name of the Lord***.

3:4 And the king went to Gibeon to sacrifice there, ~~;~~ for ***Gibeon*** ~~that~~ was ~~the~~ ***in a*** great high place***;*** ~~:~~ ***and Solomon offered upon that altar, in Gibeon,*** a thousand burnt offerings ~~did Solomon offer upon that altar~~.

3:5 ***And*** ~~In Gibeon~~ the LORD ***hearkened unto Solomon, and*** appeared ***un***to ~~Solomon~~ ***him*** in a dream by night, ~~:~~ and ~~God~~ said, Ask what I shall give thee.

3:6 And Solomon said, Thou hast ~~shewed~~ ***showed*** unto thy servant David, my father, great ~~mercy,~~ ***things*** according ***to thy mercy,*** ~~as~~ ***when*** he walked before thee in truth, and in righteousness, and in ~~uprightness~~ ***uprighteousness*** of heart with thee; and thou hast kept for him this great kindness, that thou hast given him a son to sit on his throne ~~, as it is~~ this day.

3:7 And now, O LORD my God, thou hast made thy servant king, instead of David, my father, ~~:~~ ***over thy people.*** and ~~I am but a little child: I~~ I know not how to ***lead them, to*** go out, or come in ***before them***.

3:8 and ***I,*** thy servant***, am as a little child,*** ~~is~~ in the midst of thy people ~~which~~ ***whom*** thou hast chosen, a great people, that cannot be numbered, nor counted for multitude.

3:9 Give therefore thy servant an understanding heart to judge thy people, that I may discern between good and bad***;*** ~~:~~ for who is able to judge this thy ***people,*** so great a people?

3:12 Behold, I have done according to thy ~~words:~~ ***word;*** lo, I have given thee a wise and an understanding heart; so that there was none ***made king over Israel*** like ***unto*** thee before thee, neither after thee shall any arise like unto thee.

3:14 And if thou wilt walk in my ways, to keep my statutes, and my commandments, ***then I will lengthen thy days, and thou shalt not walk in unrighteousness,*** as ***did*** thy father David. ~~did walk, then I will lengthen thy days~~.

4:23 Ten fat oxen, and twenty oxen out of the pastures, and ~~an~~ ***a*** hundred sheep, beside harts, and roebucks, and ~~fallowdeer~~ ***fallow deer***, and fatted fowl.

1st KINGS

5:3 Thou knowest how that David my father could not build ~~an~~ ***a*** house unto the name of the LORD his God, for the wars which were about him on every side, until the LORD put them under the soles of his feet.

5:5 And, behold, I purpose to build ~~an~~ ***a*** house unto the name of the LORD my God, as the LORD spake unto David my father, saying, Thy son, whom I will set upon thy throne in thy room, he shall build an house unto my name.

6:1 And it came to pass in the four hundred and eightieth year after the children of Israel were come out of the land of Egypt, in the fourth year of Solomon's reign over Israel, in the month ***of*** Zif, which is the second month, that he began to build the house of the LORD.

6:2 And the house which king Solomon built for the LORD, the length thereof was ~~threescore~~ three-score cubits, and the breadth thereof twenty cubits, and the height thereof thirty cubits.

6:26 The height of ~~the~~ one cherub was ten cubits, and so was it of the other cherub.

7:2 He built also the house of the forest of Lebanon; the length thereof was ~~an~~ ***a*** hundred cubits, and the breadth thereof fifty cubits, and the height thereof thirty cubits, upon four rows of cedar pillars, with cedar beams upon the pillars.

7:8 And his house where he dwelt had another court within the porch, which was of the like work. Solomon made also ~~an~~ ***a*** house for Pharaoh's daughter, whom he had taken to wife, like unto this porch.

7:26 And it was an hand-breadth thick, and the brim thereof was wrought like the brim of a cup, with flowers of lilies***;*** ~~:~~ it contained two thousand baths.

8:13 I have surely built thee ~~an~~ ***a*** house to dwell in, a settled place for thee to abide in for ever.

8:16 Since the day that I brought forth my people Israel out of Egypt, I chose no city out of all the tribes of Israel to build ~~an~~ ***a*** house, that my name might be therein; but I chose David to be over my people Israel.

8:17 And it was in the heart of David my father to build ~~an~~ ***a*** house for the name of the LORD God of Israel.

8:18 And the LORD said unto David my father, Whereas it was in thine heart to build ~~an~~ ***a*** house unto my name, thou didst well that it was in thine heart.

8:20 And the LORD hath performed his word that he spake, and I am risen up in the room of David my father, and sit on the throne of Israel, as the LORD promised, and have built ~~an~~ ***a*** house for the name of the LORD God of Israel.

10:10 And she gave the king ~~an~~ ***a*** hundred and twenty talents of gold, and of spices very great store, and precious stones***;*** ~~:~~ there came no more such abundance of spices as these which the queen of Sheba gave to king Solomon.

10:29 And a chariot came up and went out of Egypt for six hundred shekels of silver, and an horse for ~~an~~ ***a*** hundred and fifty***;*** ~~:~~ and so for all the kings of the Hittites, and for the kings of Syria, did they bring them out by their means.

1st KINGS

11:4 For it came to pass, when Solomon was old, that his wives turned away his heart after other gods***;*** ~~:~~ and his heart was not perfect with the LORD his God, ***and it became*** as ~~was~~ the heart of David his father.

11:6 And Solomon did evil in the sight of the LORD, ***as did David his father,*** and went not fully after the LORD~~, as did David his father~~.
11:7 Then did Solomon build ~~an~~ ***a*** high place for Chemosh, the abomination of Moab, in the hill that is before Jerusalem, and for Molech, the abomination of the children of Ammon.

11:18 And they arose out of Midian, and came to Paran: and they took men with them out of Paran***;*** ~~,~~ and they came to Egypt, unto Pharaoh king of Egypt; which gave him ~~an~~ ***a*** house, and appointed him victuals, and gave him land.

11:33 Because that they have forsaken me, and have worshipped Ashtoreth the goddess of the Zidonians, Chemosh the god of the Moabites, and Milcom the god of the children of Ammon, and have not walked in my ways, to do that which is right in mine eyes, and to keep my statutes, and my judgments, ***and his heart is become as David his father; and he repenteth not*** as did David his father***, that I may forgive him***.
11:34 Howbeit, I will not take the whole kingdom out of his hand, ~~:~~ but I will make him prince all the days of his life, for David my servant's sake, whom I chose, because he kept my commandments and my statutes ***in that day.*** ~~:~~
11:35 But I will take the kingdom out of his son's hand, and will give it unto thee~~, even~~ ten tribes.
11:36 And unto his son will I give one tribe***.*** ~~, t~~***T***hat David my servant may have a light ~~alway~~ ***always*** before me in Jerusalem, the city which I have chosen me to put my name there.

11:38 And it shall be, if thou wilt hearken unto all that I command thee, and wilt walk in my ways, and do ~~that is~~ right in my sight, to keep my statutes and my commandments, as David my servant did ***in the day that I blessed him***; ~~that~~ I will be with thee, and build thee a sure house~~,~~ as I built for David, and ~~will~~ give Israel unto thee.
11:39 ***And for the transgression of David, and also for the people, I have rent the kingdom, ~~a~~A***nd ***for this*** I will for this afflict the seed of David, but not for ever.

12:2 And it came to pass, when Jeroboam the son of Nebat, who was yet in Egypt, heard of it, (for he was fled from the presence of king Solomon, and Jeroboam dwelt in Egypt, ~~;~~)

12:16 So when all Israel saw that the king hearkened not unto them, the people answered the king, saying, What portion have we in David? neither have we inheritance in the son of Jesse***;*** ~~:~~ to your tents, O Israel***;*** ~~:~~ now see to thine own house, David. So Israel departed unto their tents.

12:21 And when Rehoboam was come to Jerusalem, he assembled all the house of Judah, with the tribe of Benjamin, an hundred and four-score thousand chosen men, which were warriors, to fight against the house of Israel, to bring the kingdom again to Rehoboam the son of Solomon.

12:31 And he made ~~an~~ ***a*** house of high places, and made priests of the lowest of the people, which were not of the sons of Levi.

13:18 He said unto him, I am a prophet also, ***even*** as thou ~~art;~~ ***,*** and an angel spake unto me by the word of the LORD, saying, Bring him back with thee into

1st KINGS

thine house, that he may eat bread and drink water*, that I may prove him;* ~~.~~ ~~But~~
and he lied ***not*** unto him.

13:26 And when the prophet that brought him back from the way heard thereof, he said, It is the man of God, who was disobedient unto the word of the LORD*;* ~~:~~ therefore the LORD hath delivered him unto the lion, which hath torn him, and slain him, according to the word of the LORD, which he spake unto him.

14:8 And rent the kingdom away from the house of David, and gave it thee, ~~:~~
~~and yet thou hast~~ ***because he kept*** not ***my commandments. But thou hast not***
been as my servant David~~, who kept my commandments, and who~~ ***when he***
followed me with all his heart~~,~~ ***only*** to do ~~that only which was~~ right in mine eyes;

15:3 And he walked in all the sins of his father, which he had done before him*;* ~~:~~ and his heart was not perfect with the LORD his God, as ~~the heart of~~ ***the Lord commanded*** David his father.

15:5 Because David did ~~that which was~~ right in the eyes of the LORD, and turned not aside from ~~any thing~~ ***all*** that he commanded him***, to sin against the Lord; but repented of the evil*** all the days of his life, save only in the matter of Uriah the Hittite***, wherein the Lord cursed him***.

15:11 And Asa did ~~that which was~~ right in the eyes of the LORD, as ~~did~~ ***he commanded*** David his father.
15:12 And he took away the sodomites out of the land, and removed all the idols that his fathers had made***; and it pleased the Lord***.

18:4 For it was so, when Jezebel cut off the prophets of the LORD, that Obadiah took ~~an~~ ***a*** hundred prophets, and hid them by fifty in a cave, and fed them with bread and water.)

18:13 Was it not told my lord what I did when Jezebel slew the prophets of the LORD, how I hid ~~an~~ ***a*** hundred men of the LORD's prophets by fifty in a cave, and fed them with bread and water?

18:37 Hear me, O LORD, hear me, that this people may know that thou art the LORD God, and that thou ~~hast turned their~~ ***mayest turn*** their heart back again.

20:20 And they slew every one his man*;* ~~:~~ and the Syrians fled; and Israel pursued them*;* ~~:~~ and Ben-hadad the king of Syria escaped on ~~an~~ ***a*** horse with the horsemen.

2nd KINGS

1:9 Then the king sent unto him a captain of fifty with his fifty. And he went up to him***;*** ~~:~~ and, behold, he sat on the top of ~~an~~ ***a*** hill. And he spake unto him, Thou man of God, the king hath said, Come down.
1:10 And Elijah answered and said to the captain of fifty, If I be a man of God, then let fire come down ~~from~~ ***out of*** heaven, and consume thee and thy fifty. And there came down fire ~~from~~ ***out of*** heaven, and consumed him and his fifty.

1:12 And Elijah answered and said unto them, If I be a man of God, let fire come down ~~from~~ ***out of*** heaven, and consume thee and thy fifty. And the fire of God came down ~~from~~ ***out of*** heaven, and consumed him and his fifty.

1:14 Behold, there came fire down ~~from~~ ***out of*** heaven, and burnt up the two captains of the former fifties with their fifties***;*** ~~:~~ therefore let my life now be precious in thy sight.

4:9 And she said unto her husband, Behold now, I perceive that this is ~~an~~ ***a*** holy man of God, which passeth by us continually.

4:43 And his servitor said, What, should I set this before ~~an~~ ***a*** hundred men? He said again, Give the people, that they may eat***;*** ~~:~~ for thus saith the LORD, They shall eat, and shall leave thereof.

5:23 And Naaman said, Be content, take two talents. And he urged him, and bound two talents of silver in two bags, with two changes of garments, and laid them upon two of his servants; and they bare them before ~~him~~ ***them***.

8:10 And Elisha said unto him, ***Thou wilt*** ~~G~~***g***o, ***and*** say unto him, Thou mayest certainly recover***;*** ~~:~~ howbeit***,*** the LORD hath ~~shewed~~ ***showed*** me that he shall surely die.

18:33 Hath any of the gods of the nations delivered at all ~~his~~ ***this*** land out of the hand of the king of Assyria?

21:7 And he set a graven image of the grove that he had made in the house, of which the LORD said to David, and to Solomon his son, In this house, and in Jerusalem, which I have chosen out of all tribes of Israel, will I put my name for ever***.*** ~~:~~

25:5 And the army of the Chaldees pursued after the king, and overtook him in the plains of Jericho***;*** ~~:~~ and all his army ~~were~~ ***was*** scattered from him.

1st CHRONICLES

5:7 And his brethren by their families, when the genealogy of their generations ~~was~~ were reckoned, were the chief, Jeiel, and Zechariah,

5:21 And they took away their cattle; of their camels fifty thousand, and of sheep two hundred and fifty thousand, and of asses two thousand, and of men ~~an~~ ***a*** hundred thousand.

6:69 And Aijalon with her suburbs, and Gath-rimmon with her suburbs***;*** ~~:~~

8:40 And the sons of Ulam were mighty men of ~~valour~~ ***valor***, archers, and had many sons, and sons' sons~~, an~~ ***a*** hundred and fifty. All these are of the sons of Benjamin.

10:13 So Saul died for his transgression which he committed against the LORD, ~~even~~ ***or*** against the word of the LORD, which he kept not, and also for asking counsel of one that had a familiar spirit, to ~~enquire~~ ***inquire*** of it;

11:11 And this is the number of the mighty men whom David had; Jashobeam, an Hachmonite, the chief of the captains***;*** ~~:~~ he lifted up his spear against three hundred slain by him at one time.

12:25 Of the children of Simeon, mighty men of ~~valour~~ ***valor*** for the war, seven thousand ~~and~~ one hundred.

12:37 And on the other side of Jordan, of the Reubenites, and the Gadites, and of the half tribe of Manasseh, with all manner of instruments of war for the battle, ~~an~~ ***a*** hundred and twenty thousand.

14:1 Now Hiram king of Tyre sent messengers to David, and timber of cedars, with masons and carpenters, to build him ~~an~~ ***a*** house.

15:5 Of the sons of Kohath; Uriel the chief, and his brethren ~~an~~ ***a*** hundred and twenty***;*** ~~:~~

15:7 Of the sons of Gershom; Joel the chief, and his brethren ~~an~~ ***a*** hundred and thirty***;*** ~~:~~

15:10 Of the sons of Uzziel; Amminadab the chief, and his brethren ~~an~~ ***a*** hundred and twelve.

17:1 Now it came to pass, as David sat in his house, that David said to Nathan the prophet, Lo, I dwell in ~~an~~ ***a*** house of cedars, but the ark of the covenant of the LORD remaineth under curtains.

17:4 Go and tell David my servant, Thus saith the LORD, Thou shalt not build me ~~an~~ ***a*** house to dwell in***;*** ~~:~~
17:5 For I have not dwelt in ~~an~~ ***a*** house since the day that I brought up Israel unto this day; but have gone from tent to tent, and from one tabernacle to another.
17:6 Wheresoever I have walked with all Israel, spake I a word to any of the judges of Israel, whom I commanded to feed my people, saying, Why have ye not built me ~~an~~ ***a*** house of cedars?

1st CHRONICLES

17:10 And since the time that I commanded judges to be over my people Israel. Moreover I will subdue all thine enemies. Furthermore, I tell thee that the LORD will build thee ~~an~~ ***a*** house.

17:12 He shall build me ~~an~~ ***a*** house, and I will stablish his throne for ever.

17:20 O LORD, there is none like thee, neither is there any God ~~beside~~ ***besides*** thee, according to all that we have heard with our ears.

17:25 For thou, O my God, hast told thy servant that thou wilt build him ~~an~~ ***a*** house***;*** ~~:~~ therefore thy servant hath found in his heart to pray before thee.

18:3 And David smote Hadarezer king of Zobah unto Hamath, as he went to ~~stablish~~ ***establish*** his dominion by the river Euphrates.
18:4 And David took from him a thousand chariots, and seven thousand horsemen, and twenty thousand footmen***;*** ~~:~~ David also houghed all the chariot horses, but reserved of them ~~an~~ ***a*** hundred chariots.

21:3 And Joab answered, The LORD make his people ~~an~~ ***a*** hundred times so many more as they be***;*** ~~:~~ but, my lord the king, are they not all my lord's servants? why then doth my lord require this thing? why will he be a cause of trespass to Israel?

21:5 And Joab gave the sum of the number of the people unto David. And all they of Israel were a thousand thousand and ~~an~~ ***a*** hundred thousand men that drew sword***;*** ~~:~~ and Judah was four hundred three-score and ten thousand men that drew sword.

21:15 And God sent an angel unto Jerusalem to destroy it***.*** ~~:~~ ~~a~~***A***nd ***the angel stretched forth his hand unto Jerusalem to destroy it; and God said to the angel, Stay now thine hand, it is enough; for*** as he was destroying, the LORD beheld ***Israel***, ~~and~~ ***that*** he repented him of the evil***;*** ~~;~~ ~~and said to~~ ***therefore the Lord stayed*** the angel that destroyed, ~~It is enough, stay now thine hand. And the angel of the LORD~~ ***as he*** stood by the threshing-floor of Ornan, the Jebusite.

21:20 ***Now Ornan was threshing wheat, and his four sons with him;*** ~~A~~***a***nd Ornan turned back, and saw the angel; and ~~his four sons with him~~ ***they*** hid themselves. ~~Now Ornan was threshing wheat.~~

22:6 Then he called for Solomon his son, and charged him to build ~~an~~ ***a*** house for the LORD God of Israel.
22:7 And David said to Solomon, My son, as for me, it was in my mind to build ~~an~~ ***a*** house unto the name of the LORD my God***;*** ~~:~~
22:8 But the word of the LORD came to me, saying, Thou hast shed blood abundantly, and hast made great wars***;*** ~~:~~ thou shalt not build ~~an~~ ***a*** house unto my name, because thou hast shed much blood upon the earth in my sight.

22:10 He shall build ~~an~~ ***a*** house for my name; and he shall be my son, and I will be his father; and I will establish the throne of his kingdom over Israel for ever.

22:14 Now, behold, in my trouble I have prepared for the house of the LORD ~~an~~ ***a*** hundred thousand talents of gold, and a thousand thousand talents of silver; and of brass and iron without weight; for it is in abundance***;*** ~~:~~ timber also and stone have I prepared; and thou mayest add thereto.

1st CHRONICLES

25:31 The four and twentieth to Romamti-ezer, ~~he,~~ his sons, and his brethren, were twelve.

28:2 Then David the king stood up upon his feet, and said, Hear me, my brethren, and my people***;*** ~~:~~ As for me, I had in mine heart to build an house of rest for the ark of the covenant of the LORD, and for the footstool of our God, and had made ready for the building***;*** ~~:~~
28:3 But God said unto me, Thou shalt not build ~~an~~ ***a*** house for my name, because thou hast been a man of war, and hast shed blood.

28:10 Take heed now; for the LORD hath chosen thee to build ~~an~~ ***a*** house for the sanctuary***;*** ~~:~~ be strong, and do it.

29:16 O LORD our God, all this store that we have prepared to build thee ~~an~~ ***a*** house for thine holy name cometh of thine hand, and is all thine own.

2nd CHRONICLES

1:17 And they fetched up, and brought forth out of Egypt a chariot for six hundred shekels of silver, and an horse for ~~an~~ ***a*** hundred and fifty***;*** ~~:~~ and so brought they out horses for all the kings of the Hittites, and for the kings of Syria, by their means.

2:1 And Solomon determined to build ~~an~~ ***a*** house for the name of the LORD, and ~~an~~ ***a*** house for his kingdom.

2:3 And Solomon sent to Huram the king of Tyre, saying, As thou didst deal with David my father, and didst send him cedars to build him ~~an~~ ***a*** house to dwell therein, ***therefore,*** even so deal with me.
2:4 Behold, I build ~~an~~ ***a*** house to the name of the LORD my God, to dedicate it to him, and to burn before him sweet incense, and for the continual ~~shewbread~~ ***showbread***, and for the burnt offerings morning and evening, on the sabbaths, and on the new moons, and on the solemn feasts of the LORD our God. ***And*** ~~T~~***t***his ~~is an~~ ordinance ***shall be kept in Israel*** for ever ~~to Israel~~.
2:5 And the house which I build ~~is~~ ***shall be a*** great ***house;*** ~~:~~ for great is ***the Lord*** our God above all gods.
2:6 But who is able to build him ~~an~~ ***a*** house, seeing the heaven and heaven of heavens cannot contain him? who am I then, that I should build him ~~an~~ ***a*** house, save only to burn sacrifice before him?
2:7 Send me now therefore a man cunning to work in gold, and in silver, and in brass, and in iron, and in purple, and crimson, and blue, and that ~~can~~ ***has*** skill to grave with the cunning men that are with me in Judah and in Jerusalem, whom David my father did provide.
2:8 Send me also cedar trees, fir trees, and algum trees, out of Lebanon***;*** ~~:~~ for I know that thy servants ~~can~~ ***have*** skill to cut timber in Lebanon; and, behold, ***I will send*** my servants ~~shall be~~ with thy servants,

2:12 Huram said moreover, Blessed be the LORD God of Israel, that made heaven and earth, who hath given to David the king a wise son, endued with prudence and understanding, that might build ~~an~~ ***a*** house for the LORD, and ~~an~~ ***a*** house for his kingdom.

2:17 And Solomon numbered all the strangers that were in the land of Israel, after the numbering wherewith David his father had numbered them; and they were found ~~an~~ ***a*** hundred and fifty thousand and three thousand and six hundred.
2:18 And he set three-score and ten thousand of them to be bearers of burdens, and four-score thousand to be hewers in the mountain, and three thousand and six hundred overseers to set the people ~~a~~ ***at*** work.

3:4 And the porch that was in the front of the house, the length of it was according to the breadth of the house, twenty cubits, and the height was ~~an~~ ***a*** hundred and twenty***;*** ~~:~~ and he overlaid it within with pure gold.

3:16 And he made chains, as in the oracle, and put them on the heads of the pillars; and made ~~an~~ ***a*** hundred pomegranates, and put them on the chains.

4:5 And the thickness of it was ~~an~~ ***a*** hand-breadth, and the brim of it like the work of the brim of a cup***;*** ~~,~~ with flowers of lilies; and it received and held three thousand baths.

4:8 He made also ten tables, and placed them in the temple, five on the right side, and five on the left. And he made ~~an~~ ***a*** hundred ~~basons~~ ***basins*** of gold.

2nd CHRONICLES

5:12 Also the Levites which were the singers, all of them of Asaph, of Heman, of Jeduthun, with their sons and their brethren, being arrayed in white linen, having cymbals and psalteries and harps, stood at the east end of the altar, and with them ~~an~~ ***a*** hundred and twenty priests sounding with trumpets***;*** ~~:~~)

6:2 But I have built ~~an~~ ***a*** house of habitation for thee, and a place for thy dwelling for ever.

6:5 Since the day that I brought forth my people out of the land of Egypt I chose no city among all the tribes of Israel to build ~~an~~ ***a*** house in, that my name might be there; neither chose I any man to be a ruler over my people Israel***;*** ~~:~~

6:7 Now it was in the heart of David my father to build ~~an~~ ***a*** house for the name of the LORD God of Israel.
6:8 But the LORD said to David my father, Forasmuch as it was in thine heart to build ~~an~~ ***a*** house for my name, thou didst well in that it was in thine heart***;*** ~~:~~

6:17 Now then, O LORD God of Israel, let ~~thy~~ ***the*** word be verified, which thou hast spoken unto thy servant David.

7:5 And king Solomon offered a sacrifice of twenty and two thousand oxen, and ~~an~~ ***a*** hundred and twenty thousand sheep***.*** ~~:~~ ~~s~~***S***o the king and all the people dedicated the house of God.

7:12 And the LORD appeared to Solomon by night, and said unto him, I have heard thy prayer, and have chosen this place to myself for ~~an~~ ***a*** house of sacrifice.

7:22 And it shall be answered, Because they forsook the LORD God of their fathers, which brought them forth out of the land of Egypt, and laid hold on other gods, and worshipped them, and served them***;*** ~~:~~ therefore hath he brought ~~all this~~ evil upon them.

9:9 And she gave the king ~~an~~ ***a*** hundred and twenty talents of gold, and of spices great abundance, and precious stones***;*** ~~:~~ neither was there any such spice as the queen of Sheba gave king Solomon.

9:14 ***Besides*** ~~Beside~~ that which chapmen and merchants brought. And all the kings of Arabia and governors of the country brought gold and silver to Solomon.

11:1 And when Rehoboam was come to Jerusalem, he gathered of the house of Judah and Benjamin ~~an~~ ***a*** hundred and four-score thousand chosen men, which were warriors, to fight against Israel, that he might bring the kingdom again to Rehoboam.

12:3 With twelve hundred chariots, and three-score thousand horsemen***;*** ~~:~~ and the people were without number that came with him out of Egypt; the ~~Lubims~~ ***Lubim,*** the ~~Sukkiims~~ ***Sukkiim***, and the Ethiopians.

13:3 And Abijah set the battle in array with an army of valiant men of war, even four hundred thousand chosen men***;*** ~~:~~ Jeroboam also set the battle in array against him with eight hundred thousand ~~chosen~~ men, being mighty men of ~~valour~~ ***valor***.

2nd CHRONICLES

14:9 And there came out against them Zerah the Ethiopian with ~~an~~ ***a*** host of a thousand thousand, and three hundred chariots; and came unto Mareshah.

16:2 Then Asa brought out silver and gold out of the treasures of the house of the LORD and of the king's house, and sent to ~~Ben-hadad~~ ***Benhadad*** king of Syria, that dwelt at Damascus, saying,

16:8 Were not the Ethiopians and the ~~Lubims~~ ***Lubim*** a huge host, with very many chariots and horsemen? yet, because thou didst rely on the LORD, he delivered them into thine hand.

17:18 And next him was Jehozabad, and with him ~~an~~ ***a*** hundred and four-score thousand ready prepared for the war.

18:20 Then there came out a ***lying*** spirit, and stood before ~~the LORD~~ ***them***, and said, I will entice him. And the LORD said unto him, Wherewith?
18:21 And he said, I will go out, and be a lying spirit in the mouth of all his prophets. And the LORD said, Thou shalt entice him, and thou shalt also prevail***;*** ~~:~~ go out, and do even ***so; for all these have sinned against me.***
18:22 Now therefore, behold, the LORD hath ~~put~~ ***found*** a lying spirit in the mouth of these thy prophets, and the LORD hath spoken evil against thee.

20:2 Then there came some that told Jehoshaphat, saying, There cometh a great multitude against thee from beyond the sea on this side Syria; and, behold, they ~~be~~ ***are*** in Hazazon-tamar, which ~~is~~ ***was called*** En-gedi.

20:6 And said, O LORD God of our fathers, ~~art not~~ thou God ***who are*** in heaven***;***
~~?~~ and rulest ~~not thou~~ over all the kingdoms of the heathen***;*** ~~?~~ and in ~~thine~~ ***thy*** hand ~~is there not~~ ***thou hast*** power and might, so that none is able to withstand thee***;*** ~~?~~
20:7 ~~Art not~~ ~~t~~***T***hou our God~~, who~~ didst drive out the inhabitants of this land before thy people Israel, and gavest it to the seed of Abraham thy friend for ever. ~~?~~

20:11 Behold, ~~I say, how~~ they reward us ***not***, ~~to~~ ***but have*** come to cast us out of thy possession, which thou hast given us to inherit.

20:17 Ye shall not ~~need~~ ***go*** to fight in this ~~battle~~ ***day;*** ~~:~~ set yourselves, stand ye still, and see the salvation of the LORD with you, O Judah and Jerusalem***;*** ~~:~~ fear not, nor be dismayed; ~~to morrow~~ ***to-morrow*** go out against them***;*** ~~:~~ for the LORD will be with you.

20:29 And the fear of God was on all the kingdoms of those countries, when they had heard that the LORD ***had*** fought against the enemies of Israel.

22:2 ~~Forty and two~~ ***Two and twenty*** years old was Ahaziah when he began to reign, and he reigned one year in Jerusalem. His mother's name also was Athaliah the daughter of Omri.

24:9 And they made a proclamation through Judah and Jerusalem, to bring in to the LORD the collection ~~that~~ Moses the servant of God laid upon Israel in the wilderness.

2nd CHRONICLES

24:15 But Jehoiada waxed old, and was full of days when he died; ~~an~~ ***a*** hundred and thirty years old was he when he died.

24:22 Thus Joash the king remembered not the kindness which Jehoiada his father had done to him, but slew his son. And when he died~~,~~ he said, The LORD look upon ~~it~~ ***me***, and require ~~it~~ ***me***.

25:6 He hired also ~~an~~ ***a*** hundred thousand mighty men of ~~valour~~ ***valor*** out of Israel for ~~an~~ ***a*** hundred talents of silver.

25:18 And Joash king of Israel sent to Amaziah king of Judah, saying, The thistle that ~~was~~ ***grew*** in Lebanon sent to the cedar that ~~was~~ ***grew*** in Lebanon, saying, Give thy daughter to my son to wife***;*** ~~:~~ and there passed by a wild beast that was in Lebanon***;*** ~~,~~ and trode down the thistle.

26:11 Moreover Uzziah had ~~an~~ ***a*** host of fighting men, that went out to war by bands, according to the number of their account by the hand of Jeiel the scribe and Maaseiah the ruler, under the hand of Hananiah, one of the king's captains.

27:5 He fought also with the king of the Ammonites, and prevailed against them. And the children of Ammon gave him the same year ~~an~~ ***a*** hundred talents of silver, and ten thousand measures of wheat, and ten thousand of barley. So much did the children of Ammon pay unto him, both the second year, and the third.

28:6 For Pekah the son of Remaliah slew in Judah ~~an~~ ***a*** hundred and twenty thousand in one day, which were all valiant men; because they had forsaken the LORD God of their fathers.

28:9 But a prophet of the LORD was there, whose name was Oded***;*** ~~:~~ and he went out before the host that came to Samaria, and said unto them, Behold, because the LORD God of your fathers was wroth with Judah, he hath delivered them into your hand, and ye have slain them in a rage that reacheth up unto heaven.

29:32 And the number of the burnt offerings, which the congregation brought, was three-score and ten bullocks, ~~an~~ ***a*** hundred rams, and two hundred lambs***;*** ~~:~~ all these were for a burnt offering to the LORD.

30:16 And they stood in their ~~place~~ ***places*** after their manner, according to the law of Moses the man of God***;*** ~~:~~ the priests sprinkled the blood, which they received of the hand of the Levites.

31:16 ~~Beside~~ ***Besides*** their genealogy of males, from three years old and upward, even unto every one that entereth into the house of the LORD, his daily portion for their service in their charges according to their courses***;*** ~~:~~

33:10 And the LORD spake to Manasseh, and to his people***;*** ~~:~~ but they would not hearken.

2nd CHRONICLES

34:16 And Shaphan carried the book to the king, and brought the ***word of the*** king ~~word~~ back again, saying, All that was committed to thy servants, they do ~~it.~~

36:3 And the king of Egypt put him down at Jerusalem, and condemned the land in ~~an~~ ***a*** hundred talents of silver and a talent of gold.

36:23 Thus saith Cyrus king of Persia, All the kingdoms of the earth hath the LORD God of heaven given me; and he hath charged me to build him ~~an~~ ***a*** house in Jerusalem, which is in Judah. Who is there among you of all his people? The LORD his God be with him, and let him go up.

EZRA

No JST changes to the Book of Ezra.

NEHEMIAH

4:8 And conspired all of them together to come and ~~to~~ fight against Jerusalem, and to hinder it.

6:11 And I said, Should such a man as I flee? and who is ~~there~~ ***mine enemy***, that~~;~~ ~~being~~ ***such as man*** as I ~~am,~~ would go into the temple to save his life? I will not go in.

6:13 Therefore ~~was he hired, that I~~ should ***I*** be afraid ***of him he hired***, and do ~~so~~ ***as he said***, and sin, and that they might have ~~matter~~ ***me*** for an evil report, that they might reproach me.

7:10 The children of Arah, ~~six~~ ***seven*** hundred ~~fifty and two~~ ***seventy and five***.
7:11 The children of Pahath-moab, of the children of Jeshua and Joab, two thousand and eight hundred and ~~eighteen~~ ***twelve***.

7:13 The children of Zattu, ~~eight~~ ***nine*** hundred forty and five.

7:15 The children of ~~Binnui~~ ***Bani***, six hundred forty and ~~eight~~ ***two***.
7:16 The children of Bebai, six hundred twenty and ~~eight~~ ***three***.

7:18 The children of Adonikam, six hundred ~~threescore and seven~~ ***sixty and six***.
7:19 The children of Bigvai, two thousand ~~threescore and seven~~ ***fifty and six***.
7:20 The children of Adin, ~~six~~ *four* hundred fifty and ~~five~~ ***four***.

7:22 The children of Hashum, ~~three~~ ***two*** hundred twenty and ~~eight~~ ***three***.
7:23 The children of Bezai, three hundred twenty and ~~four~~ ***three***.
7:24 The children of ~~Hariph~~ ***Jorah***, ~~an~~ ***a*** hundred and twelve.

7:32 The men of Beth-el and Ai, ~~an~~ ***two*** hundred twenty and three.

7:37 The children of Lod, Hadid, and Ono, seven hundred twenty and ~~one~~ ***five***.

NEHEMIAH

7:38 The children of Senaah, three thousand ~~nine~~ ***six*** hundred and thirty.

7:44 The singers~~:~~ ***of*** the children of Asaph, ~~an~~ ***a*** hundred forty and eight.
7:45 The porters***;*** ~~:~~ the children of Shallum, the children of Ater, the children
of Talmon, the children of Akkub, the children of Hatita, the children of Shobai,
~~an~~ ***a*** hundred thirty and ~~eight~~ ***nine***.

7:62 The children of Delaiah, the children of Tobiah, the children of Nekoda,
six hundred ~~forty~~ ***fifty*** and two.

10:29 They clave to their brethren, their nobles, and entered into ***an oath that*** a
curse~~, and into an oath , to~~ ***should come upon them if they did not*** walk in God's
law, which was given by Moses the servant of God, and to observe and do all the
commandments of the LORD ~~our Lord~~ ***their God***, and his judgments and his
statutes***.*** ~~;~~
10:30 And that ~~we~~ ***they*** would not give ~~our~~ ***their*** daughters unto the people of the
land, nor take ~~their~~ ***the*** daughters ***of the people*** for ~~our~~ ***their*** sons***.*** ~~:~~

ESTHER

No JST changes to the Book of Esther.

JOB

1:6 Now there was a day when the ~~sons~~ ***children*** of God came to present
themselves before the LORD, and Satan came also among them.

2:1 Again there was a day when the ~~sons~~ ***children*** of God came to present
themselves before the LORD, and Satan came also among them to present himself
before the LORD.

4:8 Even as I have seen, they that ~~plow~~ ***plough*** iniquity, and sow wickedness,
reap the same.

16:1 I was at ease, but he hath broken me asunder***;*** ~~:~~ he hath also taken me by
my neck, and shaken me to pieces, and set me up for his mark.

39:14 Which leaveth her eggs in the earth, and warmeth them in ***the*** dust,

---

PSALMS

10:6 He hath said in his heart, I shall not be moved***;*** ~~:~~ ~~for I shall~~ never be in adversity.
10:7 His mouth is full of cursing and deceit***;*** and ***his heart is full of*** fraud***;*** ~~:~~ ***and*** under his tongue is mischief and vanity.

10:10 He croucheth ***to the strong ones***, and humbleth himself, that the poor may fall by his ~~strong ones~~ ***devices***.

10:13 ~~Wherefore doth t~~***T***he wicked ~~contemn~~ ***condemn*** God***;*** ~~?~~ ***wherefore*** he ~~hath said~~ ***doth say*** in his heart, Thou wilt not require ~~it~~ ***iniquity at my hand***.
10:14 ***O Lord,*** ~~T~~***t***hou hast seen ~~it~~ ***all this***; for thou beholdest mischief and spite, to requite it with thy hand***.*** ~~:~~ ~~t~~***T***he poor committeth himself unto thee; thou art the helper of the fatherless.
10:15 ***O Lord, thou wilt*** ~~B~~***b***reak ~~thou~~ the arm of the wicked, and ***of*** the evil ~~man;~~ ~~:~~ ***and*** seek out his wickedness ~~till~~ ***until*** thou find none ***that remaineth***.
10:16 The LORD ~~is~~ ***shall be*** King for ever and ever ***over his people;*** ~~:~~ ~~the heathen are perished~~ ***for the wicked shall perish*** out of his land.

11:1 ~~In the LORD put I my trust: How say ye to my soul, Flee as a bird to your mountain?~~ ***In that day thou shalt come, O Lord; and I will put my trust in thee. Though shalt say unto thy people, for mine ear hath heard thy voice; thous shalt say unto every soul, Flee unto my mountain; and the righteous shall flee like a bird that is let go from the snare of the fowler.***
11:2 For~~, lo,~~ the wicked bend their bow***;*** ~~;~~ ***lo,*** they make ready their arrow upon the string, that they may privily shoot at the upright in heart ***to destroy their foundation***.
11:3 ~~If~~ ***But*** the foundations ***of the wicked shall*** be destroyed, ***and*** what can ~~the righteous~~ ***they*** do?
11:4 ***For*** ~~T~~***t***he LORD ***when he shall come into*** ~~is in~~ his holy temple, ***sitting upon*** ~~the LORD's~~ ***God's*** throne ~~is~~ in heaven, ~~:~~ his eyes ***shall pierce the wicked.*** ~~b~~***B***ehold, his eyelids try~~,~~ the children of ***men, and he shall redeem the righteous, and they shall be tried..***
11:5 The LORD ~~trieth~~ ***loveth*** the righteous, ~~:~~ but the wicked, and him that loveth violence, his soul hateth.
11:6 Upon the wicked he shall rain snares, fire and brimstone, and ~~an~~ ***a*** horrible tempest, ~~:~~ ~~this shall be~~ the portion of their cup.

12:1 ***In that day thou shalt*** ~~H~~***h***elp, ***O*** LORD***, the poor and the meek of the earth.*** ~~;~~ ~~f~~***F***or the godly man ***shall*** ~~ceaseth~~ ***cease to be found***; ~~for~~ ***and*** the faithful fail from among the children of men.
12:2 They ***shall*** speak vanity every one with his ~~neighbour:~~ ***neighbor;*** with flattering lips, ~~and~~ with a double heart do they speak.
12:3 ***But*** ~~T~~***t***he LORD shall cut off all flattering lips, ~~and~~ the tongue that speaketh proud things, ~~:~~
12:4 Who have said, With our tongue will we prevail, ~~;~~ our lips are our own, ~~:~~ who ~~is~~ ***shall be*** lord over us?
12:5 ***Therefore, thus saith the Lord, I will arise in that day, I will stand upon the earth, and I will judge the earth*** ~~F~~***f***or the oppression of the poor, for the sighing of the needy ; ~~;~~ ***and their cry hath entered into mine ear.*** ~~Now will I arrise, saith the Lord;~~ ***Therefore the Lord will sit in judgment upon all those who say in their hearts,*** ~~I will set him in safety from him that~~ ***We all sit in safety; and*** puffeth at him.
12:6 ~~The~~ ***These are the*** words of the LORD***; yea,*** ~~are~~ pure words, ~~:~~ ~~as~~ ***like*** silver tried in a furnace of earth, purified seven times.
12:7 ***Thou shalt save thy people, O Lord;*** ~~T~~***t***hou shalt keep them ~~, O LORD,~~ ***;*** thou shalt preserve them from ***the wickedness of*** ~~this generation~~ ***their generations*** for ever.

PSALMS

12:8 The wicked walk on every side, ~~when~~ ***and*** the vilest men are exalted***; but in the day of their pride thou shalt visit them***.

13:1 How long***, O Lord,*** wilt thou ~~forget~~ ***withdraw theyself from*** me, ~~O LORD? for ever?~~ ***H***ow long wilt thou hide thy face from ***me, that I may not see thee? Wilt thou forget me, and cast me off from thy presence for ever?***
13:2 How long shall I take counsel in my soul, having sorrow in my heart daily? ~~h~~***H***ow long shall mine enemy be exalted over me?
13:3 Consider ~~and hear~~ me, O LORD***; and hear my cry, O*** my God***;*** ~~:~~ ***and*** lighten mine eyes, lest I sleep the ~~sleep~~ of death ***of the ungodly***;
13:4 Lest mine enemy say, I have prevailed against him***.*** ~~;~~ ~~and~~ ~~t~~***T***hose that trouble me***,*** rejoice when I am moved.

14:1 The fool hath said in his heart, ***there is no man that hath seen God Because he showeth himself not unto us, therefore*** there is no God. ***Behold,*** ~~T~~ ***t***hey are corrupt***;*** ~~;~~ they have done abominable works, ~~there is~~ ***and*** none ~~that~~ ***of them*** doeth good.
14:2 ***For*** ~~T~~***t***he LORD looked down from heaven upon the children of men~~,~~***and by his voice said unto his servant, Seek ye among the children of men,*** to see if there ~~were~~ ***are*** any that ~~did~~ ***do*** understand~~, and seek~~ God. ***And he opened his mouth unto the Lord, and said, Behold, all these who say they are thine.***
14:3 ***The Lord answered, and said,*** They are all gone aside, they are ~~all~~ together become filthy***,*** ~~:~~ ***thou canst behold*** ~~there is~~ none ***of them*** that ~~doeth~~ ***are doing*** good, no, not one.
14:4 ~~Have all the~~ ***All they have for their teachers are*** workers of iniquity***, and there is*** no knowledge~~?~~ ***in them. They are they*** who eat up my people***.*** ~~as they~~ ***They*** eat bread~~;~~ and call not upon the LORD.
14:5 There ~~were they~~ ***are*** in great fear, ~~:~~ for God ~~is~~ ***dwells*** in the generation of the righteous. ***He is the counsel of the poor, because they are ashamed of the wicked, and flee unto the Lord, for their refuge.***
14:6 ~~Ye have shamed~~ ***They are ashamed of*** the counsel of the poor~~;~~ because the LORD is his refuge.
14:7 Oh that ***Zion were established out of heaven,*** the salvation of Israel***.*** ~~were come out of Zion!~~ ***O Lord, when wilt thou establish Zion?*** ~~w~~***W***hen the LORD bringeth back the captivity of his people, Jacob shall rejoice, ~~and~~ Israel shall be glad.

15:1 LORD, who shall abide in thy tabernacle? who shall dwell in thy holy hill ***of Zion*** ?

15:4 In whose eyes a vile person is contemned; but he ~~honoureth~~ ***honoreth*** them that fear the LORD***;*** ~~:~~ ~~He that sweareth to his own hurt~~ ***sweareth not falsely to hurt any man***, and changeth not.

16:2 ~~O my soul,~~ ~~t~~***T***hou hast said unto ~~the LORD,~~ ***me that*** ~~T~~***t***hou art ~~my~~ ***the*** Lord ***my God, and,*** ~~:~~ my goodness ***is*** extendeth ~~not to~~ ***unto*** thee;
16:3 ~~But~~ ***And*** to ***all*** the saints that ~~are~~ ***dwell*** in the earth, and ~~to~~ the excellent, in whom is all my delight.
16:4 ***And the wicked, there is no delight in them;*** ~~T~~***t***heir sorrows shall be multiplied ***upon all those who*** ~~that~~ hasten ~~after~~ ***for to seek*** another god***;*** ~~:~~ their drink offerings of blood will I not ~~offer~~ ***accept***, nor take up their names into my lips.
16:5 ~~The LORD is~~ ***Therefore thou, Lord, art*** the portion of mine inheritance, and of my cup***;*** ~~:~~ thou maintainest my lot.

PSALMS

17:1 ~~Hear the~~ ***Give me*** right ***words***, O LORD***; speak, and thy servant shall hear thee;*** attend unto my cry, ***and*** give ear unto my prayer~~. , that goeth~~ ***I come*** not ***unto thee*** out of feigned lips.

17:3 Thou hast proved mine heart; thou hast visited me in the night; thou hast tried me***;*** ~~; and~~ ***thou*** shalt find nothing ***evil in me,*** ~~;~~ ***for*** I am purposed ~~that~~ my mouth shall not transgress ~~:~~
17:4 ~~C~~concerning the works of men***.*** ~~; b~~***B***y the word of thy lips I have kept ~~me from~~ ***out of*** the paths of the destroyer.

17:6 I have called upon thee, for thou wilt hear ~~me~~, O God***,*** ~~:~~ ***my speech, and***: incline thine ear unto me~~, and hear my speech~~.
17:7 Shew thy marvellous loving-kindness, O thou that savest ~~by thy right hand~~ them which put their trust in thee***, by thy right hand*** from those that rise up ~~against them~~.

17:9 ~~From the wicked that oppress me, from m~~***M***y deadly enemies ~~, who~~ compass me about***;*** ~~:~~

17:13 Arise, O ~~L~~*l*ord, disappoint him, cast him down***.*** ~~:~~ ~~d~~***D***eliver my soul from the wicked~~, which is~~ ***by*** thy sword***;*** ~~:~~
17:14 ~~F~~***f***rom men ~~which are~~ ***by*** thy ***strong*** hand***.*** ~~;~~ ***Yea,*** O Lord, from men of the world***;*** ~~; which have~~ ***for*** their portion ***is*** in ~~this~~ ***their*** life, and whose belly thou fillest with thy ~~hid treasure~~ ***good things;*** ~~:~~ they are full of children, ***and they die*** and leave the rest of their ~~substance~~ ***inheritance*** to their babes.

18:3 I will call upon the LORD, ~~who~~ ***for he*** is worthy to be praised***;*** ~~:~~ so shall I be saved from mine enemies.

18:30 ~~As for~~ ***O*** God, ~~his way is~~ ***thy ways are*** perfect***;*** ~~:~~ the word of the LORD is tried***;*** ~~:~~ he is a buckler to all those ~~that~~ ***who*** trust in him.

18:32 ~~It is~~ ***Our*** God that girdeth me with strength, and maketh my way perfect***?*** ~~:~~

18:41 They cried, but ~~there was~~ ***found*** none to save ~~them~~***;*** ~~:~~ ~~even~~ unto the LORD, but he answered them not.

19:3 ~~There is n~~***N***o speech nor language ***can be***, ~~where~~ ***if*** their voice is not heard.

19:13 Keep back thy servant also from presumptuous ~~sins~~ ***acts***; let them not have dominion over me***;*** ~~:~~ then shall I be upright, and I shall be innocent from the great transgression.

22:1 My God, ~~my God,~~ why hast thou forsaken me? ***My God, hear the words of my roaring;*** ~~why art~~ thou ~~so~~ ***art*** far from helping me***.*** ~~, and from the words of my roaring?~~
22:2 O my God, I cry in the daytime, but thou ~~hearest~~ ***answerest*** not; and in the night season, and am not silent.
22:3 But thou art holy~~, O thou~~ that inhabitest ***the heavens; thou art worthy of*** the praises of Israel.

22:6 But I***,*** ~~am~~ a worm, ~~and~~ ***am loved of*** no man; a reproach of men, and despised of the people.

22:10 I was cast upon thee from the womb***;*** ~~:~~ thou ~~art~~ ***wast*** my God from my mother's ~~belly~~ ***breasts***.

PSALMS

22:12 Many ~~bulls~~ ***armies*** have compassed me***;*** ~~:~~ strong ~~bulls~~ ***armies*** of Bashan have beset me ~~round~~ ***around***.
22:13 They gaped upon me with their mouths, ~~as~~ ***like*** a ravening and a roaring lion.

22:21 Save me from the lion's mouth***,*** ~~:~~ for thou hast heard me ***speak*** from the ***secret places of the wilderness, through the*** horns of the unicorns.

22:31 They shall come, and shall declare his righteousness unto a people that shall be born, ~~that~~ ***what*** he hath done ~~this~~.

24:7 Lift up your heads, O ye ~~gates~~ ***generations of Jacob***; and be ye ~~lift~~ ***lifted*** up ~~; ye everlasting doors; and the Kind of glory shall come in~~.
24:8 ~~Who is this King of glory?~~ ***And*** ~~T~~***t***he LORD strong and mighty***;*** ~~,~~ the LORD mighty in battle***, who is the king of glory, shall establish you for ever. And he will roll away the heavens; and will come down to redeem his people; to make you an everlasting name; to establish you upon his everlasting rock***.
24:9 Lift up your heads, O ye ~~gates~~ ***generations of Jacob***; ~~even~~ lift ~~them~~ up ***your heads***, ye everlasting ~~doors~~ ***generations,*** ~~;~~ and the ***Lord of hosts, the king of kings;*** ~~King of glory shall come in.~~
24:10 ~~Who is this King of glory? The LORD of hosts, he is the King of glory.~~ ***Even the king of glory shall come unto you; and shall redeem his people, and shall establish them in righteousness.*** Selah.

27:3 Though ~~an~~ ***a*** host should encamp against me, my heart shall not fear***;*** ~~:~~ though war should rise against me, in this ~~will I be~~ ***I am*** confident.

27:13 ~~I had fainted, u~~***U***nless I had believed to see the goodness of the LORD in the land of the living***, thou wouldst deliver my soul into hell***.
27:14 ***Thou didst say unto me,*** Wait on the LORD***,*** ~~:~~ be of good courage, and he shall strengthen ~~thine~~ ***thy*** heart***;*** ~~:~~ wait, I say, on the LORD.

30:5 For his anger ***kindleth*** ~~endureth but~~ ***against the wicket; they repent, and in*** a moment~~;~~ ***it is turned away, and they are in his favor, and he*** ~~in his favour is~~ ***he giveth them*** life***;*** ~~:~~ ***therefore,*** weeping may endure for a night, but joy cometh in the morning.

30:9 ~~What profit is there in my blood, w~~***W***hen I go down to the pit***,my blood shall return to the dust.*** ~~? Shall the dust~~ ***I will*** praise thee***;*** ~~?~~ ***my soul*** shall ~~it~~ declare thy truth***; for what profit am I, if I do it not***?

30:12 To the end that my glory may ***give glory to thy name, and*** sing praise to thee, and not be silent. O LORD my God, I will give thanks unto thee for ever.

32:1 Blessed ~~is he~~ ***are they*** whose ~~transgression is~~ ***transgressions are*** forgiven, ~~whose sin is~~ ***and who have no sins to be*** covered.

32:3 When I kept silence, ***my spirit failed within me; when I opened my mouth,*** my bones waxed old through my ~~roaring~~ ***speaking*** all the day long.
32:4 For day and night thy ~~hand~~ ***Spirit*** was heavy upon me***;*** ~~:~~ my moisture is turned into the drought of summer. Selah.

32:8 ***Thou hast said,***I will instruct thee and teach thee in the way which thou shalt go***;*** ~~:~~ I will guide thee with mine eye.

PSALMS

33:1 Rejoice in the LORD, O ye righteous***;*** ~~:~~ ~~for~~ ***to*** praise ***the Lord*** is comely for the upright ***in heart***.
33:2 Praise the LORD with ~~harp:~~ ***thy voice;*** sing unto him with the psaltery and ***harp,*** an instrument of ten strings.

33:4 For the word of the LORD is ~~right;~~ ***given to the upright,*** and all his works are done in truth.

33:9 For he spake, and it was ~~done~~ ***finished***; he commanded, and it stood fast.

33:12 Blessed ~~is~~ ***are*** the ~~nation~~ ***nations*** ~~whose God is the LORD:~~ and the people whom ~~he~~ ***the Lord God*** hath chosen for his own inheritance.

33:19 To deliver their soul from death, and to keep them alive in ***a time of*** famine.

35:12 They rewarded me evil for good***,*** ~~to the~~ ***for the purpose of*** spoiling of my soul.

36:1 The ~~transgression of the~~ wicked ***who live in transgression,*** saith ~~within my heart~~ ***in their hearts***, ***There is no condemnation; for*** ~~that~~ there is no fear of God before ~~his~~ ***their*** eyes.

36:2 For ~~he flattereth himself in his~~ ***they flatter themselves in their*** own eyes, until ~~his iniquity be~~ ***their iniquities are*** found to be hateful.
36:3 The words of ~~his~~ ***their*** mouth are ***full of*** iniquity and deceit***.*** ~~:~~ ~~he~~ ***The wicked man*** hath left off to be wise, and to do good***;*** ~~:~~
36:4 He deviseth mischief upon his bed; he setteth himself in a way that is not good~~; he abhorreth not evil~~.
36:5 ~~Thy mercy,~~ O LORD, ~~is~~ ***thou art*** in the heavens; ***they are full of thy mercy.*** ~~and thy faithfulness reacheth unto~~ ***And the thoughts of a righteous man ascendeth up unto thee whose throne is far above*** the clouds.
36:6 ***He is filled with*** ~~T~~***t***hy righteousness ~~is~~ like the great mountains***,*** ~~;~~ ***and with*** thy judgments ~~are~~ ***like*** a great deep***.*** ~~:~~ O LORD, thou preservest man and beast.

36:12 ~~There~~ ***They*** are the workers of iniquity ~~fallen~~ ***and shall fall;*** ~~:~~ they ~~are~~ ***shall be*** cast down, and shall not be able to rise.

37:38 But the transgressors shall be destroyed together***;*** ~~:~~ the end of the wicked shall ***come, and they shall*** be cut off.

38:7 For my loins are filled with a loathsome ~~disease~~ ***distress;*** ~~:~~ and ~~there is~~ no soundness ***is found*** in my flesh.
38:8 I am feeble***,*** and ~~sore~~ broken***, and very sore.*** ~~:~~ I have ~~roared~~ ***wept*** by reason of the disquietness of my heart.

38:11 My lovers and my friends stand aloof ~~from~~ ***because of*** my sore; and my kinsmen stand afar off.

39:9 I was dumb, ~~I~~ ***and*** opened not my mouth; because thou didst ~~it~~ ***chasten me***.
39:10 Remove thy stroke away from me***,*** ~~:~~ ***or*** I ~~am~~ ***shall be*** consumed by the blow of ~~thine~~ ***thy*** hand.

PSALMS

40:2 He brought me up also out of ~~an~~ ***a*** horrible pit, out of the miry clay, and set my feet upon a rock, and established my ~~goings~~ ***doings***.

41:3 The LORD will strengthen him upon the bed of languishing***;*** ~~:~~ thou wilt make all ***his pains to cease, when he is laid in*** his bed ~~in his~~ ***of*** sickness.

42:2 My soul thirsteth for ***to see*** God, for ***to see*** the living God***;*** ~~:~~ when shall I come and appear before ***thee, O*** God?
42: 3 My ears have been ~~my meat~~ ***poured out unto thee*** day and night, while ~~they~~ ***mine enemies*** continually say unto me, Where is thy God?
42:4 When I remember ~~these things~~ ***mine enemies***, I pour out my soul ~~in me~~ ***to thee;*** ~~:~~ for I had gone with the multitude***;*** ~~,~~ I ***also*** went with them to the house of God, with the voice of joy and praise, with ~~a~~ ***the*** multitude that kept holyday.

46:1 God is our refuge and strength, a ~~very~~ present help in trouble.
46:2 Therefore will not we fear, though the earth ***shall*** be removed, and though the mountains ***shall*** be carried into the midst of the sea;
46:3 ~~Though~~ ***And*** the waters thereof roar***,*** ~~and be~~ ***being*** troubled, ~~though~~ ***and*** the mountains shake with the swelling thereof. ~~Selah~~.
46:4 ***Yet*** ~~T~~***t***here ~~is~~ ***shall be*** a river, the streams whereof shall make glad the city of God, the holy place of the tabernacles of the ~~m~~***M***ost High.
46:5 ***For Zion shall come, and*** God ~~is~~ ***shall be*** in the midst of her; she shall not be moved***;*** ~~:~~ God shall help her~~, and that~~ right early.
46:6 The heathen ***shall be enraged*** ~~raged~~, ***and*** ~~the~~ ***their*** kingdoms ~~were~~ ***shall be*** moved***,*** ~~:~~ ~~he uttered~~ ***and the Lord shall utter*** his voice, ***and*** the earth ***shall be*** melted.
46:7 The LORD of hosts ~~is~~ ***who shall be*** with us***,*** ~~;~~ the God of Jacob is our refuge. Selah.
46:8 Come, behold the works of the LORD, what desolations he ~~hath made~~ ***shall make*** in the earth ***in the latter days***.
46:9 He maketh wars to cease unto the end of the earth; he breaketh the bow, and cutteth the spear in sunder; he burneth the chariot in the fire***,*** ~~.~~ ***and saith unto the nations,***

46:11 The LORD of hosts ~~is~~ ***shall be*** with us***,*** ~~;~~ the God of Jacob ~~is~~ our refuge. Selah.

49:7 None ~~of them~~ can by any means redeem his brother, nor give to God a ransom for him~~:~~
49:9 ~~T~~***t***hat he should still live for ever, ~~and~~ ***that it ceaseth*** not ***for ever to*** see corruption.
49:8 ~~(~~For the redemption of their soul ***is through God, and*** ~~is~~ precious***.*** ~~, and it ceaseth for ever:)~~

(NOTE the reversal of verses 8 and 9.)

49:10 For he seeth ~~that~~ wise men die***;*** ~~,~~ likewise the fool and the brutish person perish, and leave their wealth to others***;*** ~~.~~
49:11 Their inward thought ~~is, that~~ ***of*** their houses ~~shall continue~~ for ever***;*** ~~,~~ and their dwelling places***,*** to all generations***.*** ~~; they call their~~ ~~l~~***L***Lands ***they called*** after their own names***, and they are honorable***.
49:12 Nevertheless***,*** man ~~being~~ in honour abideth not***,*** ~~:~~ he is ***also*** like the beasts that perish.
49:13 This ***I speak of them who walk in*** their way***, and forsaketh the Almighty*** ~~is~~ ***in*** their folly: yet their posterity approve their sayings. Selah.

PSALMS

50:21 These things hast thou done, and I kept silence; thou thoughtest that I was altogether such ~~an~~ ***a*** one as thyself***;*** ~~:~~ but I will reprove thee, and set ~~them~~ ***covenants*** in order before thine eyes.
50:22 Now consider this, ye that forget God, lest I tear you in pieces, and there be none ~~to~~ ***can*** deliver.

52:7 Lo, ~~this is~~ the man ~~that~~ ***who*** made not God his strength; but trusted in the abundance of his riches, and strengthened himself in his wickedness.

52:9 I will praise thee for ever, because thou hast done ~~it~~ ***wonderful works;*** ~~:~~ ~~and~~ I will wait on thy name; for ~~it is~~ ***thou art*** good before thy saints.

53:1 The fool hath said in his heart, There is no God. ***Such are*** ~~C~~corrupt ~~are they~~, and ***they*** have done abominable iniquity***.*** ~~:~~ ~~t~~***T***here is none that doeth good.

53:3 Every one of them is gone back***;*** ~~:~~ they are altogether become filthy***.*** ~~;~~ ~~there is none that doeth good, no, not one~~.
53:4 ~~Have~~ ~~t~~***T***he workers of iniquity ***have*** no knowledge***;*** ~~?~~ ~~who~~ ***they*** eat up my people as they eat bread***;*** ~~:~~ they have not called upon God.
53:5 ***There is none that doeth good, no not one.*** There were they in great fear***,*** ~~where no fear was:~~ for God hath scattered the bones of him that encampeth against ~~thee~~ ***him.*** ~~:~~ ***O Lord,*** thou hast put ~~them~~ to shame ***those who have said in their hearts there was no fear***, because ~~God hath~~ ***thou hast*** despised them.
53:6 Oh that ***Zion were come,*** the salvation of Israel***;*** ~~were come~~ ***for*** out of Zion ***shall they be judged,*** ~~!~~ ~~W~~***w***hen God bringeth back the captivity of his people***.*** ~~;~~ ***And*** Jacob shall rejoice***;*** ~~,~~ ~~and~~ Israel shall be glad.

55:12 For it was not an enemy that reproached me***, neither he that hated me that did magnify himself against me***; ***if so,*** then I could have borne it***;*** ~~:~~ ~~neither was it he that hated me that did magnify himself against me; then~~ I would have hid myself from him***;*** ~~:~~
55:13 But it was ~~thou,~~ a man mine equal, my guide, and mine acquaintance.

55:20 ~~He hath~~ ***They have*** put forth ~~his~~ ***their*** hands against such as be at peace with ~~him~~ ***them;*** ~~:~~ ~~he hath~~ ***they have*** broken ~~his~~ ***the Lord's*** covenant.
55:21 The words of ~~his~~ ***their*** mouth were smoother than butter, but war was in ~~his~~ ***their*** heart***.*** ~~:~~ ~~his~~ ***Their*** words were softer than oil, yet ~~were~~ they ***have*** drawn swords.

56:3 What***?*** ~~time I~~ am ***I*** afraid***?*** ~~,~~ I will trust in thee.

58:10 The righteous shall rejoice when he seeth the vengeance***;*** ~~:~~ he ~~shall~~ ***will*** wash his feet in the blood of the wicked.

82:2 How long will ye ***suffer them to*** judge unjustly, and accept the persons of the wicked? Selah.

90:13 Return ***us***, O LORD***.*** ~~,~~ ~~h~~***H***ow long ***wilt thou hide thy face from thy servants***? and let ~~it~~ ***them*** repent ***of all their hard speeches that they have spoken concerning*** thee ~~concerning thy servants~~.

PSALMS

92:13 Those that ~~be~~ ***he*** planted in the house of the LORD shall flourish in the courts of our God.

102:18 This shall be written for the generation to come***;*** ~~:~~ and the people which shall be ~~created~~ ***gathered*** shall praise the LORD.

104:1 Bless the LORD, O my soul. O LORD my God, thou art very great; thou art clothed with ~~honour~~ ***power*** and majesty.

104:26 There go the ships***;*** ~~:~~ ~~there is that leviathan, whom~~ ***and*** thou hast made ***leviathan*** to play therein.

105:42 For he remembered his holy promise~~, and~~ ***unto*** Abraham his servant.

106:4 Remember me, O LORD, with the ~~favour~~ ***favor*** ~~that thou bearest unto~~ ***of*** thy people***;*** ~~:~~ ~~O~~ ***oh*** visit me with thy salvation;

106:7 Our fathers understood not thy wonders in Egypt; they remembered not the multitude of thy mercies; but provoked ~~him~~ ***thee*** at the sea, ~~even~~ at the Red sea.

106:45 And he remembered for them his covenant, and ~~repented~~ ***spared his people*** according to the multitude of his mercies.

107:11 Because they rebelled against the ~~words~~ ***works*** of God, and contemned the counsel of the ~~m~~***M***ost High***;*** ~~:~~

109:3 They compassed me about***; they spake against me*** also***,*** with words of hatred; and fought against me without a cause.
109:4 ~~For~~ ***And, notwithstanding*** my love***,*** they are my adversaries***;*** ~~: but I give myself unto~~ ***yet I will continue in*** prayer ***for them***.

109:6 Set thou a wicked man over ~~him~~ ***them;*** ~~:~~ and let Satan stand at his right hand.
109:7 When ~~he~~ ***they*** shall be judged, let ~~him~~ ***them*** be condemned: and let ~~his~~ ***their*** prayer become sin.
109:8 Let ~~his~~ ***their*** days be few; ~~and~~ let another take ~~his~~ ***their*** office.
109:9 Let ~~his~~ ***their*** children be fatherless***;*** ~~,~~ and ***let their wives widows*** ~~his wife a widow~~.
109:10 Let ~~his~~ ***their*** children be continually vagabonds, and beg***;*** ~~:~~ let them seek ~~their bread~~ also out of their desolate places.
109:11 Let the extortioner catch all that ~~he hath~~ ***they have***; and let the ~~strangers~~ ***stranger*** spoil ~~his labour~~ ***their labor***.
109:12 Let there be none to extend mercy unto ~~him~~ *them,* ~~:~~ neither let there be any to ~~favour his~~ ***favor their*** fatherless children.
109:13 Let ~~his~~ ***their*** posterity be cut off~~; and~~ in the generation following***;*** let their ~~name~~ ***names*** be blotted out.
109:14 Let the iniquity of ~~his~~ ***their*** fathers be remembered ~~with~~ ***before*** the LORD; and let not the sin of ~~his mother~~ ***their mothers*** be blotted out.

109:16 Because ~~that he~~ ***they*** remembered not to ~~shew~~ ***show*** mercy, but persecuted the poor and needy man, that ~~he~~ ***they*** might even slay the broken in heart.

PSALMS

109:17 As ~~he~~ ***they*** loved cursing, so let it come unto ~~him~~ ***them;*** ~~:~~ as ~~he~~ ***they*** delighted not in blessing, so let it be far from ~~him~~ ***them***.
109:18 As ~~he~~ ***they*** clothed ~~himself~~ ***themselves*** with cursing like as with ~~his garment~~ ***their garments***, so let it come into ~~his~~ ***their*** bowels like water, and like oil into ~~his~~ ***their*** bones.
109:19 Let it be unto ~~him~~ ***them*** as ~~the~~ ***a*** garment which covereth ~~him~~ ***them***, and for a girdle wherewith ~~he is~~ ***they are*** girded continually.
109:20 ~~Let t~~***T***his ***shall*** be the reward of mine adversaries, from the LORD***;*** ~~;~~, and of them ~~that~~ ***who*** speak evil against my soul.
109:21 But do thou ~~for~~ ***deliver*** me, O ~~GOD the~~ Lord ***my God***, for thy name's sake***;*** ~~:~~ because thy mercy is good, ***therefore*** deliver thou me.

110:6 He shall judge among the heathen, he shall fill ~~the places~~ ***their streets*** with ~~the~~ ***their*** dead bodies; he shall wound the heads over many countries.

112:1 Praise ye the LORD. Blessed is the man ~~that~~ feareth ***who*** the LORD, ~~that~~ ***and*** delighteth greatly in his commandments.

112:8 His heart is established, he shall not be afraid, until he see ~~his desire~~ ***judgment executed*** upon his enemies.

115:1 Not unto us, O LORD, not unto us, but unto thy name ~~give~~ ***be*** glory, for thy mercy, and for thy truth's sake.

115:9 O Israel, trust thou in the LORD***;*** ~~:~~ he is ~~their~~ ***thy*** help and ~~their~~ ***thy*** shield.
115:10 O house of Aaron, trust in the LORD: he is ~~their~~ ***thy*** help and ~~their~~ ***thy*** shield.
115:11 Ye that fear the LORD, trust in the LORD***;*** ~~:~~ he is ~~their~~ ***your*** help and ~~their~~ ***your*** shield.

119:15 I will meditate ~~in~~ ***upon*** thy precepts, and have respect unto thy ways.

119:20 My ~~soul~~ ***heart*** breaketh, for ~~the longing that it hath unto~~ ***my soul longeth after*** thy judgments at all times.
119:21 Thou hast rebuked the proud***;*** ~~that~~ ***they*** are cursed~~, which~~ ***who*** do err from thy commandments.

119:33 Teach me, O LORD, the way of thy statutes; and I shall keep it ~~unto~~ ***to*** the end.

119:48 My hands also will I lift up unto thy commandments, which I have loved; and I will meditate ~~in~~ ***upon*** thy statutes.

119:78 Let the proud be ashamed; for they dealt perversely with me without a cause***;*** ~~:~~ but I will meditate ~~in~~ ***upon*** thy precepts.

119:109 My soul is continually in ~~my~~ ***thy*** hand***;*** ~~: yet do I~~ and I do not forget thy law.

119:126 ~~It is~~ ***And the*** time ~~for thee~~, ***O*** LORD, ***for me*** to work***;*** ~~:~~ for they have made void thy law.

119:130 The entrance of thy words giveth light; ~~it giveth~~ ***they give*** understanding unto the simple.

PSALMS

121:4 Behold, he that keepeth Israel shall neither slumber nor sleep.
121:3 He will not suffer thy foot to be moved***;*** ~~:~~ he that keepeth thee will not
slumber.

(NOTE: JST reversal of verse order for verses 3 & 4)

124:1 ~~If it had not been the LORD who w as on our side,~~ ~~n~~***N***ow may Israel say~~,~~;
124:2 If ~~it had not been~~ the LORD ~~who~~ was ***not*** on our side~~;~~ when men rose up
against us~~,~~ ~~:~~
124:3 Then they had swallowed us up quick~~;~~ when their wrath was kindled
against us~~.~~ ~~:~~
124:4 Then the waters had overwhelmed us, the stream had gone over our soul***;*** ~~:~~

124:7 Our soul is escaped as a bird out of the snare of the fowlers***;*** ~~:~~ the snare
is broken, and we are escaped.

125:1 They that trust in the LORD ~~shall be as~~ in mount Zion, ~~which~~ cannot be
removed, but ~~abideth~~ ***abide*** for ever.

125:4 Do good, O LORD, unto ~~those that be~~ ***the*** good, and ~~to them that are~~
unto the upright in their hearts.

135:14 For the LORD will judge his people, and he will ***not*** repent himself
concerning his servants.

135:21 Blessed be the LORD out of Zion***;*** ~~,~~ ~~which dwelleth at~~ ***Blessed be the
Lord out of*** Jerusalem. Praise ye the LORD.

137:5 If I forget thee, O Jerusalem, let my right hand forget ~~her~~ ***its*** cunning.

137:7 Remember, O LORD, the children of Edom in the day of Jerusalem; who
said, Rase it, ~~rase it,~~ even to the foundation thereof.

138:2 I will worship toward thy holy temple, and praise thy name for thy loving-
kindness and for thy truth***;*** ~~:~~ for thou hast magnified thy word above all thy name.

138:8 The LORD will perfect ~~that which concerneth me: thy mercy,~~ ***me in
knowledge, concerning his kingdom. I will praise thee*** O LORD, ~~endureth~~ for
ever***;*** ~~:~~ ***for thou art merciful, and wilt not*** forsake ~~not~~ the works of thine own
hands.

139:16 Thine eyes did see my substance, yet being unperfect; and in thy book all
my members were written, which in continuance were fashioned, when as yet ~~there
was~~ ***I knew*** none of them.

141:5 ~~Let~~ ***When*** the righteous smite me ***with the word of the Lord*** ~~;~~ it shall be
a kindness***;*** ~~:~~ and ~~let him~~ ***when they*** reprove me~~,~~ ~~;~~ it shall be an excellent oil,
~~which~~ ***and*** shall not ~~break~~ ***destroy*** my ~~head~~ ***faith;*** ~~:~~ for yet my prayer also shall
be ***for them. I delight not*** in their calamities.

PSALMS

142:4 I looked on my right hand, and ~~beheld~~ ***behold***, but there was no man that would know me***;*** ~~:~~ refuge failed me; no man cared for my soul.

143:3 For the enemy hath persecuted my soul; he hath smitten my life down to the ground; he hath made me to dwell in darkness, as those that have ~~been~~ long ***been*** dead.

PROVERBS

1:26 I also will laugh at your calamity***;*** ~~;I~~ will mock when your fear cometh;

11:1 A false balance is ***an*** abomination to the LORD***;*** ~~:~~ but a just weight is his delight.

11:20 They that are of a froward heart are ***an*** abomination to the LORD***;*** ~~:~~ but such as are upright in their way are his delight.

18:22 Whoso findeth a ***good*** wife ~~findeth a good thing, and obtaineth favour~~ ***hath obtained favor*** of the LORD.

22:12 ***For t***~~T~~he eyes of the LORD preserve knowledge***;*** ~~:~~ ~~and~~ ***but*** he overthroweth the words of the transgressor.

30:30 A lion**,** which is strongest among beasts~~,~~ and turneth not away ~~for~~ ***from*** any;

ECCLESIASTES

No JST changes in the Book of Ecclesiastes.

SONG OF SOLOMON

The Song of Solomon was eliminated from the Inspired Version

See: Bible Dictionary, p 776

See: Joseph Smith Translation of the Bible, (Extent of Changes,) Encyclopedia of Mormonism, p 766, Daniel H. Ludlow.

ISAIAH

See entire text in full context, pages 123-225.

JEREMIAH

2:24 A wild ass used to the wilderness, that snuffeth up the wind at her pleasure; in her occasion who can turn her away? all they that seek her will ~~not~~ weary themselves; in her month they shall find her.

3:2 Lift up thine eyes unto the high places, and see where thou hast not been ~~lien~~ ***lain*** with. In the ways hast thou sat for them, as the Arabian in the wilderness; and thou hast polluted the land with thy whoredoms and ~~with thy~~ wickedness.
3:3 Therefore ~~the~~ ***thy*** showers have been withholden, and there hath been no latter rain; and thou hadst a whore's forehead, thou refusedst to be ashamed.

5:19 And it shall come to pass, when ye shall say, Wherefore doeth the LORD our God all these things unto us? then shalt thou answer them, Like as ye have forsaken me, and served strange gods in your land, so shall ye serve strangers in ~~a~~ ***the*** land that is not yours.

7:5 For if ye throughly amend your ways and your doings; if ye throughly execute judgment between a man and his ~~neighbour~~ ***neighbor***;

12:5 If thou hast run with ~~the~~ ***our*** footmen, and they have wearied thee, then how canst thou contend with horses? and if in the land of peace, wherein thou trustedst, they wearied thee, then how wilt thou do in the swelling of Jordan?

16:2 Thou shalt not take thee a wife, neither shalt thou have sons ~~or~~ ***nor*** daughters in this place.

18:8 If that nation, against whom I have pronounced, turn from their evil, I will ~~repent of~~ ***withhold*** the evil that I thought to do unto them.

18:10 If it do evil in my sight, that it obey not my voice, then I will ~~repent of~~ ***withhold*** the good, wherewith I said I would benefit them.

18:14 Will ~~a man~~ ***you not*** leave the snow ***of the fields*** of Lebanon***;*** ~~which cometh from the rock of the field? or~~ shall ***not*** the cold flowing waters that come from another place ***from the rock,*** be forsaken?

19:7 And I will make void the counsel of Judah and Jerusalem in this place; and I will cause them to fall by the sword before their enemies, and by the hands of them that seek their lives***;*** ~~:~~ and their carcases will I give to be meat for the fowls of the heaven, and for the beasts of the earth.
19:8 And I will make this city desolate, and ~~an~~ ***a*** hissing; every one that passeth thereby shall be astonished and hiss***,*** because of all the plagues thereof.

23:14 I have seen also in the prophets of Jerusalem ~~an~~ ***a*** horrible thing***;*** ~~:~~ they commit adultery, and walk in lies***;*** ~~:~~ they strengthen also the hands of evildoers, that none doth return from his wickedness***;*** ~~:~~ they are all of them unto me as Sodom, and the inhabitants thereof as Gomorrah.

24:7 And I will give them ~~an~~ ***a*** heart to know me, that I am the LORD***;*** ~~:~~ and they shall be my people, and I will be their God***;*** ~~:~~ for they shall return unto me with their whole heart.

JEREMIAH

25:9 Behold, I will send and take all the families of the north, saith the LORD, and Nebuchadrezzar the king of Babylon, my servant, and will bring them against this land, and against the inhabitants thereof, and against all these nations round about, and will utterly destroy them, and make them an astonishment, and ~~an~~ ***a*** hissing, and perpetual desolations.

25:18 To wit, Jerusalem, and the cities of Judah, and the kings thereof, and the princes thereof, to make them a desolation, an astonishment, ~~an~~ ***a*** hissing, and a curse; as it is this day;

25:31 A noise shall come even to the ends of the earth; for the LORD hath a controversy with the nations***;*** ~~,~~ he will plead with all flesh; he will give ~~them that are~~ ***the*** wicked to the sword, saith the LORD.

26:3 If so be they will hearken, and turn every man from his evil way, ~~that I may repent me of~~ ***and repent, I will turn away*** the evil~~,~~ which I purpose to do unto them because of the evil of their doings.

26:5 To hearken to the words of my servants, the prophets, whom I sent unto you, ~~both rising~~ ***commanding them to rise*** up early, and sending them ~~, but ye have not hearkened~~;
26:6 Then will I make this house like Shiloh, and will make this city a curse to all the nations of the earth***; for ye have not hearkened unto my servants the prophets.***

26:13 Therefore now, amend your ways and your doings, and obey the voice of the LORD your God, ~~;~~and ~~the LORD will~~ repent, ~~him of~~ ***and the Lord will turn away*** the evil that he hath pronounced against you.

26:18 Micah the Morasthite prophesied in the days of Hezekiah king of Judah, and spake to all the people of Judah, saying, Thus saith the LORD of hosts; Zion shall be ~~plowed~~ ***ploughed*** like a field, and Jerusalem shall become heaps, and the mountain of the house ***of the Lord*** as the high places of a forest.
26:19 Did Hezekiah, king of Judah, and all Judah put him at all to death? ~~D~~***D***id he not fear the LORD~~,~~ and ~~besought~~ ***beseech*** the LORD~~,~~ and ~~the LORD repented him of~~ ***repent? and the Lord turned away*** the evil which he had pronounced against them. ~~?~~ Thus ***by putting Jeremiah to death we*** might we procure great evil against our souls.
26:20 ~~And~~ ***But*** there was ~~also~~ a man ***among the priests, rose up and said,*** that ~~prophesied in the name of the LORD~~ , Urijah the son of Shemaiah of Kirjath-jearim, ~~who~~ prophesied ***in the name of the Lord, who also prophesied*** against this city, and against this land, according to all the words of Jeremiah:

27:7 And all nations shall serve him, and his son, and his son's son, until the very time of ~~his land~~ ***their end*** come***;*** ~~:~~ and ~~then~~ ***after that*** many nations and great kings shall serve themselves of ~~him~~ ***them***.

27:11 But the nations that bring their neck under the yoke of the king of Babylon, and serve him, those will I let ***still*** remain ~~still~~ in their own land, saith the LORD; and they shall till it, and dwell therein.

28:8 The prophets that have been before me and before thee of old prophesied both against many countries, and against great kingdoms, of war, and of evil, and ~~of~~ pestilence.

JEREMIAH

29:12 Then shall ye call ~~upon~~ ***unto*** me, and ye shall go and pray unto me, and I will hearken unto you.

29:18 And I will persecute them with the sword, with the famine, and with the pestilence, and will deliver them to be removed to all the kingdoms of the earth, to be a curse, and an astonishment, and ~~an~~ ***a*** hissing, and a reproach, among all the nations whither I have driven them***;*** ~~:~~
29:19 Because they have not hearkened to my words, saith the LORD, which I sent unto them by my servants the prophets, ~~rising up~~ ***commanding them to rise*** early***,*** and sending them; but ye would not hear, saith the LORD.

30:12 For thus saith the LORD, ~~T~~***t***hy bruise is incurable, ~~and thy wound is~~ ***although thy wounds are*** grievous.
30:13 ~~There~~ ~~I~~***I***s ***there*** none to plead thy cause, that thou mayest be bound up*?* ~~:~~: ~~thou~~ ***Hast thou*** no healing medicines***?*** ~~.~~
30:14 ***Have*** ~~A~~***a***ll thy lovers ~~have~~forgotten thee***,*** ~~;~~ ***do*** they ***not*** seek thee ~~not;~~ ***?*** ~~f~~***F***or I have wounded thee with the wound of an enemy, with the chastisement of a cruel one, for the multitude of thine ~~iniquity~~ ***iniquities***; because thy sins ~~were~~ ***are*** increased.
30:15 Why criest thou for thine affliction? ***Is*** thy sorrow ~~is~~ incurable***? It was*** for the multitude of thine ~~iniquity~~ ***iniquities,*** ~~:~~ ***and*** because thy sins ~~were~~ ***are*** increased~~;~~ I have done these things unto thee.
30:16 ~~Therefore~~ ***But*** all they that devour thee shall be devoured; and all thine adversaries, every one of them, shall go into captivity; and they that spoil thee shall be a spoil, and all that prey upon thee will I give for a prey.

31:32 Not according to the covenant that I made with their fathers***,*** in the day that I took them by the hand to bring them out of the land of Egypt; which my covenant they brake, although I was ~~an~~ ***a*** husband unto them, saith the LORD***;*** ~~:~~

33:11 The voice of joy, and the voice of gladness, the voice of the bridegroom, and the voice of the bride, the voice of them that shall say, Praise the LORD of hosts***;*** ~~:~~ for the LORD is good; for his mercy endureth for ever~~: and of~~ ***unto*** them that shall bring the sacrifice of praise into the house of the LORD. For I will cause to return the captivity of the land, as at the first, saith the LORD.
33:12 Thus saith the LORD of hosts; Again in this place, which is desolate without man and without beast, and in all the cities thereof, shall be ~~an~~ ***a*** habitation of shepherds causing their flocks to lie down.

34:14 At the end of seven years let ye go every man his brother ~~an~~ ***a*** Hebrew, which hath been sold unto thee; and when he hath served thee six years, thou shalt let him go free from thee***;*** ~~:~~ but your fathers hearkened not unto me, neither inclined their ear.
34:15 And ye were now turned, and had done right in my sight, in proclaiming liberty every man to his neighbour; and ye had made a covenant before me in the house which is called by my name***.*** ~~:~~

35:14 The words of Jonadab the son of Rechab, that he commanded his sons not to drink wine, are performed; for unto this day they drink none, but obey their father's commandment***;*** ~~:~~ notwithstanding I have spoken unto you, ~~rising~~ ***commanding you to rise*** early***,*** and speaking ***to you,*** ~~;~~ but ye hearkened not unto me.

JEREMIAH

35:15 I have sent also unto you all my servants the prophets, ~~rising~~ ***commanding them to rise*** up early, and sending them, saying, Return ye now every man from his evil way, and amend your doings, and go not after other gods to serve them, and ye shall dwell in the land which I have given to you and to your fathers: but ye have not inclined your ear, nor hearkened unto me.

37:4 Now Jeremiah came in and went out among the people***;*** ~~:~~ for they had not put him into prison.

37:16 When Jeremiah was entered into the dungeon, and into the cabins, and ~~Jeremiah had~~ ***he*** remained there many days***.*** ~~;~~

40:1 The word ~~that~~ ***which*** came to Jeremiah from the LORD, after that Nebuzar-adan the captain of the guard had let him go from Ramah, when he had taken him being bound in chains among all that were carried away captive of Jerusalem and Judah, which were carried away captive unto Babylon.

42:10 If ye will still abide in this land, then will I build you, and not pull ~~you~~ down***;*** ~~, and~~ I will plant you, and not pluck ~~you~~ up***;*** ~~:~~ ~~for I repent me of~~ ***and I will turn away*** the evil that I have done unto you.

42:14 Saying, No; but we will go into the land of Egypt, where we shall see no war, nor hear the sound of the trumpet, nor have hunger of bread; and there will we dwell***;*** ~~:~~

42:21 And now I have this day declared it to you***,*** ~~;~~ ~~but~~ ***that*** ye have not obeyed the voice of the LORD your God, nor ~~any thing~~ ***anything*** for the which he hath sent me unto you.

44:4 Howbeit I sent unto you all my servants the prophets, ~~rising~~ ***commanding them to rise*** early and sending them, saying, Oh, do not this abominable thing that I hate.

45:5 And seekest thou great things for thyself? seek them not***;*** ~~:~~ for, behold, I will bring evil upon all flesh, saith the LORD***;*** ~~:~~ but thy life will I give unto thee for a prey in all places whither thou goest.

46:26 And ~~I~~ will deliver them into the hand of those that seek their lives, and into the hand of Nebuchadrezzar king of Babylon, and into the hand of his servants***;*** ~~:~~ and afterward it shall be inhabited, as in the days of old, saith the LORD.

48:34 From the cry of Heshbon even unto Elealeh, and even unto Jahaz, have they uttered their voice, from Zoar even unto Horonaim, as ~~an~~ ***a*** heifer of three years old***;*** ~~:~~ for the waters also of Nimrim shall be desolate.

51:37 And Babylon shall become heaps, a dwelling-place for dragons, an astonishment, and ~~an~~ ***a*** hissing, without an inhabitant.

52:23 And there were ninety and six pomegranates on a side; and all the pomegranates upon the network were ~~an~~ ***a*** hundred round about.

LAMENTATIONS

No JST changes in the Book of Lamentations.

EZEKIEL

14:9 And if the prophet be deceived when he hath spoken a thing, I the LORD have ***not*** deceived that prophet***;*** ~~,~~ ~~and~~ ***therefore*** I will stretch out my hand upon him, and will destroy him from the midst of my people Israel.

18:32 For I have no pleasure in the death of him that dieth, saith the Lord GOD***;*** ~~:~~ wherefore turn ~~yourselves, and live ye~~ ***ye and live***.

21:7 And it shall be, when they say unto thee, Wherefore sighest thou? that thou shalt answer, For the tidings***,*** ~~;~~ because it cometh***;*** ~~:~~ and every heart shall melt, and all hands shall be feeble, and every spirit shall faint, and all knees ~~shall~~ be weak as water***;*** ~~:~~ behold, it cometh, and shall be brought to pass, saith the Lord GOD.

23:17 And the Babylonians came to her into the bed of love, and they defiled her with their whoredom, and she was polluted with them, and her mind was alienated from ***me by*** them.

23:22 Therefore, O Aholibah, thus saith the Lord GOD; Behold, I will raise up thy lovers against thee, ~~from~~ ***by*** whom thy mind is alienated ***from me***, and I will bring them against thee on every side;

23:28 For thus saith the Lord GOD; Behold, I will deliver thee into the hand of them whom thou hatest, into the hand of them ~~from~~ ***by*** whom thy mind is alienated***;*** ~~:~~

29:7 When they took hold of thee by thy hand, thou didst break, and rend all their shoulder***;*** ~~:~~ and when they leaned upon thee, thou brakest, and madest all their loins to be at a stand.

35:6 Therefore, as I live, saith the Lord God, I will prepare thee unto blood, and blood shall pursue thee***;*** ~~:~~ ~~sith~~ ***since*** thou hast not hated blood, even blood shall pursue thee.

36:20 And when they entered unto the heathen, whither they went, they profaned my holy name, when they said to them, These are the people of the Lord, and are gone forth out of ~~his~~ ***this*** land.

36:36 Then the heathen that are left round about you shall know that I the LORD build the ruined places, and plant that ~~that~~ ***which*** was desolate***;*** ~~:~~ I the LORD have spoken it, and I will do it.

40:31 And the arches thereof were toward the utter court; and palm trees were upon the posts thereof***;*** ~~:~~ and the going up to it had eight steps.

EZEKIEL

40:37 And the posts thereof were toward the utter court; and palm trees were upon the posts thereof, on this side, and on that side***;*** ~~:~~ and the going up to it had eight steps.

40:39 And in the porch of the gate were two tables on this side, and two tables on that side, to slay thereon the burnt offering and the sin offering and ~~the~~ trespass offering.

42:1 Then he brought me forth into the utter court, the way toward the north***;*** ~~:~~ and he brought me into the chamber that was over against the separate place, and which was before the building toward the north.

42:3 Over against the twenty cubits which were for the inner court, and over against the pavement which was for the ~~utter~~ ***outer*** court, was gallery against gallery in three stories.

42:7 And the wall that was without over against the chambers, toward the ~~utter~~ ***outer*** court on the forepart of the chambers, the length thereof was fifty cubits.
42:8 For the length of the chambers that were in the ~~utter~~ ***outer*** court was fifty cubits***;*** ~~:~~ and, lo, before the temple were ~~an~~ ***a*** hundred cubits.
42:9 And from under these chambers was the entry on the east side, as one goeth into them from the ~~utter~~ ***outer*** court.

42:14 When the priests enter therein, then shall they not go out of the holy place into the ~~utter~~ ***outer*** court, but there they shall lay their garments wherein they minister; for they are holy; and shall put on other garments, and shall approach to those things which are for the people.

44:8 ~~And y~~***Y***e have not kept the charge of mine holy things***;*** ~~:~~ but ye have set keepers of my charge in my sanctuary for yourselves.

44:19 And when they go forth into the ~~utter~~ ***outer*** court, even into the ~~utter~~ ***outer*** court to the people, they shall put off their garments wherein they ministered, and lay them in the holy chambers, and they shall put on other garments; and they shall not sanctify the people with their garments.

46:20 Then said he unto me, This is the place where the priests shall boil the trespass offering and the sin offering, where they shall bake the meat offering; that they bear them not out into the ~~utter~~ ***outer*** court, to sanctify the people.
46:21 Then he brought me forth into the ~~utter~~ ***outer*** court, and caused me to pass by the four corners of the court; and, behold, in every corner of the court there was a court.

47:2 Then brought he me out of the way of the gate northward, and led me about the way without unto the ~~utter~~ ***outer*** gate by the way that looketh eastward; and, behold, there ran out waters on the right side.

48:35 It was round about eighteen thousand measures***;*** ~~:~~ and the name of the city from that day shall be ***called***, ***Holy; for*** ~~T~~***t***he LORD ~~is~~ ***shall be*** there.

DANIEL

2:48 Then the king made Daniel a great man, and ***he*** gave him many great gifts, and made him ruler over the whole province of Babylon, and chief of the governors over all the wise men of
Babylon.

3:4 Then ~~an~~ ***a*** herald cried aloud, To you it is commanded, O people, nations, and languages,

3:27 And the princes, governors, and captains, and the king's counsellors, being gathered together, saw these men, upon whose bodies the fire had no power, nor was ~~an~~ ***a*** hair of their head singed, neither were their coats changed, nor the smell of fire had passed on them.

4:23 And whereas the king saw a watcher and ~~an~~ ***a*** holy one coming down from heaven, and saying, Hew the tree down, and destroy it; yet leave the stump of the roots thereof in the earth, even with a band of iron and brass, in the tender grass of the field; and let it be wet with the dew of heaven, and let his portion be with the beasts of the field, till seven times pass over him;

5:2 Belshazzar, ~~whiles~~ ***while*** he tasted the wine, commanded to bring the golden and silver vessels which his father Nebuchadnezzar had taken out of the temple which was in Jerusalem; that the king~~,~~ and his princes, his wives, and his concubines, might drink therein.

5:28 ~~PERES~~ ***UPHARSIN***; Thy kingdom is divided, and given to the Medes and Persians.

6:1 It pleased Darius to set over the kingdom ~~an~~ ***a*** hundred and twenty princes, which should be over the whole kingdom;

6:5 Then said these men, We shall not find any occasion against this Daniel, except we find it against him concerning the law of ~~his~~ God.

8:2 And I saw in a vision; and it came to pass, when I saw, that I was at Shushan in the palace, which is in the province of Elam; and I saw in a vision, and I was by the river ~~of~~ Ulai.

8:5 And as I was considering, behold, ~~an~~ ***a*** he goat came from the west on the face of the whole earth, and touched not the ground***;*** ~~:~~ and the goat had a notable horn between his eyes.

8:12 And ~~an~~ ***a*** host was given him against the daily sacrifice by reason of transgression, and it cast down the truth to the ground; and it practised, and prospered.

9:20 And ~~whiles~~ ***while*** I was speaking, and praying, and confessing my sin and the sin of my people Israel, and presenting my supplication before the LORD my God for the holy mountain of my God;
9:21 Yea, ~~whiles~~ ***while*** I was speaking in prayer, even the man Gabriel, whom I had seen in the vision at the beginning, being caused to fly swiftly, touched me about the time of the evening oblation.

DANIEL

10:10 And, behold, ~~an~~ ***a*** hand touched me, which set me upon my knees and upon the palms of my hands.
10:11 And he said unto me, O Daniel, a man greatly beloved, understand the words that I speak unto thee, and stand upright***;*** ~~:~~ for unto thee am I now sent. And when he had spoken this word unto me, I stood trembling.

11:32 And such as do wickedly against the covenant shall he corrupt by flatteries***;*** ~~:~~ but the people that do know their God shall be strong, and do exploits.

HOSEA

3:2 So I bought her to me for fifteen pieces of silver, and for ~~an~~ ***a*** homer of barley, and an half homer of barley***;*** ~~:~~

6:1 Come, and let us return unto the LORD: for he hath torn, and ~~he~~ will heal us; he hath smitten, and he will bind us up.

6:10 I have seen ~~an~~ ***a*** horrible thing in the house of Israel***;*** ~~:~~ there is the whoredom of Ephraim, Israel is defiled.
6:11 Also, O Judah, he hath set ~~an~~ ***a*** harvest for thee, when I returned the captivity of my people.

10:6 It shall ~~be~~ also ***be*** carried unto Assyria for a present to king Jareb: Ephraim shall receive shame, and Israel shall be ashamed of his own counsel.

10:11 And Ephraim is as ~~an~~ ***a*** heifer that is taught, and loveth to tread out the corn; but I passed over upon her fair neck***;*** ~~:~~ I will make Ephraim to ride; Judah shall ~~plow~~ ***plough***, and Jacob shall break his clods.

11:4 I drew them with cords of a man, with bands of love***;*** ~~:~~ and I was to them as they that take off the yoke on their jaws, and I laid meat unto them.
11:5 He shall not return ~~into~~ ***unto*** the land of Egypt, but the Assyrian shall be his king, because they refused to return.

11:8 How shall I give thee up, Ephraim? how shall I deliver thee, Israel? how shall I make thee as Admah? how shall I set thee as Zeboim? ~~mine~~ ***My*** heart is turned ~~within me, my repentings are kindled together~~ ***toward thee, and my mercies are extended to gather thee***.

JOEL

1:6 For a nation is come up upon my land, strong, and without number, whose teeth are ***as*** the teeth of a lion, and he hath the cheek teeth of a great lion.

1:20 The beasts of the field cry also unto thee***;*** ~~:~~ for the rivers of waters are dried up, and the fire hath devoured the pastures of the wilderness.

2:13 And rend your heart, and not your garments, ***and repent,*** and turn unto the LORD your God***;*** ~~:~~ for he is gracious and merciful, slow to anger, and of great kindness, and ~~repenteth him of~~ ***he will turn away*** the evil ***from you***.

2:14 ***Therefore repent, and*** ~~W~~***w***ho knoweth ~~if~~ ***but*** he will return ~~and repent,~~ and leave a blessing behind him; ~~even~~ ***that you may offer*** a meat offering, and a drink offering unto the LORD your God?

AMOS

3:6 Shall a trumpet be blown in the city, and the people not be afraid? shall there be evil in a city, and the LORD hath not ~~done~~ ***known*** it?
3:7 Surely the Lord GOD will do nothing, ~~but~~ ***until*** he revealeth ~~his~~ ***the*** secret unto his servants the prophets.

4:3 And ye shall go out at the breaches, every ~~cow at that which is before her~~ ***one before his enemy***; and ye shall ***be*** cast ~~them into the palace~~ ***out of your palaces***, saith the LORD.

4:5 And offer a sacrifice of thanksgiving with leaven, and proclaim and publish the free offerings***;*** ~~:~~ for ~~this liketh you~~ ***thus do ye***, O ye children of Israel, saith the Lord GOD.
4:6 ~~And~~ ***Therefore*** I also have given you cleanness of teeth in all your cities, and want of bread in all your places***;*** ~~:~~ yet have ye not returned unto me, saith the LORD.

5:3 For thus saith the Lord GOD; The city that went out by a thousand shall leave ~~an~~ ***a*** hundred, and that which went forth by ~~an~~ ***a*** hundred shall leave ten, to the house of Israel.

6:10 And a man's uncle shall take him up, and he that burneth him, to bring out the bones out of the house, and ~~shall~~ ***that*** say unto him that is by the sides of the house, Is there yet any with thee? and he shall say, No. Then shall he say, Hold thy tongue***;*** ~~:~~ for we may not make mention of the name of the LORD.

7:3 ***And*** ~~T~~***t***he LORD ~~repented~~ ***said, concerning Jacob, Jacob shall repent*** for this**,** ~~: It shall not be~~ ***therefore I will not utterly destroy him,*** saith the LORD.

7:6 ***And*** ~~T~~***t***he LORD ~~repented for this: This also shall not be~~ ***said, concerning Jacob, Jacob shall repent of his wickedness; therefore I will not utterly destroy him***, saith the Lord GOD.

7:14 Then answered Amos, and said to Amaziah, I was no prophet, neither was I a prophet's son; but I was ~~an~~ ***a*** herdman, and a gatherer of sycomore fruit***;*** ~~:~~

AMOS

7:17 Therefore thus saith the LORD; Thy wife shall be ~~an~~ ***a*** harlot in the city, and thy sons and thy daughters shall fall by the sword, and thy land shall be divided by line; and thou shalt die in a polluted land***;*** ~~:~~ and Israel shall surely go into captivity forth of his land.

8:2 And he said, Amos, what seest thou? And I said, A basket of summer fruit. Then said the LORD ~~unto~~ ***with*** me, The end is come upon my people of Israel; I will not again pass by them any more.

9:8 Behold, the eyes of the Lord GOD are upon ~~the~~ ***a*** sinful kingdom, and I will destroy it from off the face of the earth; saving that I will not utterly destroy the house of Jacob, saith the LORD.

OBADIAH

No JST changes.

JONAH

1:9 And he said unto them, I am ~~an~~ ***a*** Hebrew; and I fear the LORD, the God of heaven, which hath made the sea and the dry land.

3:9 Who can tell if ***we will*** ~~God will turn and~~ repent, and ***turn unto God, but he will*** turn away from ***us*** his fierce anger, that we perish not?
3:10 And God saw their works~~,~~ that they turned from their evil way~~;~~ and ~~God~~ repented***; and God turned away*** ~~of~~ the evil~~,~~ that he had said ~~that~~ he would ~~do unto~~ ***bring upon*** them~~; and he did it not~~.

MICAH

1:6 Therefore I will make Samaria as an heap of the field, and as plantings of a vineyard***;*** ~~:~~ and I will pour down the stones thereof into the valley, and I will discover the foundations thereof.
1:7 And all the graven images thereof shall be beaten to pieces, and all the hires thereof shall be burned with the fire, and all the idols thereof will I lay desolate***;*** ~~:~~ for she gathered it of the hire of ~~an~~ ***a*** harlot, and they shall return to the hire of ~~an~~ ***a*** harlot.

6:13 Therefore also will I make thee sick in smiting thee, in making thee desolate because of thy ~~sins~~ ***sin***.

6:16 For the statutes of Omri are kept, and all the works of the house of Ahab, and ye walk in their counsels; that I should make thee a desolation, and the inhabitants thereof ~~an~~ ***a*** hissing***;*** ~~:~~ therefore ye shall bear the reproach of my people.

NAHUM

3:16 Thou hast multiplied thy merchants above the stars of heaven***;*** ~~:~~ the cankerworm spoileth, and flieth away.

HABAKKUK

1:3 Why dost thou shew me iniquity, and cause me to behold ~~grievance~~ ***grievances***? for spoiling and violence are before me***;*** ~~:~~ and there are that raise up strife and contention.

ZEPHANIAH

1:4 I will also stretch out mine hand upon Judah, and upon all the inhabitants of Jerusalem; and I will cut off the remnant of Baal from this place, and the name of the ~~Chemarims~~ ***Chemarim*** with the priests;

2:15 This is the rejoicing city that dwelt carelessly, that said in her heart, I am, and there is none ~~beside~~ ***besides*** me***;*** ~~:~~ how is she become a desolation, a place for beasts to lie down in! every one that passeth by her shall hiss, and wag his hand.

HAGGAI

2:16 Since those days were, when one came to ~~an~~ ***a*** heap of twenty measures, there were but ten***;*** ~~:~~ when one came to the pressfat for to draw out fifty vessels out of the press, there were but twenty.

ZECHARIAH

4:10 For who hath despised the day of small things? for they shall rejoice, and shall see the plummet in the hand of Zerubbabel with those seven; they are the ~~eyes~~ ***servants*** of the LORD, which run to and fro through the whole earth.

4:14 Then said he, These are the two anointed ones, that stand ~~by~~ ***before*** the Lord of the whole earth.

5:11 And he said unto me, To build it ~~an~~ ***a*** house in the land of Shinar***;*** ~~:~~ and it shall be established, and set there upon her own base.

6:5 And the angel answered and said unto me, These are the four ~~spirits~~ ***servants*** of the heavens, which go forth from standing before the Lord of all the earth.

6:7 And the bay went forth, and sought to go that they might walk to and fro through the earth***;*** ~~:~~ and he said, Get you hence, walk to and fro through the earth. So they walked to and fro through the earth.

8:7 Thus saith the LORD of hosts; Behold, I will save my people from the east country, and from the west country;

8:13 And it shall come to pass, that as ye were a curse among the heathen, O house of Judah, and house of Israel; so will I ~~save~~ ***gather*** you, and ye shall be a blessing***;*** ~~:~~ fear not, but let your hands be strong.

12:6 In that day will I make the governors of Judah like ~~an~~ ***a*** hearth of fire among the wood, and like a torch of fire in a sheaf; and they shall devour all the people round about, on the right hand and on the left***;*** ~~:~~ and Jerusalem shall be inhabited again in her own place, even in Jerusalem.

13:5 But he shall say, I am no prophet, I am an husbandman; for man taught me to keep cattle from my youth.

MALACHI

See full text on pages 229-234.

The Book of Genesis

1:1 - 1:7 11
1:8 - 1:13 12
1:14-1:22 13
1:23-1:30 14
1:31-2:4 15
2:5-2:9 16
2:10-2:20 17
2:21-2:25 18
3:1a 10
3:1b-3:5 18
3:6-3:16 19
3:17-3:24 20
4:1a 21
4:1b-4:2 22
4:3-4:7 23
4:8-4:14 24
4:15-4:24a 25
4:24b 26
4:25-4:26 27
5:1-5:2 27
5:3-5:15 28
5:168-5:21b 29
5:21c 30
5:21d 31
5:21e 32
5:21f 33
5:21g 34
5:21h 35
5:21i 36
5:21j 37
5:21k 38
5:21l 39
5:21m 40
5:21n 41
5:21o-5:24 42
5:25-5:32 43
6:1-6:2 43
6:3-6:5 44
6:6-6:17 45
6:18-6:22 46
7:1-7:7 46
7:8-7:22 47
7:23-7:24 48
8:1-8:10 48
8:11-8:21 49
8:22 50
9:1-9:10 50
9:11-9:17 51
9:18-9:24 52
10:1-10:3 52
10:4-10:21 53
10:22-10:32 54
11:1-11:4 54
11:5-11:18 55
11:19:11:27 56
11:28-11:32 60
12:1-12:3 61
12:4-12:8 62
12:9-12:13 63
12:14-12:20 64
13:1-13:16 64
13:17-13:18 65
14:1-14:17 65
14:18-14:24 66
15:1-15:16 67
15:17-15:21 68
16:1-16:16 68
17:1-17:17 69
17:18-17:27 70
18:1-18:13 70
18:14-18:32 71
18:33 72
19:1-19:14 72
19:15-19:33 73
19:34-19:38 74
20:1-20:15 74
20:16-20:18 75
21:1-21:17 75
21:18-21:34 76
22:1-22:4 76
22:5-22:24 77
23:1-23:20 78
24:1-24:22 79
24:23-24:46 80
24:47-24:67 81
25:1-25:3 81
25:4-25:24 82
25:25-25:34 83
26:1-26:12 83
26:13-26:35 84
27:1-27:27 85
27:28-27:46 86
28:1-28:2 86
28:3-28:22 87
29:1-29:2 87
29:3-29:27 88
29:28-29:35 89
30:1-30:19 89
30:20-30:41 90
30:42-30:43 91
31:1-31:24 91
31:25-31:44 92
31:45-31:55 93
32:1-32:15 93
32:16-32:32 94
33:1-33:5 94
33:6-33:20 95
34:1-34:11 95
34:12-34:31 96
35:1-35:3 96
35:4-35:26 97
35:27-35:29 98
36:1-36:23 98
36:24-36:43 99
37:1-37:7 99
37:8-37:31 100
38:32-38:36 102
38:1-38:19 101
38:20-38:30 102
39:1-39:10 102
39:11-39:23 103
40:1-40:9 103
40:10-40:23 104
41:1-41:10 104
41:11-41:37 105
41:38-41:56 106
41:57 107
42:1-42:24 107
42:25-42:38 108
43:1-43:10 108
43:11-43:33 109
43:34 110
44:1-44:24 110
44:25-44:34 111
45:1-45:15 111
45:16-45:28 112
46:1-46:11 112
46:12-46:34 113
47:1 113
47:2-47:21 114
47:22-47:31 115
48:1-48:6a 115
48:6b-48:22 116
49:1--49:2 116
49:3-49:29 117
49:30-49:33 117
50:1-50:19 118
50:20-50:24a 119
50:24b-50:26 120

The Book of Isaiah

Isaiah

1:1-1:9 124
1:10-1:24 125
1:25-1:31 126
2:1-2:5 126
2:6-2:19 127
2:20-2:22 128
3:1-3:8 128
3:9-3:23 129
3:24-3:26 130
4:1-4:6 130
5:1-5:12 131
5:13-5:25 132
5:26-5:30 133
6:1-6:6 133
6:7-6:13 134
7:1-7:4 134
7:5-7:19 135
7:20-7:25 136
8:1-8:7 136
8:8-8:20 137
8:21-8:22 138
9:1-9:8 138
9:9-9:21 139
10:1-10:13 140
10:14-10:25 141
10:26-10:34 142
11:1 142
11:2-11:9 143
11:10-11:16 144
12:1-12:6 145
13:1-13:8 145
13:9-13:21 146
13:22 147
14:1-14:9 147
14:10-14:23 148
14:24-14:32 149
15:1-15:4 149
15:5-15:9 150
16:1-16:7 150
16:8-16:14 151
17:1-17:4 151
17:5-17:14 152
18:1-18:2 152
18:3-18:7 153
19:1-19:4 153
19:5-19:18 154
19:19-19:25 155
20:1-20:4 155
20:5-20:6 156
21:1-21:11 156
21:12-21:17 157
22:1-22:8 157
22:9-22:22 158
22:23–22:25 159
23:1-23:11 159
23:12-23:18 160
24:1-24:5 160
24:6-24:20 161
24:21-24:23 162
25:1-25:8 162
25:9-25:12 163
26:1-26:10 163
26:11-26:21 164
27:1-27:13 165
28:1-28:12 166
28:13-28:24 167
28:25-28:29 168
29:1-29:4 168
29:5-29:9 169
29:10a 170
29:10b-29:11a 171
29:11b-29:12 172
29:13-29:15 173
29:16-29:24 174
30:1-30:22 175
30:23-30:33 176
31:1-31:8 176
31:9 177
32:1-32:20 177
33:1-33:2 177
33:3-33:24 178
34:1-34:2 178
34:3-34:17 179
35:1-35:6 179
35:7-35:10 180
36:1-36:16 180
36:17-36:22 181
37:1-37:15 181
37:16-37:37 182
37:8 183
38:1-38:22 183
39:1-39:8 184
40:1-40:13 184
40:14-40:31 185
41:1-41:5 185
41:6-41:29 186
42:1-42:23 187
42:24-42:25 188
43:22 188
43:23-43:28 189
44:1-44:15 189
44:16-44:28 190
45:1-45:9 190
45:10-45:25 191
46:1-46:6 191
46:7-46:13 192
47:1-47:15 192
48:1-48:10 193
48:11-48:22 194
49:1-49:8 195
49:9-49:20 196
49:21-49:26 197
50:1 197
50:1-50:11 198
51:1-51:10 199
51:11-51:21 200
51:22-51:23 201
52:1-52:2 201
52:3-52:7 202
52:8-52:13 203
52:14-52:15 204
53:1-53:7 204
53:8-53:12 205
54:1:54:4 205
54:5-54:17 206
55:1-55:12 207
55:13 208
56:1-56:11 208
56:12 209
57:1-57:10 209
57:11-57:21 210
58:1-58:2 210
58:3-58:12 211
58:13-58:14 212
59:1-59:9 212
59:10-59:21 213
60:1-60:12 214
60:13-60:22 215
61:2-61:11 216
62:1-62:12 217
63:1-63:9 218
63:10-63:19 219
64:1-64:2 219
64:3-64:12 220
65:1 221
65:2-65:12 221
65:13-65:24 222
65:25 223
66:1-66:9 223
66:10-66:20 224
66:21-66:24 225

The Book of Malachi

1:1-1:12 229
1:13-1:14 230
2:1-2:10 230
2:11-2:17 231
3:1 231
3:2-3:13 232
3:14-3:18 233
4:1-4:4 233
4:5-4:6 234

The Book of Mormon

1st Nephi

13:37 204
15:19-15:20 124
19:22-19:24 123
20:1-20:10 193
20:11-20:22 194
21:1-21:8 195
21:9-21:20 196
21:21-21:26 197

2nd Nephi

6:6-6:7 197
6:16-6:18 197
7:1 197
7:2-7:11 198
8:1-8:10 199
8:11-8:21 200
8:22-8:25 201
12:1-12:5 126
12:6-12:19 127
12:20-12:22 128
13:1-13:8 128
13:9-13:23 129
13:24-3:26 130
14:1-14:6 130
15:1-15:12 131
15:13-15:25 132
15:26-15:30 133
16:1-16:6 133
16:7-16:13 134
17:1-17:4 134
17:5-17:19 135
17.20-17:25 136
18:1-18:7 136
18:8-18:20 137
18:21-18:22 137
19:1-19:8 138
19:9-19:21 139
20:1-20:13 140
20:14-20:25 141
20:26-20:34 142
21:1 142
21:2-21:9 143
21:10-21:16 144
22:1-22:6 145
23:1-23:8 145
23:9-23:21 146
23:22 147
24:1-24:9 147
24:10-24:23 148
24:24-24:32 149
26:15-26:16 168
26:17-26:18 169
27:1-27:4 169
27:5-27:10 170
27:11-27:15 171
27:16-27:19 172
27:20-27:27 173
27:28-27:35 173
30:9-30:15 143

Mosiah

12:20-12:21 202
12:22-12:24 203
14:1-14:7 204
14:8-14:12 205
15:13-15:17 202
15:18 203
15:29-15:31 203

3rd Nephi

20:31-20:35 203
20:36-20:37 201
20:38-20:40 202
20:41-20:43 203
20:44-20:45 204
22:1-22:4 205
22:5-22:17 206
23:1-23:3 123
24:1 231
24:2-24:13 232
24:14-25:4 233

Mormon

8:23a 168
8:23b 169

The Doctrine & Covenants
The Pearl of Great Price

Doctrine & Covenants

2:1-2:3 234
110:13-110:16 234
113:1-113:2 143
113:3-113:4 142
113:5-113:6 144
113:7-113:10 201
133:46-133:53 218

History of Joseph Smith

1:19 173
1:36-1:37 233
1:38-1:39 234
1:40 142
1:59 170
1:63 171
1:64-1:65 172

The Book of Moses

1:1 -1:3 5
1:4-1:13 6
1:14-1:23 7
1:24-1:34 8
1:35-1:42 9
2:1-2:7 11
2:8-2:13 12
2:14-2:22 13
2:23-2:30 14
2:31 15
3:1-3:4 15
3:5-3:9 16
3:10-3:20 17
3:21-3:25 18
4:1-4:4 10
4:5-4:11 18
4:12-4:22 19
4:23-4:32 20
5:1-5:9 21
5:10-5:17 22
5:18-5:29 23
5:30-5:39 24
5:40-5:49 25
5:50-5:59 26
6:1-6:9 27
6:10-6:20 28
6:21-6:28 29
6:29-6:36 30
6:37-6:46 31
6:47-6:56 32
6:57-6:63 33
6:64-6:68 34
7:1-7:4 34
7:5-7:13 35
7:14-7:22 36
7:23-7:32 37
7:33-7:40 38
7:41-7:48 39
7:49-7:57 40
7:58-7:64 41
7:65-7:69 42
8:1-8:3 42
8:4-8:15 43
8:16-8:24 44
8:25-8:30 45

The Book of Abraham

1:1-1:3 56
1:4-1:12 57
1:13-1:20 58
1:21-1:29 59
1:30-1:31 60
2:1-2:5 60
2:6-2:12 61
2:13-2:20 62
2:21-2:25 63
3:1-3:8 3
3:9-3:17 4
3:18-3:23 5
3:24-3:25 9
3:26-3:28 10
4:1-4:7 11
4:8-4:13 12
4:14-4:22 13
4:23-4:30 14
4:31 15
5:1-5:4 15
5:5-5:9 16
5:10-5:13 17
5:14-55:19 18
5:20-5:21a 17
5:21b 18

Bibliography

Bible. (1920). Inspired Version, translated and corrected by the spirit of revelation by Joseph Smith, Jr., The Seer. 20th ed. Lamoni, Iowa: Reorganized Church of Jesus Christ of Latter Day Saints.

Fitzmyer, Joseph A., Brown, Raymond E., and Murphy E. Roland (Eds.). (1968). *The Jerome Biblical Commentary.* Englewood Cliffs, NJ: Prentice-Hall, Inc.

Edvalson, Fredrick M., Jr. & Smith, William B. (1977). *Inspired Version Study Guide - A Key to the Significant Changes.* Provo, UT: 70's Mission Bookstore.

Horton, George A., Jr. (1985). "Insights into the Book of Genesis." In Monte S. Nyman and Robert L. Millet (Eds.), *The Joseph Smith Translation: The Restoration of Plain and Precious Things.* Salt Lake City, UT: Bookcraft, Inc.

Matthews, Robert J. (1971). "A Review: Edwards, F. Henry, comp. *Joseph Smith's "New Translation" of the Bible." Courage: A Journal of History, Thought, and Action.* 1(2).

Matthews, Robert J. (1985). *A Plainer Translation: Joseph Smith's Translation of the Bible. A History and Commentary.* Provo, UT: Brigham Young University Press.

Millet, Robert L. (1985). "Joseph Smith's Translation of the Bible: A Historical Overview" in Monte S. Nyman and Robert L. Millet (Eds.), *The Joseph Smith Translation: The Restoration of Plain and Precious Things.* Salt Lake City, UT: Bookcraft, Inc.

Nyman, Monte S. & Millet, Robert L. (1985). *The Joseph Smith Translation: The Restoration of Plain and Precious Things.* Salt Lake City, UT: Bookcraft, Inc.

Smith, Israel A. (1985). *The Inspired Version.* Independence, MO: Price Publishing Co.

The Anchor Bible. (1970). Garden City, NY: Doubleday & Co., Inc.

The Book of Mormon.. (1981). Salt Lake City, UT: The Church of Jesus Christ of Latter-day Saints.

The Doctrine and Covenants. (1981). Salt Lake City, UT: The Church of Jesus Christ of Latter-day Saints.

The Holy Bible: King James Version. (1979). Salt Lake City, UT: The Church of Jesus Christ of Latter-day Saints.

The New Layman's Parallel Bible. (1981). Grand Rapids, Michigan: Zondervan Bible Publishers.

The Pearl of Great Price. (1981). Salt Lake City, UT: The Church of Jesus Christ of Latter-day Saints.

The Reorganized Church of Jesus Christ of Latter Day Saints. (1970). *Joseph Smith's "New Translation" of The Bible.* Introduction by F. Henry Edwards. Independence, MO: Herald Publishing House.

ABOUT THE COMPILERS

Julie M. Hite is an Assistant Professor of Educational Leadership & Foundations at Brigham Young University. She received her BS and Master of Organizational Behavior degrees from Brigham Young University and her PhD in Strategic Management at the University of Utah. For over twenty years, while focusing on her primary role as a mother, Julie has successfully developed and managed home-based entrepreneurial businesses in genealogy, computer services, and publishing throughout New England, Arizona and Utah. The mother of four daughters and one son, she has learned (with focus and determination) to successfully balance the requirements of being a faithful and thoughtful individual, caring spouse, and dedicated mother in our complex, modern world.

Steven J. Hite is an Associate Professor of Educational Leadership & Foundations at Brigham Young University. He received his BS and MS degrees at BYU and his Doctorate at Harvard University. Steven's academic career focuses on the application of educational research and evaluation to improve the efficiency, effectiveness, and equality of educational opportunities for disadvantaged individuals, families, and communities in developing countries, especially those in sub-Saharan Africa. His most cherished assets are his testimony of the Restored Gospel of Jesus Christ, his wife, Julie Melville, and his five children, Melissa, Rachel, David, Shelley, and Laurie.

R. Tom Melville is an Ordinance Worker at the Jordan River Temple, and a Gospel Doctrine teacher in the Brighton 10th Ward, Brighton (Salt Lake) Stake. He received a BS from the University of Utah, and served as a carrier Naval Aviator for five years following college. For nearly thirty years, Tom flew as a commercial pilot for both Western and Delta Air Lines, retiring in 1995. He and his wife, Pauline, then served as Senior Missionaries in the Kentucky Louisville Mission. They are the parents of two daughters (including Julie, above) and six sons, with 30 grandchildren, so far. Tom has a quiet, but firm, testimony and a great love for the scriptures. He enjoys gardening, barbershopping, and providing financial counseling to his extended family.